Victoria,
Queen of the Screen

Victoria, Queen of the Screen

From Silent Cinema to New Media

LEIGH EHLERS TELOTTE

McFarland & Company, Inc., Publishers
Jefferson, North Carolina

LIBRARY OF CONGRESS CATALOGUING-IN-PUBLICATION DATA

Names: Telotte, Leigh Ehlers, 1949– author.
Title: Victoria, queen of the screen : from silent cinema to new media / Leigh Ehlers Telotte.
Description: Jefferson, North Carolina : McFarland & Company, Inc., Publishers, 2020 | Includes bibliographical references, filmography, and index.
Identifiers: LCCN 2020022999 | ISBN 9781476679044 (paperback : acid free paper) ∞
ISBN 9781476638782 (ebook)
Subjects: LCSH: Victoria, Queen of Great Britain, 1819-1901—In motion pictures. | Victoria, Queen of Great Britain, 1819-1901—In mass media. | Queens in motion pictures. | Great Britain—History—Victoria, 1837-1901.
Classification: LCC PN1995.9.V45 T45 2020 | DDC 791.43/651—dc23
LC record available at https://lccn.loc.gov/2020022999

BRITISH LIBRARY CATALOGUING DATA ARE AVAILABLE

ISBN (print) 978-1-4766-7904-4
ISBN (ebook) 978-1-4766-3878-2

© 2020 Leigh Ehlers Telotte. All rights reserved

No part of this book may be reproduced or transmitted in any form or by any means, electronic or mechanical, including photocopying or recording, or by any information storage and retrieval system, without permission in writing from the publisher.

The front cover image is of Judi Dench in *Mrs. Brown*, 1997 (Miramax Films/Photofest)

Printed in the United States of America

McFarland & Company, Inc., Publishers
Box 611, Jefferson, North Carolina 28640
www.mcfarlandpub.com

To Orion Paul Telotte

Acknowledgments

Many thanks to Professor Jay P. Telotte of the Georgia Institute of Technology for his encouragement, guidance, and support for this project. Without his patience with my many questions and concerns, this project would not have been possible. Also, I am indebted to my daughter Gabrielle Hanson for her IT and gaming expertise, as well as her assistance in selecting illustrations. Finally, I dedicate this work to the newest of the Telotte family, my grandson Orion Paul Telotte. His strength and will to survive are reminiscent of Queen Victoria's enduring fortitude.

Table of Contents

Acknowledgments vi
Preface 1
Introduction: The Real and the Reel Victoria 3

1. Queen Victoria on the Silent Screen 11
2. Of War and Empire 36
3. Of Love and Obsession 62
4. Victoria Is Amused 91
5. Victoria Rules the Small Screen 103
6. Transformations of Victoria Into the 21st Century 137

Appendix: Select Filmography 149
Chapter Notes 195
Works Cited 215
Index 225

Preface

Through a curious coincidence, the year 2019 is not only the 200th anniversary of the birth of Victoria, Queen of the United Kingdom of Great Britain and Ireland, Empress of India, but also represents the third century of Victoria's presence on the film, television, or media screen. Historically, the *real* Victoria was the ultimate survivor, living through a reign of over 63 years, eight assassination attempts, nine childbirths in twenty years of marriage to beloved Albert, the deaths of two of those children, and ten Prime Ministers, both palatable (Disraeli) and detestable (Gladstone). The *reel* Victoria is likewise an enduring and indomitable character, beginning with the silent films of her own era, surviving and evolving into the twenty-first century in a plethora of ways and means. Victoria has been labeled the "first media monarch" and has left the legacy of a screen presence, the sheer magnitude of which has been neither chronicled nor fully appreciated. It is the goal of this book to address that very gap.

The book's methodology is to compile basic information about each film, television show, or other media featuring or presenting Queen Victoria either as a *real* person or as a *reel* character acting and reacting with other characters in a narrative plot. The Filmography gives titles, dates, production companies, countries of origin, director, writer, length, and principal cast, as well as brief summaries of story and key comments. For each entry, the information has been drawn from the most complete print or version available. It is organized in broad categories: silent actualités featuring the Queen (in chronological order), feature films presented in a theatrical environment (alphabetical order), television shows and miniseries (alphabetical order), and a miscellaneous group of twenty-first century digital media, including gaming and internet creations (alphabetical order). Excluded from the filmography are films or shows that include only passing references to Queen Victoria, such as the film *Gunga Din* (1939), whose opening shot pans a statue of the Queen but never shows her again. Also excluded are documentaries about Queen Victoria since they focus more on history and do not present Victoria as a character.

The bulk of the volume includes six chapters that describe and analyze how Queen Victoria has been leveraged as a character across time and screen media. The chapters are arranged both chronologically and by platform: silent films, films on war and empire building, films on the Victoria/Albert love story, films about Victoria's amusements, television shows and miniseries, and twenty-first century transformations (digital media, gaming, and internet). This book does not take a specific theoretical or critical approach, other than to look at the film, television show, or media through the prism of character presentation and development, commenting on elements such as costuming, camera work, music, or set design, as they enhance or shape the characterization of Queen Victoria. The book is a starting point for analysis in other disciplines of film and television studies—film history, gender studies, cultural studies, political approaches, aesthetic analysis, and genre studies. The reel Victoria of film, television, and media awaits and will no doubt survive all that future scholars and critics can say about her.

Introduction:
The Real and the
Reel Victoria

> If a character in a novel is exactly like Queen Victoria—not rather like but exactly like—then it actually is Queen Victoria, and the novel ... becomes a memoir. A memoir is history, it was based on evidence. A novel is based on evidence plus or minus x, the unknown quantity being the temperament of the novelist, and the unknown quantity always modifies the effect of the evidence, and sometimes transforms it entirely.... It is the function of the novelist to reveal the hidden life at its source: to tell us more about Queen Victoria than could be known, and thus to produce a character who is not the Queen Victoria of history.
> —E.M. Forster 52–53

As has often been observed, each generation rewrites history to reflect its own needs, whether for political motives, moral illustrations, pedagogical consumption, or simply the novelty of a new approach to well-known material. This is especially true for biography, histories, novels—as Forster sets forth—and, as this book will demonstrate, in film, television, and digital media. A case in point is the treatment of Queen Victoria, whose compelling media presence has now spanned three centuries, bringing a version of "Victoria" to new sets of eyes, generation by generation. Ultimately Queen Victoria is a protean figure, mediated and manipulated in the nineteenth century by the monarchy and political establishment, in the twentieth century by the exigencies of wartime, followed by peacetime recovery, and in the twenty-first century by preoccupation with sexuality, and overt considerations of classism and racism. As this volume will demonstrate, the key to such survival into the twentieth and twenty-first centuries rests on the ability of Queen Victoria as icon to mean many different things to many different people in many different ways.

Introduction: The Real and the Reel Victoria

Victoria's reign coincided with the explosive emergence of a publishing industry which transcended the written word and employed a visual vocabulary, using illustrations to tell the story. For the first time, a monarchy received "coverage," beginning with the traditional reporting of royal schedules (Court Circular), later supplemented with static visuals: formal paintings, daguerreotypes, and lavish illustrations of public royal events. A respectful attitude toward the monarchy still dominated at the birth of the illustrated press of the mid-nineteenth century, for example in "Queen Victoria's Visit to Birmingham," *Illustrated London News*, 3 July 1858 (Plunkett 50). Ultimately the official Diamond Jubilee photo (released in 1897, but actually taken by W. & D. Downey four years earlier) epitomized this visual hagiography. Victoria's official photography was deliberately issued without copyright and "went viral"—appearing on products ranging from penny prints to 10-guinea medallions, making it impossible "to calculate how many prints were in circulation" (Lyden 142).

However, towards the end of the nineteenth century a far less reverential view of Victoria emerged, particularly in the foreign press (e.g., France) and back home in *Punch*. The Queen became the target of political satire, evident in the highly politized caricatures of Victoria.[1] An example is "En Chine, le gâteau des Rois et ... Des Empereurs," published in *Supplément illustré du Petit Journal* on 16 January 1898. Queen Victoria is shown with enormous nose and even larger knife, contending with rivals Germany, Russia, France and Japan to carve up China, to the dismay of the Chinese emperor. Far from unique, these caricatures and political cartoons point to a growing discontent with endless foreign wars, grinding poverty in Great Britain, and the role of the monarchy.

In contrast to the satirical vein in print media, the nascent film industry avidly leaped at the huge spectacle of Victoria's Diamond Jubilee (1897) and funeral (1901), producing a large number of reverential silent films, produced for and delivered to mass audiences both within England and worldwide. Media preoccupation with royalty took root before the twentieth century, as is demonstrated by the persistent presence of Queen Victoria in the early days of the emerging film industry. A perennial icon, Queen Victoria is still a highly visible part of the cultural landscape, given the starring role in the numerous popular films and television series about her life, and even maintaining the familiar mantle of satirical figure in an online comic, as well as embodying the token royalty role in video games.

Chapter 1 will show how nineteenth-century film celebrated Victoria as a symbol of order, benevolent government, and family, ultimately presenting her as the grandmother of the Empire. Great affection could be generated by projecting these cultural needs onto such a charismatic personality, as noted by historian Peter Carlson:

Introduction: The Real and the Reel Victoria 5

The Reverential: Queen Victoria's "1897" Diamond Jubilee photograph, which was deliberately released without copyright, in order to ensure maximum distribution.

[Buffalo Bill] Cody introduced Her Majesty to several Sioux performers. "She shook hands with all of us," Black Elk remembered. "Her hand was very little and soft. We gave a big cheer for her and then the shining wagons came in and she got in one of them and they all went away".... Decades later, in 1931, Black Elk—who had witnessed both the Battle of Little Bighorn in 1876 and the massacre at Wounded Knee—in 1890—recalled the Queen fondly, "We liked Grandmother England because we could see that she was a fine woman, and she was good to us. Maybe if she had been our Grandmother, it would have been better for our people" [Carlson 3].

This reaction seems hopelessly out of touch for a twenty-first century audience unused to and likely appalled by the notion of a unifying cultural symbol that even the "oppressed" groups bought into. Although a key manifestation of British and Irish radicalism focused on anti-monarchism, a majority of the British people responded positively, if not enthusiastically, to her appeal. Ironically, as Paul Thomas Murphy demonstrates in his history *Shooting Victoria*, the eight assassination attempts on Victoria failed to achieve the intended destruction, but instead spurred an increased support for the monarchy and admiration for Victoria's personal courage.

The short silent films of the late nineteenth century (often termed "actualités") reveal much about how the monarchy marketed itself and how an eager public consumed the pro–Victoria message. Given the newness of experiencing film projected in a theater, the immediate impact of "look, there's the Queen!"

The Not-So-Reverential: Queen Victoria and rivals (Germany, Russia, France, Japan) are carving up China in "En Chine, le gâteau des Rois et ... Des Empereurs" *Supplément illustré du Petit Journal*, 16 January 1898.

drew in audiences and distributed Victoria's moving image on a mass scale impossible prior to 1895. Perhaps taking a clue from her great-great-grandmother, Queen Elizabeth II reportedly has stated, "I have to be seen to be believed." The groundwork for such a deliberate media strategy was laid out by Victoria, who in her old age was willing to go out in public before the cameras, albeit with cameras kept at a respectful distance. As Chapter 1 will demonstrate, the emergence of this film practice parallels and can be viewed in the context of nineteenth century industrialization. Victoria's royal patronage of still photography, stereography, railroads, telegraphs, telephones, to name just a few of the inventions she patronized, segued into her embrace of the silent film industry to bring her in touch with her people.

Queen Victoria's tenure received more complex treatment in the twentieth century. Chapter 2 examines films presenting Victoria in the context of empire building and wartime, which coincided with every year of her long reign. During the build-up to World War I, Victoria appears as the benevolent symbol of empire, as in the silent Crimean war films *The Victoria Cross* (1912) and *Balaclava* (1928). The anxieties created by impending World War II are reflected in the Anna Neagle vehicle *Sixty Glorious Years* (1938), while a number of Disraeli-focused films (such as *The Prime Minister*, 1941) center on the Suez Canal purchase as critical to empire building. *The Lady with a Lamp*, 1951, staring Anna Neagle as Florence Nightingale presents Victoria in a flattering light. In contrast, a negative view of Victoria appears in propaganda films from other countries, notably Germany (*Uncle Kruger*, 1941) and China (*The Opium War*, 1997).

During the second part of the twentieth century, the representation of Queen Victoria splits into various directions, with several recurring themes examined in Chapter 3, including the perennially popular Victoria and Albert love story, various characters' obsession with the Queen, and darker fantastical portrayals that bridge genres from horror to comedy. In romance, *Victoria the Great* (1937) led the way with Anna Neagle and Anton Walbrook playing the royal couple, but in this film the love story is overshadowed by key political events, notably Albert's 1861 deathbed effort to avert war with the United States during the Civil War. Post-World War II German films put the couple solely in a personal light, such as the escapist *Victoria in Dover* (1954) with a luminously charming Romy Schneider. And 2009's *The Young Victoria* is weighted toward the personal love story, with limited political overtones. More serious themes dominate the later twentieth century: *Mrs Brown* (1997) taking on class snobbery and the politically correct *Victoria & Abdul* (2017) emphasizing Victoria's struggles against racism in her court. While all these films include Victoria's enduring passion for Albert, some films, like the 1950's *Mudlark*, reverse that lens and feature a character obsessed with Victoria. Such obsession turns deadly in *From Hell* (2001), wherein a detective unravels murder cases that implicate the Queen in an effort to suppress a threat to her monarchy.

Several animated feature films also delve into a man's obsession with taking control over Victoria: *The Great Mouse Detective* (1986) with its mechanical replicant of the Queen and *Van Helsing: The London Assignment* (2004) where the mad scientist restores Victoria's youth and gets her under his control. Chapter 3 also looks at a dark comedy in the 2012 animated feature *The Pirates! In an Adventure with Scientists!* which reveals Victoria's malevolent identity as a member of a private dining club that eats endangered animals, a vision suggesting a thoroughly jaundiced view of Queen Victoria.

Chapter 4 takes up the theme of Victoria's amusements, offering a corrective to the cliché of the dour widow whose disapproval begins and ends with "We are not amused." Dancing is a favorite pastime in several films such as the Anna Neagle–Anton Walbrook films *Victoria the Great* and *Sixty Glorious Years*, Romy Schneider's *Victoria in Dover*, and is featured in the highland reel scene in *Mrs Brown*. Victoria's taste in opera and music is featured in *The Story of Gilbert and Sullivan* (1953) and is a key plot point in *The Young Victoria* where Victoria and Albert first clash in their musical tastes and gradually fall in love to the tunes of Franz Schubert. Literary tastes are also explored in *The Young Victoria*, with Albert dutifully reading the Sir Walter Scott books that Victoria likes. Less highbrow—and less well known—is Victoria's enthusiasm for *tableaux vivants*, as dramatized in *Victoria & Abdul* where her Indian protégé Abdul is shown as the King of Persia, to the racist chagrin of the Victorian court. Victoria's love of wild west shows appears in *Buffalo Bill* (1944) as well as circus in both *Barnum* (1986) and the musical *The Greatest Showman* (2017). And Victoria's interest in science and technology is addressed in *Jules Verne's Rocket to the Moon* (alternate title *Those Fantastic Flying Fools*, 1967) and *The Story of Alexander Graham Bell* (1939). All these films are a notable counter to the stereotype of Victoria as the sourpuss widow immune to pleasure.

Chapter 5 looks at how television has presented Victoria in five general categories: politics and war, family history, the Victoria and Albert love story, farce comedy, fantasy, and time travel. Political overtones are evident in the miniseries *Around the World in 80 Days* (1989), which emphasizes Victoria's role in international diplomacy. Two war-oriented series portray Victoria and her government in a highly negative light: *Rhodes* (1996) which shows her ministers as greedy and corrupt in their dealings with British South Africa and *Shaka Zulu* (1986), the South African miniseries that pulls no punches depicting Victoria as a ruthless empress determined to deny autonomy to the Zulu nation. The 1980 miniseries *Disraeli: Portrait of a Romantic* takes a biopic format to Disraeli's life and his partnership with Victoria to build the British empire. Historical miniseries take advantage of the plethora of material about Victoria's family, notably *Edward the Seventh* (1975), in which Queen Victoria dominates most of the episodes, just as she dominated her son's life. A small role for Victoria as dynastic matchmaker appears in *The Fall of Eagles* (1974), as well as an outing as the difficult-to-live-with mother of Princess Beatrice in an episode of the police drama *Cribb*. Victoria's disapproval of her son's many mistresses is shown in the *Lillie* miniseries (1978) and the Daisy Grenville episode of *The Edwardians* (1973). The Victoria and Albert love story takes a sexy turn in two twenty-first century miniseries: *Victoria & Albert* in 2001 and *Victoria* seasons 1–3 (2016 to 2019). Both series leverage the nostalgia of costume drama with detailed attention to character development, building gradually over multiple episodes. The Daisy Goodwin miniseries *Victoria*

Introduction: The Real and the Reel Victoria 9

in particular benefits from impressive sets, costumes, and stunning CGI recreations of Victorian London, offset by its reinterpretations (some critics say misrepresentations) of history through the prism of twenty-first century preoccupations with sexuality and political correctness.

In contrast to the in-depth characterizations in several miniseries, British farce comedy often treats Victoria as a one-note joke: notably in *Blackadder's Christmas Carol* (1988), as well as in "Queen Victoria Handicap" (where all contestants are dressed as the Queen) and the "Poetry Reading" skit from *Monty Python's Flying Circus* (Victoria appears with Albert's coffin in tow). In an unusual twist, Queen Victoria appears in a ghost story; in the "Poor Butterfly" episode of *Journey to the Unknown* (1968), a stranger wanders into an isolated haunted manor house and meets the Queen who resides as the ghostly lady of the manor. Not surprisingly, a number of time travel television shows leverage Queen Victoria as a character; the *Bewitched* episode "Aunt Clara's Victoria Victory" (1967) brings Victoria forward in time into Samantha's mid-century modern living room, and *A Curse on the House of Windsor* (1994) has a time traveling Queen Victoria offering advice to Queen Elizabeth in 1992. In *Voyagers!* the time travelers go back into the past to prevent a mistake in history (a marriage between Victoria's granddaughter and a Russian duke). Perhaps the most famous time-traveling show featuring the Queen is the *Doctor Who* Episode 2.2 "Tooth and Claw" (2006) where Rose and the Doctor meet Queen Victoria at the Torchwood estate and defeat a group of monks who want to turn her into a werewolf. In the end, Victoria banishes the Doctor from Britain and stands ready to fight for her cultural values and the empire's safety, a world where faith in God and country are still viable choices, as the Doctor's world apparently is not.

Chapter 6 examines how the rise of new media has introduced transformative approaches to the character of Queen Victoria. The simplest approach is to create a clone of Victoria, as in the "Meltdown" episode of *Red Dwarf* (1991), wherein a mindless Victoria is sent to kill a clone of Hitler and dies alongside him. *The Wild Wild West Revisited* (1979) pits the real Victoria against a villain who has created a clone of her in order to rule the world. The steampunk television series *The Secret Adventures of Jules Verne* (2000) includes a politically engaged Queen Victoria, who manipulates Secret Service agents to defeat the evil League that wants to assassinate her. A much darker view of Victoria appears in the anime series *The Black Butler* (2008–09), where the Queen is cast as unbalanced after her husband's death. Attempting to anchor herself in the past, she has part of Albert's dead body grafted to her neck, which transmutes her into a living figure fused with a rotting corpse. Video games pick up Queen Victoria for empire building play: *Assassin's Creed Syndicate* (2015) and *Civilization VI* (2016).

Since 2006, a daily webcomic entitled *New Adventures of Queen Vic-*

toria has the Queen comment on the cultural and historical phenomena of the twenty-first century with obvious disdain.[2] A particularly philosophical example is Victoria creating fake posts which overwhelm the internet collapsing it "into a black hole of metatextual irony" (15 September 2018). Thus, Victoria has the last laugh on the platform that transformed her persona for the internet generation.

This book chronicles the long journey from silent actualités where we look at Victoria from afar, through fictionalized narratives where we watch her life unfold, to a topsy-turvy internet Queen Victoria who looks at us and is both amused and exasperated by what she finds. Contemporary criticism has posited that no character can be reduced to a single meaning, a principle, as we shall see, amply demonstrated by the varied representations of Queen Victoria. Given the richness of her character and biography and the multiple interpretations of her iconic status put forth in film, television, and twenty-first century new media, we can safely assume that Queen Victoria will continue to fascinate and reflect British and indeed world-wide culture well into the future.

1

Queen Victoria on the Silent Screen

On 23 November 1896, Queen Victoria, family, and guests sat down to an evening's entertainment at Windsor Castle. On the program were several films by the French Lumière brothers and Robert Paul, as well as Birt Acres' film (now lost) of the 1896 Derby. Most notably this screening included a film taken by W. & D. Downey (the official photographers of the British royal family) in October 1896 at Balmoral showing Queen Victoria, Czar Nicholas, and his wife Alexandra (Christie 29). Afterwards, the Queen recorded in her reaction in her journal:

> After tea went to the red drawing-room, where so-called "animated pictures" were shown off, including the groups taken in September at Balmoral. It is a very wonderful process, representing people, their movements and actions as if they were alive [*QVJ*, Hibbert 334].

In this simple statement, Queen Victoria demonstrates her well-known ability to capture the pulse of the British public. Quick to capitalize on the growing popularity of silent films, she became the subject of over a hundred cataloged film titles. The content of these short films includes royal family movies; films of important public events; propaganda films showing the crown's support for war; films recording the Queen's compassionate visits to wounded soldiers; films showing Victoria's travels to specific locations throughout Great Britain, Scotland, and Ireland; and finally films of the two largest public events of her reign: the Diamond Jubilee of 1897 and her funeral in 1901.

The year 1896 was a key turning point for the British film industry. London enjoyed much of this industry's growth and witnessed an explosion in film viewing opportunities. While Londoners had access to a Kinetoscope parlor opened in 1894 (Musser 82), the smaller city of Nottingham had a Kinetoscope on exhibition in a shop as early as February 1895 (Brown and Anthony 11). The limitations of the Kinetoscope were quickly surpassed by film projection, opening up new opportunities to reach a mass audience. Entrepreneurs rushed to promote their film projection devices. Birt Acres and Arthur Melbourne-Cooper showed their Kineopticon device to the Royal Photographic Society on 14 January 1896 at the Empire Theatre. Acres later become the first cinematographer to seek royal patronage and filmed the Prince and Princess of Wales on 27 June 1896, a film now lost (Christie 28). The Lumière Cinématographe device was demonstrated in February 1896, and Robert Paul exhibited his Theatrograph device (later the Animatograph). By the end of 1896, London audiences could see films mixed with live performances at the Egyptian Hall on Piccadilly or the Alhambra Theatre of Varieties in Leicester Square.

The royal family was quick patronize the new movie theaters. At the Alhambra Theatre in June 1896, the Prince of Wales viewed Robert Paul's film of the 1896 Derby, which was won by the Prince's horse Persimmon only a day before the showing, Paul having printed his film on a rush basis (Christie 28). The Palace Theatre of Varieties, which used the American Biograph projector, began screening films in 1897. A Palace program for 25 September 1899 shows a typical mixture of entertainment: a music hall offering of classical music, comedians, mimics, singers, dancers, and acrobats, followed by the "The American Biograph" show of seventeen titles, including one featuring Victoria: "Honourable Artillery Company Review, Queen in Carriage" (Brown and Anthony 47). In 1898, the London County Council issued the first set of regulations concerning film showings (Fletcher np), and by 1908, just seven years after Queen Victoria's death, London film goers could choose from a wide variety of venues: "variety theaters ... churches, chapels, mission halls, Salvation Army hostels, workhouses, public halls, schools, shops and fairgrounds" (O'Rourke np).[1] Distribution beyond London was achieved through traveling shows: "Travelling 'bioscope' shows, which toured the national fair circuit, were also frequent visitors to London..." (O'Rourke np). Town and country clearly were demanding more and more films of every variety.

As these distribution channels proliferated rapidly, the demand for content intensified. The type of films shown from 1896 to 1901 were typically a mixture of actualities—scenes from real life of short duration (typically up to two minutes)—or short one-take narratives. As audiences gradually became more sophisticated, Georges Méliès' narrative films were distributed to an international audience, his fantasy or *féeries* (fairy stories) becoming quite popular.[2] In March 1896, Auguste and Louis Lumière presented their Cinématographe film program at London's Empire Theatre of Varieties; their slate of short films was so popular that it ran for 18 months. The Lumière program was more down to earth compared to Méliès; it included such content as "fishing for goldfish," "horse trick riders" or "baby's breakfast." Other filmmakers ventured into historical subjects and political commentary. In 1895, the Thomas Edison Production Company released Alfred Clark's notorious film *The Execution of Mary Stuart*, using live actors and the shock effect of a severed head, achieved via a stop motion trick shot with a dummy (Barry np). In 1896, the Alhambra Theatre showed two films of Tom Merry, the "Lightning Cartoonist," drawing caricatures of Kaiser Wilhelm II (Victoria's grandson) and Bismarck. Tom Merry was the stage/pen name of William Mecham (1853–1902), whose act was high speed drawing of subjects taken from the audience or famous figures. Merry's two other known films recorded his caricatures of former Prime Ministers William Gladstone (1896) and Lord Robert Salisbury (1896).

Filmmakers were quick to realize that the British monarch was a popular and sellable screen presence. Consequently, Queen Victoria quickly became as ubiquitous a film subject as she had been in print media from 1837 to 1896. The first short films "starring" Victoria appeared in 1896, peaked in 1897 for the Diamond Jubilee, and continued through her funeral in 1901. Over one hundred films about Queen Victoria were produced during this period and have survived, either as catalog entries or videos readily available on the internet (see Filmography). These films featuring Queen Victoria are what we would today call "newsreels" or shorts. Due to limitations of the late nineteenth century film cameras, these films are very short indeed, often 1–2 minutes. Some of these surviving films are longer and were the product of editing shorter takes into a longer film, some up to 15 minutes in length.

These royal silent films represent both an extension of Victoria's coverage in print media from 1838 to 1896 and a deliberate leveraging of film's immediacy. During the decades of print media coverage, John Plunkett notes a conscious effort to promote a "reflexive awareness of Victoria-as-image ... with the constitutional politics that the royal press coverage helped to promote." (Plunkett 8). Victoria and Albert established a pattern of royal public events that is still being followed today and received extensive coverage in the nineteenth century's newspapers and graphic periodicals. Such publications as *News of the World*, *Lloyd's Weekly Newspaper*, the *Weekly Times*, the *Illustrated London News*, and the *Illustrated Times* began circulation in the 1840s. The press coverage of Victoria's public appearances became "bound up with a new style of monarchy.... There was a crucial symbiotic relationship between the civic publicness of Victoria and the publicity that these events received. The movements of Victoria and Albert provided an ever-greater individual focus on their lives" (Plunkett 14).

This personal image of Victoria appears in a group of silent films that today we would call home movies, with the exception that they were taken by a professional cinematographer, not by a family member. This impulse to show the personal side of the monarch arose from the widely distributed engravings of the young glamorous Victoria and later the royal family from 1838 to 1896 (Plunkett 79–82).³ Given Victoria's awareness and approval of the broad dissemination of her personal image in print media, it comes as no surprise that after her marriage both she and Albert developed a strong interest in photography in general, and family photography specifically. Prince Albert was first photographed via daguerreotype in 1842, a dark room was installed in Windsor Castle (Christie 24), and Victoria and Albert were patrons of the Photographic Society, contributing £50 in 1855. They commissioned photographs of their children in *tableaux vivants* in 1854 (Plunkett 147).

On the commercial side, by the 1860s there were numerous posed images of the royal family intended for public consumption, often in the form of *cartes-de-visite*, a number of which were exhibited in August 1860. Between 1862 and 1900, the top four the most photographed subjects were (in descending order): the Princess of Wales, the Prince of Wales, the actress Ellen Terry, Queen Victoria (Plunkett 157). While the photographic prominence of Alexandra Princess of Wales over her husband the Prince of Wales makes an interesting parallel with Princess Diana and Prince Charles in the twentieth century, the ultimate impact was to humanize the royal family and promote the monarchy. In fact, many of Victoria's photographs were unflattering, testifying to her willingness to show herself as a real person, visibly human, and far removed from the previous Hanoverian monarchy's royal aggrandizement in their formal portraits. Furthermore, many of Victoria's still photographs show her mourning for her departed husband Albert, a situation familiar to her British subjects.⁴

Arising from the royal family's interest in still photography, a natural extension occurs in 3 October 1896 with the first of the royal home movies. *Scenes at Balmoral* filmed by W. & D. Downey has the distinction of being the earliest film currently available for viewing (see Filmography), but also clearly a family record, not unlike a contemporary family's movies (8 mm, VHS, digital) of family vacations. In this film, we see Victoria riding in a small pony cart holding her dog in her lap, followed by her relatives Czar Nicholas and his family walking the grounds.⁵ While Victoria and family appear only in long shot, the impact on the cinema audience of seeing English and Russian monarchs on vacation cannot be underestimated. The detail of Victoria holding her white Pomeranian in her lap, while several other dogs run around freely, adds the same humanizing touch as found earlier still photographs of the royal family. Victoria's journal for that date makes clear that this filming was an arranged event:

> At twelve went down to below the terrace, near the ballroom, and we all were photographed by Downey by the new cinematograph process, which makes moving pictures by winding off a reel of films. We were walking up and down [Hibbert, *QV Letters and Journals* 334].

1. Queen Victoria on the Silent Screen

Queen Victoria appears in her first silent home movie, filmed at Balmoral by Downey.

A noteworthy point is that this journal entry represents an early example, arguably the earliest, of a "making of the movie" commentary by a principal actor, now a commonplace addition to DVD/Blu-ray sets. Victoria was undoubtedly ahead of her times.

Several other family vacation films are located in Scotland: *The Queen and the Emperor and Empress of Russia at Balmoral* (1896, W. & D. Downey), *Arrival of the Queen and the Emperor and Empress of Russia at Mar Lodge* (1896, W. & D. Downey), and *Clans Receiving the Queen* (1898). Others feature Victoria with relatives: *The Queen and Royal Family* (1897, Watson & Sons Motorgraph), *The Queen, Princess and Escort* (1897, Watson & Sons Motorgraph), and *The Queen and Princess of Battenburg* (1899, Warwick Trading Co.).

As early as 1896, Victoria grasped that these highly personal films, by their foregrounding of family, friends, relatives, and pets, would have appeal to her family, though the explicit intention to distribute en mass to British film audiences has been debated by film historians. Ian Christie notes "there is no evidence that this intimate family footage was widely, if ever, seen outside the royal family until modern times" (Christie 31). In contrast, Richard Brown and Barry Anthony in their history of the British Mutoscope and Biograph Company have documented the public presentation of two royal family films (in which Victoria does not appear): *Afternoon Tea in the Gardens of Clarence House* (1897), showing several of Victoria's relatives; and *Children of the Royal Family Playing Soldiers* (1900), shown at the Palace Theatre, also made available for home display on a Kinora reel (a miniature version of the Mutoscope), and the subject of "making of the movie" article in *Harmsworth Magazine,* October 1900 (Brown and Anthony 57–59, 285). Regardless of whether intended for public or private consumption, Victoria would have given permission for filming in such intimate family settings and, as her journal indicates, was acutely aware of the cameras. Furthermore, these films deliver the moving image of Victoria with far more immediate and personal impact than earlier engravings and still photography could achieve. The potential of films to make her come *alive* to her people was not lost on Victoria, and over the next two years she appears in a range of films that were seem intended for public distribution.

Garden parties were the subject of at least three films.[6] The most personal and revealing is *Queen Victoria at Garden Party* (1898, British Pathé), which is one of the few viewable online (see Filmography). At this time three years before her death, Victoria suffered rheumatism that severely limited her mobility, and consequently she needed assistance to move in and out of her carriages. In this film, the royal carriage drives up, Victoria puts away her parasol, and then the camera, placed at a discrete distance, records the image of the Queen being assisted out of the carriage by an unidentifiable man and woman. This 1898 film evidences an enormous change in the royal attitude toward press coverage over the decades. On 6 October 1873, the *Printer's Register* reported that "a carriage of reporters was following Victoria on a drive through Fort William, only to be caught unawares when the royal carriage stopped and suddenly turned around. The reporters' carriage was forced into a ditch in order to let Victoria pass. She reportedly had a hearty laugh at their expense" (Plunkett 221). While the Queen was amused, this incident underscores her realization of the potentially deleterious impact of intrusive press coverage and an initial, albeit somewhat crude, attempt to cope with reporters. By the time of the 1898 garden party film, the roles are reversed. Victoria clearly has the upper hand through her control over the placement of film cameras at a respectful distance, while at the same time creating a cinematic record to show the monarchy interacting with people on a personal level. The garden party films testify to her willingness to show herself being assisted out of her carriage, foregrounding her human frailty. It is a touchingly personal and courageous image of the monarchy that was unthinkable for previous Hanoverian monarchs, or even twenty-five years prior.

Less personal, but more expansive in scope are the short films that record public royal events. Their visual grammar arose out of the earlier illustrated

1. Queen Victoria on the Silent Screen

This engraving from *Illustrated London News*, 26 September 1858, of Queen Victoria's visit to Leeds, offers a sneak preview of the cinematic technique of shooting a scene from different angles and distances to achieve a desired effect.

press coverage of royal events: engraved illustrations of royal visits emphasizing the sweeping vistas of large crowds and reducing the royal personages to barely recognizable figures, visible in long shot of a carriage. For example, the *Illustrated London News* of 26 September 1858 presents two views of Victoria's visit to Leeds. The first image shows the back of the Queen's coach as it enters the city through an arch, and the second image is equivalent of a film reverse shot, showing the front of the horses and carriage, reducing Victoria to a tiny figure in an open coach (Plunkett 49).

Even more emphasis on the crowds is evident in Queen's visit to Liverpool as reported by the *London Illustrated News* on 18 October 1851: a vast crowd fills the public square in front of the Town Hall without clearly showing a royal presence, and only the caption connects this image with Queen Victoria. Film coverage of royal events carried out this visual approach of extreme long shots that emphasize the vast scope of the event, while downplaying images of Queen Victoria as a person.

A number of royal visit films document the grimmest aspects of the historical and political contexts of Victoria's reign. During the last years of her reign, the Queen made numerous appearances to review her troops, which

This engraving from the *Illustrated London News*, 18 October 1851, shows Queen Victoria's arrival at the town hall in Liverpool.

were dutifully captured on film. British Mutoscope & Biograph's *The Coldstream Guards* aka *The Military Review at Aldershot* (1897) was filmed by William K.L. Dickson. While the film is lost, there is an extant photograph of Dickson filming at Aldershot on 1 July 1897. "His note on the back of the photograph reads: 'Kodak picture I took at Aldershot Showing Roped off enclosure or stand given me by the Duke of Connaught Queen's Royal carriages adjoin'" (Brown and Anthony 190). The still photo shows Dickson and camera perched high above the parade route at a prearranged location for the shooting. Surviving footage shows the Queen reviewing the troops before deployment to Africa for the Second Boer War. In *Review of the Life Guards by the Queen* (1899, Warwick Trading Co.), the camera focuses on the rows of marching soldiers, and the Queen is barely visible on the left side of the frame, while she acknowledges salutes. In *Queen Victoria with Horse Guards* (1899, British Mutoscope & Biograph Co.), the camera focuses on the parade of the mounted Horse Guards (a cavalry regiment in the British Army and part of the Household Cavalry); the royal carriage is briefly shown at the end of the film. The Queen is showing her support for these soldiers by joining her carriage into the soldiers' parade.

At least seventeen other films were made (catalog titles only, not viewable online) where Victoria is reviewing the troops between 1897 and 1900. While these films are unfortunately not available for viewing, their titles are descriptive of the content.[7] More importantly, they show that Victoria was aware of and leveraged the power of film as propaganda, to demonstrate the monarch's care for her military troops, and to deliver this cinematic spectacle to the British public at large. Ultimately, the people viewing the films and the Queen participating in the cinematic event are joining together to honor and support the military engaged in the prolonged and deadly guerrilla war. At the beginning of the Boer War, the popularity of these films was enormous: "For about a year, from the end of 1899, Anglo-Boer War-related films regularly accounted for slightly more than half of the total Biograph presentation at the Palace.... Filming troops leaving for the front and being reviewed by the Queen was an effective way to demonstrate national unity" (Brown and Anthony 129).[8]

The Queen's Dublin films are an early examples of government propaganda exploiting this royal visit to acknowledge and celebrate the role of Irish soldiers in this war. *The Queen's Visit to Dublin* (1897, unknown production company) shows Victoria in an open carriage with two larger Highlanders standing at the back. After the carriage stops, the camera is close enough to reveal Victoria nodding at the crowds. Three years later during the Second Boer War, *The Queen's Visit to Dublin* (1900, British Pathé) was shot from a much further back vantage, and the Queen is barely visible in the open carriage, greeting the local dignitaries. At the right side of the screen, a man steps out and is seen waving his arms at the crowd, whether as protest or encouragement is not clear. While this film "does not register the dissent it provoked among Irish nationalist and home-rule campaigners," it was enthusiastically received in Belfast (Christie 37). This particular royal visit was in part a response to the unpopularity of the Second Boer War in 1900. These films' images of large crowds surrounding and supporting the Queen was clearly an attempt to influence public opinion in favor of the British government's war policy.

The importance of the 1900 Dublin visit is reflected by the fact that several other film companies made records of the same event (catalog titles only, not viewable online): *The Queen's Visit to Dublin* (1900, Warwick Trading Co.), *The Queen's Entry Into Dublin* (1900, Northern Photographic Works), *Queen Victoria in Ireland* (1900, Williamson Kinematograph Co.), and *Queen Victoria's Last Visit to Ireland* (1900, British Mutoscope & Biography Co.). Three films focus on the reception at Phoenix Park: *The Queen Entering Phoenix Park* (1900, British Mutoscope & Biograph Co.), *Presenting Bouquet to Queen in Phoenix Park* (1900, British Mutoscope & Biograph Co.), and *Great Review by the Queen in Phoenix Park* (1900, Robert W. Paul). The Phoenix Park films are especially noteworthy in their visualization of spectacle: thousands (estimated 40,000 to 52,000) of Irish children greeting the Queen.[9] In her journal for 7 April 1900, Victoria reveals that she knew how to stage an impressive event, even at this very late stage in her life: "Drove ... to the public part of the Phoenix Park, where 52,000 school-children from all parts of Ireland were assembled with their masters and mistresses. It was a wonderful sight, and the noise of the children cheering was quite overpowering. I drove down the line so that they could all see me" (Hibbert 344). Victoria consciously positioned her carriage for the cameras as well, thus extending the impact empire-wide. Taken as a body, these Dublin films are early examples of propaganda films and foreshadowed the activities of the British War Propaganda Bureau during World War I.

Victoria's involvement with the military takes on a more humanitarian role in two films taken during the Second Boer War: *The Queen's Arrival at Netley* (1899, Haydon & Urry) and *The Queen Leaving Netley Hospital* (1901, Haydon & Urry). Victoria's involvement with Netley was extensive. Netley Hospital was started in 1856 at Victoria's suggestion, in response to news accounts of poor conditions in military hospitals during the Crimean War. Not only did she lay the corner stone in 1856, she made twenty-three visits to Netley throughout her reign, the first being in 1863, her first public appearance in public after the death of Prince Albert, which testifies to the personal importance she placed on this kind of event.[10] In 1898 her visit to Netley received coverage in *The Indian Medical Gazette*:

It has created a sensation of lively satisfaction among the soldiers under treatment in the Royal Victoria Hospital, and, in the Army at large, a feeling in which the public heartily participate that the aged sovereign of the British Empire, bowed with years and crippled with infirmity, should in mid-winter undertake a long journey and undergo the fatigue of a prolonged progress through the corridors and wards of a huge hospital for the purpose of personally ascertaining the condition of those who had bled and suffered for their country [*Indian Medical Gazette*].[11]

Echoing the sentiments described in this press coverage, the two Netley films underscore the power of the cinema to reinforce public appreciation and promote the impact of the monarchy's care for soldiers wounded in the Boer War. Compared to earlier static images of Victoria visiting wounded soldiers, such as an 1856 painting by Jerry Barrett showing the royal family on a hospital visit, the greater immediacy of film brings home the point more effectively, allowing the British film audiences to see their Queen in action, leading a war effort and personally caring for the wounded.

Other films associated Victoria with specific locations around or near London, and occasionally far from London. While none of these films are available for viewing, their descriptive titles demonstrate the Queen's willingness to be filmed in a wide range of circumstances. No longer the reclusive Widow of Windsor, Victoria was filmed at a large variety of locations between 1897 and 1901. Victoria's filmic presence in venues familiar to the British public were the staple stock of no less than eight film companies, resulting in twenty film titles. Victoria seems perpetually on the go, with film crews in tow:

- *The Queen Entering the Borough* (1897, Chard's Vitagraph)
- *The Queen at Temple Bar* (1897, Chard's Vitagraph)
- *The Queen's Carriage and Escort* (1897, Warwick Trading Co.)
- *Queen's Carriage and Indian Escort Arriving at St. Paul's* (1897, two parts, Paul's Animatograph Works)
- *The Queen, Princess and Escort* (1897, Watson & Sons Motorgraph)
- *Queen and Escort in Churchyard* (1897, Paul's Animatograph Works)
- *Arrival of the Queen from Windsor* (1897, Warwick Trading Co.)
- *The Queen at Sheffield* (1897, Riley Brothers), located in Yorkshire
- *Her Majesty the Queen in State Carriage* (1898, Prestwich Manufacturing Co.)
- *Visit of the Queen to South Kensington* (1899, Paul's Animatograph Works)
- *The Queen Arriving and Leaving the Lawn* (1899, Warwick Trading Co.)
- *The Queen and Royal Household with Bodyguard* (1899, Warwick Trading Co.)
- *Arrival of the Queen and Bodyguard* (1899, Warwick Trading Co.)

- *The Queen's Drive Through Windsor* (1899, Warwick Trading Co.)
- *Queen and Royal Family Entering Their Carriages* (1899, Warwick Trading Co.)
- *Departure from Folkestone of the Queen* (1899, British Mutoscope & Biograph Co.), located in Kent.
- *The Queen Leaving Buckingham Palace* (1900, British Mutoscope & Biograph Co.)
- *The Queen Leaving Windsor Castle* (1900, British Mutoscope & Biograph Co.)
- *The Queen's Visit to London* (1900, Robert W. Paul)
- *The Queen in Her State Carriage* (1901, Haydon & Urry)—Queen Victoria's last public appearance

British film audiences could scarcely have avoided seeing their Queen during those five years, testifying to continued public interest, commercial exploitation of that interest, and the monarchy's leveraging of "the Queen coming and going" films to convey a message showing her engagement with and accessibility to the public.

A subset of these "Queen coming and going films" show Victoria arriving at a specific location by railway, and in fact the royal family were seasoned railway travelers.[12] Two films recorded such travels: *Queen Victoria's Arrival at Ballater* (1897) and *Queen Victoria's Departure from Ballater for Balmoral* (1897). The town of Ballater, located 12 km west of Balmoral Castle, was used by the royal family for access to their vacation home.[13] This railway station was a branch line from Aberdeen on the Great North of Scotland Railway, which Victoria and Albert began using in 1853 to travel to Balmoral. The two films of the Queen getting off a train coach at Ballater underscore Victoria's ability to exploit the railroads for personal pleasure, but also to be seen by the British people as visiting many different parts of Great Britain.

More importantly Victoria railway films imply her endorsement of the progress resulting from nineteenth-century industrialization. "The railroads were a revolution that cut across class boundaries" resulting in the family holiday as a Victorian institution enjoyed by all levels of society (Gill 227). By taking her family holidays via railway, the Queen is able to personally visit many parts of the country, promoting her image as constitutional monarch and exemplar of family values. Unlike her Hanover predecessors who were bound to London, royal palaces, and courts, Victoria used the railway to get out and about, to be seen by any and all of her subjects (either in person or on film at a theater), and to enjoy family vacations while still conducting the business of state, anticipating twentieth-century telecommuting! In 1897 for the Diamond Jubilee, the Great Western Railway provided the Queen with a new Royal Train consisting of six coaches, indicating how essential railway travel had become.[14] The "Queen at Ballater" films, in essence industrialized moving images, reinforce how the melding of two technologies worked together for Victoria's benefit. A surviving railway artifact shows how Victoria's travels became a media event; on 10 March 1898, the London and SW

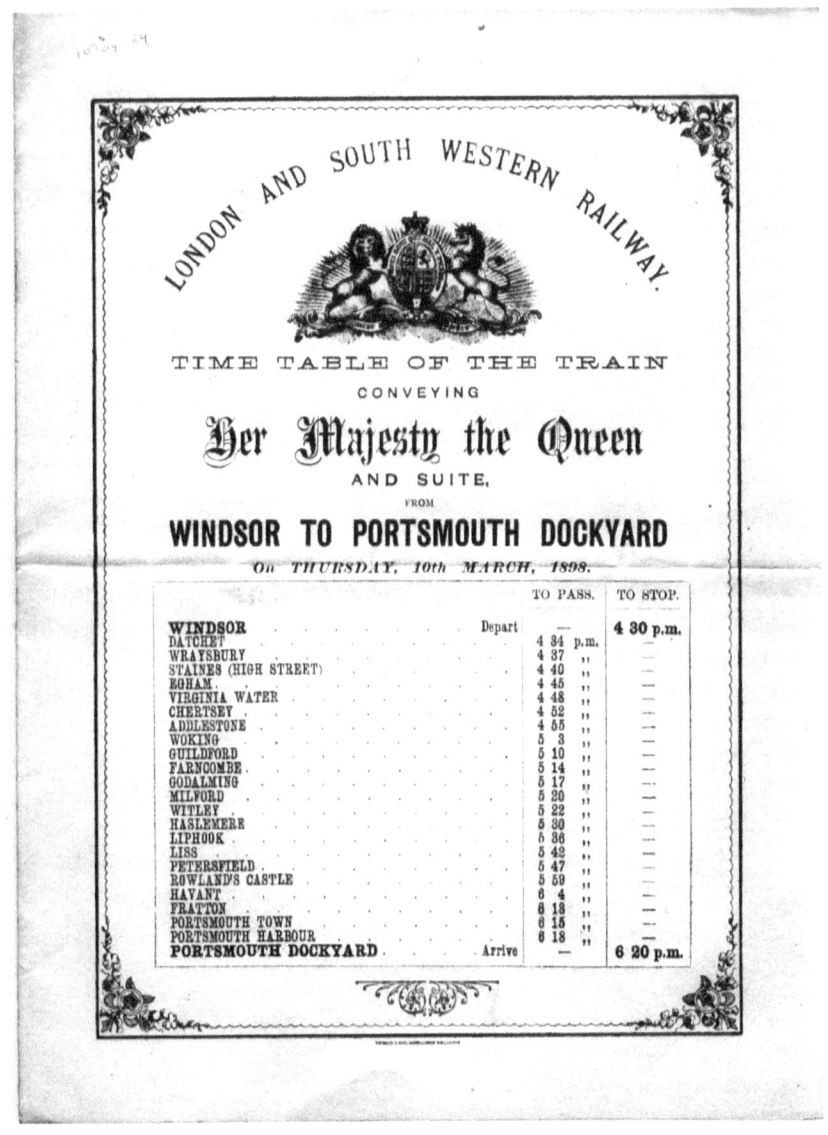

A Media Event: The railway timetable of Queen Victoria's trip on 10 March 1898 from Windsor to Portsmouth, published by the London and South Western Railway.

Railway publicized one trip on a handbill: *Time Table of the Train Conveying Her Majesty the Queen and Suite, from Windsor to Portsmouth Dockyard.* The twenty-two stations between Windsor and Portsmouth Dockyard were listed with the precise time of the train's appearance, so that people were given the opportunity to view the royal train as it passed through.[15] Thus, the railway media events complement the impact of the Queen at Ballater films, engaging monarch and people via a shared use of technology.

Two public engagement films document another key aspect of Victoria's understanding and endorsement of her country's industrialization. These films record the monarch's laying of a corner stone: *Queen Victoria Laying Corner Stone* (1899, British Mutoscope & Biograph Co.) and *Her Majesty the Queen Arriving at South Kensington on the Occasion of the Laying of the Foundation Stone of the Victoria & Albert Museum* (1899, British Mutoscope & Biograph Co.) These are likely both the same event: the laying of the foundation stone for the Aston Webb Building of the Victoria and Albert Museum on 17 May 1899. On this occasion, the name of the museum was officially changed from the South Kensington Museum (founded 1852) to the Victoria and Albert Museum. Over the years, it expanded its collections from the initial focus on applied art and science to a broader range of educational resources, including a school of design. In addition to the films of the ceremony, the *London Gazette* on 19 May 1899 reported the Queen's brief remarks ending in "I rejoice that I have been able to take a personal part in the completion of a Scheme ... which will, I trust, continue to be a powerful factor in the industrial enlightenment and the artistic training of My people." These films (surviving only as catalog titles) gave the national film audience a powerful endorsement of industrial progress, as well as promoting the museum itself. The marketing message is clear: "come see where the Queen laid the foundation stone." This the "Cornerstone" films jointly benefit both institutions, museum and monarchy and represent an early example of films leveraged for their advertising potential.

The Diamond Jubilee of 1897 received the most intensive cinematic coverage of any royal event heretofore. As Plunkett notes, it was

> one of the first major public events to be filmed. It was a key event in the development of the British film industry. The Diamond Jubilee pictures proved highly successful and were a standard feature of many variety programmes in both London and the provinces. They received showings in cities as far apart as New York, Melbourne, Cape Town, and Paris [Plunkett 240].

The day—Tuesday, 22 June 1897—was declared a bank holiday in Britain, Ireland, and India. Memorials were erected in Maidenhead, Chester, the Seychelles, Manchester, Penang, Malaysia, and New Zealand (Sully np). Ever mindful of media impact reaching across the globe, Victoria, before starting her carriage procession, sent out a telegram to every part of the British

Empire: "From my heart I thank my beloved people. May God bless them" (McKernan np).

Victoria's use of the telegraph is characteristic of her embrace and endorsement of technology. Just as she and Albert were enthusiastic photographers and patrons of the Great Exhibition of 1851, the telegraph helped Victoria disseminate her Jubilee message across the globe. Among the spectators was that most American of pundits Mark Twain, on reporting assignment for the Hearst newspapers. From his perspective as an American not particularly enamored with the concept of monarchy, Twain focused on the march of industrialization during Victoria's reign:

> Since the Queen first saw the light she has seen invented and brought into use (with the exception of the cotton gin, the spinning frames, and the steamboat) every one of the myriad of strictly modern inventions which, by their united powers, have created the bulk of the modern civilization and made life under it easy and difficult, convenient and awkward, happy and horrible, soothing and irritating, grand and trivial, an indispensable blessing and an unimaginable curse. She has seen all these miracles, these wonders, these marvels piled up in her time, and yet she is but seventy-nine years old. That is to say, she has seen more things invented than any other monarch that ever lived [Twain 1047].[16]

The Jubilee procession was designed as a massively participatory event, in which both the spectators in person and the spectators in film theaters could enjoy. The route began at Buckingham Palace, through Hyde Park, Piccadilly, Charing Cross, and Ludgate Circus to St. Paul's Cathedral, where specially erected outdoor seating was provided at the west steps (McKernan np). During a 20-minute service at St Paul's Cathedral, Victoria remained in her carriage, due to her frailty.[17] Accompanying the Queen were 50,000 troops and sixteen carriages full of dignitaries, including Victoria's grandchildren, her second daughter Princess Helena, her third daughter Princess Christian of Schleswig-Holstein, and the Princess of Wales. Behind them rode the Prince of Wales, the old Duke of Cambridge, and Prince Arthur, Duke of Connaught, who arranged the procession. All levels of society were engaged, especially Victoria's poorest subjects who enjoyed a street feast; 400,000 in London and 100,000 in Manchester received free ale and pipe tobacco. That night, a chain of beacons was lit across Britain, St Paul's was illuminated, and pubs remained open until 2:30 AM, at special government order (Sully np). Several days after the main Jubilee procession, a Diamond Jubilee military review was filmed by British Mutoscope and Biograph on 1 July 1897: *The Diamond Jubilee Review at Aldershot, showing H.R.H. the Princess of Wales Taking Snapshots* (Brown and Anthony 246). This film's title embodies the self-reflexive nature of the Diamond Jubilee event, in essence royalty captured on film taking still photographs of a royal parade.

Given the international importance of the Jubilee, it is not surprising that London received nearly three million visitors. Mark Twain, who later published his observations in the *San Francisco Examiner* and the *New York Times*, was clearly impressed by the international impact of the procession: "I was not dreaming of so stunning a show. All the nations seemed to be filing by. They all seemed to be represented.... The procession was the human race on exhibition" (Twain 1050). Anticipating a huge potential for domestic and international sales, film companies eagerly paid for rights to filming locations. Nearly forty cameramen from twenty film companies were stationed along the route from Buckingham Palace to St. Paul's Cathedral, and their output was thousands of feet of film:

> Among them was one of the pioneers of British film, Robert Paul ... with a camera on a swivel base that he announced he would use for panning shots. John Le Couteur, with his bulky 60mm Demenÿ camera, was positioned on the steps of St. Paul's itself. There were cameramen from European firms.... Gaumont, Lumière, Joly-Normandin from France and Dr. J.H. Smith of Switzerland. Hundreds of thousands would see the procession that day; hundreds of thousands more unable to be there would be able to see it on the motion picture screen [McKernan 4–5].

Of the thirty-two cataloged titles on the Diamond Jubilee, six still exist for viewing online. Unfortunately, no examples of Paul's panning shots have survived. In general, the surviving films were taken as long shots, putting the emphasis on the spectacle. The shot composition bears a strong visual similarity to the illustrations of the 1850s royal events, such as visit to Leeds in the *Illustrated London News*, 26 September 1858. In the procession films, the brief images of Victoria show a distant figure, often overshadowed by her parasol. This is quite a contrast to the personal immediacy of the Balmoral film of 1896 or garden party film of 1897. The emphasis is on commonality: the British Empire, people of all ranks and nations, coming together in a sweeping vista of stunning images.

The international interest in the Jubilee is evident in *Diamond Jubilee Procession Taken from Apsley House* (1897), photographed by John Le Couteur for the French Gaumont Company. Only 45 seconds in length, it shows the point at Hyde Park Corner where the procession made a right turn. The camera in use was the 60mm camera invented by Georges Demenÿ for Gaumont. Le Couteur, who was the agent for the Demenÿ/Gaumont equipment, claimed to have spent over £200 filming the Jubilee with three cameramen (Idler 102). The film clearly shows the horse riders and carriages before they make the turn. In the foreground a band faces away from the camera and towards the street. Unfortunately, this film did not capture an image of Victoria, and the other Jubilee films shot by Le Couteur have not survived.

Much more of the spectacle appears in the 4:27 minute *Queen Victoria's Diamond Jubilee Procession* (1897), photographed by the British Cinematograph Company using the Joly-Normandin camera.[18] This camera recorded the procession on St. James's Street, with horse riders and backs of heads of standing spectators, horse drawn artillery, carriages of dignitaries, the military band on horseback with their instruments (trombones and drum especially), and one of the Indian representatives with his turban clearly visible. The film's images capture the elaborate decorations on St. James's Street, with forty Venetian masts topped with the Imperial crown and festooned with garlands. Two huge Corinthian columns were placed at either end, shown clearly in the film, as the camera captures the parade winding around a corner (McKernan np). These parade film give some inkling of scope and impact of the Diamond Jubilee procession.

The participants in the procession ranged from political to royal to military. Mark Twain noted that the procession's length before he saw the Queen. "At last when the process had been on view an hour and a half, carriages began to appear ... containing the Ambassadors Extraordinary, in one of them Whitelaw Reid, representing the United States. Then six containing Ministers foreign and domestic; princes and princesses, and five four-horse carriages freighted with offshoots of the family" (Twain 1051). This variety is evident in the Lumière Company's nine separate titles (only still shots exist). Two titles—*Queen's Arrival from Windsor* (# 488) and *Crowd following the Queen's Carriage (# 489)*—were taken on 20 June 1897 when Victoria left Windsor and arrived at Paddington to encounter large crowds. On 22 June, Alexander Promio, the photographer for Lumière, filmed multiple shots of dignitaries (numbers from Lumière Catalog): *Foreign Princes* (# 491), *Ambassadors* (# 492), *Life Guards and Dragoon's Band* (# 493), *Naval Field Battery and Guns* (# 494), *Colonial Premiers and Colonial Troopers* (# 495), *Royal Horse Artillery with Guns* (#496). And finally, the Queen, seen in the Lumière film *Her Majesty the Queen and her Escort* (# 490), sitting under her white parasol. From his vantage at the Strand, Twain recalled "a landau driven by eight cream-colored horses, most lavishly upholstered in gold stuffs, with postilions and no drivers ... came along, followed by the Prince of Wales, and all the world rose to its feet and uncovered. The Queen-Empress was come" (Twain 1051).

The main ceremony at St. Paul's Cathedral was the most prized location for film companies, who paid dearly for access to this site. They included Robert Paul and assistant Mr. Hunt, and John Le Couteur for Gaumont (McKernan np). Not all film companies succeeded in producing viable film, as Paul later recalled:

> Large sums were paid for suitable camera positions, several of which were secured for my operators. I myself operated a camera perched on a narrow ledge in the Church yard. Several continental operators came over, and it was related of one that, when the Queen's carriage passed he was under his seat changing film, and of another, hang-

ing on the railway bridge at Ludgate Hill, that he turned his camera until he almost fainted, only to find, on reaching a dark room, that the film had failed to start [Christie 34].

Fortunately for posterity, Paul was able to capture a clear shot of Queen Victoria, under the white parasol, bowing her head right and left, in his film *Queen Victoria's Diamond Jubilee* (1897). In addition to his motion picture crew, Le Couteur had a still film camera set up at from St Paul's and achieved some measure of success with it. In an interview in the *Idler*, "M. Le Couteur produced a magnificent print of the photo ... he himself took on Jubilee Day from his special sentry-box like erection on the steps of St. Paul's. It is claimed to be the finest photo of Her Majesty secured on that ever-to-be remembered occasion" (Holland 102). This image shows the Queen's face peering out from the white parasol.

After the short 20-minute ceremony at St. Paul's, the procession returned to Buckingham Palace. One of Robert Paul's cameramen shot *Queen Victoria's Diamond Jubilee from York Road* (1897). The quality of this shot is not as good, since the camera is shaking up and down as two groups of horsemen pass from left to right on York Road, just before Westminster Bridge. Much clearer is the Prestwich *Queen Victoria's Diamond Jubilee Procession* (1897), taken from the other side of Westminster Bridge (McKernan np). This film

This still from the Lumière film *Her Majesty the Queen and her Escort (Le Cortege La Reine, # 490)*, June 1897, shows Queen Victoria hidden under her white parasol, surrounded by military escorts and crowds.

1. Queen Victoria on the Silent Screen

has a yellowish tint with a sharp focus. It shows the cream-color horses pulling the Queen's carriage, Victoria under her white parasol, and at the right the Prince of Wales on horseback.

An unknown production company shot *Queen Victoria's Diamond Jubilee location unknown* (1897), believed to be in the City of London area; one shot in this film shows Victoria looking towards the camera. R. J. Appleton's *Queen Victoria's Diamond Jubilee Procession* (1897), which has not survived, was taken on the procession route outside St. George's Church, and is noteworthy for its speedy distribution. Appleton used a special van to develop and print his film on the train journey to Bradford, where he screened it on the same evening of the Jubilee. This lost film was said to show the Queen smiling.[19]

The quality of these Jubilee films may disappoint the modern audience accustomed to high-resolution extreme close-ups of celebrities. The poor quality is partially attributable to the limitations of outdoor photography in 1897 and to the locations permitted for camera setups. Other limitations of focus are apparent. Queen Victoria viewed several of the Lumière films and recorded in her journal for 23 November 1897 that "they were very wonderful, but I thought them a little hazy & rather too rapid in their movements" (Christie 36). Regardless of technical limitations of the time, the cinematic emphasis on the spectacle was the real attraction for the British audiences. Ticket sales were hot. During 1897 alone, Biograph's regional showings included forty-four theatrical engagements, some one day long, others lasting multiple days, such as 5 July through 20 September at the Winter Gardens Theatre in Blackpool (Brown and Anthony 315). Film distributors took note of the extreme interest by raising their prices to theater exhibitors: "several filmmakers ... increased the 'standard' 1s per foot rate for films of the Queen's Diamond Jubilee in 1897, and then returned to the old price level when less salable products followed" (Brown and Anthony 18). Interest in Jubilee films was clearly widespread, driving up ticket sales:

> The general impression given by reviews from the late-1890s is that audiences outside of London were infused with a post–Jubilee euphoria, more interested in witnessing the scenes that confirmed themselves as citizens of the world's mightiest Empire than as inhabitants of workaday regional centres. An advertisement for the Empire Palace, Edinburgh, on 23 August 1897 listed.... *Her Majesty the Queen's The Diamond Jubilee Festivities* ... with a note proudly proclaiming "IMPORTANT—These Pictures were exhibited before His Royal Highness the Prince of Wales ... who highly complemented the exhibitor on the superiority of his Subjects" [Brown and Anthony 207–08].

As a cinematic event, the Diamond Jubilee provides early examples of differential pricing and celebrity endorsement being leveraged in a widely distributed marketing campaign.

While these Jubilee films could not offer close-ups, it is interesting to

The cover from a souvenir commemorative program for the Diamond Jubilee: *Her Majesty's Glorious Jubilee 1897, The Record Number of a Record Reign*, published by the *Illustrated London News*.

note that film goers had access to more intimate visual artifacts of the event, in essence, souvenirs. The official Diamond Jubilee photograph of Queen Victoria was notable since it was the first time the monarchy officially endorsed a photograph of the Queen. Taken by Downey in dated 1893, four years before the Diamond Jubilee, it "was deliberately not registered for copyright, a decision that allowed it to be reproduced at will. Wholly protean, the image appeared on biscuit tins, commemorative plates, and souvenir artifacts of every description." (Plunkett 197). It is not hard to image the film audiences watching the spectacular films of the Diamond Jubilee procession while munching on the contents of the Queen Victoria Regina biscuit tins. Victorians may not have enjoyed popcorn at the film theater, but official Jubilee biscuits seem a suitable parallel of the convergence of the film and gustatory experiences. Not surprisingly, the marketing potential for Jubilee items was enormous. Surviving souvenirs include Jubilee postage stamps, coins, postcards, teapots, tea cups, mugs, jugs, spoons, medals, pins, pendants, vases, glass bottles, buttons, handkerchiefs, cards with various images of the Queen and the procession or the royal family tree, books, bookmarks, and lavishly illustrated commemorative programs published by the *Illustrated London News*.[20]

A little over three years after the Diamond Jubilee, Queen Victoria's health was in serious decline. On 22 January 1901, surrounded by family, supported by her grandson Kaiser Wilhelm and her long-time personal physician Dr. James Reid, she died at 6:30 PM at Osborne House, the family home designed by Prince Albert where she typically spent Christmas and New Year (Reid 212). Victoria's death was announced to a stunned nation: "people gathered anxiously on street corners, traffic came to a halt and bells tolled. This was the end of an era" (Bourke np). In New York, the stock market closed, telegrams poured into Osborne House, and assessments of her impact were many, including personal grief, comments about her as a mother of nations, praise for her iconic status as a model of decorum, and statements attesting to her near divine status and to her inspirational impact on the nescient women's rights movement (Baird 485–88). Many felt the loss of an icon of stability. Laurence Housman, the playwright best known today for his 1934 play *Victoria Regina*, wrote "The most dramatic thing about Queen Victoria was her duration: in the moving age, to which she gave her name, she remained static" (Housman 370). The notion of Victoria as a fixed point in a moving universe contrasts ironically with the near obsessive interest of the film industry to record her funeral in moving images and distribute these films as widely as possible.

The media interest had started as early as 19 January 1901 when an official public bulletin was issued indicating the Queen's decline, followed by the ominous "The Queen is sinking" message issued at 4 PM on 22 January (Baird 481–3). Her funeral on 2 February 1901 was a global media event, extensively recorded and presented to film audiences. The opportunity for spectacle drew the attendance of two major film companies: British Mutoscope & Biography Company and British Pathé, each with three film titles apiece, plus several unknown filming companies. Public interest was high, and the

Warwick Trading Company, which exhibited their own films as well as those from other companies, posted record viewership in February 1901: the "films of Queen Victoria's funeral procession ... transformed the normally quiet February month into the best results yet achieved by the company," resulting in net sales of more than double that of February 1900 (Brown and Anthony 20–21).

At least nine of approximately twenty film titles are viewable online (see Filmography; duplicates are noted). British Mutoscope made shorter film clips (only descriptions available): the coffin at Trinity Pier being loaded into the royal yacht Alberta, the procession taken from Earl Gray's Gardens, and the naval brigade drawing the cortege gun carriage. These three films were distributed to audiences in the United States, appearing in the *American Mutoscope and Biograph Catalogue* 1902. The longest films were made by British Pathé's, such as *Funeral of Queen Victoria A, B, C and D* (1901), most likely shot separately and then later edited into longer films.

The Pathé "A," "B" and "D" films are duplicates, with a running time of about 15 minutes each. Subtle timing differences and reversed images in some scenes suggest that Pathé created three prints of the same film (see Filmography). The first scene is the funeral procession on the Isle of Wight where Osborne House was located. Next, we see the royal yacht Alberta on route to the mainland, and a puff of smoke from a cannon is visible. One oddity is that from the beginning through the yacht scene, both the "A" and "B" films reverse the images: soldiers' medals, rifles and swords are on the wrong side (i.e., on the right of the body when they should be on the left near the heart), the drummers are wearing their drums on the wrong side, and the royal yacht moves from left to right across the frame. However, the "D" film corrects this mistake: the yacht moves right to left across the frame, and the soldiers wear their medals on the left.

After the sea scene the Pathé film includes several different shots of the funeral procession through the streets of London, passing through two turns, one at the Marble Arch giving a good view of King Edward VII and Kaiser Wilhelm. The next scene cuts to the coffin's arrival at Windsor, where the gun carriage is pulled by seamen (after the horses had broken their traces), followed by an assortment of military groups, the Yeomen Warders (Beefeaters), and a group of Scotsmen in kilts. Next the Pathé film shows the coffin's arrival at St. George's Chapel and the pallbearers carrying it up the steps. This scene is composed of two shots from different angles. The first camera produced rather dark and fuzzy images, but did capture a strange shot of a woman breaking out of the procession on the steps to hug a bystander at the left. The hug appears in the center of the frame. The second camera gives a reverse angle shot, in much clearer detail, of the ceremonious removal of the three-crown covering from the coffin on the gun carriage and then the movement of both up the chapel steps. The most endearing shot occurs in London where a stray dog runs in front of the marchers for a few brief seconds.[21] Between both the hugging woman and the stray dog, Victoria would have approved and most likely laughed.

Other companies were involved in filming the funeral, with mixed results. *Funeral of Queen Victoria—The Marble Arch* (1901) was taken by an unknown film company. It is a very dark and fuzzy version of the parade past the Marble Arch, taken further back from the filming position of Pathé; it omits the left turn after this point in the procession, and King Edward is barely visible on horseback. Cecil Hepworth's *Queen Victoria Funeral Procession* (1901) is much more successful and surprising modern. Considered one of the most creative figures in British silent cinema, Hepworth was stationed to film the departure of Queen Victoria's coffin from the Isle of Wight on 1 February 1901. He positioned his camera from a lower, close-angled position than those seen in the Pathé "A" and "B" films, resulting in a more personal, dramatic touch. At 0:16 minutes there is a medium shot of royal physician Sir James Reid's face, grief clearly marked on his features, as he marched on the left side of the procession.

Other companies merely leveraged clips from Victoria's funeral for use in compilations of disparate topics. A bizarre example exists in the Huntley Film Archives # 3221, which sandwiches a four-second clip of the Queen's funeral between Edison's *The Burning Stable* and a shot of a lightning sketch artist drawing a cartoon. The motive behind such a compilation is baffling, although it does testify to the public interest in seeming films of the Queen's funeral, as well as the liberties taken by film exhibitors eager to catch the public interest in current events.

The most interesting film of the funeral is the 5-minute Pathé "C" film, which provides shots of the coffin with three crowns and its white drapery (the color dictated by the Queen's express directions for her funeral). The Pathé "C" film also shows King Edward VII (on a black horse) and her grandson Kaiser Wilhelm (on a white horse) parading through London.

Unique among the surviving funeral films, the Pathé "C" film then cuts to the Great Western Railway's Windsor station where a long shot shows sailors waiting at train station as the royal funeral train pulls in. Discretely, the film skips over images of the coffin's removal from the train and next presents a long sequence showing the sailors pulling the gun carriage away from the train station, followed by the King and Kaiser on foot, followed by many groups of military units. This train shot captures Victoria's last railroad journey, on the Great Western Rail from Paddington Station in London to Windsor.[22] The *Railway News* for 9 February 1901 reported that the royal train was "composed of an engine and eight vehicles ... viz.: Engine, brake van, saloon, funeral car, Royal saloon, saloon, bogie first-class carriage, bogie first-class carriage, and brake ... this was the first occasion on which the dead body of a British Monarch was born on the way to its last resting-place by railway." In the Pathé "C" film, only the engine with its funeral drapery barely visible and the first two of the saloon cars are in frame, set against a rather dark background. As was the case in the Golden Jubilee films, the emphasis is on the crowd, and this film delivers clear images of the many military units involved, befitting the funeral of a soldier's daughter, as Victoria called herself in her funeral directions.[23] Touchingly, the Great Western was the railway on which Victoria took her first ride in 1842 with Prince Albert and her last, nearly 59 years later as her coffin moved towards to its final resting place next to her beloved consort.

All these films are of course silent, and serendipitously that very silence reflects the reaction of the crowds watching the funeral procession. In a letter dated 2 February from Windsor Castle, Sir James Reid, Victoria's personal physician, noted both his sorrow and the reactions of the watching crowds: "My last journey with Bipps [his nickname for the Queen] is over, and I feel rather sad.... There was an imposing assemblage at Victoria

Queen Victoria's coffin is pulled by sailors at Windsor train station. Note two of the marchers are looking directly at the camera, thus acknowledging the camera as participant in the event. From the *Pathé A film* (1901).

Station.... I walked on the left side of the gun carriage...—a very slow march—two hours I think till we reached Paddington, immense crowds all the way.... Not a sound anywhere we passed" (Reid 219).[24] While the films show there was music in the funeral procession, the real crowds apparently watched in respectful silence, while the "reel" experience for the global audience was told in silent imagery—an instance of cinematic art mimicking life.

The technical advances achieved during Victoria's reign—railways, telegraphy, still photography, motion pictures—come together powerfully in the films of the Golden Jubilee and especially Victoria's funeral. And the fleeting human touches—stray dog running across the procession, hugging woman on the chapel steps, the face of her grieving friend and physician—enhance the impact, visually speaking to the audience, a media construct that draws them into the reality of the event. In the next generation of films where an actress portrays the Queen, Victoria finds her voice on screen, as she leads her country in time of war.

2

Of War and Empire

In a letter to Lord Beaconsfield (Disraeli) on 28 July 1879, Queen Victoria demonstrated both an astute grasp of military matters and a steely determination to involve herself in her government's response to the many wars fought during her reign:

> One great lesson is again taught us, but it is never followed: never let the Army and Navy down so low as to be obliged to go to great expense in a hurry.
> This was the case in the Crimean War. We were not prepared. We had but small forces at the Cape: hence the great amount having to be sent out in a hurry.... If we are to maintain our position as a first-rate Power ... we must, with our Indian Empire and large Colonies, be prepared for attacks and wars, somewhere or other, continually. And the true economy will be to be always ready. Lord Beaconsfield can do his country the greatest service by repeating this again and again, and by seeing it carried out. It will prevent war [Hibbert, *QV Letters and Journals* 259].

Such a comment about war and empire is far from unique in Victoria's correspondence and journals. Quite the reverse is the case. During Queen Victoria's reign 1837 to 1901, it is difficult to find a year without a war being waged somewhere on the globe by British forces. In 1900 the "sun never sets" empire held sway over nearly one quarter of the world (both land mass and population). Attempting to expand markets for British manufacturing spurred by the industrial revolution, Disraeli's government aggressively pursued imperial expansion into Asia, India, and Africa, while retaining Canada, Australia, and New Zealand. As a consequence, the British military were on a perpetual wartime footing. Many of these wars have been the subject of movies, such as *Zulu* (1964) and *Zulu Dawn* (1979).[1] The focus for this chapter is on feature films where first, Queen Victoria is character portrayed by an actress, rather than just a passing reference or limited presence; second, one of the Victorian era-empire building wars is a subject, if not *the* subject. Therefore, feature films such as *The Campbells are Coming*, Francis Ford's 1915 spectacular about the siege of Lucknow, or the well-known Errol Flynn vehicle *Charge of the Light Brigade* (1936) will not be dealt with since Victoria does not appear in either film.[2] This chapter will discuss the films in the chronological order of the war they portray.

The earliest Victorian-era war appearing as the subject of a feature film occurred in 1839–42. Known as the First Opium War, this dispute centered on British trading rights in China, diplomatic relations, and the administration of justice in deliberately isolationist China. After nearly two centuries of a large trade imbalance, nineteenth-century British merchants began importing opium (up to 30,000 chests annually) at massive profits. Worried about both the drain of silver on their economy and a growing number of addicts, the Daoguang Emperor (Qing Dynasty) appointed a viceroy Lin Zexu to root out opium trade. In 1839 Lin confiscated and destroyed about 20,000 chests of opium and closed the port of Canton to foreign trade, actions that precipitated war with England. The British Navy defeated the Chinese and forced the Qing dynasty to sign the Treaty of Nanking 1842 that ceded Hong Kong to the British Empire and opened an additional five ports to foreign trade. This treaty is infamous in the China was the first of the "unequal treaties" leading to the so-called "Century of Humiliation" at the hands of European powers.

In coordination with the 1997 handover of Hong Kong from Britain to China, *The Opium War* (aka *Yapian zhanzheng*) was released in the same year. Directed by Jin Xie, it was shot in Hengdian World Studios (known as "Chinawood") where the streets of nineteenth-century port city Guangzhou were recreated. Told from the Chinese point of view, this epic of the First Opium War runs 154 minutes, including multiple well-staged battle scenes, altogether costing £7,000,000 and using 50,000 extras (Higgens 1). The key British characters are villains, especially the merchant Denton (Bob Peck, best known for *Jurassic Park*) who is crude, brutal, immoral, and grasping. Charles Elliot (Simon Williams, of *Upstairs Downstairs* fame) is portrayed as a military officer in the film, in contradiction to the historical record of Elliot's non-military services as Superintendent for British Trade in China. In the film, Elliot scoffs at Chinese military capability, boasts of the British Navy's might, and lusts after Chinese women. In a key scene, Elliot is given Lin Zexu's letter to Queen Victoria, which was published in Canton and openly accused the British of poisoning the Chinese (De Bary and Lufrano 201–204). Elliot refuses to deliver the letter and condescendingly tucks it back into the Chinese courier's shirt. To balance the tone, however, many British politicians are shown speaking against the war, notably during a debate in Parliament highlighting Gladstone's famous speech against the ethics of the Opium War. Interestingly, the Daoguang Emperor comes in for criticism as well; the film shows him as indecisive, with a limited understanding of the larger world and the potential impact of industrialization on England's ability to wage war. Lin Zexu (Guoan Bao) is treated more heroically, and at the end of the film, when going into exile, he sends a globe to the Emperor with a prescient message that China cannot afford to be out of touch with the larger world.

Compared to the treatment of English villains in *The Opium War*, Victoria is shown as a decisive monarch, determined to promote the expansion of the British Empire. Victoria (Debra Beaumont) has four scenes of about four minutes of screen time. After a scene of the British cabinet discussion in favor of war, the film cuts to Windsor park where the Queen is informed by Foreign Secretary Lord Palmerston (Benjamin Whitrow) and Prime Minister Melbourne (Corin Redgrave) that the Chinese have destroyed £8,000,000 worth of opium and are trying to drive the English out of China. While appearing quite young and pretty, Victoria clearly is on top of events and displays an aggressive attitude to her ministers saying "I hear you are already assembling marine forces" as she walks away snapping her horse whip. To emphasize Britain's technical superiority, the next scene shows Victoria cutting a ribbon to open a new railroad, a foreshadowing of the battles later in the film where British technology—warships, cannons, and rifles—are vastly superior to Chinese weaponry. Victoria's imperialism is demonstrated in the scene where she approves the design of the first British stamp, known as the 1839 Black Penny. Prince Albert (James Innes-Smith) comments that this stamp will be used world-wide, thus underscoring British colonial ambitions.

In a later meeting with Melbourne and Palmerston, Victoria asks them for an assessment of viceroy Lin Zexu and then states her political assessment that this war has evolved from a dispute about lost property (20,000 chests of opium) into a dispute about free trade, which Victoria declares is essential to the British Empire. Imperialist and strong, the Queen tells her ministers (as opposed to taking advice from them): "we must teach them a lesson on free trade. Britain has the responsibility to open up this last and largest territory in the East.... Whoever gets hold of China will have the entire East." The aggressiveness of Victoria in *The Opium War* pointedly contrasts with the vacillating and weak Chinese Emperor, who cedes Hong Kong to the British and turns on Lin Zexu, today seen as both a national hero and as the scapegoat for the lost war.

Duleep Singh (1838–1893), the last Maharajah of the Sikh Empire, is the subject of the 2017 film *The Black Prince*. A subject rarely covered in film, with the exception of an occasional documentary, Duleep's tragic story is told against the background of the First and Second Anglo-Sikh Wars (1845–46 and 1848–49). Queen Victoria (Amanda Root) has a secondary role as a substitute mother figure to Duleep (Satinder Sartaaj) and appears in a limited number of scenes. The film is notable for its extremely slow pace, flashbacks to bloody events in the Punjab, boring shots of a moody exiled king (he is asked "what troubles you" by multiple people on multiple occasions), nearly non-existent character development, and poor box office performance (total gross of approximately $633,000, meaning the film most likely did not make back its production and distribution costs). On the positive side, the production values are high, featuring gorgeous costumes, slow pans of beautiful landscapes and historical buildings, and most notably Shabana Azmi's powerful characterization of Duleep's mother, Maharani Jindan, who calls on him to regain his kingdom and Sikh roots. Ultimately, *The Black Prince* does not give much sense of interior life of the main character, or any other character for that matter. Queen Victoria is shown as a kindly sort, encouraging Duleep to smile during his portrait session for a painting now hanging at Osborne House (Hibbert, *Personal* 192). She engages him in Christian prayer, fondly refers to him as her "black prince" and helps to convince the government to allow Duleep to return to India to meet his mother. The tea scene between Victoria, Duleep, and Maharani Jindan is arguably the best in the film, certainly the one with the most sense of life. The Queen is smiling graciously, while the Maharani makes snarky comments in Punjabi about the tea service having been stolen from her family and the Queen's rudeness in not offering food to her visitors.

As *The Black Prince* progresses, Victoria's political power diminishes. In another tea scene set in the beautiful Buckingham Palace gardens, Duleep tells her that he wants his Punjab kingdom back, and Victoria warns him "what you seek is now gone," a fact which the rest of the film makes evident. Finally, in a scene completely lacking in historical credibility, Victoria humbles herself to apologize: "all I wanted was the love of a child. Forgive me, my

Queen Victoria (Amanda Root) invites Duleep (Satinder Sartaaj) and his mother Rani Jindan (Shabana Azmi) to tea. Rani Jindan is not amused. From *The Black Prince* (2017).

son, for we have wronged you and now I am so helpless." All historical evidence contradicts such a statement on Victoria's part; in fact, Duleep begged Victoria's forgiveness in 1891 for his dissipated life (Hibbert, *Personal* 447, Mallet 48). By glossing over key historical events, *The Black Prince* reduces its plot to the political struggle of Sikh versus British and passes up the opportunity to delve into the cultural and psychological conflicts haunting the protagonist.

Made to order for British war films, the Charge of the Light Brigade occurred 25 October 1854 during the Battle of Balaclava in the Crimean War. Given its potential for cinematic spectacle, the heroism of a doomed assault, and the tragedy of command miscommunications, the Charge of the Light Brigade appears in multiple films and documentaries. Well known films such as the 1912 *The Charge of the Light Brigade* (a 12-minute short from Edison Studios, directed by J. Searle Dawley), the feature length in 1936 of same title (Warner Brothers, directed by Michael Curtiz, starring Errol Flynn and Olivia de Havilland) and the 1968 film of the same title (directed by Tony Richardson, starring Trevor Howard and John Gielgud), do not include Queen Victoria as a character and therefore will not be discussed in this book.

The historical record of the Crimean War demonstrated a transformation in Queen Victoria's response to this conflict. Initially reluctant about English involvement, once war was declared, Victoria became a highly engaged war-time monarch, constantly bombarding her ministers with concerns about poor preparation. As early as 30 November 1854, Victoria decided to create the Victoria Cross, with directions that show real thought to make the award meaningful and personal to her soldiers:

> The medal should have the word "Crimea" on it, with an appropriate device ... and clasps—like to the Peninsular Medal, with the names Alma and Inkerman inscribed on them, according to who had been in one or both battles. Sebastopol, should it fall, or any other name of a battle which Providence may permit our brave troops to gain, can be inscribed on other clasps hereafter to be added [from a letter to the Duke of Newcastle, Hibbert 127].

This medal takes on a notable patriotic status in the silent film *The Victoria Cross*. Capitalizing on audience awareness of an impending World War I, this 15-minute film, directed by Hal Reid for the Vitagraph Company, was released in the USA on 27 April 1912 and on 16 May 1912 in UK. Starring Edith Storey as Ellen Carson and Wallace Reid as Lt. Cholmo[n]deley, it features the women characters more than might be expected for a war film. The first two scenes are dominated by women: a dance scene followed by a confrontation between Ellen, the lieutenant, and her disapproving father, Colonel Carson; and the hospital scene where Ellen approaches Florence Nightingale (Julia Swayne Gordon). After much persuasion, Nightingale accepts Ellen as a nursing volunteer. The scene shifts to the English camp in the Crimea, where the colonel is receiving battle orders and is immediately interrupted by women: Nightingale and her nurses. The remaining half of the film, about six minutes, is the staging of the charge of the Light Brigade, handled as crossing cutting between four distinct elements: the battlefield shots, Ellen's observation of the charge through her binoculars, her emotional reactions, and title cards with lines from the Tennyson poem.[3] The battle is shown in conventional long shots with a static camera with the horsemen moving in and out of frame. In contract, Ellen's view of the battle is framed as two semicircles, to mimic her view in the binoculars, effectively mediating the battle action through a single perspective. Ellen's emotional reactions are consistently shown in medium shot, full screen, static camera, while her hand movements of binoculars mimic the direction of the charge. During the battle, she sees her father fall from his horse and the Lt. Cholmodeley [sic] rescue him.

A quick title-card cut to England brings *The Victoria Cross* to another woman-dominated scene where Queen Victoria awards the Victoria Cross to Lt. Cholmodeley [sic]. The staging of the Queen's two minutes of screen time is similar to the long shots familiar to audiences of the earlier movies of her Di-

In the silent *The Victoria Cross* (1912), the heroine Ellen Carson (Edith Storey) views the Charge of the Light Brigade through her binoculars.

amond Jubilee. The Queen, nodding her head to the assembly, arrives at a parade ground at the back of the frame, as a carriage drawn by four white horses moves toward the film viewer and out of frame. After a title card explains that the Victoria Cross was made "from cannon captured in the Crimean War," a medium shot shows Victoria walking across the front of the frame towards the soldiers and pinning the medal on the Lieutenant. He wears it in the final scene where the father gives his blessing to the happy couple. *The Victoria Cross* consistently presents the women as the frame of reference, both narratively and visually—the feminine world of the ballroom, the humanitarian campaign of Nightingale's nurses, the heroine's binocular observations of the charge, and film's final image of the Victoria Cross.

A much more elaborate silent film about the Crimean War, *Balaclava* was shot at a critical juncture of the British film industry's transition to sound films. In an instance of art imitating life, this film was itself a battle to get produced and released. Originally shot for Gainsborough Pictures by Maurice Elvey in 1928 as a silent film, the reconstruction of the Charge of the Light Brigade was shot at Aldershot, Salisbury Plains, and Long Valley, "the nearest thing available to the 1854 battlefield" noted in *Kine Weekly* 8 November 1928 (Brown 1–2). Production plans evidently included sound, as British Acoustic van trucks were present at the battlefield shooting.[4] Due to internal disagreements over whether the British Acoustic sound could be synchronized effectively for theatrical presentation, Gainsborough Studios withheld the film, added synchronized sound scenes (shot by a new director Milton Rosmer), and released as a talkie on April 1930 in London. Starring Cyril McLaglen (younger brother of Victor McLaglen) and Benita Hume, the film employs a familiar plot device: a British officer John Kennedy (McLaglen) is falsely accused of murder by a rival officer and is dishonorably discharged from the army. He rejoins as an enlisted man and is posted as a cavalryman to the siege of Sebastopol during the Crimean War. There he encounters Jean MacDonald, a young English woman (Benita Hume), who is living in Crimea for reasons not clearly shown.

Jean discovers a Russian spy and courageously rides out to the British regiment to warn them. In a fit of narrative economy, the film uses her warning to move directly to the famous Charge of the Light Brigade to take the Balaclava Heights. The action leading up to the charge, particularly the mistaken order "There is your enemy. There are your guns," is effectively staged. Kennedy fights valiantly both on foot and on horseback. At one point, the film uses cross cutting between Kennedy's frenzied face in close-up and the confusion of battle in long shot. *Balaclava* ends with a confession from the real murderers, thus exonerating Kennedy who embraces Jean joyously. Unfortunately, only a truncated (35 minute) silent version in readily available, and Queen Victoria does not appear in this incomplete version. Film pro-

2. Of War and Empire 43

JAWS OF HELL starring Cyril MacLaglen

John Kennedy (Cyril McLaglen) attempts to charm Jean McDonald (Benita Hume) in *Balaclava* (1928).

gram notes from a 1972 showing by the Theodore Huff Film Society mention that Queen Victoria is treated harshly (Huff np). Most likely, Victoria, the Tsar, and Lord Palmerston (all credited for this film), appeared in the sound footage and are shown as political manipulators, as opposed to the brave members of the Light Brigade. Arguably, 1928 audiences retained vivid memories of the shocking horrors of World War I, and were prepared to take a negative view of the governments that brought the world into such a destructive war.[5]

The Crimean War was notable for the involvement of women in the field, as well as Victoria's participation as an involved war-time monarch. Victoria avidly followed the newspaper accounts of the "Lady with the Lamp." A January 1850 letter from Queen Victoria to Florence Nightingale expresses the strong feminist stance that the famous nurse inspired in Victoria:

> I need hardly repeat to you how warm my admiration is for your services, which are fully equal to those of my dear and brave soldiers, whose sufferings you have had the privilege of alleviating in so merciful a manner. I am, however, anxious of marking my feelings in a manner which I trust will be agreeable to you, and therefore send you with this letter a brooch, the form and emblems of which commemorate your great

and blessed work.... It will be a very great satisfaction to me, when you return at last to these shores, to make the acquaintance of on who has set so bright an example to our sex [Hibbert 135].

Victoria's admiration of Nightingale appears in two films. A Kay Francis vehicle *The White Angel* (1936) includes a brief nod to Queen Victoria. The brooch award scene is staged with Nightingale (Kay Francis) rehearsing her speech and the Nightingale Pledge to a large portrait of the Queen. Then we see Nightingale turn and curtsy as the Queen (an uncredited Fay Holden) enters the room, obscured by a row of footmen. Only the Queen's hand is visible, as she gives the commemorative brooch over to an official, who pins it on Nightingale. The film ends with a close-up of the front of the Nightingale brooch. The reverse of the Nightingale brooch, designed by Prince Albert, states "To Miss Florence Nightingale as a mark of esteem and gratitude for her devotion towards the Queen's brave soldiers. From Victoria R. 1855."

In *The Lady with a Lamp* (1951), the meeting between Queen Victoria and Florence Nightingale is dramatized quite differently. The film's timeline is framed by the 1907 presentation of the Order of Merit to an elderly Nightingale, who was the first woman to receive this honor. Within that frame, the bulk of the film focuses on Crimean War, with brief mention of Nightingale's later work in setting up the nursing school at St. Thomas' Hospital in 1861. The film benefits from Anna Neagle starring as Florence Nightingale, with a strong supporting cast: Michael Wilding as Lord Sidney Herbert, Gordon Jackson as Dr. Anson, and Felix Aylmer as Lord Palmerston. A staging of the Charge of the Light Brigade (with lines from the Tennyson poem superimposed over the image), is highly effective; the editing of the war scenes was praised by *TV Guide* (1951), as was Neagle's characterization of Nightingale as a "sincerely moving study" (*Variety*, December 1950). Immediately after the Charge scene, the film shows a field reporter making notes that resulted in an October 1854 editorial excoriating the death rate at Scutari Hospital. Two themes appear multiple times during film: Nightingales' conflicts with patronizing or indifferent male officials and her revolutionary insistence on strict sanitation. Two scenes show the famous lamp, the first handled dramatically in a long shot of a nighttime ward and Nightingale descending a staircase in the far back center of the frame, the light streaming from her lamp. In the second lamp scene, Nightingale reads a letter from Queen Victoria to her wounded soldiers.

The Lady with a Lamp does not stage the brooch scene. Instead, Nightingale returns to England and meets Queen Victoria (Helena Pickard) and Prince Albert (Peter Graves, the British actor, not the American TV star) at Balmoral. Dressed simply for a family holiday in Scotland, the Queen thanks Nightingale for her work with "our noble and sick soldiers" and listens with interest to her pitch for continued reform in living conditions for British troops in India.

In a follow-up scene, Victoria and Albert discuss political topics such as the proposal of a Royal Commission for India. Albert warns that Nightingale's ideas will cause "consternation" in the War Office (as it did), to which Victoria takes a strong stand that the commission is the right course of action and that she wishes that Nightingale had been in the War Office.

Queen Victoria's role as war-time monarch during the Crimean War receives a more contemporary and politically imbued slant in the 1938 *Sixty Glorious Years* (aka *Queen of Destiny*). The second of two Victoria biopics, starring Anna Neagle as Queen Victoria and Anton Walbrook as Prince Albert and produced by Herbert Wilcox, *Sixty Glorious Years* is a follow-up to the successful 1937 *Victoria the Great*. The earlier 1937 film focuses predominately on the

This poster for *The Lady with a Lamp* (1951) shows Anna Neagle as Florence Nightingale. Note the curious graphic design: typeface letters in sharp set against a deliberately grainy background.

domestic and personal; Wilcox called it a "tribute to the woman" (Chapman 75). In contrast, the 1938 film intercuts the personal with political events, specifically foreign wars in the Crimea and the Sudan receiving as much as 20 percent of the screen time. The fact that the entire *Sixty Glorious Years* was shot in Technicolor is significant (only the last section of *Victoria the Great* on the Diamond Jubilee was in color). In 1938 only about a dozen films (out of over 390 released in UK and USA) were done in color, due to the huge expense of the patented Technicolor process and availability of the patented Technicolor cameras.[6] James Chapman notes that *Sixty Glorious Years* "was one of the first British features made in three-strip Technicolor—the cinematographer, as on *Victoria the Great*, was Freddie Young, working under the nominal supervision of American 'color director' Natalie Kalmus—and must therefore be presumed to have been an even more expensive production than its predecessor [about £150,000], though there is not clear indication of its cost" (Chapman 67, 79).

Sixty Glorious Years was considered important enough to warrant such considerable effort and expense. While the color enhances the many non-political domestic scenes around Victoria and Albert's marriage, it is the handling of the Crimean War where use of color dramatically underscores the action and highlights the political importance of its anti-appeasement message. Released in the UK on 14 October 1938 at a London premier, the political context for this film is Neville Chamberlain's policy of appeasement to Germany and the Munich Agreement 29 September 1938, which allowed Germany to annex portions of Czechoslovakia and bring, in Chamberlin's words, "peace with honor," tragically followed in less than a year by Hitler's invasion of Poland and the British declaration of war in September 1939. Director/producer Wilcox acknowledged his awareness that his second Victoria film was made "at a time critical to our national history.... I sought out Sir Robert Vansittart at the Foreign Office, who for years had advocated a strong line towards Germany" (Chapman 79). Vansittart, ousted from the Foreign Office because of "his implacable hostility to Chamberlain's appeasement policy" (Downs 98), wrote a screenplay (presciently completed before the Munich agreement) which takes a clear stance against appeasement and, more

A magazine advertisement for *Sixty Glorious Years* (1938) describes the film as "A Cavalcade of British Nation Building," and touts the use of Technicolor, and the reappearance of stars Anna Neagle and Anton Walbrook, who reprise their roles from *Victoria the Great* (1937).

thoughtfully, provides a nuanced balance of the arguments for waging war with an understanding of the horrors of war.

Sixty Glorious Years makes extensive use of title cards to convey the historical context of the Crimean War: "The clouds of war gather over Europe when the designs of the Czar upon Turkey—'The Sick Man of Europe'—threatened to involve England, where the Queen's and Prince Albert's policy of conciliation 'exasperated' the Foreign Minister, Lord Palmerston." The first scene in the Crimean sequence shows Lord Palmerston as the war monger; he characterizes the royal couple as "two innocents" (an obvious swipe at the Foreign Office appeasers in 1938), ignores a letter from the Czar offering peace, and delivers a fiery speech in favor of war with Russia. In contrast, Albert's strong stance for peace is based on an actual letter from the Prince which characterized "talk of the inevitability of war as 'like living in a madhouse'" (Downs 101). Finally, Queen Victoria is convinced by the Lord John Russell that war in the Crimea is inevitable after she and Albert witness street mobs waving signs "Albert the Traitor" and accusing him of being a foreign agent. The film then moves forward to the drawn-out Siege of Sebastopol and shows the tide of political opinion on the home front transitioning from a previous bellicose attitude towards an anti-war, anti-government mindset. Using cross cutting, the camera first focuses on a newspaper headline which

In *Sixty Glorious Years* (1938) Albert (Anton Walbrook), center, and Victoria (Anna Neagle), far right, visit the wounded and discover the lack of medicine and food during the Crimean War.

reads "Appalling Conditions in Crimea" and then follows up with a scene of starving soldiers lying in the snow, lamenting their lack of ammunition. In the next scene, Victoria and Albert visit a military hospital and are shocked when one soldier informs them of the lack of chloroform for amputations.[7] While the soldiers in the hospital cheer the Queen, a group of three women make scathing comments that Victoria has not sacrificed a son or husband, though they are somewhat mollified when they observe her weeping about the soldiers' conditions. As Stephen Fielding notes "this senseless sacrifice provokes the Queen to tears ... showing even her most skeptical subjects that she truly cares for them" (Fielding 74).

The alternation of critical vs. reverential attitudes toward crown and government continues through the last major scenes for the Crimean War in *Sixty Glorious Years*.[8] Immediately following the image of a weeping Queen, the film presents a full Technicolor treatment of the Charge of the Light Bridge (25 October 1854). While brief, about a minute of screen time, the impact of showing battle action in color is not inconsiderable, compared to the more well-known *Charge of the Light Brigade* (1936) filmed in black and white. Using the inevitable quote from Tennyson, the long shot montage of cannon, horses, smoke, and doomed soldiers captures the scope of the engagement, and the color enhances the emotional impact by making it very real—less about individual heroes (as in the Errol Flynn film) and more about the collective heroism of the brigade and the utter waste begot by the incompetence of their military officers. The final scenes move forward to 1856 to show Queen Victoria establishing the Victoria Cross, specifying its composition of base metal from cannons and the words "for valor." She awards it to a Crimean commander, followed by a presentation of the special brooch award to Florence Nightingale. Bringing in the Nightingale brooch as the last statement ends this sequence on a note of political consensus for the British people; it balances humanitarian efforts to ease suffering with a call to sacrifice for coming conflict of World War II looming on the political horizon.[9]

After the Crimean War, the cinematic treatment of war, or at least potential for war focuses on the Trent Affair of November 1861. The earlier Anna Neagle—Anton Walbrook film *Victoria the Great* (1937) primarily explores the relationship of Victoria and Albert, and that aspect will be discussed in the next chapter. One exception is its treatment of the Trent Affair, included for both topical appeal to audiences in the United States and for the opportunity to show Prince Albert sacrificing his health to save Great Britain from a costly war. At the beginning of the American Civil War, Britain had issued a proclamation of neutrality on 13 May 1961. Over the next five months, the two sides traded barbs: Secretary of State William Seward declared the intention to treat as hostile any country that recognized the Confederacy and put in place a blockade of Southern ports, while Britain sent 3,000 troops to Canada in anticipation of an invasion by the United States. Given such heightened tensions, in November 1861 a U.S. Navy warship stopped the British steamer *Trent* in international waters and seized two Confederate envoys—James Murray Mason and John Slidell—on their way to Europe to lobby for diplomatic recognition, as well as financial and military support. American reaction was jubilant: legal pundits applauded the legality of the arrests. British opinion was swift: this was an insult to national honor and a violation of maritime law.

Victoria the Great summarizes this international crisis in about ten minutes of screen time (nearly 10 percent of film's length) by dramatizing Prince Albert's efforts to revise the government's belligerent dispatch to U.S. President Lincoln.[10] The first scene shows Prime Minister Palmerston lecturing a colleague about the outrage to British national dignity. When asked if he should send his strongly worded dispatch to the Queen for review, his caustic reply is that the Queen and Prince think foreign policy is their realm (which they did), there isn't time to send it up to Balmoral, and that he wants to send troops to Canada, with an eye to dissolution of the United States. Victoria and Albert receive an anonymous letter, its text shown as a title card, urging them to return to London to avert war with the United States. In the ensuing confrontation with Palmerston, Albert hotly defends himself against Palmerston's accusation that he is a "foreign" influence and the "best hated man in the country." The Queen resorts to a cutting line "Lord Palmerston we are not amused" (the sole instance of this iconic line in the entire film) and gives him a direct order to hold off on the dispatch. Gravely ill, Albert stays up all night revising the dispatch and then collapses. The scene shifts to Washington, D.C., where President Lincoln tells his cabinet that the matter is closed and gives the Queen and Prince the credit for the temperate and diplomatic tone of the message. Ultimately, *Victoria the Great*'s emphasis is more on the physical and emotional toll that the Trent Affair took on Prince Albert and secondarily on the contrast between Victoria's political decisiveness and Albert's physical decline. Such tight focus on their partnership throughout the Trent crisis scenes increases the emotional impact of Albert's deathbed scene. Contrary to historical fact, this deathbed scene is staged with only Victoria in attendance to witness his passing on 14 December 1861.[11] Her solitary figure walks out of the room and down a long hallway, visually implying the isolation and narrowing of her life after Albert's death.

While several films dealing with Victoria's reclusive "Widow of Windsor" phase will be discussed in the next chapter, several other feature films take a radically opposite approach to Victoria's later life. Specifically, these films examine and celebrate British imperialism by featuring the partnership between Prime Minister Benjamin Disraeli and Queen Victoria to expand the British empire. By 1875, the opportunity to gain British control over the

Suez Canal presented itself. Constructed from 1859 to 1869, the canal shortened the journey from the Indian Ocean and North Atlantic Oceans by up to 3,700 miles and avoided the treacherous waters of the Cape of Good Hope. By 1875, the bankrupt Khedive Pasha sold his country's Canal shares worth £4,000,000 to the United Kingdom, while France still controlled the majority of the shares. Prime Minister Disraeli came under heavy criticism from William Gladstone for essentially cutting the deal (including a loan from the Rothschilds) without referring to or obtaining permission from Parliament. Britain gained full control of the Suez Canal in 1882 and held that control until 1956.

British empire-building via the Suez Canal is a key narrative point in Louis N. Parker's 1911 play *Disraeli*, which starred George Arliss on Broadway. The play was adapted into three feature films: *Disraeli* (1916), an unsuccessful film starring Dennis Eadie, all prints of which were destroyed by the producer Arrigo Bocchi in 1921 when George Arliss bought the film rights in preparation for his silent version; *Disraeli* (1921), a silent version of the play, starring George Arliss and Florence Arliss; and *Disraeli* (1929), a talkie starring George Arliss and a young Joan Bennett. These films based on the Parker play devote the bulk of the screen time to the efforts of Disraeli's wife to help him complete the Suez purchase, an interesting parallel to the Victoria-Albert partnership and one which has a woman playing a central role in political events. As a result, the play's version of Queen Victoria is limited in scope. The 1911 playbill and 1921 film credits do not include Victoria. The 1916 film credits Mrs. Henry Lytton as Queen Victoria; however, since this film is lost, there is no way to verify the amount of screen time for or attitude towards the Queen. The 1929 film has Margaret Mann (uncredited) as Queen Victoria in a non-speaking role: the final scene is a reception in honor of Disraeli and his wife, held in an anteroom. The Queen appears when the doors are opened to show her enthroned at a distance, and the film ends with a glorification of Queen and Empire.[12]

The Suez Canal is also a key element of *Sixty Glorious Years* (1938), which, not surprisingly for a biopic, puts Victoria at the center of political intrigue. First, the film shows Disraeli discussing with Lord Darby the possible sale of Suez Canal shares and stating the need for quick action. Later at dinner, Disraeli and the Queen have a whispered conversation, clearly aware that others at the dinner party are attempting to eavesdrop. Victoria agrees with Disraeli that the Canal must be bought quickly, without going through Parliament and firmly declares because the Canal is "an artery of the British Empire," the opportunity outweighs the unconstitutionality of bypassing Parliament to make the purchase. Also given the 1938 release date, the Suez scene in *Sixty Glorious Years* again reflects the concerns of a nation facing imminent war by demonstrating to the 1938 audience how prescient Victoria and

2. Of War and Empire 51

Disraeli were in 1875 to acquire that shipping lifeline for Great Britain. The scene conveys an implicit condemnation of the appeasement policy of Neville Chamberlain's government during the years leading up to World War II.

The Prime Minister (1941) takes the Suez discussion into much greater detail and echoes the overall anti-appeasement message of *Sixty Glorious Years*. Directed by Thorold Dickinson, *The Prime Minister* starts out much like the Arliss plays, focusing on the personal relationship of young Disraeli and Mary Anne, his gradual rise to power, his relationship with Queen Victoria and Prince Albert, and Mary Anne's declining illness. Compared to the Arliss film, *The Prime Minister* gives Queen Victoria more to do, and notably Fay Compton as the Queen receives fifth billing (much higher than the 1916 *Disraeli* film).[13] The love story of Disraeli and Mary Anne (starring John Gielgud as Disraeli and Diana Wynyard as Mary Disraeli) concludes with a scene involving a compassionate and thoughtful Queen Victoria. Coming immediately after a title card touting the series of 1870s social reforms implemented by Disraeli and the Conservative Party (affordable housing, sanitation codes, reforms in education, legal rights for factory workers), Queen Victoria offers Disraeli a peerage as an earl, which he declines for political reasons but asks that his wife receive the title of Viscountess Beaconsfield. He tells the Queen that he would be "nothing without her [Mary Anne]." After looking nostalgically at a picture of Prince Albert, thus drawing a parallel between both couples, the Queen brings Mary Anne out from behind a curtain to congratulate her and expresses concern for her illness. Aware that she has stomach cancer, Mary Anne begs the Queen to not let Disraeli give up after her death.

About three quarters through, *The Prime Minister* shifts from the domestic and personal to Disraeli's influence on international affairs. In a scene set in 1875 scene, Disraeli's cabinet discusses the purchase of the Suez Canal shares and Cyprus. Disraeli warns that Russia wants to invade Constantinople and that Bismarck cannot be trusted, but receives a skeptical response from these British politicians. The film

Fay Compton as Queen Victoria in *The Prime Minister* (1941).

glosses over the issues about the unconstitutionality of funding for the Suez Canal purchase and instead moves to British preparation for the Congress of Berlin of 1878. Although the now widowed Disraeli is reluctant to attend, Victoria bluntly tells him that the other British politicians are too inexperienced to deal with Bismarck. In a bold move that goes against the supposedly non-political role of a constitutional monarch, Victoria shows Disraeli a letter from her daughter Victoria Crown Princess of Prussia warning of Germany's plans to invade France while Russia invades the Balkans and Constantinople. With Victoria's explicit backing, Disraeli cautions his cabinet against "appeasement to an autocrat" and that autocrats [technically 1878 Russia, but really Germany in context of this 1941 film] recognize only arguments backed by force. The cabinet is not convinced and decides to continue a policy of appeasement. Disraeli confers with Queen Victoria who fumes against these "mad blind fools." She approves his plan to mobilize the Indian Army in secret and bring them through the Suez Canal, and writes a letter to the Viceroy of India to initiate this action. In this astonishing scene, Queen Victoria has not only correctly anticipated a major war but also has taken unconstitutional steps to put Great Britain on a war footing, without referring to Parliament—a strong anti-appeasement message for the 1941 British audience, showing the monarchy saving the nation while the elected government dallies.[14]

The Congress of Berlin receives significant screen time in *The Prime Minister*. Disraeli and German Chancellor Otto von Bismarck are shown trying to outmaneuver each other. In a comically staged scene, Bismarck and Disraeli have a private three-hour dinner ("more goulash, Mr. Disraeli?"), ending with cigars, presented in an elaborate ritual. This scene has basis in historical fact. Disraeli reported to the Queen that "I dined with [Bismarck] alone ... and then we talked and smoked. If you do not smoke under such circumstances, you look like a spy, taking down his conversation in your mind. Smoking in common puts him at his ease" (Pakula 349). In the end, the Prime Minister outwits the German Chancellor, resulting in Bismarck's famous comment about Disraeli "der alte Jude, das is der Mann." The Prime Minister comes away with Germany's agreement to pull back from supporting Russia, granting Great Britain her key point of continued Turkish rule over Constantinople, as well as gaining control over the strategically placed island of Cyprus.

The final scene of *The Prime Minister* is Queen Victoria's reception of Disraeli who declaims "I have brought you peace with honor"–a clear reference to Prime Minister Neville Chamberlain's similar statement on returning from the 1938 Munich Agreement with Germany.[15] The irony would have been clear to 1941 audiences. Chamberlain's conference gave away huge territory to Germany, and World War II began within a year, while Disraeli came home bringing "Peace with honor and Cyprus too," as the joke went at the time, a peace that was maintained for nearly 30 years until the outbreak of World War I. The film ends on a triumphant patriotic note: Victoria gives Disraeli the Order of the Garter, and they go out on the balcony of Buckingham Palace where crowds sing "God Save the Queen" and Disraeli murmurs "if only she [Mary Anne] could have been here."[16]

The Sudan Campaign (aka the Mahdist War, 1881–99), in particular the fall of Khartoum in January 1885, is effectively dramatized in *Sixty Glorious Years*. By 1881, British interests in the Egypt were threatened by conflict between the Khedive of Egypt supported by Great Britain, and the revolutionary forces of religious leader Muhammad Ahmad bin Abd Allah, who proclaimed himself the "Mahdi" or "Guided One" of Islam. General Charles Gordon led a campaign against the Madhi, but by late May 1884, his troops were hopelessly surrounded by nearly 50,000 Mahdist soldiers at Khartoum, the capital of the Sudan. Complicating the situation, communications between Khartoum and the outside world were severely hampered by the cutting of the telegraph lines to Cairo. For three months, Gladstone's government procrastinated, due in part to his stance against "a war of conquest against a people struggling to be free" (Farwell 280). Finally, Gladstone's government authorized a relief expedition in late August, which was delayed by formidable geographic barriers and determined Mahdist forces, arriving two days too late.

Sixty Glorious Years picks up the story with a title card setting up the situation: "The Sudan—where General Gordon was besieged in his heroic stand against the fanatical native leader—the Mahdi—whose conquering hordes—in revolt against Egyptian rule—brought terror and bloodshed to countless millions." In the next scene, while a British soldier patrols the fort walls at Khartoum, Gordon is showing refusing to evacuate and puts his hope in relief from Queen and government. Back in England, Queen Victoria confronts Gladstone to protest the tardy efforts to relieve Khartoum, and Gladstone merely stonewalls telling her "everything has been done that can be done."[17] The narrative moves to 26 January 1885 when Khartoum falls, after a 313-day siege. Based visually on George Joy's well-known painting *General Gordon's Last Stand*, Gordon is shown kissing the Bible and going outside onto a balcony, where he is speared in the chest.[18]

In *Sixty Glorious Years*, Queen Victoria gets the final word by taking a strong and brazenly public method to chastise her Prime Minister: she sends Gladstone an uncoded telegram (later reported in the press), shown as a title card in the film: "It is too fearful to consider that the fall of Khartoum might have been prevented and many precious lives saved by earlier action" (Hardie 84). Immediately after this stunning rebuke, the film moves to a long shot of a victory parade depicting the liberation of Khartoum in 1898. The image is superimposed with a title card "It was not until thirteen years later that the Mahdi was defeated at the Battle of Omdurman [just across the Nile], and his conqueror—General Kitchener—triumphantly entered Khartoum." Throughout the Khartoum sequence, *Sixty Glorious Years* celebrates Queen Victoria's attitudes, in opposition to a government that considered her actions unconstitutional and "provoked Gladstone into declaring that he 'would never set foot in Windsor again'" (Hibbert, *Personal* 371). The film celebrates the Queen's stature as a soldier's daughter and protector of her country's honor, expressing frustration at an inert, inept, inactive government. The parallels to the 1938 Munich Convention and Chamberlain's policy of appeasement are inescapable and played to the hilt by the film's glorification of Queen Victoria's forceful intervention.[19]

The triumphant relief of Khartoum in 1898 was soon eclipsed by the atrocities committed by British troops during the Second Boer War (1899–1902). The British use of scorched earth tactics and concentration camps had catastrophic impacts on the civilian population and were the target of excoriating attack in *Uncle Kruger* aka *Ohm Kruger* (1941).[20] The most notorious of the Nazi propaganda films against Great Britain, this biopic of Paul Kruger (starring Emil Jannings as Paul "Ohm" Kruger) is told in flashback.[21] A dying Kruger tells his story to a nurse in a Swiss hospital, beginning with the buildup to the Second Boer War. Kruger is consistently presented sympathetically as the patriotic President of the South African Republic (i.e., the Transvaal), and is contrasted with the sly, cunning, and despicable Cecil Rhodes, Prime Minister of the British Cape Colony (Ferdinand Marian). Rhodes sends out his equally crafty henchman Jameson to incite unrest and smuggle guns to black Africans, an event known as the Jameson Raid of 1895–96. In another scene, the film shows ostentatiously hypocritical British missionaries, with smirking, pious looks on their faces as they distribute rifles and Bibles to black Africans. A furious Kruger arrests Jameson, thundering "only an Englishman would smuggle weapons into a foreign country," the first of several such anti–British declamations throughout the film. After Rhodes discovers the presence of gold in Boer territory, he starts buying up land, and Kruger in response passes laws restricting land sales without government approval remarking "If Cecil Rhodes is involved, it stinks of gold."

In *Uncle Kruger*, Queen Victoria (played by Hedwig Wangel, noted German character actress with a sonorous voice) is brought into the film first as a looming presence of her portrait, referred to as the "White Mother" by black leader Lobengula, who admits to Kruger that his people received their guns from British missionaries. The scene shifts to London where Joseph Chamberlain, Colonial Secretary, has an audience with an old and ailing Queen Victoria. He tries to convince her to "make changes" in South Africa, meaning British domination over Kruger's Transvaal and the Orange Free State. She counters all his arguments and then in a coughing fit, asks for her medicine which is revealed as a very large glass of scotch poured into her glass by

2. Of War and Empire   55

John Brown. Weakened by illness and alcoholism, the Queen finally responds when Chamberlain tells her of gold. Victoria is show as mercenary and grasping: "If there is gold to be found there, then this land belongs to us? Do the missionaries have enough guns and ammunition?" Finally thinking "agreements are cheaper than war," and "my government can trick an uneducated farmer," Queen Victoria decides to invite Kruger to a meeting in London, a scene that dramatizes the Anglo-Boer conflicts, but has no basis in historical fact.[22]

In a formal presentation scene, *Uncle Kruger* shows Queen Victoria as feeble, using a cane and assistance from the Prince of Wales to step down from her throne. After the British sign an agreement with Kruger allowing them to mine for gold, the next scene jumps forward in time to Rhodes and Jameson discussing how Kruger duped the government. Victoria gets scant respect from her two minions: Jameson calls her "an old frump," and Rhodes fumes that Kruger "managed to trick the best brains of the English government and even our good old 'up to every trick' Queen." Debating tactics, they decide on bribery, and Rhodes directs Jameson to the checkbook sitting "under the Bible." After several montages of Boer mobilization, including a parade featuring a caricature of Queen Victoria, the film moves to Field Marshall Kitchener, who in 1899 implements his scorched earth policy and concentration camps: "no more humanitarian sentimentality." Scenes of farmhouse burning and attempted rape are crosscut with Kruger struggling with increasingly blindness, desperately planning a trip to gain support in Europe, and paying an emotional farewell to his wife.

Uncle Kruger jumps forward to 1901 with the news that Queen Victoria is dying. A profligate Prince of Wales is depicted at Paris chorus girl review (very short skirts and derriere bumps right at the camera lens) when he gets the summons back to England. On her deathbed, Victoria gives final advice to her son: "Something terrible is coming our way." The camera moves to a close-up of her haggard dying face: "You have to be very clever and very careful, my son. Always make sure the nations hate each other. For the day they stop arguing with each other will be the day of our downfall."[23]

As if this wasn't enough condemnation of the British, *Uncle Kruger* piles more on: the burning of a farm owned by Kruger's son, his execution forcibly witnessed by his wife, a massacre of women and children at a concentration camp, and a final searing image of a baby crawling out from its dead mother's arms. Once the flashback ends, the dying Kruger delivers one more anti–British oration: "Eventually the day of retribution will come.... Great and powerful nations will revolt against the British tyranny. They will knock England down to the ground. God will be with them. And they shall clear the way for a better world." Strong stuff, this condemnation of Great Britain's use of concentration camps, but also exceeding ironic, conveniently overlooking the historical record of approximately 6 million Jewish deaths, up to 17 million victims overall in German concentration camps (Niewyk and Nicosia 52).

Another film that deals with the Second Boer War is as far from the tone of *Uncle Kruger* at it is possible to get. *The Little Princess* was released on 11 March 1939, four days before Germany occupied Czechoslovakia, and six months before the invasion of Poland. A charming, albeit escapist, Shirley Temple vehicle, *The Little Princess* is based on a novel by Frances Hodgson Burnett and provides a sympathetic view of England's involvement in the Boer War and of Queen Victoria, in particular. Little Sara Crewe (Shirley Temple) is left in a London girls' boarding school by her captain father who is ordered to the Boer War and listed as dead during the siege of Mafeking (1900). Refusing to give up hope, she scours the hospital wards and encounters Queen Victoria (Beryl Mercer), who is visiting wounded soldiers.

Sara Crew (Shirley Temple) meets a sympathetic Queen Victoria (Beryl Mercer) in this lobby card for *The Little Princess* (1939).

Every bit the Grandmother of the nation, dressed in her iconic black, with small white headband, the Queen is confined to a wheelchair, but alert and compassionate. Observing the ruckus of attendants trying to get Sara out of the ward, she imperiously interrupts, beacons the child over, and tells one of her colonels to help Sara search the wards. The dialog of this encounter is typical of the light tone that pervades *The Little Princess*:

"What is your name?," asks Shirley.
"Victoria, what is your name?"
"O Your Majesty" [kissing the Queen's hand],
"I hope you will find your father, dear."

Sara does find her father, after several instances of misdirection, and they both salute Queen Victoria as she is leaving the hospital while the soundtrack plays "God Save the Queen," followed by "Rule Britannia" during the credits. Described by *Variety* (31 December 1938) as "saccharine to the nth degree," this film's contrast to the savagery of war in *Uncle Kruger* is like night and day. Supportive of England and ending with the same patriotic music as *The Prime Minister*, this Temple vehicle delivers Hollywood fantasy (e.g., the dream sequence and ballet with Shirley as princess and Arthur Treacher as court jester). Dressed up in Technicolor (a first for a Temple film), *The Little Princess* peddles a mixture of bland pro–British sentiment and escapism to 1939 American audiences cushioned by the U.S. government's isolationism from the impending horrors of World War II.

An alternative view of British empire building is captured in two British films about the efforts of Scottish missionary-explorer David Livingstone to bring education, sanitation, and Christianity to Africa: the 1925 silent epic *Livingstone*, directed and starring M.A. Wetherell, and the 1936 *David Livingstone*, essentially a talkie remake, starring Percy Marmont, directed by James A. FitzPatrick. The 1925 silent film is subtitled *A Film Biography of the Great African Explorer*, which sums up the overall approach. *Livingstone* captured the "expressions of popular imperialism" (Rapp and Weber 3–17) by first endorsing the explorer's religious ideals as justification for exploration aimed at opening up new markets for British commerce and, second, by dramatizing his strong stance against slave trade, which the film shows being run by the Portuguese, Arabs, and Mohammedan black Africans. For example, after discovery of Lake Nyasa, Livingstone is shown writing (via a title card): "If only I could establish a steamer on this lake to trade in European goods, I know I could ring the death-knell of this abominable slave trade."

A key scene in Livingstone's campaign against slavery involves Queen Victoria. The audience actually occurred in 13 February 1858, when Livingstone had returned to England to drum up support for additional expeditions. The scene first has Victoria asking Livingstone to tell her about his African discoveries. Both are shown in long shot, but greater impact occurs as this conversation (title cards again) is crosscut with location footage taken during an 1923–24 expedition: spectacular shots of Victoria Falls as well as impressive safari shots of eland and antelope herds.[24] The Queen is particularly pleased that the falls are named after her and is seen smiling (in long shot).

The scene then moves on to Livingstone's condemnation of the African slave trade—"God's image, carved in ebony, is sold for a few shillings in the slave market at Zanzibee. For every one of these poor slaves sold, ten die of disease, ill treatment or a broken heart before they reach the coast." Livingstone's speech is crosscut with a scene in a slave market where slave

Promotional pamphlet for the silent *Livingstone* (1925) directed by M.A. Weatherall, whose 1923 African location footage for this film predated the better-known safari footage used in *Trader Horn* (1931). This scene shows Stanley (right) greeting Livingstone (left).

merchants inspect and bid for the captured Africans. Responding to the raw power of Livingstone's depiction of African slavery, the Queen endorses his campaign to abolish the slave trade.

Livingstone's audience with the Queen ends on a lighter note. When Victoria asks if the Africans were curious about her, Livingstone replies "Yes, your Majesty. I said you had much wealth—and they wanted to know how many cows you had." Victoria laughs heartily at this, again all in respectful long shot. This scene is the last of the limited amount of levity in the film (there were earlier semi-comic scenes of Livingstone's courtship of Mary Moffett). The remainder of the film moves into Livingstone's final explorations, his meeting with Stanley, his search for the source of the Nile, his death and burial. A last title card proclaims "And now the body broken in the service of humanity rests in Westminster Abbey amongst the greatest of our British Dead" and the final images of the Abbey's exterior and nave, where Livingstone is buried, bring the film's conclusion to an emphatically visual celebration of a humanitarian British Empire.

A final glorious celebration of British Empire appears in both the

Wilcox-Neagle biopics *Victoria the Great* (1937) and *Sixty Glorious Years* (1938). Undoubtedly consuming a major portion of an estimated production cost of £150,000 (Chapman 67), the final 10 minutes or so of *Victoria the Great* shifts into Technicolor to cover the last twenty years of Victoria's reign, handled via a title cards and a shot of the British flag. These title cards foreground the film's political agenda, specifically its concern "to validate the institution of monarchy in the wake of the Abdication Crisis of 1936" (Chapman 64). The first title card (dated 1877) in this sequence celebrates the Queen's "innate sense of ruling that was to guide her through the most glorious period in the history of the British Empire." Splashed with Technicolor, a triumphant scene—staged outdoors with Victoria enthroned in long shot at the center of the frame, flanked by green verdure—shows Disraeli proclaiming Victoria Regina et Imperatrix, after a speech summarizing the progress, interestingly couched as a balance between global industrialism (the telegraph, railways, factories, shipping to "the four corners of the world") and social reform (children no longer slaving in mills, women no longer working in mines, "more kindliness between rich and poor.")²⁵

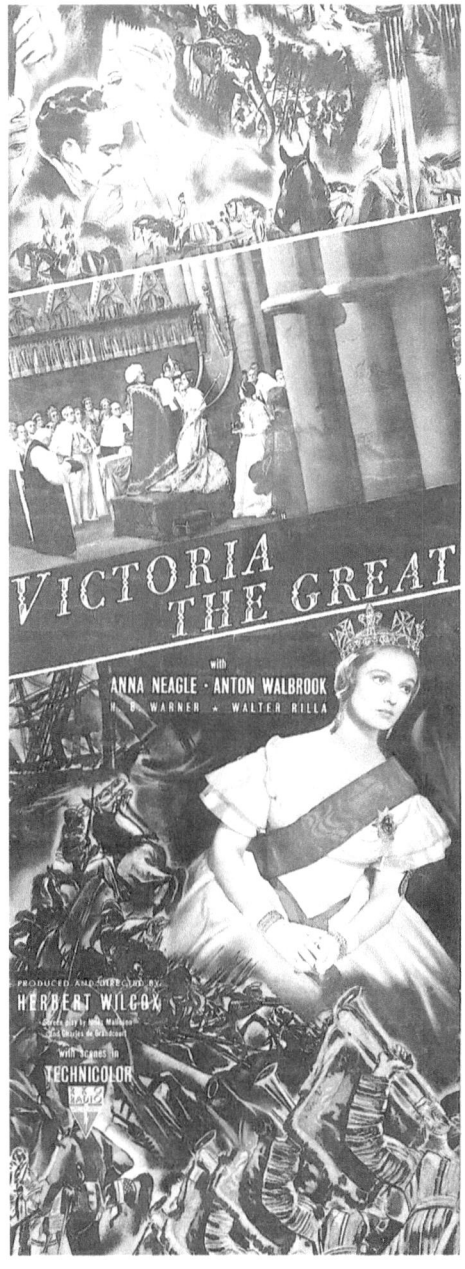

This poster for *Victoria the Great* (1937) celebrates the Queen and empire. While the poster is in color, the small print notes "with scenes in Technicolor."

Victoria embraces all her subjects and more specifically speaks to the equality of Indian subjects with all British subjects and declaring herself the grandmother of a grand family blessed with "democracy, tolerance and freedom." This recapitulation of British progress not only echoes the article by Mark Twain, discussed in Chapter 1, but also as Chapman points out "this emphasis on industrial and social progress is reminiscent of the publicity of the National Government in the 1930s (Chapman 74)," thus positioning *Victoria the Great* squarely in the political concerns of 1937: fallout from the 1936 Abdication Crisis and recovering the monarchy's image as unifying symbol for the nation. Continuing the imperial theme, the next title card jumps forward to 22 June 1897, the Diamond Jubilee "when from every corner of the British Empire, her people gathered to give thanks for the sixty years of her glorious reign." Wilcox and his photographer Freddie Young deliberately recreated several of the long shots from the silent films of the Diamond Jubilee. This is clearly evident in the long shots of the procession, no doubt taken from the similar vantage points as the 1897 footage. A concession to the contemporary [1938] audience's expectations of more visual intimacy, several medium shots present Victoria bowing her head under her parasol, and later weeping and whispering to herself "Albert, you've done all this." An extreme long shot of crowds singing "Praise God from Whom All Blessings Flow" and "God Save the Queen" is followed by the Archbishop's touting the stability of the monarch "more secure on your throne than any other nation." To top off this spectacle, *Victoria the Great* concludes with a stunning iconic image, the young Victoria and the old Victoria, girl and grandmother to the nation stand side by side, then look at each other, and finally look directly at the camera, while a loud fanfare of Elgar's "Pomp and Circumstance" swells.[26]

In contrast to this emphasis on visual spectacle, *Sixty Glorious Years* presents the Diamond Jubilee in a more personal context for Victoria. A title card positions the Jubilee within the history of British military triumphs by imposing the following text over the statue of Nelson in Trafalgar Square: "From Pole to Pole a mighty shout, Echoes from sea to sky. For Sixty Glorious Years she reigned." A series of crosscuts show street scenes of celebration, a band of black singers praising the British Navy, and the formal Jubilee procession. Contrasting this broad spectacle with the individual, a montage superimposes the image of Queen Victoria's face on moving images of passing faces, mimicking the procession's movement throughout London. A long shot of the ceremonies at St. Paul's concludes with two hymns, and we see Victoria returning to Buckingham Palace. She visits an ill servant who is eager to get the Queen's impressions. Victoria muses "I didn't know they loved me so much," a sentiment that is echoed in the final sequence of the film covering the Queen's final illness, death and funeral.

Such congruence of personal and monarchical, of humanitarian progress and brutal empire-building wars, of propaganda both for and against the British monarch, sums up the impact of the Victorian war and empire building films.[27] These films are not particularly subtle and certainly suffer from limited analysis of Queen Victoria's character and motivation. The surface is shown broadly, often epically, foregrounding the political and imperialistic world which the Queen inhabits. In the next chapter, we will see films that delve more deeply into Victoria's personality, relationships, passions, and obsessions.

3

Of Love and Obsession

Victoria and Albert—the grand love story of the nineteenth century—was made to order for biopic feature films. Victoria's emergence from an unhappy childhood, constant pressure from family, politicians, and grasping courtiers, her initial resistance to marriage, her emerging passion for Albert, their partnership in a tempestuous marriage, his untimely death at age 42, her obsession with mourning, and her close (platonic or otherwise) relationships with male servants in her later years—all are elements exploited in various feature films from 1936 to 2019.[1] This chapter will focus on feature biopic films of young Victoria, the older widowed Victoria, and her slow emergence from mourning. Given the intensity of Victoria's emotional life, not surprisingly the Queen also appears in films that examine obsession, ranging from gruesome, to comic, to heartwarming. In contrast to the more conventional biopics, these films reverse the emotional situation and foreground other characters' obsessions with Victoria, in some cases relegating the Queen to a one-dimensional object of pursuit.

The two Herbert Wilcox productions—Anna Neagle films, *Victoria the Great* (1937) and *Sixty Glorious Years* (1938)—when considered together as one body of work, intertwine the love story with political events.[2] As discussed in Chapter 2, the 1938 film puts most, but not all, of its emphasis on events during Victoria's reign (Crimean War, Sudan, Suez Canal); its goal was to bolster the British film audience's morale, damaged by the Abdication Crisis of 1936 and looming world war, by appealing to patriotism and glorifying of the Empire. In contrast, *Victoria the Great* (1937) is mainly focused on the love story, with the exception of the Trent Affair, as discussed in the previous chapter.

Victoria the Great begins with the Queen's accession to the throne and coronation, and then devotes considerable screen time to the love story. Victoria (Anna Neagle) feels the pressures on her to marry from all quarters: family, politicians, and society, dramatized by street gossip between two carriage drivers. When Lord Melbourne suggests Prince Albert (Anton Walbrook), Victoria ticks off his shortcomings: he is self-willed, doesn't dance,

3. Of Love and Obsession

goes to bed too early, is too straight-laced, and bookish. In a parallel scene, Albert enumerates her shortcomings: she is too frivolous, dances all night, and is like an insect who "devours her mate immediately after the wedding night." More parallels are drawn in the following scenes. First, two tempests: Victoria's temper tantrum when told the Prince doesn't want to travel to En-

Young Queen Victoria (Anna Neagle) impatiently, and a bit apprehensively, waits for Prince Albert (Anton Wolbrook) in *Victoria the Great* in a "Movie of the Week" advertisement in *Life Magazine,* 4 October 1937.

gland, contrasted with a real storm at sea in the English Channel while Albert and brother Ernest suffer sea sickness, and Albert muses "How can one live happily in a country that is so difficult to get to?"

The parallel scenes in *Victoria the Great* show the Queen stomping off after waiting an hour for the Prince, compared to Albert shivering in a blanket, his luggage lost, and complaining that he doesn't want to meet his cousin. Their subsequent meeting is embarrassed and awkward; Albert sits stiffly on a coach, and Victoria says, "courage cousin, I'm not going to eat you," unconsciously recalling Albert's earlier remark. Finally, they come together in a ballroom scene and dance the waltz together, at first self-consciously, as they are being closely watched by Baroness Lehzen, Lord Melbourne and the Duchess of Kent (all of whom have differing political stakes), and ultimately fluidly and gracefully. When Victoria compliments Albert's dancing, he tells her that he isn't going home.[3]

A particularly effective anachronism occurs in *Victoria the Great*, which seems ironic as the film was vaunted for the over "six months ... spent in intensive research before the script was finally completed" (Chapman 67) and for Anton Walbrook's physical similarity to Prince Albert,[4] but the anachro-

Queen Victoria (Anna Neagle) and Prince Albert (Anton Wolbrook) assess each other upon first meeting in *Victoria the Great* (1937).

nism was deliberately inserted as plot point in the proposal scene. Meeting in a library in October 1839, Victoria and Albert stand awkwardly with a table between them. To stall for time, Victoria shows Albert a photograph album of the family and explains the process of having a photograph taken. No such photographs existed that early, 1842 being the date of the first daguerreotype of Prince Albert and 1844 for Queen Victoria and her oldest daughter. By including this discrepancy, *Victoria the Great*'s proposal scene underscores the young Queen's status as the first media monarch, her progressiveness in keeping up with the latest technology, and also gives its 1937 audience a familiar point of reference.

A similar anachronism emphasizes Victoria and Albert's modernity. In *Victoria the Great* Victoria and Albert are shown leaving on their honeymoon from London to Winsor Castle via the railway, when in fact they made the journey via carriage.[5] The *Motion Picture Reviews* praised the scene for using "not a copy but the very train they used" (December 1937), thus foregrounding Victoria and Albert's role in legitimizing the progress of the Industrial Age (despite the obvious anachronism). In pointed contrast with the royals, conservative, backward looking Lord Melbourne complains that railways are bad for the country because they allow mixture of social classes. Shown at their ease in the royal coach, the couple makes chitchat which summarizes this intersection of romantic love and industrial progress; Victoria remarks on the speed (15 miles per hour!), and Albert tenderly teaches her the German name for honeymoon "die Flitterwochen." A comic bit rounds out the lessons of industrial progress. Before departure, the royal coachman had confronted the locomotive's engineers to demand his privilege to ride on a high seat behind the "cab," i.e., the engine. The final shot of the honeymoon ride shows the coachman's face covered in soot as the train chugs along.

Victoria the Great continues the love affair through the early years of the marriage up to the birth of the first baby. More examples of parallel structure underscore the growing tensions in the marriage, notably shown via Albert's musical abilities. The film's presentation of his proficiency on the piano is based on historical fact, giving these scenes a convincing authenticity and emotional impact. According to various biographers, Albert drew on German romanticism to express feelings via music when words were either not sufficient or not allowed.[6] During their two-day honeymoon at Windsor, Albert is shown with his head in Victoria's lap as they sing a German song together. Ominously, Victoria informs her new husband that the honeymoon must be short since she has to consult with Prime Minister Peel about a proposed income tax. Eagerly, Albert tells her that he has researched the subject, only to be disregarded by his new wife. Over the months, as the honeymoon harmony wanes, Albert becomes completely fed up with being excluded from royal business. The next confrontation begins and ends with music. Albert is unhappily playing the piano when the official government box is delivered to Victoria, who explains to him that the English are suspicious of foreigners' involvement in British politics. To patch up bruised feelings, the couple sings together, and soon a more involved role for Albert emerges. After they both observe how cold the room is, Victoria asks Albert to manage the household affairs. Albert's reorganization of Buckingham Palace, while a precursor to his later achievements at Osborne and Balmoral, was a mixed achievement, in fact a kind of role reversal, and the look on Walbrook's face implies a "less than thrilled" attitude.

This marital harmony is short-lived, and again *Victoria the Great* uses music to frame the marital conflict. In the next parlor scene, the camera movement starts with a tight shot of Victoria debating the income tax with Peel ("the people won't like it," but "wars and reform cost money"). Gradually, the camera moves back to show Albert playing at a grand piano and drawing all other ladies to him in an admiring cluster. The intercutting between Albert's and Victoria's faces reveals his deliberate provocation and her jealous reaction. She huffs out of the room, announcing "we shall retire." The next scene dramatizes one of the iconic Victoria-Albert quarrels. She complains about his tobacco smoking and piano playing; he storms out, locking his bedroom door, and the quarrel ends with a contrite Victoria knocking at the door, first as the Queen and finally as "your wife." The ultimate concession appears in the next shot of Victoria and Albert working on state papers together at the famous matching desks and Victoria wondering, "How could I manage without you?" At this point, *Victoria the Great* moves on to political events (Corn Laws, Trent Affair) with Albert participating with her, without an in-depth analysis of the push-pull relationship of Queen and consort. The film does touch on a scene of Albert's humiliation when he attends Parliament and is asked to leave.[7] An intimately effective shot shows Victoria comforting her exhausted and beleaguered husband, foreshadowing his declining health and early death. The Diamond Jubilee scene ends with a simple, yet effective method of summarizing this marital tension: the visual and verbal are put at odds. After showing us the spectacle of parades, crowds, hymns, and the bowing Queen in her carriage, the camera moves in close to show Victoria quietly whispering to herself "Albert you've done all this." Outwardly she is the glorious Queen regnant and privately the devoted, sorrowing widow.

By 1938 Wilcox crafted *Sixty Glorious Years* with a "a very different ideological function. *Victoria* dealt with the anxieties produced by the Abdication Crisis; the later addressed the dangers posed to Britain by the international situation" (Harper 54). The opening title card of *Sixty Glorious Years* overtly references this purpose in its description of the stability that Victoria and Albert's marriage brings to the country:

3. *Of Love and Obsession* 67

"VICTORIA THE GREAT"—An RKO Radio Picture

Queen Victoria (Anna Neagle) comforts her exhausted husband Prince Albert (Anton Wolbrook) in *Victoria the Great* (1937).

At the turn of the nineteenth century the tide of British Monarchy was at its lowest ebb. The countryside was seething with discontent and England was never closer to revolution. This was the heritage of the young girl Queen—Victoria—when she ascended the throne in 1837. Three years later, the monarchy was firmly set in the affection of its people, and it was the Queen, "so young, so small, so dignified" that wrought the change.

Sixty Glorious Year sets up several parallel scenes that dramatize the evolution of the marriage. The first of these is the depiction of Victoria writing in her journal. Early in the film, Victoria is shown recording her decision to marry Prince Albert, contrasted with a scene where Albert expresses his uneasy feeling that he is unwelcome in England. A second journal writing scene bridges the temporal gap from the marriage in 1841 to life at Balmoral in 1852, where Victoria writes "Every year we become more attached to this Highland Paradise." A similar repetitive structure appears in the three tea pouring scenes that frame the Victoria's middle age and old age, set against the backdrop of historical events. First tea scene is set in 1857 scene, coming after the Crimean War sequence. A title card provides a quotation from Browning "Grow old along with me. The Best is yet to be." The visual frame provides two planes of action: in the foreground a middle-aged Victoria and Albert are seated at the tea table as the Queen is pouring tea for two, and through a window they observe, the next generation, their daughter Vicky and her fiancée Prince Frederick of Prussia, walking in a garden. A title card "1863 at Balmoral" coming after Albert's death scene, introduces another tea serving. Seated alone at the same table, widowed Victoria is pouring tea for two—with an empty plate for Albert on the left—set against a background of empty, wintery gardens. A third instance of Victoria's tea (title card "1870 Balmoral") completes the emotional journey from Widow to Empress. After pouring two cups, the now shabby Queen is interrupted by John Brown (Gordon McLeod), who bullies her into getting new dresses: "He wouldn't like to see you are you are now." A title card announces that Victoria is "casting aside her great grief at last," and *Sixty Glorious Years* immediately moves on to Victoria's relationship with Prime Minister Disraeli and the political events and wars that dominated the last twenty-five years of her reign.

In contrast to the Wilcox-Neagle whole-life narratives, two biopics shot in Germany and Austria focus solely on young Victoria. *Victoria in Dover* (1936) was based on a 1932 play *Mädchenjahre einer Königen* by Austrian Geza Silberer (using the pen name Sil-Vara, presumably to cover up his Jewish background), was made at a point for the German film industry when documentaries, comedies and historical drama are mixed ominously with Nazi propaganda films.[8] Taking an escapist route and avoiding the shadow of looming war, the 1936 *Mädchenjahre einer Köningen* is a highly fictionalized romantic fantasy that does not transcend its stage origins. A consistent point in all biographies of Victoria is her reluctance as a young Queen, newly freed from oppression by her mother and advisor Sir John Conroy, to jump into a marriage, which by nineteenth-century standards would have at least partially subjugated her to the husband. The film's three-act play format underscores this dilemma and quickly resolves it: Victoria frees herself from domineering mother, Victoria meets Albert, Victoria proposes to Albert.

The 1954 remake *Victoria in Dover*, starring a sixteen-year-old Romy Schneider (a year before the first of her Sissi films), emphasizes the same themes and structure. Multiple authority figures try to push the young Queen into marriage. In this film, the Duchess of Kent (Cristl Mardayn) favors the Prince of Orange or Duke Alexander of the Netherlands, while Baroness Lehzen (Magda Schneider, in reality Romy Schneider's mother) and Lord Melbourne (Karl Ludwig Diehl) agree on Prince Albert of Saxe-Coburg and Gotha (Adrian Hoven). The first hour of *Victoria in Dover* is taken up with the theme of resistance to control. Previous to the marital plotting, the film shows a direct conflict between mother and daughter where Victoria refuses the Duchess's demand to dismiss Lord Melbourne as Prime Minister. Victoria is shown girlishly and innocently going to apologize to her mother, only

3. Of Love and Obsession

to open a door and overhear Conroy plotting with her mother; Schneider's facial expression, moving from shock to fury to determination, captures the bittersweet moment of growing up and her decision to banish Conroy from her presence. Control by Conroy segues into control by Lord Melbourne, captured in two throne room scenes. The first uses dialog where Melbourne coaches Victoria through a dress rehearsal for her first speech. The second is purely visual: in an investiture scene, Victoria has difficulty lifting the dubbing sword, and Melbourne, symbolically exercising his control, holds up her wrist and guides it through the ceremony.

Victoria in Dover soon brings the young Queen into conflict with Melbourne over her desire to read the newspapers; first after he tells not to read the newspapers she just bought while riding in the park, and second when Victoria asks for the newspapers and Lehzen tells her that Lord Melbourne had confiscated all of them. In a comic bit, Victoria leans out a window to bribe a guard to bring her the papers; later the guard puts the papers on a long pole and delivers them through the window into a room while Victoria is consulting with Melbourne. The newspapers bobble in the open window, with flustered Victoria on the left and Melbourne on the right as she rushes to get him out of the room. Once she has read the papers, the camera moves into a closer shot of Victoria's weeping over news stories, leading to her later demand for laws to help the poor. The conflict vs. resistance theme is finally wrapped up in Victoria's furious outburst to the Prime Minister: "Everyone wants to marry me off, my mother, my uncle, you."

Not surprisingly for a film based on a play, *Victoria in Dover* presents the Victoria and Albert meeting within the stage convention of mistaken identity, as well as the "meet cute" movie device (personality clash, followed by embarrassing situations and misunderstandings resolved in a romantic ending).[9] After an hour of Victoria's running battles against control, the Dover sequence takes up only about 30 minutes of screen time. Victoria takes Lehzen and footman comic sidekick George (played by versatile actor Rudolf Vogel) on secret trip to Paris in order to "look over the young men" and get a point of comparison to the proposed husband. They are delayed by a storm and spend the night in a Dover inn, where Victoria is wet and shivering in a cold room. Mistaking Albert for a servant, she asks him to set a fire, which he bungles, and they finally cooperate to get a blaze going. She pumps him for information about Prince Albert, his height, looks, but Albert replies that the Prince doesn't want to marry a "stopper," i.e., a short person. To round out the "staginess" of the Dover meeting, Albert climbs up to the balcony on Victoria's room, and they both quote (in German) from *Romeo and Juliet*, act 2, scene 2 (the balcony scene). Accepting the Professor's bribe of £5 (bargained down from £30), Victoria leaves the inn still incognito.

The last "act" of *Victoria in Dover* is set in a London reception where

Victoria appears in full court dress, constricted with wide hoops and a train easily 30 feet long. With her back to the camera, she moves slowly through the court and up to her throne. Even more constricting are the conventional and stiff introductions of the competing suitors the Prince of Orange and Duke Alexander. Late and flustered, Albert runs up a staircase only to recognize her as the girl he danced with, while the Professor gasps "I offered her 30 pounds to go away." Dressed beautifully in an anachronistic costume of a wide-hooped crinoline,[10] Victoria invites Albert to dance, which begins propitiously, but ends in disagreement. They both storm out of the room, an ominous harbinger of their tempestuous marriage.

At breakfast the next morning, Victoria tells Melbourne and Lehzen that she has decided on Albert, but first asks George the footman to light fire

The German poster for *Mädchenjahre einer Königin* (*Victoria in Dover*), 1954. The film emphasizes the emotional connection between Victoria (Romy Schneider) and Albert (Adrian Hoven).

and clean the windows. George gives the bureaucratic excuse—the exterior windows are the responsibility of one department, the interior of another, the fire is laid by ... etc.—an historically accurate detail that has shown up in subsequent Victoria films. As part of her proposal to Albert, Victoria tells him she needs a strict German disciplinarian to reform the palace. After Albert barks at the footman, the pair unite in a kiss, and the film ends. All told, *Victoria in Dover* is a charming fantasy, played out against a partially historical, partially invented background, beautifully photographed in glorious Agfacolor, liberally sprinkled with comic moments, but ultimately lacking psychological depth or historical insight. Victoria is too childish and flighty and the Albert much too smooth and suave to be taken as anything other than comedic lovers in fantasy land.

3. Of Love and Obsession 71

The Young Victoria (2009) picks up many of the same scenes and themes but works them more explicitly and successfully. The narrative structure is more complex in the way it manages time. The story begins with a voice-over prologue introducing the main theme—the political struggle to control Victoria. Reminiscent of *Victoria the Great*, this biopic makes liberal use of title cards, to a degree unusual in twenty-first century films. The first two set up the conflict "1819—A child is born in a London palace" and "Caught between two Royal uncles—the King of England and the King of the Belgians—she is destined to be a Queen and to rule a great empire. Unless she is forced to relinquish powers and sign a 'regency order.'" As the adult Victoria's voice (Emily Blunt) explains "even a palace can be a prison," the screen shows a five-year-old Victoria (Grace Smith) running a stick against a railing. The voice-over describes the so-called "Kensington system," which was calculated to enforce dependence and childishness in the young girl and summarizes the family tree scene where eleven-year-old Victoria (Michaela Brooks) learns her destiny and utters the legendary vow "I will be good."[11]

Immediately after the childhood vow, time jumps forward approximately ten years to show Victoria making her coronation vows. Lighting underscores a backwards temporal leap: during the coronation scene, the face of her mother the Duchess of Kent (Miranda Richardson) is fully illuminated and then darkens as the story moves backward one year to show Sir John Conroy (Mark Strong) bullying the sick Victoria about a regency order. A long flashback, about an hour of screen time, covers the years 1837–38, including the first meeting of Victoria and Albert (Rupert Friend) engineered by Uncle Leopold (Thomas Kretschmann) and the Duchess; political maneuverings of Uncle Leopold and Baron Stockmar, Conroy and the Duchess, Lord Melbourne (Paul Bettany) and King William (Jim Broadbent), and the opposition Tories Wellington and Peel; the king's death; Victoria's proclamation; and a second look at the coronation where Albert is shown in the balcony smiling support to Victoria.[12] The remainder of the film follows a straightforward narrative through their courtship, marriage, and birth of their first child, using rapid cutting from Victoria to Albert and back again in a chronological order, suggesting the growing emotional bond between the characters. This pattern of cutting across time and space is repeated through the film, thus distinguishing itself from the Anna Neagle and Romy Schneider films which are organized as simple chronologies.

The Young Victoria addresses the political jockeying for power from 1836 to 1841, but certain choices tend to undermine this theme. Because the film maintains a tight focus on personal relationships, the power play is devoid of most historical context, existing in a vacuum to the extent that it is hard to see exactly what power the various claimants want. The pro–Coburg plotting of King Leopold and Baron Stockmar are vaguely framed; presumably, like Sir John Conroy, they are after money. The Duchess of York is merely a tool of Conroy, and her most dramatic scene is a petty dispute with King William over rooms in Kensington Palace. Melbourne is indolent and prefers to leave the status quo alone, while the Tory Prime Minister Peel is stripped of any reforming motivations and comes across as a boor—"no manners," as the Duke of Wellington says of him. The use of visual space emphasizes the control and manipulation theme. In the scene where Melbourne maneuvers King William into letting him negotiate with Conroy, Melbourne's crooked arm frames first King William in the background. Similarly, when Melbourne is pushing his selection of Whig ladies-in-waiting on the young Queen, the camera frames Victoria visually overshadowed by his crooked arm.

The only political event dramatized in *The Young Victoria* is the Bedchamber Crisis resulting from Victoria's politically naive mistake in refusing to accept Tory ladies-in-waiting. As a consequence, Prime Minister Peel is humiliated on the floor of Parliament, and nasty newspaper headlines and cartoons make their way to Albert in Coburg and presumably across Europe. The film deliberately ignores the Lady Flora Hastings affair of 1839, though the character briefly appears in the King's birthday scene. In that unfortunate affair, Lady Flora was falsely accused of pregnancy while she was actually dying of cancer, and Victoria was one of the accusers, recording in her journal that she thought Conroy was the father (Hibbert, *Personal* 78). The resulting scandal spilled over to the public press in a damaging campaign against the Queen. A deleted scene (available on the DVD disk) has Victoria visiting Lady Flora on her deathbed. By glossing over the Hastings affair and omitting the deathbed scene, the film deliberately reveals its agenda to portray the young Queen sympathetically, victimized by grasping power mongers and nobly struggling against her persecutors.

Similarly, *The Young Victoria* also elects not to address any significant role for Victoria in foreign affairs. From a historical perspective, she would have been in the loop about the Canadian Rebellion 1837–38, the First Opium War 1839–1842, the First Anglo-Afghan war (1839–42), and unrest in Jamaica over the abolition of slavery. Domestic issues are relegated to bland generalities, as in the conversation between Albert and Victoria where he shows her sketches for workers' housing and her follow-up requests to Melbourne for reports on living conditions. The casual reference to "living conditions" disguises the fact that the first three years of Victoria's reign were marred by pervasive domestic unrest: the beginning of the Chartist Movement in 1838, related riots in Birmingham, Glasgow, and an attempted uprising in Newport in 1839. Stripping this context out of the film, presumably in part due to limitations of screen time, unfortunately reduces Victoria to an object of political maneuverings by Conroy, Melbourne, Leopold, Lehzen, and Peel. These intrigues are played out in such a limited personal arena that it is often not clear exactly why they want control (other than the obvious motive of money) and, more importantly, what they might do with it.

Given the decision to foreground the love story of Victoria and Albert and downplay historical context, *The Young Victoria* does a splendid job of developing their growing relationship in a series of alternating scenes. During the build-up to their first meeting, we see Albert's archery contrasted with Victoria's painting, Victoria being bullied by Conroy, and Albert being grilled by Stockmar about Victoria's likes and dislikes. The clash between Victoria and the Duchess over attendance at the King's birthday celebration is contrasted with Uncle Leopold's direct order to Albert "no mistakes ... you are the next piece in the game." During the first meeting at Kensington Palace, the rivalry between Albert and Lehzen is set up with similar visual juxtaposition: Lehzen is escorting Princess Victoria up the stairs, per the Kensington system, and as Albert interrupts to speak with Victoria, his hand supplants Lehzen's. While they converse while ascending, his face is illuminated, showing his heartfelt yearning, while Victoria's face is shadowed, leaving her reaction ambiguous. Finally, Lehzen looks down jealously at the departing prince, and Victoria takes another peak at him from at the top of the stairs, though in the next scene she pulls back from this growing interest in Albert and states she is not ready to marry. At one point, the alternating pattern is used for narrative economy to introduce characters: Albert's lesson in English politics gives way to a visual of the King's birthday celebration with a voice-over by Stockmar that identifies key politicians—Melbourne, Peel, and the Duke of Wellington.

Employing a staple technique of historical period-piece movies, *The Young Victoria* presents the main characters as more modern in their attitudes than would be typical during the nineteenth century, which enables them to react in a manner that twenty-first century audiences can relate to. For example, the chess game being played during Albert's first visit reveals the Victoria's internal conflict. The camera's use of space makes the point: the chess pieces are in the foreground, and the manipulators (Conroy, the Duchess, Lehzen) are in the background, closely attending to the game being played out in the front of the frame. Victoria complains about feeling like a chess piece, and Albert tells her to master the rules of the game, hardly the attitude of a nineteenth-century man who was conditioned to see women only in their domestic role. She asks "don't you recommend I get a husband to play the game for me?" Albert's reply that she should "get a husband to play the game *with* you" is simply not credible within the historical context, but neatly captures what the twenty-first audience wants to hear. The film proceeds to belabor this point by visualizing Victoria's nightmare about a chess game against Conroy, one of many male oppressors at this stage of the narrative.[13]

The visualization of interior motivations in *The Young Victoria* clearly caters to twenty-first century sensibilities. Albert is shown as struggling with the lack of love in his life; after he leaves Victoria on a symbolically rainy day, the camera moves into his mind and shows his desire to rush into Victoria's bedroom and into her arms. Victoria's subjective experiences express her growing fascination with Albert: first the ballroom scene shows a fantasy of moving forward towards him without stepping (gown flapping weirdly in the breeze) and second in the slow-motion waltz as they gaze intently at each other. Ultimately, Albert becomes the epitome of the helpful partner, showing up at the coronation to offer support, sending her encouraging letters, expressing his confidence in her abilities, defending her against his brother Ernst's conclusion that she is a fool ("she is not a fool, but has listened to a fool"). After their marriage, he continues to offer his assistance, as in the scene where she is puzzling over paperwork, and he asks "Can I help?," only to be slapped down by Lehzen. When Victoria and Albert quarrel over his clandestine effort to placate in-coming Prime Minister Peel about Tory ladies-in-waiting, she accuses him of usurping her authority, and he points out her previous mistakes, i.e., the Bedchamber Crisis. This standoff is resolved when Albert is wounded while protecting Victoria during the 1840 assassination attempt, one of the film's many departures from historical fact.[14] Prompted by the shock of this event, in an unconvincingly short time screen time (back-to-back scenes), Albert reverts to the caring, supportive partner

Victoria (Emily Blunt) and Albert (Rupert Friend) in formal dress as the happy couple in *The Young Victoria* (2009).

3. Of Love and Obsession

("I am dispensable, but you are not"). Melbourne's last advice to the Queen is to let Albert share her work. The film ends with the twin work desks, Victoria's concession that they are a monarchical partnership and a final image of the happy young couple in formal dress, as title cards sum up their mutual accomplishments.[15]

Less romantic than *Young Victoria*, though equally intense, is Judi Dench's first portrayal of an older Victoria in *Mrs Brown* (1997), a dark and brooding look at the controversial, potentially scandalous relationship between the aging monarch and her ghillie / personal servant John Brown. A valiant attempt to humanize the image of the old Queen, this film focuses strictly on her domestic life from 1864 to 1883 and removes any mention of external events during this time period: various foreign wars, the rise of Bismarck, Victoria's trips abroad, her correspondence with her daughter Vicky, or the majority of domestic political events. Two key scenes make this point. First, in the scene after Brown succeeds in getting the Queen to ride, Victoria complains, "They all wish me to return to public service," and later declares she is "not interested in foreign affairs," drawing a protest from the Prince of Wales stating his belief that the royal family should be more available. While

Judi Dench as Queen Victoria in John Madden's MRS. BROWN.   Billy Connolly as John Brown in John Madden's MRS. BROWN.

MIRAMAX
A Miramax Films Release © 1997
Photo: Mark Tillie

Press photograph showing Queen Victoria (Judi Dench) and Billy Connolly as John Brown from *Mrs Brown* (1997).

the film is historically correct in pointing out Victoria's reluctance to make public appearances in the 1860s, it inaccurately suggests that she was unaware of and uninvolved in foreign affairs. Her letters and journals from this period show numerous attempts to influence, actually brow-beat, key government officials into acting as she wanted.[16] By removing the political dimension, the film's narrative is simplified and reduces Queen Victoria to Mrs Brown at the center of domestic conflicts between Brown and her family and the court.

The second way *Mrs Brown* limits its perspective is its presentation of an assassination attempt. In his capacity as royal security head, Brown had recommended a closed carriage, only to be overruled by the Queen. He is proved right during the Queen's ride in an open carriage for 27 February 1872 thanksgiving services for the Prince of Wales' recovery from typhoid fever.[17] The camera shows Victoria and Bertie driving in an open carriage, then a long shot of the would-be assassin (an Irish teenager named Arthur O'Connor), rushing towards the carriage brandishing a pistol, and Brown running at him and tackling him to the ground. This event actually occurred 29 February 1872 while the Queen was driving in Hyde and Regent's park. By conflating the two historical events, the film exaggerates Brown's role as protector and highlights Prince of Wales' jealousy of Brown's status, leading to the dinner scene where the Prince condescendingly praises Brown's actions, while Brown is standing stiffly at attention as one of the dinner attendants. Other confrontations, such as Brown physically roughing up the Prince of Wales when he is demanding access to the Queen or the letter written by the royal children against Brown, are similarly exaggerated for dramatic impact. However, the film's opening image of the Brown's bust being thrown over a parapet is a historically correct visualization of attempts by Victoria's family to downplay Brown's role after their mother's death: Princess Beatrice's burning Victoria's letters and journals after she "edits" them, or Edward's destruction of multiple memorials to Brown, including a bust, and relegating a life-size statue to an inconspicuous part of Balmoral grounds.

Other strategies in *Mrs Brown* fall a bit short. The smashing of the bust of Brown actually frames a narrative flashback that ultimately doesn't work. After the bust shatters on the ground, we see Brown off to the woods to confront intruders; the scene is shot in such dark lighting that it is never clear whether he is pursuing poachers or assassins. Brown is shown as disheveled and drunk, but this could have been the case any time from 1864 to his death in 1883. In effect, the jump forward to 1883 (in a title card), with Brown recording his security efforts in his diary, is a surprise, and only in retrospect is it clear that the bulk of the narrative has been a flashback. While the flashback's impact is undercut by the use of extremely dark lighting, this visual metaphor is applied consistently throughout the film. Faces are frequently

3. Of Love and Obsession 77

half etched in dark and light, hiding the motives and emotions of the characters. Even the scene, where Brown and a smiling Victoria visit the cottage of the Grants and the Queen lays the table, is shot with very dark lighting, suggesting that their happiness is permanently overshadowed by the world, pettiness of court life, and the demands of destiny swallowing them up.

What does work well in *Mrs Brown* is the progression of emotions for both characters. Connolly's characterization deftly balances a growing love for his Queen with his ambition and rudeness. His initial reaction to seeing the weeping Queen is shock: "Honest to God, I never thought to see you in such a state. You must miss him [Prince Albert] dreadfully." After three scenes comprising Brown's successful campaign to get the Queen outdoors to ride her white horse, Brown swaggers into the servants' dinner and usurps the butler's place at the head of the table. Later in 1866, Brown brags "there's no stopping me," an attitude which culminates in the scene where he clicks off a security checklist as the other servants are required to call him "Sir," and another scene when he threatens the staff to find out who leaked the Queen's Highlands schedule to the press. After the ghillies ball, the camera moves into a drunk Brown collapsed on the ballroom floor, suggesting that his character is on the downfall. The peak of his power ends after the meeting with Disraeli where the Prime Minister makes a case for Victoria's return to public service as a strategy to keep her safe.[18] Brown agrees reluctantly, noting "she'll think I betrayed her," which is exactly how the Queen reacts when he pleads for her to open Parliament. From that point, Brown slips through scenes of mocking censure by his fellow servants, to pneumonia and death.

Judi Dench inhabits Victoria on a wild arc from grief stricken to imperious to happy, and back, again and again. The scene where Victoria is playing piano and has commanded her children to sing "Highland Man" (all have pained looks on their faces) ends in an abrupt explosion of temper about the 1869 Irish Church Act ("How dare they ... the Irish must stay as they are"). Another notable display of temper occurs when Bertie is badgering her about her rules against smoking (confined to one room) past midnight; she flies off the handle and refuses his request, leaving Brown to dismiss the Prince ("you should go now"). A softer tone prevails in a touching scene where Victoria "confesses" to the Dean of Windsor that her grief is lessening. Gradually, she begins to wear more white lace around the face and shoulders, and her face becomes more lit up. In the dinner scene after the assassination attempt, she is wearing a diamond tiara and lots of jewels, as she announces the Devoted Service Medal for Brown. Victoria's face is fully lit as a voice-over of Disraeli's speech announces her agreement to assume a more public role. Victoria and Brown briefly glance at each other, as a visual farewell, as her destiny takes her back to London politics, and his to a decline into a diminished role. Finally, in Brown's deathbed scene, Victoria's progression back to public life is suggested by her costume—tiara, diamonds, and cascading white lace over shoulders and bodice.[19]

Judi Dench's second portrayal of the Queen in *Victoria & Abdul* (2017) takes up the final years of her life, between her Golden Jubilee in 1887 through her death in 1901. Released twenty years after *Mrs Brown* and eight years after *Young Victoria*, both of which put their emphasis on character and emotional relationships, *Victoria & Abdul* reflects a more political perspective. The film's opening title card—"based on real events … mostly"—is a fair assessment and underscores both the film's strengths and weaknesses. The realism is manifested in glorious costuming—the film was nominated for Best Costume Design Academy Award—and outstanding photography, particularly of the rain-swept Highlands and the Durbar room at Osborne House. The scene where the court first enjoys a sketching and picnic party only to be caught in a downpour captures the dreariness of a long slog back home in the pelting Highlands rain. Impressive eye candy notwithstanding, *Victoria & Abdul* is fundamentally a politically correct, twenty-first century invention, strung along a chain of somewhat historical events. Abdul Karim (played by the handsome Ali Fazal) is a fantasy figure of the wise, noble, downtrodden Indian, victim of discrimination on class, religious, and racial grounds. This Munshi is ultimately one dimensional and never changing. Chosen for his looks (especially his height) as a Diamond Jubilee attendant, he talks to his shorter companion Mohammed (Adeel Akhtar) about what an "honor" it is to be at the English court. His motivation is limited to making what Mohammed calls "nicey nice" to his new lady boss, dispensing banal philosophy ("Life is like a carpet"), and pledging to keep her safe. The film hints at a lust for power, as in the tableau vivant where Abdul plays the King of Persia and ludicrously declaims "you are all under my power." Trappings of power are applied to both Victoria and Abdul in parallel scenes. Early in the film, a state dinner is imbued with a ridiculous level of pomp and circumstance, especially when a young page runs to the kitchen announcing "She's here," whereupon the soup waiters march into the dining room. Later in the film at Osborne House, where the Household and royal family are spying on the Munshi, we hear "he's coming," just as Abdul is driven into the frame, showing off his full-dress uniform and multiple medals.

Under the Munshi's influence, Victoria grows from depressed, grumpy, and constipated, to energetic and happy with Abdul as her sounding board. In marked contrast to the psychological depth of Victoria's confessional scene in *Mrs Brown* about the process of mourning, *Victoria & Abdul* reduces Victoria's character to a simplistic one-note of depression: "Everyone I really loved has died and I just go on and on." Appointing Abdul as the Queen's Munshi, Victoria is soon happily learning Hindustani (as she called it, actually Urdu), reading the Koran, ordering mangoes (which arrive spoiled after

3. Of Love and Obsession

their long journey), redecorating Osborne House to create the Durbar Room and its Peacock throne, or singing Gilbert and Sullivan (quite badly). This emotional renaissance eventually gives way to a gradual decline, suggested in the climatic Diamond Jubilee shot, with its a long shot followed by slow regal camera movement into a medium shot of a tired, ill Queen.

Victoria & Abdul paints the royal family as one-dimensional bigots, exuding the usual clichés of classism and racism. Eddie Izzard is effective as the exasperated heir Prince Albert Edward, not understanding or even trying to accept his mother's relationship with a mere servant. The servants slam their dining hall doors to exclude Abdul and Mohammed. The ladies-in-waiting—notably Olivia Williams as Lady Jane Churchill and Fenella Woolgar as Miss Phipps—visibly shrink from Abdul. Tim Pigott-Smith gets the most screen time as the beleaguered private secretary Sir Henry Ponsonby, aware of the dangers of Victoria's fascination with the Munshi. Royal physician Sir James Reid (Paul Higgins) delivers an egregiously racist remark: "I did not do seven years in Edinburgh University to look at Indian dicks." Michael Gambon, a dead ringer for the 1900 *Vanity Fair* caricature of Lord Salisbury, is effective as a weary and distracted Prime Minister, trying to manage a fractious country and fight a difficult foreign war (the Second Boer War); he doesn't need the Munshi-mania drama at court and barks at the private secretary "What

Queen Victoria (Judi Dench) enjoys the Peacock Throne in the Durbar Room at Osborne House, while Abdul (Ali Fazal) stands at attention in *Victoria & Abdul* (2017).

the hell is going on here, Ponsonby?" In a depressing vision of human nature in the Victorian court, the other Indian servant Mohammed exhibits equal racism toward the English when he tells the Prince of Wales that Abdul is climbing the "stinking greasy pole of the shitty British Empire … and you are all quaking in your books because he's beating you at your own games." Bigotry and racism work both ways, thus corroding the fabric of society and isolating the characters in their hateful attitudes.

Like most historical films, *Victoria & Abdul* evinces a number of historical inaccuracies in the plot and setting, primarily used to heighten the emotional drama of particular scenes.[20] Most distracting is the climactic set piece where Victoria speaks directly to the camera to rebut the charges of insanity leveled at her by the Prince of Wales and Dr. Reid. Her big speech ("I am anything but insane") employs diction riddled with obvious inaccuracies and anachronisms: the British Empire did not have a "billion" citizens at this time (more like about 400,000 by the end of Victoria's reign). Victoria's medical terms ("collapsed uterus, … morbidly obese") are anachronistic and out of character for a woman who never allowed her physicians to touch her, even with a stethoscope (Reid, *Ask Sir James* 213). Additionally, there is no historical evidence that Abdul was present to comfort a dying Victoria by quoting Hindu poetry. In fact, the historical record indicated only family and close staff were present at Victoria's death, and that the Prince of Wales, now King Edward VII, invited the Munshi to see her in her coffin before the lid was closed (Reid, *Ask Sir James* 217), a gesture that does not fit in with the film's portrayal of him as persecutor of Abdul.

The film's version of the Munshi is a "fantasy view of Islam" (Robertson np) pitted against a caricatured presentation of Victorian hypocrisy and racism. The film makes no mention of how Abdul enriched himself (receiving a large estate in Agra from the Queen), grew fat, brought multiple wives to England (Baird 452), lied to Victoria about his brother-in law's theft of a brooch (Reid 131–32), and bullied Victoria about medals. At one point, mystified Bertie says "where did he get those medals?"[21] The film glosses over more serious—though never conclusively proved—questions arising from his friendship with "a young lawyer, Rafiuddin Ahmed, who was closely associated with the Muslim Patriotic League and was suspected of relaying to Afghanistan state secrets supplied to him by the Munshi" (Hibbert, *Personal* 448). Avoiding any negative reflection of the Munshi's career, *Victoria & Abdul* ends on a nostalgic note. Back in Agra, with only his memories and a miniature of Victoria, Abdul kisses the feet of her statue, a parallel to the same gesture in the film's opening state dinner scene that sums up his reverential attitude towards Victoria.[22] Unfortunately, the film missed perhaps the most telling part of the relationship. Biographer Julia Baird suggests that "part of Victoria's attachment to her Indian attendants arose from her own need for gentle physical care ... she wanted to be lifted carefully and tenderly from bed to chair, and chair to carriage. The Indians, she wrote, were 'so clever' when they lifted her, and 'they never pinch me.' What her court saw, but refused to recognize, was the value of the succor a quiet, attentive man brought to an aging Queen" (Baird 458). One leaves *Victoria & Abdul* wanting more of the intimate personal and psychological dimensions of their relationship and less of the heavy-handed, overtly political themes. The lack of emotional depth is a disservice to Victoria and Abdul.

While the Neagle, Schneider, Blunt, and Dench biopics are centered on Victoria's love for a man in her life, a number of films reverse the love story. Instead of showing Victoria in love, they examine situations where Victoria is the object of love or obsession from an unlikely quarter. The best known of these is the 1950 *Mudlark*, produced in England for Twentieth Century–Fox, starring Irene Dunne as the Queen, Alex Guinness as Disraeli, Finlay Currie as John Brown, and young Andrew Ray as Wheeler the mudlark (a boy who scavenges in river mud).

The studio Twentieth-Century Fox devised a clever promotional campaign for this film. A 1950 advertisement from *Modern Screen*, shows the mudlark in period costume, and Dunne as her glamorous self in evening gown. The intent was most likely a teaser for pulling in paying audiences to see her transformation into old Queen Victoria. Publicity stills, as well as a story in *Life Magazine* (11 September 1950), touted Dunne's 90-minute makeup sessions with layers of latex, calling attention to the Queen's double chins.[23]

The opening sequence of *The Mudlark* establishes Wheeler's obsession with Queen Victoria: he is a homeless orphan who supports himself by scrounging on the banks of the Thames, a "mudlark." When he finds a cameo of a lady attached to the body of a dead sailor he fights off several attempts by other boys to steal it, even risking his life to jump into the river to retrieve it. Rescued by a night watchman, Wheeler learns that the cameo shows Queen Victoria, "the Mother of all England," who now lives in widowed seclusion at Windsor Castle twenty miles upriver. Wheeler says "I like her face. I'd like to see her real" and sets off on a long walk through the London fog and sneaks in through a gate, just as Prime Minister Disraeli's carriage is driven into the castle. Once inside Windsor Castle, Wheeler wanders through an atmospherically lit maze of rooms and halls, punctuated by light and shadow. Goggle-eyed, awestruck, and famished (he samples fruit and other tidbits as he walks around chomping) Wheeler encounters a series of characters who all manifest obsessions of one sort or another.

At the beginning of *The Mudlark*, Queen Victoria is still obsessed with mourning the death of Prince Albert, a point visually emphasized by the initial shot of her face totally in shadow, but gradually illuminated by a candle.

Modern Screen ran this advertisement for *The Mudlark* (1950) showing a young and glamorous Irene Dunne, quite the opposite of how she appears as an aging Queen Victoria in the film.

She reacts angrily when both Disraeli (Alec Guinness) and Brown (Findlay Currie) urge her to return to public engagement. A visualization of this conflict occurs in one shot that frames Brown on the left, a bust of Albert in the center, and Queen Victoria on the right.

3. Of Love and Obsession

Brown's obsession with helping Victoria is a major theme in *The Mudlark*, shown in a series of scenes where he urges her to agree to Disraeli's request for her appearance at a commemoration of the 100th anniversary of a foundling hospital. Disraeli's obsession is, of course, political; he is shepherding a "Reform" bill through Parliament (most likely the 1880 Education Act) and desperately needs royal public engagements to tip the scales toward passage. Disraeli single-mindedly pursues this goal by repeatedly badgering the Queen, who is not amused. He gives a long speech in Parliament (expertly delivered in a single take by Guinness) using the Wheeler case as an argument for reforms to "advance the cause of British children." Another type of political obsession appears in the footman Slattery (Ronan O'Casey), who is an Irish Fenian and jokes about burning down Windsor Castle while lighting the dining room candles. After Wheeler is discovered snoring behind the window curtains, the boy blurts out in a panic that someone wants to burn down the castle, and the camera reveals Slattery slipping out the door at the back of the room.

This publicity still for *The Mudlark* (1950) shows Irene Dunne in full makeup and costume as Queen Victoria.

Brown's other obsession—whiskey—is handled comically in some of the best scenes in *The Mudlark*. Attempting to get the boy to explain how he entered the castle, Brown and Wheeler stumble through the fog. Brown takes multiple swigs from his whiskey bottle, only to fall into the coal chute, as the boy had done earlier. The two are next seen in Brown's bedroom where Wheeler observes "You're a bit sozzled, sir," and Brown replies the whiskey is "only to keep off infection, lad." As they walk out of the room into the hallway, the camera stays put until Brown returns to grab his whiskey bottle, telling Wheeler "never neglect your health." Searchers appear, only to find that Brown is "drunk as a lord," just as he keels over on the throne room floor. When Queen Victoria is informed that Brown is not available the next morning, i.e., hung over, she simply shrugs.

As *The Mudlark* progresses, Victoria shows a softening of her dour personality in the romantic subplot of Lieutenant Charles and maid of honor Lady Emily. The Queen at first sides with Emily's mother who forbids the match; on later consideration, Victoria relents, telling Emily a story about her own early crush on a soldier and implicitly approving Emily's elopement. The elopement is played out comically as Emily struggles through three attempts to elope with Charles. The first time she slips out a door and waits in the rain (he is detained to search for the mudlark). The second time she is marooned in the snow (he's off to see the Queen). Persistent and determined, she makes a third attempt which ends in a successful elopement, as the lovers disappear in the fog. Victoria's progression from widow to kindly monarch continues into the final scene, where she meets Wheeler and recognizes his obsession with her as the mother of the country. After a series of shots between the Queen and the mudlark, while Brown is lecturing ("You're still Britannia"), Victoria smiles, thanks Wheeler, asks Brown to take care of him, turns to Disraeli, and agrees to a public engagement. The final image is of Victoria in her carriage, smiling and bowing to the crowds, wearing a more festive costume, white plume on her black hat, light scarf tied around the neck, white ermine collar over her black dress.[24] The initial dark and foggy atmosphere has transitioned into a flood of light, revealing a vision of the monarch as mother of the empire, in commune with her people.[25]

A far more gruesome fate awaits Victoria in 2001's *From Hell*. Based on the graphic novel by Alan Moore and Eddie Campbell, this slasher fantasy follows the growing obsession of Inspector Abberline (Johnny Depp) with solving the 1888 Jack the Ripper murders. Set against the grim filth of Whitechapel, the film presents in graphic detail the gruesome murders of six London "unfortunates," i.e., prostitutes. The plot hinges on the Ripper's motivation to protect the royal family from a scandal. Prince Edward Albert Victor (Mark Dexter), grandson of Queen Victoria (Liz Moscrop) and heir to the throne, has secretly married a commoner—prostitute Ann Crook (Joanna Page)—in a forbidden Catholic ceremony. Subsequently, all the witnesses to the wedding, a group of six prostitutes, are brutally murdered. Abberline's dogged pursuit of the case leads him to Freemason and royal physician Sir William Gull (Ian Holm), who turns out to be the Ripper, driven to insanity in his murderous campaign to silence the witnesses.[26]

Queen Victoria appears three times in *From Hell*, each time with increasing ambiguity. First, Victoria is shown in a private meeting with Dr. Gull where she is cast as the concerned grandmother of a sick grandson, asking "How far advanced is our grandson's malady?" (syphilis) and worried that "he seems to be suffering greatly in his mind." Gull mentions his patient's depression and trembling of the hands, to which Victoria responds, "You are a true physician Sir William. In all ways you attend to the health of our empire. We are grateful," and smiles at him. Initially her comments seem innocuous, but as events degenerate into sickening violence (full frontal camera shot of a throat being slit by a long "Lister knife"), the film turns the Queen into a looming nemesis, conveniently distanced from the actual murders. Close to solving the case, Inspector Abberline takes Mary Kelly (Heather Graham) to a portrait gallery where they first see Queen Victoria's painting. Mary reacts negatively to the Queen's image: "she's a fright" whose "cold eyes" make Mary feel "like someone walking on my grave." When Mary is able to identify the portrait of Prince Edward Albert Victor as the man who married her friend Ann, Inspector Abberline realizes that the case could "shake the Empire."[27]

After the sixth and final murder Gull goes mad, and the Queen's complicity is apparent. Seated at her desk, Lord Hallsham (Peter Eyre) standing at right and a portrait of Prince Consort Albert framed in the background, Victoria wiggles her way out of blame: "We asked Sir William to remove a threat to our family and to our throne, not to engage in these ghastly rituals." Hallsham replies that the Ripper murders were "unexpected" but did remove the threat, speaking in the bland unctuous language of a courtier. In a medium shot emphasizing her cold piercing eyes, Victoria denies any responsibility: "In his way Sir William has been loyal and we are grateful for that. The rest is in your hands Lord Hallsham. We wish to hear nothing further of this." Victoria's brutal coldness to the fate of her most oppressed subjects is further suggested by the prominence of the coins placed on the eyes of the deceased ("for the ferryman" as Abberline explains), from the first Ripper victim to the dead, opium-overdosed Abberline. The film's final image of the Victorian DG penny, clearly showing the so-called "bun head" profile of the young Queen, placed over a dead man's eyes is a chilling condemnation, reducing the monarch to a bitter token of death.[28]

Several animated films present Queen Victoria as an object of obsession, but with limited character development. *The Great Mouse Detective* (1986) revolves around a quest by a little girl to rescue her kidnapped father, a toymaker. She enlists Basil of Baker Street (a mouse version of Sherlock Holmes), who uncovers a plot by arch nemesis Professor Ratigan (rat version of Moriarty) to take over as supreme ruler of all Mousedom. He forces the toymaker to create a full-size toy version of the Mouse Queen and unveils his plot at a celebration of the Diamond Jubilee (the human jubilee is shown above as guests enter Buckingham Palace, the mouse reception below). The Mouse Queen's character is limited; she appears in a newspaper touting the Jubilee, a scene at her dressing table (she is in pink, not black!) when she is kidnapped, and in a scene where she confronts the mechanical Queen and Ratigan's peg-leg bat henchman Fidget tries to feed her to the Professor's cat.

Shaking and quivering as she reads a teleprompter, the mechanical toy Queen announces that she is taking Ratigan as her new royal consort. She is connected to a wire going behind a curtain where the toymaker is forced to work the controls. In a satirical take on Prince Albert, Ratigan proceeds to read a list of 96 demands ("this is my kingdom"), deferring sarcastically to "Your Highness' permission" at the end of his speech. This film was notable for its blend of traditional hand-drawn 2D character animation with computer-generated animation of the inner clock workings of Big Ben. Basil and Ratigan have most of the screen time, and Victoria is reduced to a cypher, an image of authority without any real substance. Even the film's ending celebrating the defeat of Ratigan's plot relegates the Queen to the background: a headline in the *Illustrated London Mouse* newspaper ("Queen Honors Detective.... Medal to Be Given") is set off by a still image of the Mouse Queen, with a frozen smile on her face.

A comically gruesome take on the Queen as object of obsession appears in the animated feature 2012 *The Pirates! In an Adventure with Scientists!* which features a manipulative and malevolent Victoria (voiced by Imelda Staunton). All the characters evince obsessions, played out in a farcical, over-the-top style, visually enhanced by a fluid blend of stop-motion animation and CGI movement. Craving fame, the Pirate Captain and his amateur crew enter the Pirate of the Year contest. Charles Darwin, a member of the crew, is obsessed

In *The Great Mouse Detective* (1986), the real Victoria (voiced by Eve Bremmer) inspects the mechanical Queen Victoria, while Professor Ratigan's evil henchmen watch.

3. Of Love and Obsession

with more than science; he loves Queen Victoria and aims to win the Scientist of the Year award to impress her. While the Pirate Captain and Darwin are presented comically, thus blunting the impact of their obsessions, the Queen's obsession is pointedly gruesome. She is secretly a member of the Rare Creature Dining Club that eats endangered animals. The endangered creature turns out to be Polly, the last living dodo and the Pirate Captain's pet. Poor Polly manages to survive a convoluted narrative until she is rescued by Darin and the Captain from becoming a "Dodo à l'Orange" entrée on Queen Victoria's flagship the *QV1*.

During the end credits of *The Pirates!*, Darwin ends up on Galapagos Islands to pursue his work on evolution. Victoria is left at the mercy of the animals—panda, tiger, and rhino shown sharpening knives and waiting for her to drop onto their picnic cloth. Queen Victoria throughout is shown as short and dumpy, wearing her hair in a bun topped by a cockeyed small diamond crown. Her moods are spectacularly mercurial, turning from smiling to menacing within seconds. These mood shifts are visually underscored by the motto engraved in her throne ("I hate pirates") and the wooden Victoria statue standing near the Thames River. On one side it waves "Welcome to London," and on the backside it wields a headsman's ax with the words "unless you're a pirate." In the climactic fight, the Queen's enormous skirted posterior is revealed to be the result of an iron petticoat, which is removed to

Queen Victoria becomes deadly martial artist, after shedding her iron petticoat in *The Pirates! In an Adventure with Scientists!* (2012).

reveal the Queen as a martial artist in pantaloons, brandishing two swords. The end credits, in addition to wrapping up the fates of Darwin and Victoria, present a highly textured montage of images and jokes from the film, such as a poster advertising "Urchin throwing / Cockney baiting" and a Picasso version of the Queen's portrait. *The Pirates* is one wild ride, not one bit historical, affording no insight into Queen Victoria (she is what she is), but very funny.[29]

The two *Around the World in 80 Days* films (1956 and 2004) feature an obsession with betting. In the 1956 film, Fogg (David Niven) wagers £20,000 that he can circumnavigate the globe in 90 days. Queen Victoria follows his progress. After an exterior establishing shot of Windsor Castle the camera shows a breakfast tray with newspaper headline "Fogg" being delivered to Queen Victoria; only her hand reaching for the paper is shown on screen. In the 2004 version of the movie, the Queen (Kathy Bates) is more involved. In a scene set at the front of the Royal Academy, the villainous Lord Kelvin (Jim Broadbent) tries to arrest Fogg (Steve Coogan) and Passepartout (Jackie Chan). Kelvin insults the Queen just as she is walking up behind him. Having discovered Kelvin's fraudulent dealings with the Chinese and his attempts to arrest Fogg, the Queen sends the villain to jail. Because the Queen has 20 quid riding on Fogg, she divulges the correct date so that he can win the bet, and she gets the payoff.

In *Around the World in 80 Days* (2004) Queen Victoria (Kathy Bates) uncovers Lord Kelvin's (Jim Broadbent) various plots and sends him to jail.

3. Of Love and Obsession

The 2004 animated short *Van Helsing: The London Assignment* is a prequel to the feature film *Van Helsing* (video release 2004). Monster fighter Van Helsing (voiced by Hugh Jackman) discovers that the mad scientist Dr. Jekyll / Mr. Hyde / Jack the Ripper is in love with Queen Victoria. He has been murdering young woman to steal their souls, which he uses to concoct a potion designed to turn Victoria into a young woman. Gruesome murders and fight scenes are presented atmospherically, as Van Helsing chases the monster through the fog-obscured London streets, into the underground railway, and high up onto the Golden Jubilee balloon. Queen Victoria is first presented as a 70-year-old woman, imposed upon by her royal physician, whose medicine makes her "feel better and better after each of your visits." Transformed into the 20-year-old Queen, Victoria is unable to remember her past and is completely dominated by Dr. Jekyll. One image underscores this domination; as they escape in the balloon, the screen shows a split facial image with Victoria on the left and Jekyll's face on the right, as if reflected in Jekyll's knife. Beyond that image, there is little more to this Victoria, other than her ability to dangle on ropes and survive mayhem. After Van Helsing rescues her, the Queen turns back to her old self at daybreak, cannot remember events during her youthful enchantment, declares "we are not amused," and calls for her guards.[30]

The *Van Helsing* film's ending on "we are not amused" perpetuates the stereotypical reductive view of the old Queen. The themes of love and obsession have moved from the hagiographic romances about Victoria and Albert, through the politically infused visions of Victoria, John Brown, and the Mun-

The split images of young Victoria and Dr. Jekyll are projected onto the escape balloon in *Van Helsing: The London Assignment* (2004).

shi, to films where other characters pursue Victoria, sometimes with positive results (*The Mudlark*), more often with sinister intent as in *From Hell* and *The Pirates!* Contrary to the dour, malevolent, grumpy caricature presented in these more recent animated films, the historical record attests that Victoria was capable of and appreciative of humor, as we will see in the next chapter in a number of feature films that highlight her capacity for amusement.

4

Victoria Is Amused

Queen Victoria was known as a keen consumer of a wide variety of entertainment, ranging from dancing, opera, classical music, novels, poetry, theater, to popular shows. The image of the dour, elderly widow is completely at odds with the historical record. Particularly in her younger, formative years, Victoria was known for her ability to express happiness. Even during her later years, her smile was extraordinary; an American visitor to the 1897 Diamond Jubilee noted: "I watched her while she was talking and I never saw a smile make such a difference to a face. Hers is quite beautiful and lights up her whole face" (Hardy 147). This smile was captured by court photographer Charles Knight in 1898 and published on a carte de visite as "her Majesty's Gracious Smile." Biographer Hibbert notes that "often she would laugh until the tears rolled down her cheeks" (Hibbert, *Personal* 471). Her sense of humor was reputed to border on the slapstick: "According to Lord Ganville ... the Queen was herself much amused by such mishaps as a man squashing his hat by sitting on it or by a misfortune such as experienced by the wife of the Secretary of the Office of Works who, when she rose from her curtsy, her dress gave a loud crack like a pistol shot, much to the Sovereign's amusement" (Hibbert, *Personal* 101). Hence it is not surprising that several feature films, eschewing the clichéd image of the stern, "we are not amused" monarch, dramatize Queen Victoria's myriad amusements.[1]

The dancing Queen appears in *Victoria the Great* (1937) in a scene introduced by a title card: "Court Circular Windsor Castle October 11, 1839," announcing a ball in honor of the Coburg cousins, with music by Mr. Johann Strauss and company. Albert is shown complaining to his brother Ernest about his discomfort about this arranged meeting. Victoria (Anna Neagle) dances first with Ernest and then sends a servant to Albert (Anton Walbrook) to waltz: "Her Majesty will dance with you." At first Albert is stiff, saying he wants to leave the next day and prefers reading to dancing. Soon they begin to waltz beautifully, Victoria compliments Albert's dancing, and he says he is not going home. In contrast to this film's use of waltzes, the historical record shows that Victoria and Albert danced quadrilles together during their courtship because at this time the waltz was considered too modern and too physically intimate for a sovereign. By foregrounding a "modern" dance against historically accurate costumes and sets, the film suggests that Victoria and Albert are socially progressive, in touch with a dance form that 1937 audiences would perceive as romantic and personal, as opposed to the formality of the quadrille.[2]

In *Sixty Glorious Years* (1938) the waltz scenes are more prominently featured and effectively frame the couple's personal lives. The first occurs at the celebration of Victoria and Albert's wedding in 1840. The newly wed pair are seated watching others dance, and they jest about whether it is appropriate for a married woman to do the waltz. Shortly thereafter, they join in the waltz, splendidly performed by Neagle and Walbrook against the background of a magnificent ballroom set. The later waltz scene occurs at their daughter Vicki's wedding in 1858 where Victoria and Albert have the same "should we or shouldn't we" conversation and then move to the dance floor. As Downs notes, the waltz scenes "frame the entire life of Victoria and Albert ... for the second one [waltz scene] is followed immediately by his collapse and subsequent death" (Downs 99).[3]

Victoria in Dover (1954) also picks up the waltz motif and debate about the dance's propriety, though in only one scene. After Victoria and Albert's incognito meeting in the inn at Dover, the scene shifts to the parlor, where a friendly and flirtatious Albert (Adrian Hoven) teaches Victoria (Romy Schneider) how to waltz, as Johann

As this 1898 candid photograph by Charles Knight indicates, Queen Victoria had a ready smile and was clearly capable of expressing her amusement. The caption reads "Her Majesty's Gracious Smile, an instantaneous photograph from life."

4. Victoria Is Amused

In this scene from *Victoria in Dover* (1954) two couples dance the "immodest" waltz. Albert's tutor Professor Landmann (Paul Höbiger) and Victoria's governess Baroness Lehzen (Magda Schneider) dance in the foreground while Victoria (Romy Schneider) and Albert (Adrian Hoven) embrace in a waltz behind them.

Strauss, Sr., plays on the piano.[4] His tutor Landmann and her governess Lehzen discuss the waltz as "an immodest dance" just before they start dancing it. Strauss, it seems, has conquered royal protocol.

More recent films feature dance scenes that evoke the emotions of key characters. *Mrs Brown* (1997) shows Queen Victoria and John Brown dancing a reel at the Highland ghillies ball. The lighting in this scene emphasizes the ambiguity surrounding their relationship. The frame puts full lighting on Victoria (Judi Dench) and Brown (Billy Connelly), as they whirl in the center of the ballroom while the rest of the court is cloaked in shadow. The next few shots intercut the disapproving reactions of Victoria's family and courtiers with the dancing, suggesting their dark suspicions about the nature of Victoria and Brown's relationship.

In *The Young Victoria*, dancing is a key element in Albert's courtship of his cousin. Before Albert's arrival, the Queen's fondness for dancing is established by the score used in various public ball and court scenes, specifically Johann Strauss, Sr.'s waltzes which were so popular during the 1837–1838 time period of the film: "Walzer à la Paganini" and "Tausendapperment Walzer," as well as his "Contredanses, Op 44." During his first visit, Albert (Rupert Friend) makes a critical error by declining Victoria's (Emily Blunt) invitation to waltz with her. Once back in Coburg, Albert practices the waltz with his dancing master ("eins, zwei, drei, turn as you go"). On Albert's second visit, the ballroom scene paves the way to the couple's more permanent pairing.

During the buildup to the waltz, Victoria's growing attraction to Albert is made apparent. Entering the ballroom, she floats towards him without actually walking, as if pulled forward by her growing entrancement with her cousin. They dance a slow-motion waltz to the aria "Della crudele Isotta" from Donizetti's comic opera *L'Elisir d'Amore*. This aria tells the story of a strong love potion: the lover Tristan drinks a love potion which causes Isotta (Isolda) to fall in love with him. The love potion seems to work quickly, and Victoria and Albert's emotional rapture is visualized by the slow motion of their movements and their intent gaze at each other, against an out-of-focus background of all the other dancers.[5]

A key element of *The Young Victoria*'s appeal is its skillful blend of contemporary and classical music, resulting in a highly entertaining experience for the audience and at the same time enhancing characterization by contrasting the characters' personal, interior feelings with their public roles of Queen and suitor. The modern "Only You" song (sung by Sinead O'Connor) evokes the intensity of Victoria and Albert's consuming passion for each other. George Frideric Handel's "Coronation Anthem No 1" (aka "Zadok the Priest" and used in every British monarch's coronation since 1727) appears in the two separate coronation scenes that frame the flashback covering Victoria's oppressed childhood in Kensington Palace through first her meeting with Albert. On an equally historical note, Albert is coached by Stockmar on Victoria's amusements under the Kensington System (dolls, books, music, opera, or sketching). After he is told Victoria's favorite opera is *I Puritani*, the film cuts to an opera scene where Victoria reveals her romantic nature by silently singing along to *I Puritani*'s love duet "Vieni, vieni fra queste braccia" ("Come to my arms"). The brief excerpt from the aria features only the man's part of this duet and thus "emphasizes the disconnect between Victoria and Albert at the present moment of the film" (Salazar np). The musical disconnect continues during their first visit. Albert's clumsy effort to mention what he thinks is her favorite opera ends poorly, as she rudely shuts him down "I used to like *I Puritani*, now I like *Norma*."[6]

The Young Victoria adds complexity by using music to suggest the growing attachment of Victoria and Albert, contrasted with political dissention surrounding the young Queen. A second opera scene foregrounds Victoria's political mistakes arising from her partisan support of Prime Minister Melbourne early in her reign. During the singing of "What Power Art Thou?" (aka "The Cold Song") in Henry Purcell's *King Arthur or the British Worthy*, the insult "Mrs. Melbourne" is hurled at Victoria, the implication being that she is *not* worthy of wearing the British crown. During the long-distance phase of Victoria and Albert's relationship, *The Young Victoria* uses romantic piano music to bridge the time and space between the two. Having earlier told Albert that she didn't "mind" Schubert, Victoria gradually becomes intrigued with Schubert and flattered by Albert's gift of sheet music. Schubert's "Ständchen" ("Serenade," D 957, no. 4) is a plea to a lover to make the singer happy, which of course expresses Albert's feelings. Suffering later from the political fallout of the Bedchamber Crisis, Victoria plays this same piece while her voice-over, reading a letter to Albert, conveys her sadness about her shortcomings and reveals her growing love for Albert.[7]

Victoria's fondness for theatrical music is explored in *The Story of Gilbert and Sullivan* (1953). A traditional 1950s biopic, the film covers the joint careers of ambitious young "serious" composer Arthur Sullivan (Maurice Evans) and dramatist W.S. Gilbert (Robert Morley), following their collaboration on *The Sorcerer*, *H.M.S. Pinafore*, *The Pirates of Penzance*, and *Iolanthe*. Tensions flare between the two artists, especially when Sullivan is working on a cantata based on Longfellow's *The Golden Legend* simultaneously with Gilbert's libretto of *The Mikado* (subject of the 1999 film *Topsy-Turvy*). Queen Victoria (Muriel Aked) attends the premiere of *The Golden Legend* (1886), likes Sullivan's work, and asks him to compute a grand opera. The film has unfortunately not aged well, resulting in instances of unintended humor. Commenting on derisive audience reaction in a recent showing, Jamie Moffat noted "the room dissolved into laughter at the film's archaic conventions and often hammy acting ... yes, it does look a bit like Queen Victoria is reading the newspaper during *The Golden Legend*, though I know she's meant to be following the score. That scene got the biggest laugh of the night" (Moffat 3). Doggedly pursuing its biopic narrative, the film balances the high and lowbrow musical tastes of the protagonists. For example, Sullivan's grand opera *Ivanhoe* is based on Sir Walter Scott's novel (one of the Queen's favorite authors), and he presents a bound copy to the Queen. Finally, Queen Victoria commands a private performance of *The Gondoliers* (Gilbert and Sullivan's last great success) at Windsor Castle on 6 March 1891, which was the first theatrical entertainment at Windsor since the death of Prince Albert. *The Story of Gilbert and Sullivan* demonstrates that Victoria could appreciate both highbrow and lowbrow entertainment.[8]

Another kind of theatrical amusement frequently performed in Victoria's court was the *tableau vivant*, originally a presentation of static posed scenes and later by the Victorian era sometimes incorporating limited speech and movement. *Victoria & Adbul* presents a farcical version of this entertainment to underscore the tensions permeating Victoria's court during the period of her patronage of the Munshi. The scene begins with a direct view of the front-row audience, the Queen (Judi Dench) flanked by Prime Minister Salisbury (Michael Gambon) and the Prince of Wales (Eddie Izzard). A smiling Queen tells Bertie to change seats and invites the fully veiled Mrs. Munshi to sit next to her, which infuriates Bertie. A quick cut to behind the curtain reveals the ladies-in-waiting Miss Phipps (Fenella Woolgar) and Lady

The King of Persia *tableau vivant* features the Munshi (Ali Fazal) flanked by Miss Phipps (Fenella Woolgar) and Lady Churchill (Olivia Williams), much to the horror of Victoria's (Judi Dench) family and court in *Victoria & Abdul* (2017).

Churchill (Olivia Williams) adjusting their costumes. Echoing the conflicting attitudes of Bertie and the Queen, Lady Churchill complains "I've never been so humiliated in my life, but Miss Phipps is having fun: "Actually I am rather enjoying it."

The Munshi's tableau is announced as "A Scene in Ancient Persia," and the curtain reveals Abdul standing in the center, with Miss Phipps on the left waving a large fan in front of him and Lady Churchill on the right pouring wine into his cup. After proclaiming, "I am the Sultan of Persia, the King of all Kings," Abdul shares a brief smile with Victoria, Lord Salisbury looks around aghast, and Ponsonby takes a pill. The scene gets funnier. The two ladies execute a deep curtsy to the Sultan and declare "Your highness, we bestow on you all the riches of the Orient." Bertie begins to look worried as Abdul the Sultan concludes: "You are all under my power." Salisbury looks on with open-mouth horror, Ponsonby has a "oh no" look on his face, and the beaming Queen jumps up clapping "bravo, the Munshi." Salisbury's parting shot to Ponsonby sums up the court's reaction: "What the hell is this Munshi-mania? I'm trying to keep an empire together. I want this whole sodding mess knocked on the head." These class and racial tensions, epitomized by the characters' conflicting reactions to the tableau, continued to simmer until the dramatic scene where the Queen faces down her household about the Munshi.[9]

Literature was another source of great pleasure to Victoria, as is evident in comments sprinkled throughout her journal. *The Young Victoria* shows Albert receiving coaching from his tutor Baron Stockmar about Victoria's tastes including her favorite author Sir Walter Scott. In an awkward first meeting with his cousin, Albert robotically blurts out that he spent the long sea voyage reading *The Bride of Lammermoor* (1819), after an awkward pause "by Sir Walter Scott," to which Victoria coolly replies "quite," and brother Ernest (Michiel Huisman) whacks him on the arm in disapproval of his faux pas. While historically accurate regarding Victoria's enthusiasm about Scott's writings, Albert's literary choice underscores his ineptitude during this first meeting, particularly regarding the content of the novel he professes to like. *The Bride of Lammermoor's* heroine is forced into an arranged marriage, stabs her bridegroom on the wedding night, runs mad, and dies, arguably, a storyline that is the worst possible choice for beginning a courtship of the future Queen of England.[10]

Literature is mentioned briefly in *Mrs Brown*. At one point, John Brown is quizzing the Queen's maids to find out what she is reading. The reply is "Lord Tennyson," possibly a reference to his poem "In Memoriam A.H.H." which Victoria found comforting after Albert's death. Both Prince Albert and Queen Victoria read Tennyson with pleasure. Albert was responsible for Tennyson's appointment as Poet Laureate in 1850, and as late as summer 1861 he was urging his daughter Vicky (Empress Frederick) to illustrate Tennyson's "Idylls of the King" (Pakula 158). *Mrs Brown* unfortunately handles the Tennyson reference as a quick throw-away and misses an opportunity to provide more dimension and backstory to Victoria's interest in the poet, which included her commissioning Tennyson for the verses carved on Brown's tombstone (Baird 406) and on a plaque at the base of a statue of Brown (Rappaport 79).

In contrast to poetic flights of Tennyson, *The Great McGonagall* (1975) provides a farcical take on Victoria's lowbrow literary taste. Scottish William McGonagall (Spike Milligan) wants to become England's Poet Laureate, but his poetry is terrible. In fact, he has been often lampooned as the worst poet in English literature. Rebuffed when he tries to present his poetry to the Queen (Peter Sellers), McGonagall fantasizes about meeting her. In the dream sequence, he appears after Victoria's nonsensical statement, "That sounds like the unknown Scottish poet William McGonagall." She appoints him Poet Laureate ("Tennyson will have something to say about this"). They waltz to the "Blue Danube," with Sellers reportedly kneeling on roller skates to appear short enough. McGonagall sings "I can feel you under my kilt," whereupon the Queen says, "Stop, I can hear Albert playing on his organ." *The Great McGonagall* is a poorly constructed concoction of skits, buffoonery, and cheap jokes, the absolute nadir of lowbrow taste.

While Victoria was an accomplished sketch artist and avid collector of artwork, her taste ran to the conventional and representational. A notable exception was her taste for nudes and the exotic Indian art and architecture incorporated in the Durbar Room at Osborne House.[11] Her dislikes were equally emphatic, and a recent film shows Victoria expressing a decided dislike for a particular painting. In *Mr. Turner*, a 2014 biopic of J. M. W. Turner, the young Queen Victoria (Sinead Matthews) attends an art exhibition and rejects Turner's abstract work, which eschewed form and representation. "In the film Queen Victoria calls Turner's *Sunrise with Sea Monsters* (1845) a 'dirty yellow mess'" (Green). The painting's lack of form did not appeal to her. Apparently, this film has the history right on this point; Victoria pointedly passed over Turner (Timothy Small) for a knighthood, which embittered him.

While not appreciative of abstract art, the Queen enjoyed spectacles of varying types, specifically Buffalo Bill's Wild West show. *Buffalo Bill* (1944) is a highly fictionalized version of William Frederick "Buffalo Bill" Cody's (Joel McCrea) career from his service as a civilian scout, his advocacy for Indian rights, to the establishment of his show. The film ends with a montage of the performances around the world as Buffalo Bill's hair gradually whitens. His wild west show performs for Queen Victoria (Evelyn Beresford, uncredited), who is shown in an extreme long shot. She is smiling and applauding from the royal box, flanked by family, with two turban-clad Indian and two Scottish attendants. As "God Save the Queen" is played, two horse riders parade in front of Victoria, one carrying the United States flag and the other carrying the British flag.

Queen Victoria (Peter Sellers) and Scottish "poet" William McGonagall (Spike Milligan) in *The Great McGonagall* (1975).

4. Victoria Is Amused 99

Beresford also appears as Queen Victoria (uncredited again) in the 1950 musical comedy *Annie Get Your Gun*, loosely based on sharpshooter Annie Oakley (Betty Hutton) and her rivalry with Frank Butler (Howard Keel) in Buffalo Bill's Wild West show. Queen Victoria has a more active role in *Annie Get Your Gun*, appearing first in a long shot of the royal box, dressed in large tiara with elaborate white lace cascading down her shoulders. As the show unfolds, the film uses crosscutting between the action and Queen Victoria's reactions. In the last of these medium shots Victoria stares open-mouthed at seeing Annie's swinging upside-down shot. To the tune of "Rule Brittania," the camera pulls back from a close-up of Annie wearing the medal presented to her. The Queen tells her "you are a very remarkable young lady." Annie attempts a handshake, but is stopped by Cody and instead manages a curtsy, thus completing her character's development from "Little Sure Shot," the rough back-country girl-sharpshooter to a Victorian lady, at least one who can curtsy when not firing at targets.[12]

Queen Victoria was known for enjoying the circus, and two films show her meeting with Phineas T. Barnum and his star attraction General Tom Thumb.[13] In the flashback biopic *Barnum* (1986) starring Burt Lancaster, the

Queen Victoria (Evelyn Beresford, uncredited) eyes Annie Oakley (Betty Hutton) in *Annie Get Your Gun* (1950).

impresario describes his 1844 international tour to London when he presented Tom Thumb to the Queen (Bronwen Mantel). The scene begins with a high angle shot of Barnum and General Thumb walking down a long red carpet, and intercutting shows the Queen on her throne surrounded by courtiers, followed by a medium shot of a young, beautiful, and regal Victoria. Hampered by protocol that requires the visitor to speak through a courtier, Thumb addresses the Queen directly and asks to shake hands with the young Prince of Wales. Thumb then goes into his stage act, pretending to be Napoleon and teasing the Duke of Wellington: "A few more horses and I would have beaten you English," to the great amusement of all. The Queen presents a glittering watch and chain to Thumb, who impulsively hugs her and she responds with a warm smile. In a scene set 38 years later, Barnum causes outrage in London by purchasing Jumbo the great elephant, triggering a montage of angry newspaper headlines and a shot of the old widowed Queen uttering "we are not amused."[14]

The 2017 musical *The Greatest Showman* also includes the meeting between the Queen (Gayle Rankin) and Tom Thumb (Sam Humphrey). Unlike the 1986 *Barnum*, *The Greatest Showman* dispenses with any pretense towards historical accuracy in order to promote decidedly twenty-first century attitudes. Desperate to drum up business in London, his manager obtains an invitation for Barnum (Hugh Jackman) to meet the Queen. Instead of just Barnum and General Tom Thumb (as was the case in actual 1844 meeting), this film has Barnum and his entire group of "oddities" attending as a group, deliberately emphasizing the film's major themes of family unity and courageous struggles against racism and exploitation. Walking into the royal presence, their reception is quite frosty at first. Some courtiers betray shock at the bearded Lady and the trapeze artist whose bare legs are partially covered by a long cape. Breaking protocol, Barnum addresses the Queen directly. When Victoria says she has heard about, "your little colonel," Tom Thumb jumps out from behind Barnum and bows, "General, Ma'am." Victoria remarks on his short stature, whereupon the General replies in very improper (by Victorian standards) twenty-first century diction: "Well, you're not actually reaching the top shelf yourself, sweetheart." Barnum looks appalled, but the Queen, taken back a moment, bursts out in uproarious guffaws, followed at a few seconds later by her court. *The Greatest Showman* suffers from a fundamental disconnect between its feel-good themes of acceptance and anti-exploitation versus what Barnum is actually doing in the Queen Victoria scene. Barnum is exploiting the prestige of royalty for commercial reasons, thus undercutting his stance as the noble hero protecting his "family." This scene reduces Barnum to a questionable sideshow barker, while the monarchy fares no better. Queen Victoria is presented as a simplistic cardboard figure, animated only by raucous laughter.[15]

4. Victoria Is Amused

In *Jules Verne's Rocket to the Moon* (aka *Those Fantastic Flying Fools*, 1967), Queen Victoria (Joan Sterndale-Bennett) is caught up in the enthusiasm for scientific progress. This comedy opens with two parallel scenes involving the Queen, in which her award to an inventor results in disaster. First, she commends the Duke of Barset's electricity: "We would like to congratulate him for being the first man to illuminate his house completely by electricity." When she throws the switch, sparks fly, and the house burns down. The next scene involves a suspension bridge engineered by Sir Charles Dilworthy; when Victoria cuts the ribbon, the bridge collapses. Invoking the optimism of the age, the narrative moves on to another grand scheme. Phineas T. Barnum is involved with German Professor Von Bulow's plan to send a rocket to the moon, by dropping the rocket into a shaft onto a powerful explosive, similar to the cannon launch device in the Jules Verne's 1865 novel *From the Earth to the Moon*. Barnum sees the opportunity to make money, raises funds, and ultimately brings in a second inventor, Gaylord (Troy Donahue), who has invented round-trip rockets. Queen Victoria comes to the launch of the "moonship" and awards Gaylord a medal, delivered by Joan Sterndale-Bennett in a masterpiece of comedic timing: "As the first person to attempt an astronautical voyage from the earth to the moon, we award you this decoration and wish you bon voyage... [significant pause]. Oh and a safe return." She then tries to give the Professor a medal, but since he is being carried off on a stretcher, she neatly drops the medal onto him. Misleading title not withstanding (very little Jules Verne), the Queen is presented as royal patroness of scientific progress.

The Story of Alexander Graham Bell (1939) also features Victoria's patronage and endorsement of new communication technology. Beginning in 1873, this fictionalized biopic dramatizes Bell's romantic, financial, and scientific struggles. By 1878 his company is losing money, and Bell (Don Ameche) decides to travel to England to demonstrate his telephone to Victoria, reasoning "if the Queen will install telephones in the palace, the whole world will follow suit, just as they copy her hats." Fortunately, his wife (played by the ever-elegant Loretta Young) has the good taste not to copy Victoria's bonnets. Bell has more success after receiving an invitation to Osborne House on 14 January 1878. The scene shows the Queen (Beryl Mercer) seated at a small round table, with the telephone device in front of her.[16] She states "Sir William Thompson [knighted by the Queen for his work on the transatlantic telegraph] tells us that your telephone is a marvelous instrument, Mr. Bell." When Bell claims that his device can transmit a conversation with Sir Thomas Biddulph in Osborne Cottage (just under a half mile away), a medium shot captures the Queen's skeptical reception of this claim. She hesitates: "You expect me to speak into that? Perhaps you should speak into it. After all, you don't converse with a wire." When the reply comes through clearly, the

Queen is visibly impressed. Victoria next displays a keen sense of scientific method by requiring a second proof: "Ask him the time," and after hearing his reply, issues her first telephone command: "Sir Thomas, your watch is two minutes slow. Set it." Congratulating Bell, Victoria decides to have the telephone installed in Buckingham Palace. She observes that "Americans are a very inventive people," and upon learning that Bell was born in Edinburgh, she smiles "the Scots are very inventive too. Now have it say something else, Mr. Bell." Such enthusiasm for an invention is most definitely in the historical tradition of both Queen Victoria and Prince Albert, patrons of the 1851 Great Exhibition of the Works of Industry of All Nations, and Victoria's use of the communications technologies available in her era.[17]

As these films demonstrate, Victoria was not only very amused by the traditional entertainment of the nineteenth century (opera, novels, poetry, theatricals, tableaux vivants, circus), she was also looking to the future and derived much enjoyment in trying out and patronizing new inventions that would shape the future world. Motion pictures used for royal propaganda purposes (Chapter 1), the telegrams demanding information and action during various war crises, such as the death of General Gordon at Khartoum (Chapter 2), Victoria's discussion of the photographic process as a lead-in to the proposal scene in *Victoria the Great* (Chapter 3), and the endorsement of the telephone (Chapter 4)—all these key cinematic elements show an engaged, vibrant, and very "amused" Queen Victoria. The next chapters will show how the entertainment technology of the twentieth and twenty-first centuries have both leveraged these character traits and transformed the representation of Queen Victoria in unexpected ways.

5

Victoria Rules the Small Screen

Queen Victoria on the small screen may at first seem like an oxymoron, her character being so much larger than life, ever imperial and daunting. It is, perhaps, the very iconic nature of Victoria that attracted television writers, directors, and producers in the first place. From the 1950s to the present, Queen Victoria has appeared in more television productions than feature films, with each distinct era reinventing her figure to the tune of contemporary culture and obsessions. This chapter will focus solely on fictionalized productions and will not discuss television documentaries or televised versions of stage plays.[1] In contrast to the biopic films like *Victoria the Great, Sixty Glorious Years, The Young Victoria, Mrs Brown,* or *Victoria & Abdul,* television productions featuring the Queen as a character take a broader and more contemporary approach, falling into six broad categories: politics, empire-building and war; family history; series focusing on the Victoria and Albert love story; farce comedy; fantasy and time travel.

The several television series in the late 1980s to early 1990s show Queen Victoria as an engaged political player shaping the Empire. First, the Pierce Brosnan / Eric Idle series *Around the World in 80 Days* (1989) takes on an element of international diplomacy. At the beginning of Episode 1.3, Queen Victoria (Anna Masse) is informed by her ministers of Phileas Fogg's contribution to improving relations with Burma, despite the suspicion that he is also a bank robber. Cutting off her squabbling ministers, Victoria declares her confidence in British institutions ("Mr. Fogg cannot escape British justice") and immediately pivots to a pragmatic perspective: "Can't there be some graceful way out of this for the sake of our Burmese relationship and the dreadful disappointment it would bring to our British subjects?" While a temporary solution appears (the news that Fogg was lost at sea), the point is that Victoria demonstrates astute political savvy and underscores the late twentieth-century perspective that politics imbues all aspects of society.

A similar political slant is evident in the "Responsible Government"

(31 March 1991) episode of Canadian *Heritage Minutes*. A young, beautiful, and fashionably dressed (white silk and elaborate coiffure) Queen Victoria discusses foreign affairs with Lord Melbourne, specifically the government response to the Canadian Rebellions of 1840. Victoria (Bronwen Mantel) decides in favor of a proposal to grant some degree of self-rule, called "responsible government," to the Canadian provinces.[2] While arch-conservative Melbourne (Harry Hill) is shocked at Victoria's willingness to give up royal power, the young Queen takes a progressive stance. She decisively states her confidence that the responsible government arrangement will bring harmony to the colonies. Shrewdly she asks, what would be the consequence of denying her assent. When told another rebellion might occur, she affirms her approval of responsible government for Canada. It is significant Prince Albert is not involved; Victoria is shown as an informed and politically savvy decision maker in her own right, a status clearly aligned with twentieth-century feminist ideals, rather than based on historical fact.

The political perspective of twenty-first century television is also evident in the 2001 show *Station Jim*, which dramatizes a plot to assassinate Queen Victoria. Loosely based on the dog known as Station Jim, a canine collector at a railway station from 1894 to 1896, this show has socialist, anti-royalist revolutionaries hiring a sharpshooter to kill Victoria as she arrives at a railway station. The station dog amuses the Queen (Prunella Scales) with the tricks he formerly performed in a circus. Then, recognizing the would-be assassin as his former cruel master in the circus, Station Jim attacks the revolutionary and saves Queen Victoria.[3]

Two television series take an historical approach to the British Empire in Africa heavily filtered through late-twentieth century unease over the legacy of imperialism. The result is revisionist histories that put the British in a highly negative light. The 1996 *Rhodes* series covers the career of Cecil Rhodes (Martin Shaw), who became the wealthiest man in the Western world and founded the nation of Rhodesia. In "The Price of My Blood" Episode 1.4 (6 October 1996), Rhodes will stop at nothing to get an exclusive gold mining concession from King Lobengula of Matabeleland (now part of Zimbabwe). The episode begins with Rhodes receiving word that Lobengula wants to repudiate the Ruud Concession for mining, on the grounds that an oral agreement restricting the British grantees' activities was fraudulently omitted from the written concession. Shown as greedy, cynical, conniving, and racist, Rhodes takes counter measures, including a plot to delay the London arrival of two emissaries from Lobengula to Queen Victoria. Rhodes plants a confederate as a language interpreter for these emissaries, the implication being that the translations will hurt the Africans' cause.

The one scene with Queen Victoria (sympathetically played by Margaret Heale) begins with the two emissaries, dressed in western clothing, walking apprehensively into the Windsor Castle. The Queen enters regally, dressed in black with white headdress, but also pointedly wearing a large gold necklace, thus hinting at potentially ambiguous motives, since the Ruud Concession was about gold mining. Graciously welcoming them, she treats them politely (in stark contrast to Rhodes' attitude) and comments, "We hope you are not suffering from the cold," to which the translated reply is "How could they possibly be cold in the presence of the great white Queen?," which draws a smile from Victoria. She sits down with Lobengula's emissaries and gives them honest advice against the Ruud Concession ("It is not wise to put so much power in the hands of one man") and offers to help their cause: "We shall prepare a letter for you to take to your King leaving him in no doubt that any Englishman who enters Matabeleland to dig for stones does so without our blessing and without our authority."

Arriving in London, Rhodes works to undermine Victoria's edict, by lying in a government hearing, bribing politicians with company shares worth millions, and influence peddling—offering to name new towns after Prime Minister Salisbury, the Duke of Abercorn (later the chairman of Rhodes' company) and the Duke of Fife (later married to Victoria's granddaughter). In the end, the British government overrides the Queen and grants Rhodes a royal charter to create the British South Africa Company in 1889 and to expand northward as far as he wished. The one brief scene with Queen Victoria is arguably the only point in this episode where a British person is shown acting unselfishly and generously. She is presented as a beacon of light but ultimately powerless, her humanitarian effort thwarted by the British establishment, who are no more than a pack of corrupt ministers and greedy entrepreneurs.

In the 1986 South African television series, *Shaka Zulu* Queen Victoria is depicted far more negatively than she appeared in *Rhodes*. The series is set up as an extended flashback, with Episode 1, "Epilogue: Death of an Empire," the only scene with Queen Victoria covering her meeting with the King Cetshwayo, who had been defeated and captured at the end of the Anglo-Zulu War. Cetshwayo petitions the Queen, hoping to negotiate his return to control over Zululand. Seated on her throne, awash in white lace and pearls, the Queen looks haughtily down on the captive king as she listens to her advisors who argue for and against Cetshwayo's plea. A professor gives Victoria a brief history of the long-dead Shaka Zulu, whom he describes as "One of the greatest military geniuses in history, certainly on the level of a Caesar or an Alexander the Great." Arguing that Shaka Zulu's messianic stature among his people is still a threat to the British Empire, another advisor recommends "a progressive destruction and dislocation of the military and economic system" of the Zulu kingdom. After King Cetshwayo, a half-nephew of Shaka Zulu, reveals his ability to speak English, the Queen dismisses her advisors.

Without hesitation, she informs him "we cannot give you back your realm. Shaka Zulu is more alive today than ever. His military strength still prevails. You are the king, but it is his spirit which rules your people. We are a practical woman, your highness. We will not form an alliance with a legend." The rest of the series uses flashbacks to cover Shaka's birth, exile, innovations in warfare, assumption of the throne, building of the Zulu Empire, first contact with Europe, and the events that led to his downfall. *Shaka Zulu*'s version of Queen Victoria is unflinchingly negative, that of the ruthless British empress determined to maintain control over the Cape Colony and to deny autonomy to the Zulu nation.[4]

Television attitudes toward the British Empire were not monolithically negative, however. The outstanding exemplar of a positive perspective on empire building is the Ian McShane four-part series *Disraeli: Portrait of a Romantic*.[5] Released in 1978 in UK and 1980 on *Masterpiece Theatre* in the USA, the series employs the same biopic formula used in the Anna Neagle films of the late 1930s: a personal love story (in this case Disraeli and Mary Anne Lewis) is featured against a chronological narrative based on political events. Disraeli's key partnership with Queen Victoria shapes the overall narrative. Filmed for British ATV, the series provides excellent costuming and superior acting, but suffers from heavy preponderance of generic interior sets and reliance on 1970s television visuals: poor videotape quality and repeated sequences of medium shot, close-up, medium shot, close-up, talking heads, and limited camera movement. Poor production values are not the only drawback; the series moves the story along by condensing events over five decades, suffering at times from confusing jumps forward in time, without a title card to provide historical or temporal context. An unintentional result of the missing historical context is particularly apparent in the early scenes that depict the young Disraeli's world without clearly introducing or delineating who is who. The series seems pitched at a British audience presumably familiar with the events and characters of the 1830s to 1880s. American audiences viewing the series on *Masterpiece Theatre*, even with Alistair Cooke's introductions, may well have been more befuddled.[6]

Despite these drawbacks, *Disraeli: Portrait of a Romantic* succeeds in its well-drawn development of the relationship between Disraeli and his wife Mary Anne (Mary Peach) and in turn their relationship with Queen Victoria (Rosemary Leach). Episode 1 "Dizzy" covers his early life as a dandy, his affairs with several women, his growing interest in politics despite anti–Jewish prejudice, multiple failed attempts to get elected, and finally his successful election. Queen Victoria does not appear in Episode 1 and is only mentioned as Disraeli and friends drink a toast to the new "Queen to the little tips of her toes." Balancing the personal with politics, Episode 2 "Mary Anne" covers Mary Anne Lewis' widowhood and her marriage of political convenience with Disraeli. Mary Anne is shown as politically savvy but poorly educated; in a discussion with Disraeli about a copyright bill, it is clear that she has never read or even heard of John Milton, to his great surprise (later in Episode 4, a bust of Milton is shown in their study).

In Episode 2 political events of 1838 to 1851—Disraeli's rise from back bencher to his 1851 appointment as Chancellor of the Exchequer—are set off against the disapproval of Queen Victoria and Prince Albert. The Prince deplores Disraeli's morals, they both find his speeches against Peel to be "offensive, near treasonous" and they are not in favor of Disraeli's 1851 appointment. When Lord Darby presents his cabinet to the Queen, Disraeli kisses her hand as Victoria won't condescend to look at him.

In Episode 3 "The Great Game," the Queen and Prince Albert come around to Dizzy's side. During the Indian Rebellion in 1858, Dizzy dreads reporting to them: "Facing Queen Victoria and Prince Albert is like looking down the barrel of a double shotgun." Fortunately, the interview is successful as Dizzy explains his government's decision to transfer rule from the East India Company to the crown (Victoria looks pleased), appoint a Viceroy, guarantee religious customs, and pursue a policy of "justice tempered with mercy" (Albert looks impressed). After lavishly praising the new Houses of Parliament designed by Prince Albert (following his own advice "when you come to royalty, lay it on with a trowel"), the royal couple is smitten. Victoria thinks he is "handsome," and Albert takes back his negative opinion: "what an extraordinary man. Our views are so surprisingly similar."

Mary Anne Disraeli makes a similar good impression on the Queen during a weekend at Windsor. In the ladies' drawing room, Mary Anne is at first ignored until Princess Alice kindly talks with her. The Queen ap-

Rosemary Leach as Queen Victoria in the television series *Disraeli: Portrait of a Romantic* (1980).

Queen Victoria (Rosemary Leach) glowers at Disraeli (Ian McShane) after he is made Chancellor of the Exchequer in Episode 1.2 of *Disraeli: Portrait of a Romantic* (8 June 1980).

pears just as Alice is recommending a statue of Apollo in the British Museum as "absolute perfection of form" (presumably nude), and Mary Anne blurts out "you should my Dizzy in the bath." Victoria laughs uproariously, and when Prince Albert approaches and asks what the joke is, she says "I couldn't possibly tell you." Episode 3 continues to develop the Disraeli—monarch relationship. The widowed Queen appears in three scenes, showing her growing respect for and reliance on Disraeli, beginning with his first administration as Prime Minister and ending with her offer of a peerage, which he declines and instead requests the title Lady Beaconsfield for Mary Anne in her own right.

Episode 4 "The Chief" of *Disraeli* continues the personal and political counterpoint. After Mary Anne's death, Disraeli moves into a political partnership with the Queen, who is pleased with his appointment of "exceptionally able men. Our voice should be hear again in foreign affairs," touching on one of her chief complaints against Gladstone. After receiving a letter from the Prince of Wales about the opportunity to buy a controlling interest in the Suez Canal ("that is unusually perceptive of him," she grouses), the

5. Victoria Rules the Small Screen

Queen tells Disraeli "it must be done," and Disraeli delivers. This episode features Disraeli's recognition of the long-term political ramifications of the Russo-Turkish War 1877–78. Despite declining health, Disraeli attends the 1878 Congress of Berlin, where he bests the Russians and German Chancellor Bismarck (Brewster Mason) and returns with British control over the island of Cyprus. Queen Victoria sends him flowers, and in their follow-up meeting, she makes the old man sit down in her presence: "I am proud to have you as my friend and chief minister." Her white headdress and cascading lace symbolizing her newfound political life, the Queen waxes nostalgic for the loss of Prince Albert, and Disraeli concurs in his feelings towards the loss of his wife. Both have succeeded in their political agendas and faced loss in their personal lives. In another time jump forward to 1881 (sans title card), the Queen sends flowers to Disraeli, who is on his death bed. He declines a visit from Victoria because "she would only ask me to take a message to Albert." The episode ends with the image of a weeping Queen, dressed completely in black, placing flowers on Disraeli's grave. She turns slowly and walks alone away from the grave of her friend and political partner.

A number of television biopics relegate Empire to a secondary status and instead explore the dynamics of power played out within Queen Victoria's family. The best example is *Edward the Seventh* (1975). While covering Edward's entire life, this series provides a detailed and complex role for Queen Victoria (Annette Crosbie). In fact, Victoria appears in 10 of the 13 episodes, effectively making the series as much about the mother as it is about the son.[7] Like *Disraeli: Portrait of a Romantic*, the *Edward* series is hampered by 1970s production values: poor studio sets with painted views in the windows (especially in the early episodes), heavy reliance on generic television camera work (boring repetition of establishing shot, alternating mediums shots, end of scene close-ups), limited and ineffective location scenes (such as Danish Princess Alix riding her horse through generic grounds), and costumes that seem almost perfunctory and uninspired. However, the series compensates for these drawbacks with its strong characterizations and careful development of the characters, especially of Bertie and Victoria. Beginning with Victoria's furious reaction to the knowledge of her second pregnancy, the first episode sets up the initial conflicts between Albert and Victoria over her "uncontrollable rage" and her quick contrition, followed by promises of reform and subsequent failure to achieve the level of emotional control that Albert demands. Episode 1 develops Albert's successful ouster of Baroness Lehzen and his campaign to "help" Victoria with her state paperwork, leaving Albert the "master in my own house." At the end, Victoria is submissively and anxiously listening to plans for Bertie's education. The camera looks down on the worried Queen, as she is framed by Baron Stockmar and Prince Albert as they naïvely draw up plans more appropriate to an intellectually gifted and industrious student, e.g., more like Prince Albert himself, or Princess Royal Vicky, than poor Bertie turns out to be. An ominous note ends the episode: at Christmas the father takes a toy horse away from his heart-broken infant son and substitutes an educational toy—an abacus.

Episodes 2 through 4 of *Edward the Seventh* cover the basics of Victoria's and Albert's life from 1854 through 1861: the on-going disaster of Bertie's poor scholarship, Victoria's periodic tantrums (for example, when she feels excluded by Albert and their daughter Vicky), the parents' skepticism when they read reports of Bertie's successful tours in the United States and France, Victoria's admission to her mother that "I dread the idea of Bertie becoming King," Bertie's plea for an Army assignment (as opposed going to college at Cambridge) which is rejected by Albert who lectures his son about "honesty and morality," the parents' effort to find a wife to "settle him down," Albert's shock on learning of Bertie's affair with a musical hall actress, and Albert's decline and death as Victoria looks on helplessly. The earlier power struggle between husband and wife has morphed into a status quo of Victoria's acquiescence to Albert's opinions and actions, ceding to him the power behind the throne until his untimely death.

Episodes 5–10 cover the remainder of Victoria's life and her determination to hold tight to her royal prerogatives. Now that she doesn't have to share power with Albert, she declines to allow the Prince of Wales a meaningful role, to his growing frustration. After a montage of the Wales' successful public appearances, the Queen expresses jealousy of their reception complaining to Lord Palmerston that Bertie goes "about begging for admiration ... a puppet running around for show. My nerves will not allow me to appear in public. You will not let them [Bertie and Alix] compete with me for popularity." Political events are discussed but never staged. For instance, the Prussian-Danish War over Schleswig-Holstein is presented through the prism of a family conflict: Bertie's support of his wife's native Denmark and Victoria's preference for German interests. Also mentioned in passing are the French defeat in Mexico and execution of Emperor Maximilian, the end of the Russo-Turk War (without mentioning Disraeli's efforts at the Congress of Berlin), Bertie's dislike of the Prussians especially Bismarck's influence over cousin Willie (later the Kaiser), and the Second Boer War. Bertie's various affairs and mistresses receive much more time than politics. Lillie Langtry, Daisy Grenville, Alice Keppel, Agnes Keyser, among others, make an appearance, though none are shown in bed with the Prince. The Prince of Wales also makes two courtroom appearances for the Mordaunt and Aylesford divorce cases and is involved in the Tranby Croft gambling scandal. Victoria gives her wayward son the best advice after the first of these scandals: "your life is like a city set up on a hill.... People delight in believing the worst of us," which Bertie promptly disregards.[8]

On occasion, *Edward the Seventh* overcomes some of its production constraints that unfortunately result in far too many talking heads, predictable alteration of medium and close-up shots, the same drawing and ball room sets, over and over again. A welcome change occurs in a scene staged

Queen Victoria (Annette Crosbie) glowers at her wayward son Bertie (Timothy West) in *Edward the Seventh* (1975).

at Albert's mausoleum, though the use of a tomb setting as a visual "breath of fresh air" is arguably ironic. In the 1863 episode, Victoria takes Bertie and Alix to the tomb to get Albert's approval of their marriage; the young couple are both quite a bit taken back from this communication from beyond the grave. Later in 1897, Victoria and daughter Vicky, Empress Frederick, visit the tomb; the Queen says she misses Albert every day, but is sustained by the public's encouragement to "go it old girl." The complexity of Queen Victoria is evidenced by the balancing of the mourning scenes with a number of family scenes showing Victoria's pleasure in her grandchildren. Most noteworthy is the tea scene where misbehaving grandson Georgie imitates a little dog, and Grandma sends him under the table where the doggies go. Soon Georgie emerges, sans shirt and barking "woof, woof," and Bertie and the Queen both collapse in laughter, ending with her statement "I never want my house without grandchildren." A political dimension is brought out in scenes showing the Queen's dislike of Gladstone, such as her complaint that "he speaks to me as if addressing a public meeting." Their relationship is summed up in a camera angle in an audience scene: a high angle shot looks down at the Queen's glowering face as Gladstone voice lectures on and on. The depth of her anti–Gladstone animus is effectively visualized by the scene where Victoria explodes when she hears that Bertie had attended Gladstone's funeral. She screams and sweeps her desk clear, leaving only a bust of Albert perched precariously on the desktop.

The most cinematic effects in *Edward the Seventh* are reserved for Episode 10 in a short clip of silent films of the Diamond Jubilee, first presented with a clicking sound and with the camera pulling back to show the royal family watching "home movies." Bertie remarks that this "remarkable invention" takes snapshots and brings them to life via a "projector." An effective cinematic set piece occurs during the Queen's deathbed scene; first the camera slowly pans over the faces of her family gathered around the bed, and after her death, the camera slowly pulls back as the lighting remains solely on the dead Queen, leaving her family in shadow around the bed. Episode 11 of *Edward the Seventh* reprises the home movie theme when the family is viewing a short clip of Queen Victoria's funeral, and one of the young family members calls out "oh there is Uncle Bertie" riding behind the cortege. While not in keeping with dignified mourning, this comment attests to the power of the cinematic experience to pull its audience into the action on screen.

A far more limited role for Queen Victoria appears in the 1974 series *The Fall of Eagles*, covering the collapse of three European dynasties. Two episodes about the Romanovs and Hohenzollerns dynasties touch on Victoria's family. Episode 1.2 "The English Princess" (22 March 1974) opens with the wedding of Princess Victoria (Gemma Jones) and German Crown Prince Frederick (Denis Lill), introduced via a voice-over with visuals taken from contemporary illustrations. The first scene with actors shows Prince Albert (Frank Thornton) and Queen Victoria (Perlita Neilson) discussing the match. The Queen is worried, "If only she were going to a happier court. It's a dreadful moment for a mother," while Albert is confident in Vicky's training and abilities. Upon leave taking, both parents give their daughter advice: Victoria tells her to "number your letters dear," and Albert advises "find liberal minds in Prussia and read the English newspapers." The scene ends with a tight medium shot of Victoria's face showing great anxiety for her daughter, with son Bertie (Mike Elles) looking over her shoulder while nonchalantly eating candy. The only other interaction between mother and daughter are letters, such as Victoria's comments to Vicky about the perils of childbirth and much later Vicky's letter about the horrors of the Prussian-Austria war.

Even more limited is Queen Victoria's role in "The Last Tsar" Episode 1.5 in *The Fall of Eagles* series (12 April 1974). The emphasis on this biopic is Tsarevich Nicholas (Charles Kay), his reservations about becoming Tsar, his affair with a ballerina, and his proposal to Princess Alix of Hesse. Queen Victoria (Mavis Edwards) has just one scene, when she arrives in Coburg to attend a grandson's wedding. Informed by her granddaughter Elisabeth that Tsarevich Nicholas wishes to marry her sister Alix of Hesse, the Queen expresses her approval: "Oh this will be a fine match for her. You should speak to her. We must all speak." Warned that Nicholas' father and uncles do not approve of a match with a German princess, Queen Victoria brushes aside with an imperial dismissal "That is not important," a historical miscalculation as both sisters Elisabeth and Alix married into the Russian nobility and were ultimately executed by the Bolsheviks. Queen Victoria's scene ends as the episode moves on to Nicholas' elevation to Tsar and the beginnings of Russian revolution, with Patrick Stewart as Lenin, hoping that Nicholas will be the last Tsar. Both episodes seem an awkward fit in a series entitled the *Fall of Eagles* since they put in play the forces that led to the fall of the Romanovs and Hohenzollerns dynasties, without actually showing the fall. The assumption is that audiences in 1974 had sufficient historical knowledge to fill in the gaps, but such an assumption would be unlikely with today's television audience.[9]

A similar exploration of family history with broader political implications appears in "The Hand That Rocks the Cradle" Episode 2.3 (12 April 1981) of the *Cribb* police series. Set in 1897, the year of the Diamond Jubilee, an anarchist group plots against Queen Victoria (Jessica Spencer). First they sabotage her grandson's pram as a means to gain entrance into the palace. Due to disabled brakes, the pram rolls loose, careens down terrace steps, and nearly runs into an unamused Queen. The royal family disagrees on a replacement nurse: Queen Victoria favors former royal nurse Mrs. Innocent (Rosalie Crutchley), and the parents Princess Beatrice (Irene Richard) and Prince Henry of Battenberg (Scott Fredericks) favor a young Miss Temple

(Jane Temple), who turns out to be in league with the anarchists. Queen Victoria dominates a humorous scene where she overrules Beatrice's objections to Mrs. Innocent. Brow-beaten Beatrice says that Mrs. Innocent frightened her and dosed her with Gregory Powder, a laxative made from rhubarb, magnesia, and ginger (mercifully no longer sold). Outraged, the Queen replies dismissively in a grand dictatorial tone: "and what is wrong with Gregory Powder?" Poor Beatrice has to suffer through her mother's shifting opinions. At one point, Victoria tells Beatrice that she wants to invite to the Jubilee those divorced ladies who were "not to blame," but Lord Salisbury had objected. Later she abandons her progressive stance and reverts to a conservative disapproval of women doctors and the women's suffrage movement. When Beatrice informs her mother that Mrs. Innocent and Lady Musgrove attended a women's suffrage meeting, Victoria vents against the movement and says "Lady Musgrove ought to get a good whipping." The "Hand That Rocks the Cradle" episode presents a limited vision of Victoria, but the episode does capture several of Queen Victoria's well-known opinions and mannerisms.[10]

A much different approach to the royal family's history is presented in the 1978 *Lillie* series, specifically the two episodes covering the Prince of Wales' affair with Lillie Langtry (Francesca Annis, reprising her role from the 1975 *Edward the Seventh* series). Queen Victoria appears in a small but decisively disapproving role, and the conflict is presented without a larger political dimension, leaving more focus on her moral objections to Bertie's behavior. Queen Victoria (Sheila Reid) is apparently well aware of what was going on. At the beginning of Episode 1.5, Bertie complains to his younger brother Leopold that "Mama" disapproves of his lifestyle, won't give him useful work, and blames him for not being "an imitation of my father." Gleeful that this frees up his time for other pursuits, Bertie aggressively pursues Lillie. Prince Leopold is also among Lillie's admirers and has a sketch of her on his bedroom wall. When Queen Victoria barges into his bedroom, she removes the sketch muttering, "She is much too pretty. This has no place here. I shall see it disposed of." A cut to Leopold's face registers his dismay. In Episode 1.6, Bertie manages to get Lillie presented at court, but Queen Victoria is frosty. When Lillie does a deep curtsy, Victoria is slow to hold out her hand to be kissed and in a tight close-up, stares straight ahead, refusing to make eye contact with Lillie. The Queen is most definitely not amused.[11]

A highly cynical attitude towards Victoria society is exploited in Episode 1.7 of *The Edwardians* (1973), which is based on the scandal surrounding Bertie's affair with Francis Evelyn "Daisy" Greville, later Countess of Warwick. In a flashback, "Babbling Brooke," aka the Socialist Countess, dictates her memoirs covering her colorful life as part of the Prince of Wales' Marlborough house set, her nine-year tenure as royal mistress, and her later interest in Socialism and associated causes. Queen Victoria (Mollie Maureen) is presented negatively throughout. The opening scenes are set up like a Broadway stage with an open area in the front and in the back a balcony with two curving staircases. This spatial dichotomy is used to suggest that the Queen is distant and self-absorbed. Victoria sits on a throne at the back corner of the balcony, weeping over a portrait of Albert. Still on the balcony, the Queen awkwardly receives Daisy (Virginia McKenna) at court (forced small talk such as "are you fond of music?") and next tries to engineer an arranged marriage of Daisy and her hemophiliac son Prince Leopold. Daisy declines the proposition by running away. The last two appearances of Queen Victoria, perched on a throne in the background, reveal her as a looming figure of disapproval—first about Bertie's involvement in a card-cheating scandal (the Tranby Croft affair 1890) and finally about his affair with Daisy and her Socialist antics. Casting off her passive role as a spectator of corruption, the Queen actively conspires to espouse a cynical world view: she instructs Lord Albemarle (whose son is the husband of the new royal mistress Alice Keppel) "find him another woman, a discrete one this time." The artificial, stagey design underscores the rampant corruption of this society, starting from the Queen at the top (literally in the staging) down to the Cockney chimney sweeps (at the front of the camera frame) who provide a satiric Greek chorus to the aristocratic goings-on. The ultimate impression is of a superficial, hypocritical society, a whirlwind in which anything goes, as long as embarrassing behavior stays out of the public eye.[12]

While television has repeatedly placed Queen Victoria within a range of contexts involving war, politics, empire building, family drama, and morality, the love story of Victoria and Albert has received somewhat less attention on television. Only two major series—*Victoria and Albert* in 2001 and *Victoria* Seasons 1, 2, and 3 in 2017 to 2019—tackle this subject, in contrast to multiple theatrical films on the love story. Moving beyond the political perspectives of the 1970s to 1990s series that, in some cases, leveled harsh criticism at the Queen and British government on political grounds, the twenty-first century series return to the formula of the Victoria and Albert love story, foregrounded against select political events of the era.

The 2001 the television series *Victoria & Albert* was pointedly conceived as a contrast to the 1997 Judi Dench film *Mrs Brown* that portrayed the older Queen. Producer David Cunliff explicitly "wanted to get beyond the politics, paint a more rounded, human picture of Victoria and show what her relationship with her husband was really like…. It was definitely stormy and passionate" and his intent was to "be a breath of fresh air for a viewing public fed images of Queen Victoria as a grim monarch."[13] This deliberate attempt to play off against a four-year-old film (*Mrs Brown*) and ignore the complex portrayals of young Victoria and Albert of the 1930s and 1950s films seems curiously myopic, a sign of popular culture with limited half-life and inability to value the perspectives of previous eras. Looking forward, the television *Victoria & Albert* seems to have paved the way in certain critical elements for the 2017–2019 *Victoria* series.[14]

Broadcast by the BBC in 2001 as two 100-minute episodes, *Victoria & Albert* covers their first meeting in 1837 through Albert's death in 1861. The series is framed as a reminiscent flashback for the old Queen (Joyce Redman in her last role), as she adjusts the combs on Albert's dresser in the Blue Room at Windsor, the room in which he died. Previously a footman had been using a measuring stick to lay out the combs, and the Queen actually moves them off kilter, a most human touch. Using typical television camera conventions, the focus goes into a tight close-up of the Queen's face as she thinks back on her life with Albert. Part 1 covers familiar territory: Victoria's first unsuccessful meeting with Albert; growing tension between Conroy, mother, and daughter; King William's birthday celebration where he pointedly insults the Duchess; Albert's reluctance to marry; Victoria's accession; her infatuation with Lord Melbourne and rejection of mother and Conroy; Albert's second visit; the proposal and wedding; and the first major row over Lehzen's mismanagement of the household. Part 2 covers more time, 1840 to 1861 using two 10-year jumps forward: the Oxford assassination attempt; birth of the first two children; the Boy Jones sneaking into the palace; Sir Robert Peel; dismissal of Lehzen after the debacle of Princess Vicky's serious illness; the Christmas traditions introduced by Albert; Bertie's affairs with an actress; Albert's confrontation with Bertie; and Albert's decline and death. The overall emphasis is on the personal and familial, with only passing references to politics, such as the concessions to Peel suggested by Prince Albert to remove the Whig Lady Standish ("Hetty") from Victoria's ladies-in-waiting at the beginning of Peel's second government in 1841.

Shot more like a film, the *Victoria & Albert* series pays much more attention to setting, visual composition, and camera movement, resulting in overall higher production values than earlier series. Visual complexity is evident in its use of dynamic exteriors, a welcome change from the monotony of talking heads trapped in interior sets common in earlier Victoria series. *Victoria & Albert* begins with a visual dichotomy between two planes of action: the exterior croquet scene where Victoria (Victoria Hamilton) and Albert (Jonathan Firth) irritate one another, contrasted with an interior shot of the rival manipulators Baroness Lehzen and Baron Stockmar who are watching the outdoor scene. Even more dynamic is the use of camera movement in outdoor settings. The camera moves ahead or around Baron Stockmar and Prime Minister Melbourne as they walk and talk through the Baron's role as private secretary and Melbourne's definitive "you'll have to let her go and leave her to me." Similarly, the camera follows and leads in a scene between

Uncle King Leopold and Stockmar; as they stroll the grounds of his castle, they debate whether to send Albert back for a second visit. The most impressive camera movement occurs in the Christmas scene where Albert, dressed as bear, chases his children, and they in turn chase him through corridors and upstairs, camera moving with them.

Shot composition in *Victoria & Albert* is a key element used to underscore conflict and increase emotional tension. After learning that she is now Queen, the camera frames Victoria in the right foreground as she declares "I will do my utmost to do my duty," while her moth-

Queen Victoria (Victoria Hamilton) and Prince Albert (Jonathan Firth) in a publicity still from *Victoria & Albert* (2001).

er's face looms menacingly in the left background. The immediate next shot has Victoria moving across a dark room and opening shutters to stream light into the frame. A similar pattern of framing occurs in the wedding night scene where Victoria is framed with empty mirror on the right side, immediately followed by the couple's embrace. Low angle shots underscore specific ominous points: the deathbed of King William, and later Conroy manipulating the Duchess into his plan to demand a large monetary payoff from the new Queen. Camera angles enhance Victoria's final confrontation with the Duchess and Conroy. A high angle shot of the Duchess and Conroy waiting in hallway is a giveaway that they are not going to succeed. The camera goes to medium shots of Conroy demanding action on his outrageous demands and finally to a tight close-up on Victoria's face, holding back the tears in her eyes, as she reverts to the royal third person: "The Queen owes you nothing," effectively dismissing both Conroy and her mother from power over her.

Given a total of 200 minutes screen time, *Victoria & Albert* has the luxury of developing character over time-sequenced scenes. A well-acted development of Albert's love for Victoria is handled through gradual details:

his initial disagreement with Victoria over late hours and Bryon's poetry (immoral lifestyle), second meeting where he now claims to like Byron and quotes "She walks in beauty," his scene with Stockmar where he honestly questions his motives for the marriage, his discussion with secretary Anson about the nature of love, and finally the scene where he tells Victoria how much he loves her. Victoria's development is similarly slow. Initially dominated by her mother, she defies Conroy about the letter from the King, and celebrates her first Privy Council meeting by skipping down the hall, quite probably the inspiration for Emily Blunt's skipping to escape from the grim old councilors in *The Young Victoria*.[15] Her gradual maturation is measured by the diminishing frequency of temper tantrums, her increasing ability to handle paperwork with Albert's assistance, her eventual agreement with Albert about the moral tone of her court, her forgiveness and reconciliation with her mother, her generous recognition of Albert's contributions to the Great Exhibition, and her pointed criticisms of Bertie's poor scholarship and anger over his excessive smoking. Diana Rigg's Lehzen also develops slowly; first shown as the loyal servant defending her charge against an arranged marriage, Lehzen is later denounced by the Duchess as interloper plotting to separate mother and daughter. When Albert is angry about the household arrangements controlled by Lehzen, she deftly dismisses the Prince's complaints, using the excuse that the dirty household windows are cleaned by separate departments, also a point of contention in *The Young Victoria* film. Part 1 ends with Victoria taking sides with her old governess, visually emphasized in a tight camera shot of Lehzen's triumphantly smug face. In Episode 2, Lehzen's power gradually slips away. Her loss of control over the household and impending dismissal are presaged by a clear visual clue: as she lurks in the background shadows of a hallway, the Queen directs the placement of the Victoria and Albert twin working desks.

The second part of *Victoria & Albert* is more episodic and relies on title cards to bridge time gaps: "Ten Years Later Windsor Castle 1851" or the camera panning over the model of the Crystal Palace with a sound bridge of a band playing, ending in a title card "The Great Exhibition 1861." Costuming, ever a strength in British television series, reinforces the passage of time. In particular, Victoria's dresses and hairdos begin with the simple white Princess dresses (high waist, small puff sleeves, ankle length skirt), followed by the young Queen's dresses of pale green and purple; for her second meeting with Albert, she wears a dress in cream with small roses, matching necklace, and small crown. After marriage, she sports bolder designs with strong stripes or hats with large plumes. By middle age, her dresses are heavy silk in dark blue or olive green, outlining her thickened figure.

Victoria & Albert's emphasis on the visual is evident in the way two Christmas scenes bracket the Prince's deathbed scene. First, Princess Alice is sadly lighting candles on the tree when Bertie arrives, and she tells him that their father is not better. At the end of the episode, Victoria appears in widow black as she lights Christmas tree candles, and the camera goes to a slow-motion dissolve of her memories—their courtship, wedding night, first child. The presentation of the Prince's physical decline is somewhat undercut by the omission of political context; the camera shows Albert barely able to sign a document, without telling the audience that this is, in fact, his memorandum about the Trent Affair, which averted war with the United States as discussed in Chapter 2. Nonetheless Albert's deathbed scene is wrenching. The death scene is couched first in terms of family intimacy, especially in Albert's last words "gutes Weib" (good wife). In a brutal long shot, the camera slowly pulls back to show the entire room, Victoria still holding Albert's hand as he dies. As she is being gently pulled back by the Prince of Wales, their hands let go.

The *Victoria* series (2016–2019) starring Jenna Coleman is a fictionalized melodrama of Victoria's early life through marriage to Albert and birth of first child (1837–1840), with the Season 2 covering the birth of their heir Bertie, the Irish potato blight, repeal of the Corn Laws (1840 to 1846), and the Chartist movement of 1848. Season 3 covers 1848 revolutions in Europe, more Chartist agitation, Victoria's half-sister Feodora who stirs up trouble, the 1854 cholera epidemic in Soho, London, Victoria's conflicts with Palmerston, and the Great Exhibition of 1851. The series benefits from lush production values, particularly the excellent costuming that has become a hallmark of British historical television series. The Queen's wedding veil and jewels are a notable example of historical detail, including the orange blossom head piece, cascading lace veil and, of course, the adoring look at Albert.

The sets of Buckingham Palace, so large that they were built in a converted Yorkshire airplane hangar, were carefully designed to reproduce key elements, most notably the beautiful ballroom floor, hallways, Victoria's bedroom, and the below stairs set of the servants' hall, the dressers' work room, and the chef's kitchen. Arguably the best use of CGI is evident in the effort to make Beverley Minster look like Westminster Abbey, in particular a stunning recreation of the rose window on the north entrance. At times, other CGI effects are less successful: in the coronation scene CGI-created images of the guests are clumsily isolated on separate plane of action as the Queen's coronation procession passes by, creating a notable gap between the background of coronation observers and the procession in foreground. Equally unimpressive are the shots of blurry crowds outside the Palace as the new Queen, back to camera, waves to them. On the other hand, the use of exterior long shots as transitions between narrative sequences are stunning CGI: views of London and Buckingham Palace at different times of day, enlivened by movement (smoke or carriages) and simulation of a camera pan movement.

Victoria (Jenna Coleman) looks up adoringly at her bridegroom Albert (Tom Hughes) during their wedding in season 1 of *Victoria*, Episode 1.5 (18 September 2016).

In the *Victoria* series, several instances of high angle shots provide dramatic counterpoints to the action, such as the overhead view of whirling dancers in the ballroom at Buckingham Palace. At other times, the series unfortunately falls back on the visual cliché of television camera work: for instance, the final shot of Episode 1.2 ("Ladies in Waiting") ends with a close-up Victoria's face to imply that she is in love with Prime Minister Melbourne. Another example is the scene of Victoria's final audience with her Uncle Cambridge / King of Hanover (played to the nasty hilt by Peter Firth). The tension has been building up since the Duke was suspected of engineering an assassination attempt against his niece. When he stalks into the throne room, Cumberland's figure first appears in a long shot with his face ambiguously backlit. The camera quickly cuts to a medium shot as he delivers nasty references to the British law's softness on crime and the perils of childbirth. A close-up of Victoria's frosty reaction is followed by a slow camera pull-back as she majestically sweeps past him saying, "Uncle, I am a better monarch than you," and the camera cuts to close up of Cambridge's angry face.

One of the strengths and, ironically, the weakness of the *Victoria* series is its similarity, almost imitation of the politically correct perspective in the *Downton Abbey* series, where much of the appeal is the spectacle of modern-thinking characters (Isobel Crawley, Lady Rose MacClare, Martha

Levinson) plunked down in a historical period, with opulent sets and costumes and background references to historical events.[16] In a departure from previous television portrayals of the Queen, the *Victoria* series evinces a clearly twenty-first century obsession with sex. Brother-in-law Ernest (David Oakes) shows up in a brothel more than once, and the scene where he tries to get Albert "initiated" turns hilarious when Albert just wants to take notes based on the lady's vast experience. This brilliantly played scene (how Tom Hughes kept his countenance is a miracle) is cut against scenes of Victoria learning that married men take mistresses and finally asking her mother why this happens and, of course, not receiving a straightforward answer. Victoria and Albert are shown in bed, enjoying a healthy sex life, an unimaginable depiction of the Queen prior to the twenty-first century. The times have changed, and so 2009's *The Young Victoria* film and the 2001 *Victoria and Albert* television movie have similar bedroom scenes. Even more comic is the archly euphemistic discussion between Victoria and Lehzen on how to delay pregnancy. Jumping up and down on a sofa ("ten times?"), Victoria is ultimately caught by Albert, who primly suggests abstinence as the only sure method of birth control. As in *Downton Abbey*, political events are filtered through a familial lens, mainly in context of their impact to the immediate circle. For example, the Chartist movement is first presented in an inserted scene dramatizing a march associated with the Newport Uprising of 1839, but the issue then becomes entangled with palace soap opera. One of the convicted Chartists is a nephew of head dresser Mrs. Jennings, revealed through multiple emotionally fraught scenes. Victoria takes a progressively modern attitude in her speech advocating clemency: "I would like my reign to be merciful one." The same attitude shows up later after the assassination attempt by Oxford when Albert wants a severe punishment, but Victoria says she agrees with the insanity verdict, in contraction to the historical record showing them both appalled by the verdict.[17]

Twenty-first century politically correct attitudes are also apparent in the *Victoria* series' selection of events. Skipping over a number of serious issues such as the Canadian Rebellion or the First Afghan War (briefly mentioned by Peel), Season 1 devotes significant screen time to Albert's anti-slavery convictions and his speech to the Antislavery Society. By showing Albert actively engaged in social reform, the series glosses over his overt quest for power, to become in effect a king, which is the expectation of his father and Uncle Leopold. At times, the Albert character waffles uneasily between nineteenth-century prude and twenty-first-century husband. He lectures his brother on the risks of flirtation with a married Duchess, smugly criticizes Victoria for playing Schubert too fast and not practicing enough (when in fact Victoria just showed him up at the piano), and cautions her against going out in public during the last stages of pregnancy, echoing the conventional views, expressed also by her doctors and mother, regarding female weakness.

But in another scene that egregiously departs from historical fact, Albert seems startlingly modern in his attitude. He encourages a pregnant, restless Victoria to take a railway ride. First he sneaks off with Peel to view a locomotive, which he calls "the most magnificent thing I have ever seen," and then is elated when Victoria appears, takes a ride standing in an open carriage, and declares "I love it."[18] A contemporary print showing prince and Queen on their first railway ride on 13 June 1842, children and nanny in tow, points up how far the Victoria series has moved toward a fantasy vision of a pregnant Queen flying down the rail-line. After the Oxford assassination attempt, Albert suddenly turns from repressive consort to supportive spouse: he carries her into the palace, whispers encouragement "you know what it takes to be a monarch," patiently listens to her apprehensions, shields her from intrusions during labor, and enthuses that his daughter is "perfection. We should call her Victoria after a great Queen."[19]

Paralleling the politically correct narratives in *Victoria* is an unfortunate tendency to fall back on a soap opera style, reminiscent of *Upstairs Downstairs* series. This tendency becomes more evident in the later part of Season 1, with its entangled parallel plot lines of love stories, intrigue, and secrets among courtiers/royal family above stairs and servants below stairs. While

The Fictional: The *Victoria* miniseries presents a highly fictionalized version of the first railway ride taken by the Queen (Jenna Coleman). In a fit of feminist fantasy, this scene has a pregnant Victoria exulting in the speed ("I love it"), and leaves Prince Albert in the dust, running alongside the train. From *Victoria*, Episode 1.7 (2 October 2016).

5. Victoria Rules the Small Screen 123

The Factual: Queen Victoria's actual first railway ride occurred on 13 June 1842. This contemporary sketch shows the Queen, Prince Albert, and children, riding from Sough to Paddington in a luxurious saloon car fitted with "padded silk ceiling, blue velvet sofas, matching silk curtains, fringed lampshades, fine mahogany wooden tables and thick carpets" (Hampton np).

this choice works well during initial establishment of the multiple story lines, the end of the series suffers from a narrative marred by a choppy rhythm. The multiple story line works well in the montage of Victoria and Albert writing to each other, with a voice-over reading the text of the letters. Less successful is the excessively choppy handling of brother Ernest's flirtation with Harriet Duchess of Sutherland. The result is nearly chaotic: Peel informs Victoria and Albert of the results of the trial for would-be assassin Oxford, cut to Ernest writing a secret letter to Harriet, cut back to Victoria's statement backing the jury and deciding to return immediately to public appearances. This insertion of Ernest's clandestine (and totally fictional) flirtation dilutes the impact of Victoria's historical and politically savvy act, where she astutely uses a public appearance to reinforce confidence in the British jury system.[20] Even more choppy is the conclusion of Season 1 when the narrative is compelled to wrap up multiple story lines in a blast. The *Victoria* musical theme ("Halleluiah") plays in the background over about one minute of screen time: the upstairs flirtation of Prince Ernest and Harriet Sutherland, the Duke of Cumberland's return to Hanover, downstairs chef Francatelli leaving the palace to work on his own, dresser Nancy crying about her decision to refuse his offer of marriage, steward Penge delivering all the Queen's correspondence to Lehzen, and her triumphant glee about pulling the control over royal letters back from Albert's grasp. This overall impact is disjointed, at best, and dilutes the impact of the overall narrative.

Season 2 of *Victoria* continues the visual and narrative patterns established in Season 1: the short choppy scenes, interweaving of multiple upstairs-downstairs plot lines, lavish costuming, and CGI long shots of palace and London exteriors used to establish new sequences, such as a wintry shot of Buckingham palace in the Christmas Episode 2.9. Attention to detail is evident in the careful framing of characters against backgrounds, such as the ending of Episode 2.7 where Victoria and Albert enjoy cooking fish at home in the way they learned in Scotland, but looming above them in the background is the image of the British crown, a visual reminder of their royal obligations. Best of all, the endings of individual Season 2 episodes are more carefully crafted than in Season 1. Some end on sad notes: deaths of Melbourne and Dash the spaniel in Episode 2.3, betrayal by French King Louis Philippe at the end of Episode 2.5, and Episode 2.6's title card summarizing the impact of the Irish Potato famine. The majority of Season 2 episodes end with reconciliation. Episodes 2.1, 2.2 and 2.4 end with Victoria and Albert achieving balance in their relationship. A family reconciliation with Uncle King Leopold ends Episode 2.9 (after a series of goodbyes to Peel and Lehzen). The Christmas Episode 2.9 wraps up multiple storylines on a positive note, with Albert telling Victoria "we are no longer children."

Season 2 of *Victoria* handles political events by selectively emphasiz-

Victoria (Jenna Coleman) and Albert (Tom Hughes) enjoy a German-style Christmas with their children in *Victoria*, Episode 2.9 (25 December 2017).

ing domestic British concerns and de-emphasizing British empire building. While Robert Peel's courageous efforts to repeal of Corn Laws are foregrounded in Episode 2.8, other key foreign affairs are glossed over or given brief mention. Episode 2.6 "Faith, Hope and Charity" contrasts Dr. Trail's efforts to alleviate suffering in the 1847 Irish potato blight, with Albert's efforts to introduce improved sanitation at Buckingham Palace. The stark gloomy Irish scenes are contrasted with the comedy of Penge's and Lehzen's contrasting reactions to the Prince's installation of a water closet near the servants' hall (he is against; she is for it). Unfortunately, this episode relegates Victoria to the sidelines, glossing over the Irish press' condemnation of the "Famine Queen," as well as the fact she personally donated £2000 to the British Relief Association (worth over £206,000 or $217,000 USD in 2019 money). An even more politically correct attempt to downplay British colonial expansion is obvious in Episode 2.3 "Warp and Weft." The narrative includes an offhand reference to the 1842 Treaty of Nanking, which in fact ended the First Opium War with China and gave Great Britain control over Hong Kong. Omitting the colonial and historical context, the narrative uses this event as a lead-in to one of Victoria's miscalculations. As Albert is writing a memorandum on the Treaty of Nanking, he is interrupted by Victoria, who shows no interest in this foreign war and instead drags him into preparations for the masked ball, also known as the infamous Spitalfields silk debacle. The episode's story line is directly contrary to the historical record that shows Victoria was very much engaged and knowledgeable about the First Opium War, to the point of joking in a letter to Uncle Leopold about calling her daughter "the Princess of Hong Kong in addition to Princess Royal" (Farwell 17–18). This historical fiction in Episode 2.3 shows a Queen busily planning elaborate royal costumes, oblivious to foreign conquests and empire. While the ball scene is visually impressive, especially the cutting between the whirling dancers at the ball and the demonstrations outside the palace, the overall impact is skewed to show Victoria's political naivety and to downplay a key event towards the building of the British Empire.

The slant towards twenty-first century political correctness, particularly feminism and suppression of women, becomes apparent in the approach to the First Anglo-Afghan war taken by *Victoria* Season 2. Devoting a large amount of narrative time to a disastrous military defeat in 1842, Episode 2.1 begins with a rare title card "Afghanistan, the Khyber Pass" and shows the sufferings of defeated British soldiers freezing in the snow, the survival of only one, the Scottish physician Brydon, (subject of multiple Victorian paintings showing his solo trek from battlefield to a fort), and Victoria's fury about not receiving the bad news promptly. The historical record indicates that Victoria's role in the government's response to the army's disastrous retreat from Kabul through the Khyber Pass was limited, as she was more focused on her quarrel with Prince Albert over Lehzen's mismanagement of the nursery and Princess Vickie's serious illness, resulting in Lehzen's dismissal from service in 1842 (Erickson 95). The series moves the Lehzen dismissal much later to 1846 (Episode 2.8), thus extending the screen time devoted to Lehzen's conflicts with men—upstairs with the Prince and downstairs with steward Penge. By changing this timeline, Episode 2.1 takes a feminist slant on royal conflict, pitting Victoria against Albert, and leveraging the Khyber incident to illustrate their struggle for power. The ground for this conflict is laid in the scene where the politicians are seen looking at maps. Albert has his magnifying glass on "Khyber Pass," and ends with his statement to this all-male group "no need to trouble the Queen," who is at the time recovering from childbirth. Tension mounts when Victoria walks into her study to see an empty work desk and protests to Albert that she is recovered and wants more detail beyond his summaries of the royal box documents. When Albert informs her of the retreat from Khyber and near total loss of over 4,000 soldiers, she explodes "you have no right to keep it from me." After consulting the Duke of Wellington who tells her "The country will look to you for direction," a position reinforcing the British skepticism against Prince Albert's foreignness and their need for the Queen's leadership in time of crisis. Having heard from Wellington what she, in fact, wanted to hear, Victoria confronts Albert charging him "you have complete undermined me" and throwing a brush at him, a less than regal gesture, but effective as he retreats hastily. Albert in turn consults with his brother Ernest, who, uncharacteristically for a nineteenth-century male, suggests "perhaps Victoria doesn't like you trying to do her job."

Both pieces of advice are clearly what the twenty-first century audience wants to hear, and quite the opposite of the prevailing Victorian attitudes of female weakness, incompetence, and submission to male hegemony. While other dramatizations of Victoria and Albert's quarrels have shown her capitulation (such as, submissively knocking at his door as "your wife"), this episode takes a twenty-first century perspective on their relationship. As biographer Gill notes, "Theirs was a business partnership as well as a marriage, and they engaged in a weirdly public contest over who was the senior partner" (Gill 14). In Episode 2.1, the Queen comes out on top. At the request of her government, Victoria goes out alone to launch the HMS Trafalgar and successfully delivers her solo speech, "I am a soldier's daughter—the spirit of Trafalgar burns bright," to Wellington's approval "nicely done.... The country knows their Queen is there when it counts." The Trafalgar speech is intercut with a role reversal, by showing Albert inspecting the nursery, wrestling with an uncooperative Lehzen, and then rushing to the dockside where he stands in the background and applauds his wife's speech, yet another price of revisionist history, as contemporary illustrations showed both Victoria and Albert standing together at this launch (R. Wilson v. 1, 93).

The *Victoria* series' political correctness becomes even more heavy handed in the final episode of Season 2 about the adoption of Sarah the African princess, with maudlin scenes of weeping and wandering the darkened halls of the palace at night. Compared to Albert's speech in Episode 1.6 against slavery, based on well-drawn historical details, the anti-slavery message in Episode 2.9 segues into another bit of fantasy: the invented story of Miss Skerrett's renunciation of inheritance of 20 slaves worth £10,000. The twenty-first century preoccupation with sex adds to the fantasy: unmarried Prince Ernest's star-crossed flirtation (he was really married during this time period) with Harriet Sutherland, Mistress of the Robes (looking surprisingly young for the historical character's actual age of 40). Other inventions feed the fantasy, such as the Lord Alfred Paget—Edward Drummond romance and uncle Leopold's confession that he is Albert's father, neither of which have any historical basis (Baird 125–26). Even key visual details perpetuate a fantasy of perpetual youth. While Jenna Coleman looks right for young Victoria before her marriage, by Season 2, her appearance becomes increasingly unconvincing, compared to the well-known 1845 photograph of Victoria and daughter, which clearly shows the impact of four pregnancies in five years on the royal waistline. Coleman miraculously keeps her narrow waist through Christmas 1846, though at one point her character complains about the growing waist, but it isn't particularly evident in the costuming. Compared to the skillful costuming that created a convincing aging process for Annette Crosby's Queen Victoria in *Edward the Seventh*, the Coleman costuming is a wish fulfillment of eternal youth. And Albert's ill health, balding hairline, and bulging waist are not shown; the early 1842 daguerreotype of the Prince shows a rapidly aging, balding, middle-aged man, not the youthful Tom Hughes, who retains his hairline, figure, and athleticism, though admittedly his aggressive skating nearly ends in tragedy.[21]

The opening episode of Season 3 of *Victoria* is no better. Albert's hairline in 1848 is unchanged and retains its huge unruly mop. Victoria's face shows little trace of aging, even though the episode covers her sixth pregnancy, against a backdrop of the unsettled political events of 1848: the French Revolution that ended the Orleans monarchy and exiled King Louis Philippe, and the 1848 Chartist petitions and street demonstrations. The episode devotes as much time to family drama—Victoria's reception of Louis Philippe and her struggles to endure a surprise visit from her estranged and jealous half-sister Princess Feodora of Leiningen (Kate Fleetwood)—as it does to the political.

The Chartist political movement is shown through the prism of one "downstairs" character—Sabrina Bartlett (Abigail Turner), who provides embroidery services to the Queen's dresser and in her spare time signs up petitioners on the Chartist documents. Sabrina is a voice of pragmatism and

Queen Victoria Queen (Jenna Coleman) and her impoverished half-sister Princess Feodora of Leiningen (Kate Fleetwood) take a carriage ride. Tensions soon emerge between the two sisters in *Victoria*, Episode 3.1 (20 January 2019).

cautions against the hot-headed William Cuffay (C.J. Beckford) who is at the front of a mob that attacked Buckingham Palace, just as Victoria goes into labor with her sixth baby. Other episodes cover the royal family's enjoyment of Osborne House, the ravages of a cholera epidemic in London, a royal visit to Ireland, and Lord Palmerston's womanizing ("no girl is safe" around him, in royal steward Penge's opinion). The handling of Lord Palmerston's support for the Hungarian revolutionary Lajos Kossuth (Episode 3.3) is a distortion of history, one of so many in the *Victoria* series. Contrary to the historical records in her letters, Episode 3.3 has Victoria agreeing with Palmerston (Laurence Fox) about hosting a reception for Kossuth reception and arguing with Albert (who is opposed) to the point that they return to London not speaking to each other.[22]

While the *Victoria* series is at heart a twenty-first century political and feminist fantasy on what contemporary culture wants the Queen to be, other eras had radically different ideas. As previously discussed, twentieth-century television was heavily weighted towards presenting narratives much closer to historical record than the Coleman *Victoria* series. An alternative depiction in a number of twentieth-century television shows is Queen Victoria as a farcical figure, often the butt of the joke, sometimes as the instigator of the humor. In addition, more purely fantasy television series feature Queen Victoria as the object of a quest or search. Most transformative are the many time travel stories featuring Queen Victoria, where she either travels through time on her own or other characters travel through time to interact with her.

5. Victoria Rules the Small Screen

In marked contrast to the intensity of the romance series, the Queen Victoria figure is a perennial favorite in 1980s British television farce comedy, ever in need of a good joke and finding it in the perpetually black-clad Queen. One manifestation is verbal farce, best summed up in *Blackadder's Christmas Carol* (a standalone special aired 23 December 1988), in which a bubbly, but bumbling Queen Victoria (Miriam Margolyes) and her stupid Prince Consort (Jim Broadbent) are featured. First in the palace, Victoria, incongruously dressed in her iconic widow's black, interrupts Albert, who is busily wrapping her surprise gifts and stupidly gives away the surprises (pillow, nutcracker, shawl). On their traditional incognito Christmas adventure, the pair knock on "the great philanthropist" Blackadder's door. Victoria and Albert intend to award him £50,000 and the title Baron Blackadder for being the nicest man in England. Of course, Blackadder (Rowan Atkinson) rejects them with his typically elaborate insults: the Queen is the "shortest, fattest, dumpiest" woman and the "Empress Oink," and Albert wins the award for "stupidest" accent. The episode ends with Baldrick showing the red seal authenticating the royal identity and a freeze frame on Blackadder's iconic facial expression—a stunned/exasperated deadpan.[23]

Similar verbal farce is used in the 8 May 1983 episode of the British *Alfresco* sketch comedy series. A young and fashionable, but scatterbrained Queen (Siobhan Redmond) is taking tea with Florence Nightingale (Emma Thompson), who is back from the Crimean hospitals. While Florence makes a serious plea for better equipment and another leader like the Duke of Wellington, the Queen rattles off a series of puns, ending in "I am afraid you will find wellingtons [boots] seldom come in pairs." Responding to Nightingale's assessment that "Cardigan [commander for the Charge of the Light Brigade] is useless," the Queen veers off on names: "Lord Sandwich has allowed himself to be named after a convenience food and as for the McDonald of the McDonalds, the whole thing smacks of private sponsorship." Such verbal wit of the 1980s reduces Queen Victoria to the butt of simplistic, one-shot humor, no depth or analysis needed, thank you very much.[24]

A similarly light-hearted approach to Queen Victoria and family appears in the British sketch comedy series *Horrible Histories* (2009–2015). Based on a book series by Terry Deary, this production's aim is to interest young children in history by use of short, factual, humorous anecdotes about parts of history not covered in traditional education. For example, "Work Out with Queen Victoria" provides tips on how to keep wider than you are tall, by following these exercises: Sit and Rule (63 years), Sit and Mourn (40 years in black), Dip Away from Assassin ("you too can have a body that only looks good in black satin"). In Episode 4.2, "Victoria and Albert's Love Story" (10 April 2012), Victoria and Albert visit the Great Exhibition ("ice cream, flushing toilets, though not in the same room"), and the Queen finds, to the detriment of her

Victoria (Martha Howe-Douglas) and Albert (Jim Howick) visit the Great Exhibition where the Queen discovers that the Crystal Palace is infested with sparrows in Episode 4.2 of *Horrible Histories* (10 April 2012).

clothing, that the Crystal Palace is infested with sparrows. The Duke of Wellington suggests releasing a couple of sparrow hawks.

This scene is followed by a love ballad about Victoria and Albert's marriage. Episode 5.6 "Queen Victoria's Coronation" covers undignified snags during the ceremony, such as how the coronation ring got on Victoria's (Martha Howe-Douglas) wrong finger and how Prince Albert's moustache becomes fashionable. Episode 6.11 "Tricky Queen Vicky" summarizes Victoria's (Sarah Hadland) accession at age 18, marriage to Albert, the not-so luxurious Buckingham Palace (open sewers), and includes a Bollywood parody song "Empress of India" beginning with "It's good to be boss and Queen Victoria" and ending with her refusal to travel to India.

A more purely visual approach to farce is evident in several short skits, in which Queen Victoria is instantly recognizable and good for a quick, cheap laugh. One of the funniest is *Monty Python's Flying Circus* Episode 4.4 "Queen Victoria Handicap." In a footrace around a horse racetrack, all the contestants are dressed as Queen Victoria, and the race narrator (Eric Idle) is forced to repeat "Queen Victoria" numerous times. The "Wacky Queen Skit" In *Monty Python* Episode 1.2 uses silent footage with a voice-over describing the Queen's (Terry Jones) interactions with Gladstone (Graham Chapman), such as walking, playing with a garden hose, hiking up her skirts, running around the lawn, painting a fence right ("she's not sitting on the fence, she's painting it"), and later shoving a pie in Gladstone's face. In the "Poetry Reading" skit (*Monty Python* Episode 4.2), the Queen, with Albert's coffin in tow, interrupts Tennyson's reading of "The Charge of the

"Tricky Queen Vickie" (Sarah Hadland) performs in the Bollywood "Empress of India" number from Episode 6.11 of *Horrible Histories* (27 July 2015).

Ant Brigade" ("Half an inch onward"), and bans all poetry about ants in "Germany—er England."

More visual farce occurs in the "We Are Not Amused" Episode 4.7 of *It Ain't Half Hot Mum* (1976). This series is set at a fictional (mercifully) British base in India near end of World War II. The base's concert group puts on entertainments for soldiers prior to their departure for the front. In this episode, the chosen pageant is Queen Victoria telling the story of what the British did for India, based on a script that all agree is really bad. Gunner/Bombardier Beaumont (Melvyn Hayes) has the role of Queen Victoria in drag (first just crown and lace headdress, later a dark dress added), mainly to introduce John Brown, Disraeli, and a brief skit about the Indian Mutiny, which is described as an "industrial dispute" resolved by use of Vaseline instead of pig grease on bullets. The skit concludes with the Queen declaring "my Empire was saved" followed by a chorus line rendition of "Happy Days are Here Again." The guest, a dignified Indian deputy commissioner, is not amused, only confused by British culture, speaking for himself and many others.[25]

While the farcical images of Queen Victoria are clearly meant to gather quick laughs, a number of television series use the Queen simply as a background reference or to establish a historical context. For instance, in the 1992 animated series *Orson & Olivia*, two orphans struggle to survive in Victorian London and cross paths with Queen Victoria, as well as Charles Dickens, Lewis Carroll, and Sherlock Holmes. In one episode, they help to recover stolen crown jewels, and in another they foil an assassination plot against the Queen. The *Young Sherlock: The Mystery of the Manor House (1982)* series includes the "Eye of the Peacock" Episode 1.8, in which a teenage Sherlock (Guy Henry) foils a conspiracy against Queen Victoria (Marina McConnell) and saves a priceless diamond. In the *Hands of a Murderer* television film (1990) Sherlock recovers state secrets stolen by Moriarty and, as a reward, is presented to Queen Victoria, who is "his biggest fan." The "Poor Butterfly" Episode 1.6 (1968) of *Journey to the Unknown* places Queen Victoria (played by Fay Compton reprising her role from *The Prime Minister* 1941) in a ghost story much in the vein of the *Twilight Zone* series. The protagonist Steve Miller (Chad Everett) stumbles upon an isolated manor house and attends a costume party where everything looks as it did the 1920s. Everyone seems to know him, addressing him as John, although he has never met them. He meets a woman in a butterfly costume, who is anxious to leave the party. The lady of the manor, dressed as Queen Victoria, imperiously tells her "you can't leave, you're a house guest." Not understanding the situation, Steve goes off to get gas for his car, and when he returns, he can't find the manor house. After meeting a local couple, he learns that a disastrous fire 40 years ago killed everyone at the party and is shown the burned butterfly costume. As Steve drives away, the camera pans to a road sign for the manor house, its gate overgrown by vines, as ominous music swells.[26]

While the ghost story of "Poor Butterfly" plays out an eerie ghost story fantasy, television more frequently has presented Queen Victoria in the context of time travel stories. Not surprisingly, the earliest example of Victoria as time traveler ends in her discovery that the modern world is in moral decline and in need of fixing (by her, of course). In "Aunt Clara's Victoria Victory" Episode 3.26 (1967) of *Bewitched*, Aunt Clara (Marion Lorne) bumbles a time-travel spell, and Queen Victoria (Jane Connell) appears in Samantha's living room. This time-traveling Victoria is dictatorial, and Samantha (Elizabeth Montgomery) fears the Queen will clash with the client who is coming to dinner. While Victoria initially likes watching television, she becomes incensed by the images of bikini-clad young women, smashes the television set, and declares "we are not amused." Next she declares her intent to elevate society: "Providence obviously desires our assistance in straightening things out…. We shall begin by issuing some decrees. We will start with the western hemisphere." Before Samantha and Aunt Clara manage to send her back to the nineteenth century, Victoria gets into an argument with Darrin's client: "you remind me of Mr. Gladstone. We detest Mr. Gladstone." Most of the episode focuses on Samantha's attempts to hide Queen Victoria's presence via magic. It ends on a cliff-hanger: the spell sends Victoria back, but "now we have Prince Albert!"

Similarly, in the 1994 *A Curse on the House of Windsor*, a time traveling Queen Victoria (Miriam Margolyes, reprising her *Blackadder* role) appears in 1992. Learning of the issues facing society and the monarchy, she offers her advice to the current Queen. In a reference to 1992 as Queen Elizabeth's *annus horribilis*, the episode beings with a voice-over declaring a curse of the House of Saxe Coburg Gotha to the third and fourth generation (i.e., Elizabeth and Charles), as a camera pans over the Albert Memorial at Kensington. The next image is Queen Victoria walking out of a dark corridor (suggesting a time travel tunnel), while muttering "how dare they let his memorial rot. Our duty is clear, and we have always, whatever the personal sacrifice always, done our duty," an attitude that she soon discovers is the absolute opposite of the younger members of the twentieth-century royal family. Faithful John Brown

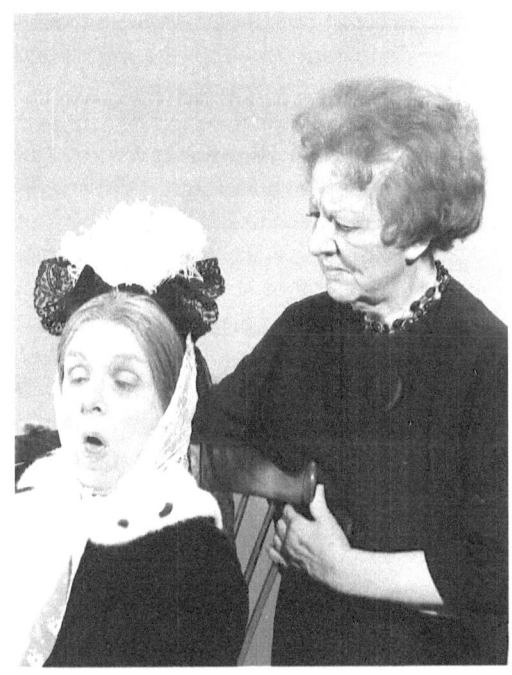

Queen Victoria (Jane Connell) is reunited with her former lady in waiting who is also Samantha's Aunt Clara (Marion Lorne) in "Aunt Clara's Victoria Victory," Episode 3.26 of *Bewitched* (9 March 1967).

(Michael Kilgarriff) drives her in a Rolls Royce ("A great improvement, where are the horses?") to the Albert Memorial, which, to her horror, is swathed in scaffolding and sheeting. After Victoria faxes (smiling and declaring the machine "miraculous") a letter of protest to the minister for heritage, much of Part 1 is a series of meetings between Victoria and real twentieth-century experts: the architect for the Memorial restoration, a couple of professors, and a constitutional historian. Victoria's questions about the neglect of the Albert Memorial are answered according to each expert's area of knowledge: high costs during a time of recession, its Gothic Revival style considered outmoded, and, most devastatingly, a symbol of the limited appeal of the monarchy that has no meaning in a late twentieth-century society.

In Part 2, John Brown drives the Queen to a bookseller, where the store window shows A.N. Wilson's *The Rise and Fall of the House of Windsor*, which posed the question "can the monarchy survive?" as well as Andrew Morton's scandal laden *Diana: Her True Story* (1992). Appalled by reading these books, Victoria interviews a radical Labor MP, her biographer Elizabeth Longford, and the editor of the *Sunday Times*. She receives a heavy dose of late 1990s negative of attitudes towards the monarchy: this Queen could be the last reigning monarch, younger royals "living out a 'soap opera ... that trivializes the monarchy,'" a public that feels "the monarchy has been undermined by its own behavior." After Brown announces "The Queen wishes to speak to the Queen" over the telephone, Queen Victoria offers sympathy to her great-great granddaughter Queen Elizabeth for the intrusions of an "unscrupulous" press and Prince Charles' shaky marriage. Victoria then proceeds to give her advice to repair the poor standing of the monarchy, strikingly similar to Victoria's response to the situation she inherited as an eighteen-year-old Queen: adopt simple family values, avoid too much access by the press (which breeds contempt), and cultivate a public image of perfection, despite personal private shortcomings. In a final gesture, Victoria and Brown consign a batch of anti-monarchy books to a Windsor fireplace, just as she gasps, "pray God they have swept the chimney!" The scene immediately cuts to an image of the 1992 Windsor Castle fire and a voice-over indicating that the government agreed in 1993 to restore the Albert Memorial. Despite this positive note of restoration, *A Curse on the House of Windsor* paints a grim vision of disintegration, from the top down, both literally in the memorial building and broadly in British society.

Two televisions series reverse the direction of time travel: time travelers going back to the Victorian age where they attempt to influence the course of history. In these shows, Queen Victoria has a small role. In the *Voyagers!* series, time travelers Phineas Bogg (Jon-Erik Hexum) and side-kick Jeffrey Jones (Meeno Peluce) repair errors in world history, as indicated by their Omni device, which takes them through time and glows red for historical error, green for correct history. One of these errors is the betrothal of Victoria's granddaughter Princess Victoria and Duke Michael of Russia. In "Buffalo Bill and Annie Play the Palace" Episode 1.12 (1983), Bogg and Jeffrey travel back in time to prevent this engagement, which coincides with a performance of Buffalo Bill's Wild West show before Queen Victoria (Lurene Tuttle). This Queen character is a bit of a rebel, enjoying a fast ride in a stagecoach ("it was wonderful") and rebuking the protocol-obsessed Russian Duke: "lately I've been up to my corset in decorum." The Russians kidnap Annie Oakley to prevent her from beating Duke Michael in a shooting match, which would humiliate him in front of the English. Phineas and Buffalo Bill free Oakley and reveal the Russian plot, whereupon Queen Victoria cancels the marriage alliance.

Queen Victoria has an even smaller role in Episode 1.8 "Pocket Watch Full of Miracles" (1990) of *Bill & Ted's Excellent Adventures*, an animation spin-off series from the 1989 film of the same name. Slackers Bill and Ted use time travel to obtain an antique watch as a birthday present for Mr. Preston, including a watch from Queen Victoria. The Queen character does not have much to do. She is shown in her carriage, comparing her watch to Big Ben and finding out she is late for being crowned Empress of India. After Bill and Ted help her get crowned in time, Victoria gives them her broken watch (inscribed "Time is Money") as a token of gratitude.

Compared to the simplistic Victoria of the *Bill & Ted* series, the "Tooth and Claw" Episode 2.2 of *Doctor Who* (2006) presents a multi-faceted, powerful, and highly engaged Queen Victoria. The Tenth Doctor (David Tennant) and companion Rose (Billie Piper) meet Queen Victoria (Pauline Collins) in 1879 Scotland. Betraying a light-hearted and shallow attitude toward Queen Victoria, Rose bets the Doctor ten quid that she can get the Queen to say "we are not amused." Rose wins by the end of the episode. The Doctor plays it rather offhand as well, first pretending to be Jamie McCrimmon (the companion to the Second Doctor), slipping briefly into a Scottish accent. Queen Victoria is shocked by Rose's skimpy attire, demanding she cover up her "nakedness" (i.e., mini-skirt, leggings, and boots) and is suspicious of the Doctor, "you who change your accent so easily." This cultural clash of twenty-first century vs. nineteenth century, is summed up in the episode's title which is a quote from Tennyson's "In Memoriam A.H.H."—a lengthy meditation on faith vs. the emerging scientific world view devoid of faith.[27] "Tooth and Claw" is a typical Whovian mixture of plots for a universal domination (the monks who want to turn the Queen into a werewolf to create an "Empire of the Wolf"), fast paced editing in multiple fight scenes, a slow-motion Hong-Kong style martial arts takeover of the Torchwood Estate, and gizmo technology that saves the day (the telescope and the Koh-i-Noor diamond which together create a concentrated light beam that kills the werewolf / alien). One of the more outstanding images is the shot of the door separating the Doctor and the werewolf, both listening intently to sounds from the other side.[28]

Although the Queen is wounded, thus passing hemophilia to her children (another Whovian historical whimsy), she rewards the Doctor and Rose with knighthoods and, aware that the Doctor is an alien, immediately banishes him from the British Empire. Queen Victoria's justification for banishment is in the same vein of Victoria-fixing society as in the *Bewitched* and *Curse on the House of Windsor* episodes: "I don't know who you are or where you're from ... you think it fun that your world is steeped with terror, and blasphemy and death.... You will leave these shores and will reflect I hope on how you came to stray from all that is good and how long you can survive this terrible life." Not getting the point, Rose and Doctor go off cracking jokes about the werewolf cells maturing in the mid twenty-first century royal house ("Princess Anne ... my god they're all werewolves"). While the cultural clash between contemporary and Victorian times is left hanging, the Queen is firmly committed to defending her version of Britain and therefore creates the

Torchwood Institute to defend Britain against aliens, including the Doctor, thus spinning off the *Torchwood* series of 2006–2011. In her warning "Great Britain has enemies beyond imagination.... If the Doctor will return Torchwood will be waiting," the *Doctor Who* Queen Victoria stands ready to fight for her cultural values and empire's safety, a world where faith in God, country and monarchy are still viable choices.

These television versions of Queen Victoria certainly underscore the contemporary need for the figure, so useful for expressing a range of messages: twentieth century's politically correct condemnations of nineteenth century politics and warfare, the on-going soap-opera of the Saxe-Coburg Gotha family history, the Victoria and Albert love story, the lighter touch of farce comedy and fantasy with a fun-loving Queen, and the twenty-first century obsessions with sexuality and social class divisions, and finally the manipulations of time travel which foreground but never resolve the discontinuity between Victorian and contemporary cultures.[29] All of these questions have been raised via television technology. In the next chapter, we will see how the new media of the internet and gaming industries both continue these themes and ultimately transform the fascination with the Queen Victoria into new creations.

Queen Victoria (Pauline Collins) disapproves of the twenty-first century in "Tooth and Claw," Episode 2.2 of *Doctor Who* (22 April 2006).

6

Transformations of Victoria Into the 21st Century

The Queen Victoria figure, first appearing as herself in late nineteenth century actualities, notably for her 1897 Diamond Jubilee, evolved through the propaganda and war films in the 1930s and 40s, into the 1950s focus on the Victoria and Albert love story, and 1970s television series exploring Victoria's family and milieu, and 1980s comedy invoking the "we are not amused" Victoria image. Reflecting a culture searching for itself, the Queen is often shown as the object of a quest, growing more intensely obsessional and dark in late twentieth-century television, eventually segueing into political correctness and multi-cultural approaches to Queen Victoria into the early twenty-first century. All of these portrayals are a recognizably human Victoria, filtered by the needs of the time—patriotic, anti-imperial, anti-establishment, romantic, political, or just good for a quick laugh. By the early twenty-first century a transformational approach to Queen Victoria emerges. In contrast to earlier depictions of the Queen, this Queen Victoria transcends mere mortality to achieve an iconic status, malleable and compelling, and with little vestiges of previous historically based representations. These transformational explorations of Queen Victoria start as early as the 1990s and become more pronounced into the early twenty-first century. Three trends of this transformation are evident: a negative or diminishing view of the Queen character, a return to Victoria as the icon for empire building, and finally political and cultural satire where Victoria turns the tables to comment on us, her viewers in the twenty-first century.

The simplest type of transformation is to turn Queen Victoria into an android or mindless clone, a non-human entity to be manipulated into situations far removed from any historical or realistic context. Episode 4.6 "Meltdown" (1991) of the science fiction television series *Red Dwarf* introduces a transporter device (nod to *Star Trek*) that deposits Rimmer (Chris Barrie), Kryten (Robert Llewellyn), Cat (Danny John-Jules), and Lister (Craig Charles) into Wax Droid Theme Park. Rimmer takes on a George Patton role as he trains the "good" droids for battle with the "evil" droids. A mute Queen Victoria (Alice De Mallet De Donas, uncredited) android appears first in the trenches with machine gun, fighting on the "good" side and then is smuggled into the villains' headquarters where she kills Hitler and in turn is killed. Throughout all the action, the Queen has no lines and mindlessly follows orders; however, an implicit comparison between Victoria and Hitler is made. The camera shows first Hitler, then Victoria, dead on the floor in the same position, with drool coming out of their mouths, thus undercutting the distinction between good and evil.

In a reversal of the android/clone situation, the television movie *The Wild Wild West Revisited* (1979) has the protagonists West (Robert Conrad) and Gordon (Ross Martin) come out of retirement in 1885 to battle the megalomaniac villain Dr. Miguelito Loveless, Jr., who has replaced world-wide government leaders with mindless clones so that he can take over the world. In this film, the clones are never shown, just talked about, and instead we see the real leaders locked up in the villain's dungeon-like jail, including a very unamused Queen Victoria (Jacquelyn Hyde). Imperiously insisting that she is the real Victoria, she orders a bumbling the British intelligence chief "get me out of here, that is an order." West and Gordon free the real leaders and blow up the villain's headquarters. Queen Victoria is last seen stalking towards a carriage that takes her to safety, dismissing her intelligence agent as a "blithering idiot." In its anachronistic mixing of Victorian era setting and characters with advanced technology (noise suppressors on guns, elevators, the atomic bomb), both the *Wild Wild West Revisited* and the television series preceding it are considered one of the origins of the steampunk genre.

A fully steampunk television series emerges in *The Secret Adventures of Jules Verne* (2000), using a notion that Jules Verne actually experienced the adventures he writes about in his books *Twenty Thousand Leagues Under the Sea*, *Journey to the Center of the Earth*, or *Around the World in Eighty Days*. Verne (Chris Demetral) travels from adventure to adventure in a dirigible owned by Phileas Fogg (Michael Praed), along with his cousin British secret agent Rebecca Fogg (Francesca Hunt) and Passepartout (Michel Courtemanche) as navigator. Episode 1.1 "In the Beginning" sets up the series' conflicts. Verne is the predictor of future technology—electricity and moon shots, for example. His futuristic visions are sought by steampunk cybernetic Count Gregory, the leader of the evil League of Darkness, which is bent on world domination through technology. Queen Victoria, who is the target of assassination by the League in several episodes, arranges for Phileas Fogg to win the dirigible and Passepartout in a card game. Episode 1.2 "Queen Victoria and the Giant Mole" sets up the partnership of Verne, Phileas, Rebecca, and Passepartout. They foil the League's plot to use a large tunneling machine (based on Verne's ideas) to kill Queen Victoria and the French Emperor, who are negotiating a peace treaty (a fictionalized version of the 1843 Entente Cordiale). In Episode 1.20 "Secret of the Realm" Count Gregory creates evil clones of Phileas, Rebecca, and a Peruvian ambassador Del Fuego. He sends them to trick Queen Victoria into revealing the secret code to the powerful Holy Grail, known only to the British monarchy since the time of Queen Boudica. Passing through a time-space-dimension travel portal, the real Rebecca, Phileas, Verne, and Passepartout foil the plot. In Episode 1.21 "The Victorian Candidate," the League kidnaps and uses hallucinogenic drug to brainwash Phileas into killing the now-widowed Victoria at Balmoral. Rebecca, a martial arts expert, breaks the brainwashing and foils the plot against the Queen's life. Steampunk attire and technology abounds, character development is limited, and the series' main attraction is the stylized action and convoluted plot situations. Used mainly as the target of plots and receiving little screen time, the Queen is reduced to a figurehead who rewards the Secret Service agents for their protection against multiple assassination plots.

Two comedic transformations of Queen Victoria are noteworthy. First, a slapstick version of the Queen is presented in the comic parody *Holmes & Watson* (2018). Moriarty has threatened to assassinate Victoria (Pam Ferris) unless Holmes (Will Ferrell) and Watson (John C. Reilly) solve a case. In a scene underscoring their technological ineptitude, Watson sets up a photographic camera on a selfie stick and poses with Holmes and the Queen. When Holmes suggests moving the camera to get better light, a bumbling Watson whacks the camera smack into Victoria's forehead, knocking her to the floor and reducing her to the status of third stooge.

In *Holmes & Watson* (2018), Holmes (Will Ferrell, right), Watson (John C. Reilly, left) and Queen Victoria (Pam Ferris) attempt a selfie.

A less obvious comic transformation of Queen Victoria comes from an unexpected source: the Pixar / Disney animated short *Your Friend the Rat* (2007). In her most bizarre role, Queen Victoria is presented as a lover of rats, in fact as a rat kisser. Released on the DVD of *Ratatouille* (2007), this short is in part styled as a homage to Disney television short *Our Friend the Atom* (1957), especially in its mixture of 2D and 3D animation with live action and stop-motion animation. Remy and Emile present a comic history of the rat's relationship with humans. For the nineteenth century, they show Jack Black, rat catcher and purveyor of pet or "fancy" rats. He presents a pet rat to Queen Victoria, who then kisses it. The rat is very amused.

The darkest view of Queen Victoria is presented in season 1 of the anime series *Black Butler* (2008–09). This anime follows the adventures of demon butler Sebastian Michaelis bound in a Faustian contract with young Earl Ciel Phantomhive. Set in 1885 Victorian England and based on the manga series by Yana Toboso, the plot revolves around the Phantomhive family known as the Queen's Watchdog, and young Ciel who inherits this role when his parents are murdered. Queen Victoria gives Ciel assignments to control and manage the British underworld, and ultimately to eliminate anything Victoria wants to get rid of. In some cases, the royal presence is mentioned but not shown, as in Episode 7 "His Butler, Merry Making," in which Ciel explains that he has the Queen's order to stop a demon hound (inspired by Conan Doyle's *The Hound of the Baskervilles*). Queen Victoria makes her first appearance at the end of Episode 1.14 "His Butler, Supremely Talented," when she arrives to

Victoria kisses the pet or "fancy" rat give to her by rat catcher Jack Black. Eeek! From *Your Friend the Rat* (2007), a Pixar/Disney short distributed on the DVD of *Ratatouille* (2007).

6. Transformations of Victoria Into the 21st Century

judge a curry cooking competition staged in the Crystal Palace. Continued in Episode 1.15 "His Butler, Competing," Victoria appears heavily veiled, face completely obscured, and communicates only through an aide Ash Landers (also called her angelic butler).

While the curry contest scene is handled comically, the veiled Victoria is an ominous note, foreshadowing the *Black Butler* Episode 1.22 "His Butler, Dissolution," in which the Queen turns into an insane villain. After Ciel confronts the Queen at the Eiffel Tower, she expresses a mad desire to exterminate and burn away everything unclean, including the house of Phantomhive and all of London. Ash reveals that Victoria's grief over Prince Albert's death nearly drove her to suicide, and he intervened to make her young again by joining part of dead Prince Albert's body to her neck. After a failed attempt to kill Ciel, Ash and the Queen set fire to the Phantomhive estate and all of London.

In the next Episode 23, "His Butler, Up in Flames," the Queen has gone completely insane, blaming the London fire on the French and is shown rotting from within because of her attachment to the past (literally, Albert's dead body). By the end of the episode, the young Victoria is dead. In the last episode of Season 1 "His Butler Fluent," an imposter old Queen Victoria is placed on the throne. *Black Butler* offers a quite astonishing version of Queen Victoria as the ultimate demented villain, a symbol of a monarchy and nation stuck in the past, rotting from within and destined for purgation by fire so a new century can begin. The false Queen speaks of rebuilding an empire from the ashes, while in the background Scotland Yard commissioner Randall says that as long as the people believe in the image of the Queen, it does not matter if she is a fake. *Black Butler* gives us the ultimate pessimistic vision of a new century based on illusion and falsehood.[1]

In marked contrast to this self-destructing Victoria, twenty-first century videogames transform the Queen into the icon and leader for global empire building, a more ambitious imperialism compared to the historically based imperialism popularized in early twentieth century films such as *Victoria the Great*.

The young Queen Victoria is mourning the death of her beloved Prince Albert in *Black Butler*, Episode 1.23 (19 March 2009).

In *Assassin's Creed: Syndicate* (2015), Queen Victoria has a small role, along the lines of the *Black Butler* anime. Set in Victorian London, the plot pits the Assassin Brotherhood, who fight for peace with liberty, despite their gory methods, against the Templars who are corrupting London, manipulating the criminal underworld, and attempting to control Britain and the world.

A regal Queen Victoria appears in *Assassin's Creed, Syndicate* (2015).

6. Transformations of Victoria Into the 21st Century   143

The game has a third person point of view, in which the player controls the twin assassins Jacob and Evie Frye. Queen Victoria is one of many historical figures featured in the plot, others include Charles Darwin, Charles Dickens, Karl Marx, Sir Arthur Conan Doyle, Alexander Graham Bell, Florence Nightingale, and Jack the Ripper.

The Queen appears at a ball in Buckingham Palace and eventually rewards the Frye characters with knighthoods for defeating the evil Grand Templar and saving her life. At other points, Queen Victoria orders the twins to solve the murder of one of her guards or to foil the "upstart Secret Society" that is hurting the people of London. In *Assassin's Creed,* Victoria's ultimate concern is the security of her country and power against the internal threats of a criminal conspiracy.

Empire building in *Civilization VI* (2016) by Sid Meier is more character-centric.[2] The player can become Victoria (or other world leaders such as Cleopatra or Eleanor of Aquitaine) and build an empire from early settlement to world power. Victory is achieved through military power, industrialization, diplomacy, and cultural influence. As Victoria, the player pursues the "Sun Never Sets" strategy to bring "Pax Britannia" world-wide. Voiced by Lucy Briggs-Owen, the Queen character appears wearing a large version of the widowhood crown, blue sash, elaborate necklace and brooch, and periodically reacts to events during the game. Queen Victoria introduces herself to the player: "Greetings. We are by the grace of God, Victoria, Queen of the United Kingdom of Great Britain and Ireland. And soon, dare I say, the empire."

Queen Victoria awards knighthoods in the video game *Assassin's Creed: Syndicate* (2015).

When Victoria approves of a player's move, she says "Please accept my warmest thanks for your kind endeavors on the continent we share." Victoria issues warnings: "You tread on dangerous waters in the face of England and her loyal colonies." A major mistake merits a Victorian denunciation: she glares directly into the player's face, yelps in disapproval, and the unvoiced text appears in the upper corner of the screen: "We will have nothing to do with your administration. You are hereby denounced." When England is attacked, the Queen comments "War? We are not amused." The *Civilization* player in effect becomes a co-ruler with Victoria and together they assemble territory, resources, and power to win this virtual version of the "Great Game."³

Queen Victoria finally has landed on the Internet, a notion whose time has come!

Queen Victoria takes the lead for England in the video game *Civilization VI* (2016).

Pab Sungenis has published a daily web comic *New Adventures of Queen Victoria* since 2006. Initially intended as a one-time response to the poor quality of humor in the *Garfield* comic strip (as in "We are not amused"), it quickly become a daily syndicated strip now available online at GoComic.com. The typical strip features Queen Victoria, clan in her widow's small crown, cascading lace headdress, sash, and heavy necklace, confronting and commenting on the cultural and historical phenomena of the twenty-first century with obvious satiric intent. A cast of characters ranges far and wide: son Bertie (frequently paired with "Mum"), Liz (Queen Elizabeth I), Mary Queen of Scots, Ann Boleyn, mad Grandpa (King George III), Oscar Wilde, Beethoven, Tesla, Carry Nation, the Virgin Mary, and Jane Austen. Emoji "bug eyes" are used to express emotion, typically anger, as in the strip where the Queen is on the telephone (long neck, 1930s style): "Thank you for calling Audible.com Customer Service. Your call doesn't mean CENSORED to us. [Victoria bug eyes] Please wait three hours before we hang up on you" (14 September 2018).

The New Adventures will sometimes include weeks with a story line, such as the time when Victoria wants to bring dead Albert onto an airplane as her "comfort" animal; after being refused, she protests that Charles gets to bring Camilla: "Why can he bring that animal on board, and we can't bring our Albert...?" Airline agent, "She's still alive. I think" (17 October 2018). Another story line ends with Victoria working at MacDonald's taking orders via headphone: "A glorious welcome to MacDonald's House of fine Scottish cuisine. Our name is Victoria. We shall be your server. Our menu today begins with your choice of cauliflower and cheddar cheese or cock-a-leekie soup. Our main course is a traditional haggis.... We need not do that to ourselves, Sir. That is what our husband Albert is for. Please drive around" (22 June 2018). Frequently son Bertie is exasperated by his mother: "Hmm [Victoria]. Let's try this, and see what.... No luck. Maybe if we... [Bertie with angry bug eyes]. Did you try to install the Windows 10 Preview? [Victoria with bug eyes]. Excuse Us for being modern!" (31 March 2015).

Some of *The New Adventures* strips are political such as Victoria's welcoming U.S. citizens fleeing the 2016 election to return to a reunited Kingdom with a caveat "Anyone using the word 'Brexit' will be shot on sight. Understood?" (1 October 2016). A more recent *New Adventures* strip comments on the *Avengers: End Game* (2019) film. The Queen wants to celebrate her 200th birthday by taking a hint from Thanos and destroying all other life in the universe. Consequently, Bertie decides *not* to give his mother the infinity gauntlet as a birthday gift. The Queen's most cutting commentary on twenty-first century culture is quite philosophical. In front of a computer screen she explains to Bertie: "we asked it to create a fake 'Fed 1,000 things to a bot' post. It created a fake 'Fed 1,000 things to a bot' post about feeding 1,000 things to a bot. That is why the Internet collapsed into a black hole of metatextual irony" (15 September 2018). This internet Queen

Victoria denounces a stupid move on the player's part in *Civilization VI* (2016).

Victoria has skewered twenty-first century culture, presaging its collapse from within, its self-destruction into a meaningless void.

Over three centuries, Queen Victoria has come full circle as a media star and branched off into previously unimagined representations. Beginning in the late nineteenth century, the media monarchy leveraged silent films and widespread marketing of print and souvenirs, touting her image as the grandmother of the British Empire and solidifying the monarchy's role in the political and cultural life of Great Britain. In the first half of the twentieth century, Victoria became the rallying image for the British people during both World Wars. By the second half of the century, Victoria's film images segued into the more domestic arena, emphasizing the Victoria and Albert love story, as well as quest stories where an individual protagonist is in search of the Queen. With an insatiable appetite for content, twentieth-century television leveraged nostalgia for period costume with extensive character development of Victoria, her family and politics of her era. In an alternate vein, television also indulged in quick comic relief skits poking fun at the old "we are not amused" widow. Twenty-first century obsessions with sex give us Victoria and Albert "tween the sheets" films and television series, paired with a tendency to project onto Victoria the aspect of a "modern" heroine fighting against racism and gender discrimination, while selectively ignoring the Victorian wars and Empire building so often explored in earlier films through the 1940s. Animation using the Queen character tends to be visually engaging but ultimately reductionist and superficial, though some of the Victoria animation is just weird fun. Media transformation of Queen Victoria into the realm of video gaming brings back the emphasis on empire building, allowing every player to be a Queen Militant, and the internet web comics turn the tables on us, allowing Queen Victoria to comment on current culture and events, with a satiric slant.

Queen Victoria wants to celebrate her 200th birthday with some peace and quiet, *Avengers* style, *The New Adventures of Queen Victoria*, 4 May 2019.

Given such a range of approaches to this pivotal character over three centuries of film and television, the reel Queen Victoria, like the real Queen Victoria of history, is a survivor. Screen media can leverage her multi-faceted image, media scholars can analyze from a multitude of critical perspectives or political agendas, journalists and reviewers can generate article upon article about the "newest" take on an iconic figure, and still Queen Victoria goes on. Her character has shown an enduring fascination for audiences and no doubt will continue its magic in media transformations yet to come.

Appendix: Select Filmography

Major sections of this select filmography / videography include:

- Actualités films featuring the "real" Queen Victoria
- Silent films using the "reel" Queen Victoria as a character (pp. 162–164)
- Theatrical release films (pp. 165–174)
- Television films, series, and episodes within series (pp. 175–192)
- Miscellaneous—video games, internet comics, audio or radio productions (pp. 192–193)

For the last four categories, the principal cast are listed, with the Queen Victoria character as the first entry, regardless of the size of her role (i.e. position in the typical credits list). In situations where the work clearly has a Queen Victoria character, but no acting credit is available, the notation "Uncredited—Queen Victoria" will be used.

Actualités Films Featuring Queen Victoria

This section includes a listing of short silent movies featuring Queen Victoria. The film titles are descriptive, but also repetitious; for example, the Diamond Jubilee attracted multiple film companies that were recording the same event and marketing under similar titles. Therefore, they are presented in chronological order, oldest first.

Where possible, I have included both IMDB link and the Catalog number from Denis Gifford's *The British Film Catalogue*. In the case of a film where a viewable copy is available online, I have given that URL, plus date of access. While these entries may be repetitious of IMDB and/or Gifford BFC entries, there is some value in providing the URL so that the reader can view the film.

Film length is given in seconds (if less than one minute in length), minutes: seconds (1:30 min = 1 minute and 30 seconds), or in meters (abbreviated "m"). Approximately 20 meters of film would have yielded a one-minute film. Where a record of the length is not available, the citation states "Unknown length."

Other sources consulted: *British Pathé Catalog, American Mutoscope & Biography Company Catalogue 1902*; Richard Brown and Barry Anthony's filmography in *A Victorian Film Enterprise: A History of the British Mutoscope and Biograph Company, 1897–1915*; and John Barnes *The Rise of Cinema in Great Britain*. I have noted instances where these sources have identified an actualité of Victoria that does not appear in IMDB.

Scenes at Balmoral (1896). W. & D. Downey (UK). 1 min. www.imdb.com/title/tt2144534/?ref_=nm_flmg_slf_86. Accessed 7 November 2017. www.youtube.com/watch?v=U5SWcoAmeBs. Accessed 6 November 2017. Possibly Huntley Film Archive, film number 17795. www.huntleyarchives.com/.

Victoria is riding in a small carriage with her white Pomeranian dog. Other dogs are running around.

Appendix: Select Filmography

Czar Nicholas II and his family are walking at Balmoral on 3 October 1896.

The Queen and the Emperor and Empress of Russia at Balmoral (1896). W. & D. Downey (UK). 36.6 m. Gifford Catalogue 00082. www.imdb.com/title/tt2271679/?ref_=nm_flmg_slf_85. Accessed 7 November 2017.

Arrival of the Queen and the Emperor and Empress of Russia at Mar Lodge (1896). W. & D. Downey (UK). 36.6 m. Gifford Catalogue 00081. www.imdb.com/title/tt2178933/?ref_=nm_flmg_slf_84. Accessed 7 November 2017.

Gordon Highlanders aka *The Military Review at Aldershot* (1897). British Mutoscope & Biograph Co. (UK). 8.23 m. www.imdb.com/title/tt0217517/?ref_=nm_flmg_slf_83. Accessed 7 November 2017.

The Queen Entering the Borough (1897). Chard's Vitagraph (UK). Unknown length. Gifford Catalogue 00167.3. www.imdb.com/title/tt2323689/?ref_=nm_flmg_slf_82. Accessed 7 November 2017.

The Queen at Temple Bar (1897). Chard's Vitagraph (UK). Unknown length. Gifford Catalogue 000167.1. www.imdb.com/title/tt2326029/?ref_=nm_flmg_slf_81. Accessed 7 November 2017.

The Queen at Sheffield (1897). Riley Brothers (UK). Unknown length. Gifford Catalogue 000286. www.imdb.com/title/tt2326027/?ref_=nm_flmg_slf_80. Accessed 7 November 2017

The Queen and Royal Family (1897). Watson & Sons Motorgraph (UK). 54.7 m. Gifford Catalogue 00183.10. www.imdb.com/title/tt2271677/?ref_=nm_flmg_slf_79. Accessed 7 November 2017.

The Queen's Carriage (1897). London Stereoscopic Co. (UK) Unknown length. Gifford Catalogue 00214.1. www.imdb.com/title/tt2268609/?ref_=nm_flmg_slf_77. Accessed 7 November 2017.

The Queen's Carriage and Escort (1897). Warwick Trading Co. (UK). 15.2 m. Gifford Catalogue 00292.3. www.imdb.com/title/tt2322629/?ref_=nm_flmg_slf_78. Accessed 7 November 2017.

Queen's Carriage and Indian Escort Arriving at St. Paul's (1897). Paul's Animatograph Works (UK). Director: Robert W. Paul. 1 min. Gifford Catalogue 00168.10. www.imdb.com/title/tt1321460/. Accessed 7 November 2017.

The Queen, Princess and Escort (1897). Watson & Sons Motorgraph (UK). 21.3 m. Gifford Catalogue 00183.3. www.imdb.com/title/tt2372423/?ref_=nm_flmg_slf_76. Accessed 7 November 2017.

Queen's Carriage and Indian Escort Arriving at St. Paul's (1897). Paul's Animatograph Works (UK). 18.3 m. Gifford Catalogue 00183.7. www.imdb.com/title/tt1321460/?ref_=fn_al_tt_1. Accessed 5 June 2019.

Returning from St. Paul's (1897). Watson & Sons Motorgraph (UK). 18.3 m. Gifford Catalogue 00183.7. www.imdb.com/title/tt2322557/?ref_=nm_flmg_slf_75. Accessed 7 November 2017

Returning, Part Two (1897). Watson & Sons Motorgraph (UK) 18.3 m. Gifford Catalogue 00183.8. www.imdb.com/title/tt2322559/?ref_=nm_flmg_slf_74. Accessed 7 November 2017.

Queen Victoria and Royal Family at State Garden Party (1897). Velograph Syndicate (UK). Unknown length. Gifford Catalogue 00207. www.imdb.com/title/tt2285667/?ref_=nm_flmg_slf_73. Accessed 7 November 2017.

Queen Victoria's Arrival at Ballater (1897). Walker (UK). Unknown length. Gifford Catalogue 00269. www.imdb.com/title/tt2349781/?ref_=nm_flmg_slf_54. Accessed 9 December 2017.

Queen Victoria's Departure from Ballater for Balmoral (1897). Walker (UK). Unknown length. Gifford Catalogue 00156. www.imdb.com/title/tt2317005/?ref_=nm_flmg_slf_55. Accessed 9 December 2017.

Queen at State Garden Party (1897). Watson & Sons Motorgraph. 77.7 m. Gifford Catalogue 00183.11. www.imdb.com/title/tt2268531/?ref_=nm_flmg_slf_53. Accessed 9 December 2017.

Appendix: Select Filmography

Queen and Escort in Churchyard (1897). Paul's Animatograph Works (UK). 12.2 m. Gifford Catalogue 00168.12. www.imdb.com/title/tt2268529/?ref_=nm_flmg_slf_52. Accessed 9 December 2017.

The Coldstream Guards aka *The Military Review at Aldershot* (1897). British Mutoscope and Biograph Co. (UK). 8.53 m. www.imdb.com/title/tt0217325/?ref_=fn_tt_tt_65. Accessed 1 March 2018.

William Dickson filmed this review for Mutoscope. There is an extant photograph of William Dickson filming at Aldershot on 1 July 1897. "His note on the back of the photograph reads: 'Kodak picture I took at Aldershot Showing Roped off enclosure or stand given me by the Duke of Connaught. Queen's Royal carriages adjoin. Another photographer with large plates ordinary camera next to us by our permission'" (Brown and Anthony 190).

Arrival of the Queen from Windsor (1897). Warwick Trading Co. (UK). 15.2 m. Gifford Catalogue 00292.1. www.imdb.com/title/tt2336201/?ref_=nm_flmg_slf_50. Accessed 9 December 2017.

Queen Victoria's Diamond Jubilee, full version (1897). 4:27 min. www.youtube.com/watch?v=pTG9NJTZFKk. Accessed 6 November 2017.

Queen Victoria's Diamond Jubilee, short version (1897). 1:15 min. www.youtube.com/watch?v=4xGqQpCbl5E. Accessed 9 December 2017.

Queen Victoria's Jubilee Procession (1897). Northern Photographic Works (UK) Unknown length. www.imdb.com/title/tt2332759/?ref_=nm_flmg_slf_72. Accessed 7 November 2017.

Queen Victoria's Diamond Jubilee Procession: Queen's Carriage (1897). George Albert Smith Films (UK). 23 m. www.imdb.com/title/tt2338169/?ref_=nm_flmg_slf_71. Accessed 7 November 2017.

Queen Victoria's Diamond Jubilee Procession: Colonials (1897). George Albert Smith Films (UK). 23 m. www.imdb.com/title/tt2361403/?ref_=ttspec_spec_tt. Accessed 27 March 2018.

Queen Victoria's Diamond Jubilee (1897). Unknown production company. Unknown length. 5. www.imdb.com/title/tt0244155/?ref_=fn_al_tt_1. Accessed 5 June 2019. www.youtube.com/watch?v=t4PDxc3acyg. Accessed Accessed 5 June 2019.

Queen Victoria's Diamond Jubilee (1897). Paul's Animatograph Works (UK). Director: Robert W. Paul. 24.4 m. www.imdb.com/title/tt2372347/?ref_=nm_flmg_slf_56. Accessed 7 November 2017. www.youtube.com/watch?v=udxoYiikhEQ. Accessed 7 November 2017.

"Robert Paul's was one of six crews to film the event, each of them paying large sums of money to secure good positions among the estimated crowd of 3 million onlookers from which to film. Paul released the film as twelve separate titles, each of which were sold for 30 shillings each…. The individual titles were: 'Head of Procession including Bluejackets,' 'Royal Carriages Passing Westminster,' 'Cape Mounted Riflemen Passing St. Paul's,' 'Royal Carriage Arriving at St. Paul's,' 'Royal Princes in St. Paul's Churchyard,' 'Queen's Carriage and Indian Escort Arriving at St. Paul's' and 'Life Guards and Princes North of St. Paul's.'"(IMDB).

Queen Victoria's Diamond Jubilee—Paul—St Paul's South—Arrival of the Queen's Carriage (1897). Paul's Animatograph Works (UK). Director: Robert W. Paul. 85 m. collections-search.bfi.org.uk/web/Details/ChoiceFilmWorks/150439011. Accessed 2 March 2018.

"Queen Victoria's Diamond Jubilee procession. The procession is seen entering St Paul's Churchyard, photographed by R.W. Paul from a position on the south side of the churchyard…. This differs from other Paul Jubilee films held in the NFTVA." (Barnes 182).

Not in IMDB.

Royal Carriages Passing Westminster (1897). Paul's Animatograph Works (UK). Director: Robert W. Paul. 1 min. Gifford Catalogue 00168.3. www.imdb.com/title/tt1321468/?ref_=fn_tt_tt_7. Accessed 2 March 2018.

"Queen Victoria's Diamond Jubilee procession, filmed from York Road, just before Westminster Bridge. Various carriages shown (not the Queen's)." (Barnes 180).

Appendix: Select Filmography

Royal Carriages Arriving at St. Paul's (1897). Paul's Animatograph Works (UK). Director: Robert W. Paul. 1 min. Gifford Catalogue 00168.8. www.imdb.com/title/tt1321467/?ref_=fn_al_tt_1. Accessed 5 June 2019.

Diamond Jubilee Procession Taken from Apsley House (1897). Gaumont / Le Couteur (UK). Cinematographer: Gustave Colley. 45 sec. Gifford Catalogue 470787. www.youtube.com/watch?v=VG55kEokxL8. Accessed 7 November 2017.
Not in IMDB.

Queen Victoria's Diamond Jubilee, location unknown (1897). Unknown production company. 38 sec. www.youtube.com/watch?v=-1pmuk-uRAJ4. Accessed 7 November 2017.
Not in IMDB.

Queen Victoria's Diamond Jubilee Procession (1897). W.C. Hughes (UK). 610 m. www.imdb.com/title/tt2268527/?ref_=nm_flmg_slf_66. Accessed 7 November 2017.

Queen Victoria's Diamond Jubilee Procession (1897). F. Harvard (UK). 23 m. www.imdb.com/title/tt2282923/?ref_=nm_flmg_slf_65. Accessed 7 November 2017.

Queen Victoria's Diamond Jubilee Procession (1897). Velograph Syndicate (UK) 54.9 m. www.imdb.com/title/tt2308881/?ref_=nm_flmg_slf_64. Accessed 7 November 2017.

Queen Victoria's Diamond Jubilee Procession (1897). Haydon & Urry. 137 m. www.imdb.com/title/tt2322545/?ref_=nm_flmg_slf_63. Accessed 7 November 2017.

Queen Victoria's Diamond Jubilee Procession—Queen in Carriage (1897). John Wrench & Sons (UK). Unknown length. www.imdb.com/title/tt2332757/?ref_=nm_flmg_slf_62. Accessed 7 November 2017.

Queen Victoria's Diamond Jubilee Procession (1897). Photographic Association (UK). Unknown length. www.imdb.com/title/tt2345691/?ref_=nm_flmg_slf_6. Accessed 7 November 2017.

Queen Victoria's Diamond Jubilee Procession (1897). Appleton. Unknown length. www.imdb.com/title/tt2359249/?ref_=nm_flmg_slf_60. Accessed 7 November 2017.

Queen Victoria's Diamond Jubilee Procession (1897). Ludgate Kinematograph Co. (UK). Unknown length. www.imdb.com/title/tt2363353/?ref_=nm_flmg_slf_59. Accessed 7 November 2017.

Queen Victoria's Diamond Jubilee Procession (1897). J.W. Rowe's Pictorialgraph (UK). Unknown length. www.imdb.com/title/tt2369231/?ref_=nm_flmg_slf_58. Accessed 7 November 2017.

Queen Victoria's Diamond Jubilee Procession (1897). J. Nevil Maskelyne (UK). Unknown length. www.imdb.com/title/tt2144330/?ref_=nm_flmg_slf_70. Accessed 7 November 2017.

Queen Victoria's Diamond Jubilee Procession (1897). Moto-Photo Supply Co. (UK). Unknown length. www.imdb.com/title/tt2146988/?ref_=nm_flmg_slf_69. Accessed 7 November 2017.

Queen Victoria's Diamond Jubilee Procession (1897). British Cinematographe Co. (UK). 4:27 min. www.imdb.com/title/tt2151854/?ref_=nm_flmg_slf_68. Accessed 7 November 2017. www.youtube.com/watch?v=pTG9NJTZFKk. Accessed 7 November 2017.

Queen Victoria's Diamond Jubilee Procession (1897). Prestwich Manufacturing Co. (UK). Unknown length. www.imdb.com/title/tt2159394/?ref_=nm_flmg_slf_67. Accessed 7 November 2017. This short film shows Queen Victoria's Diamond Jubilee, parades, and crowds.

Queen Victoria's Diamond Jubilee Procession (1897)-extract. Unknown production company. 1.58 min. www.youtube.com/watch?v=jnip7RRc3Q4. Accessed 7 November 2017.
Not in IMDB.

Jubilee Procession (1897). Watson & Sons Motorgraph (UK). 21.3 m. www.imdb.com/title/tt2336329/?ref_=nm_flmg_slf_51. Accessed 9 December 2017.

Queen Victoria's Diamond Jubilee—No Sound (1897). Unknown production

Appendix: Select Filmography   153

company. 1.22 min. www.youtube.com/watch?v=HmWyermQ8lw. Accessed 9 December 2017.
Not in IMDB.

Queen Victoria's Diamond Jubilee Procession (1897). British Mutoscope and Biograph Co. (UK).
"The Jubilee procession is shown from the Horse Guards Parade and disclosed the fact that the stands were almost empty. The pictures are good, but the procession at this part seems to have been somewhat patchy." (Brown and Anthony 245).
Not in IMDB.

The Horse Guards (1897). British Mutoscope and Biograph Co (UK). 7 m. www.imdb.com/title/tt0205138/?ref_=fn_al_tt_1. Accessed 28 February 2018.
This short film shows Queen Victoria's Diamond Jubilee, parades, and crowds, including a "splendid cavalry organization with its mounted band in the Jubilee Presentation, London." (IMDB).

Queen's Jubilee (1897). British Mutoscope and Biograph Co (UK). 80.77 m. www.imdb.com/title/tt0217752/?ref_=fn_al_tt_1. Accessed 28 February 2018.
This film shows "Mounted dignitaries and officers at the head of the line." (IMBD).

Queen's Jubilee No 2 (1897). British Mutoscope and Biograph Co (UK). 7.6m. www.imdb.com/title/tt2322547/?ref_=fn_al_tt_2. Accessed 27 February 2018.
This short film shows the Duke of Coburg's carriage (Brown and Anthony 245).

Sir Wilfred Laurier and the New South Wales Lancers (1897). British Mutoscope and Biograph Co (UK). 10.2 m. Gifford Catalogue 00293.4. www.imdb.com/title/tt0214133/?ref_=fn_tt_tt_2. Accessed 28 February 2018.
This short film shows Queen Victoria's Diamond Jubilee, parades, and crowds, including a "splendid view of the Canadian Premier escorted by one of the most famous organizations of the Great Britain Colonial Forces." (IMDB).

The Diamond Jubilee Review at Aldershot, Showing H.R.H. The Princess of Wales Taking Snapshots (1897). British Mutoscope and Biograph Co (UK). Unknown length.

"The Military Review at Aldershot is especially worthy of mention, and what strikes one particularly is its inconventionality [sic], the machine taking the pictures having evidently been moved from place to place in the very thick of the throng of royalty" (Brown and Anthony 246).
Not in IMDB.

Her Majesty's Carriage (1897). British Mutoscope and Biograph Co (UK).
This film showing Queen Victoria's carriage was listed on the Palace Theatre program for 11 October 1897 (Brown and Anthony 247).
Not in IMDB.

Fêtes du Jubilé de la reine d'Angleterre (1897). Lumière (France). Unknown length. www.bfi.org.uk/films-tv-people/4ce2b7d4cb099. Accessed 12 January 2018.
The Lumière Company is credited with nine separate films of the Diamond Jubilee. All were photographed by Alexander Promio. www.thecinetourist.net/lumiere-london.html. Accessed 12 January 2018.
The following listing includes stills available online from the Lumière films:

488. *Queen's arrival from Windsor at Paddington* aka *La reine arrivant de Windsor* (21 June 1897). catalogue-lumiere.com/la-reine-arrivant-de-windsor/. Accessed 12 January 2018. Queen Victoria arrives in a parade of cars escorted by riders, in the midst of an exuberant crowd. She is hidden under an umbrella.

489. *Crowd following the Queen's Carriage* aka *La foule suivant le cortège* (21 June 1897). catalogue-lumiere.com/-la-foule-suivant-le-cortege/. Accessed 21 January 2018. An increasingly large crowd invades the street, forcing cars to stop.

490. *Her Majesty the Queen and her Escort* aka *Le cortège: La reine* (22 June 1897). catalogue-lumiere.com/le-cortege-la-reine/. Accessed 21 January 2018. Queen Victoria rides in a carriage escorted by officers in front of a cheering crowd. She is hidden under an umbrella.

491. *Foreign Princes* aka *Le cortège: les princes étrangers* (22 June 1897). catalogue-lumiere.com/le-cortege-les-princes-etrangers/. Accessed 12 January 2018. Horsemen in colorful uniforms

advance between two hedges of soldiers standing at attention.

492. *Ambassadors* aka *Le cortège: les ambassadeurs* (22 June 1897). catalogue-lumiere.com/le-cortege-les-ambassadeurs/. Accessed 12 January 2018. This shot shows ambassadors parading in their colorful uniforms.

493. *Life Guards and Dragoon's Band* aka *Le cortège: les gardes du corps et la musique des dragons*. catalogue-lumiere.com/le-cortege-les-gardes-du-corps-et-la-musique-des-dragons/. Accessed 12 January 2018. This shot shows a parade of several bodies of musicians on horseback.

494. *Naval Field Battery and Guns* aka *Le cortège: l'artillerie de marine* (22 June 1897). catalogue-lumiere.com/le-cortege-lartillerie-de-marine/. Accessed 12 January 2018. This shot shows a parade of soldiers firing artillery, then a military music unit.

495. *Colonial Premiers and Colonial Troopers* aka *Le cortège: les cavaliers du Cap* (22 June 1897). catalogue-lumiere.com/le-cortege-les-cavaliers-du-cap/. Accessed 12 January 2018. This shot shows a parade of several cavalry units.

496. *Royal Horse Artillery with Guns* aka *Le cortège: l'artillerie à cheval* (22 June 1897). catalogue-lumiere.com/le-cortege-lartillerie-a-cheval/. Accessed 22 January 2018. This shot shows a parade of groups of riders alternating with artillery pieces drawn by horses.

The Queen's Visit to Dublin (1897). Unknown production company. 1:39 min. Huntley Film Archives, film number 11046. www.youtube.com/watch?v=MkBb3kEZbIg. Accessed 12 December 2017.
Queen Victoria visits Dublin, Ireland, on 22nd June 1897. She rides in an open carriage with two large highlanders at back of the coach. When the carriage stops by the camera position, she nods to the crowds.
Not in IMDB.

Queen Victoria at Garden Party (1897). British Pathé (UK). 2:07 min. www.youtube.com/watch?v=6jXwGKusIPM. Accessed 6 November 2017. Not in IMDB.

Queen Victoria Reviewing Troops at Aldershot (1898). C. Goodwin Norton (UK). Unknown length. Gifford Catalogue 00406. www.imdb.com/title/tt2152552/?ref_=nm_flmg_slf_49. Accessed 9 December 2017.

Queen Victoria Presenting Colours to Gordon Highlanders (1898). Walker (UK). Cinematographer: William Walker. Unknown length. Gifford Catalogue 00670. www.imdb.com/title/tt2198514/?ref_=nm_flmg_slf_48. Accessed 9 December 2017.

Queen Victoria Driving to Laffans Plain (1898). British Mutoscope & Biograph Co. (UK). Cinematographer: William Dickson. Unknown length. Gifford Catalogue 00672. www.imdb.com/title/tt2159432/?ref_=nm_flmg_slf_47. Accessed 9 December 2017.
Queen Victoria drives to Laffan's Plain. This film is listed in the Palace Theatre program for 18 July 1898 (Brown and Anthony 257).

Queen Victoria at Aldershot (1898). British Mutoscope & Biograph Co. (UK). Cinematographer: William Walker. Unknown length. Gifford Catalogue 00405. www.imdb.com/title/tt2159992/?ref_=nm_flmg_slf_46. Accessed 9 December 2017.

Her Majesty the Queen in State Carriage (1898). Prestwich Manufacturing Co. (UK). 16.8m. Gifford Catalogue 00630. www.imdb.com/title/tt2144902/?ref_=nm_flmg_slf_45. Accessed 9 December 2017.

Clans Receiving the Queen (1898). Fuerst Bros. (UK). Unknown length. Gifford Catalogue 00502.1. www.imdb.com/title/tt2151912/?ref_=nm_flmg_slf_44. Accessed 9 December 2017.

Visit of the Queen to South Kensington (1899). Paul's Animatograph Works (UK). Director: Robert W. Paul. 24.4 m. Gifford Catalogue 00753. www.imdb.com/title/tt2268430/?ref_=nm_flmg_slf_43. Accessed 11 December 2017.

The Queen Arriving and Leaving the Lawn (1899). Warwick Trading Co. (UK). 15.2 m. Gifford Catalogue 00896.1. www.imdb.com/title/tt2228362/?ref_=nm_flmg_slf_42. Accessed 11 December 2017.

The Queen and Royal Household with Bodyguard (1899). Warwick Trading Co. (UK). 45.7 m. Gifford Catalogue 00815.3.

Appendix: Select Filmography

www.imdb.com/title/tt2269508/?ref_=nm_flmg_slf_41. Accessed 11 December 2017.

The Queen and Princess of Battenburg (1899). Warwick Trading Co. (UK). 15.2 m. Gifford Catalogue 00939.4. www.imdb.com/title/tt2360654/?ref_=nm_flmg_slf_40. Accessed 11 December 2017.

The Queen's Drive Through Windsor (1899). Warwick Trading Co. (UK). 15.2 m. Gifford Catalogue 00816.1. www.imdb.com/title/tt2268442/?ref_=nm_flmg_slf_39. Accessed 11 December 2017.

The Queen's Arrival at Netley (1899). Haydon & Urry (UK). Unknown length. Gifford Catalogue 00724. www.imdb.com/title/tt2288646/?ref_=nm_flmg_slf_38. Accessed 11 December 2017.

Queen Victoria visits Netley Hospital to inspect sick and wounded from the Indian Frontier.

This film's date could possibly be a release date for an event that occurred 3 December 1898. See an article expressing appreciation for the visit: "The Queen's Visit to Netley" in *The Indian Medical Gazette*, available online at www.ncbi.nlm.nih.gov/pmc/articles/PMC5145350/?page=1. Accessed 11 December 2017.

On the same visit, the Queen participated in a demonstration of Roentgen rays (x-rays) passed through her hand and projected on a screen.

Review of the Life Guards by the Queen (1899). Warwick Trading Co. (UK). 30 m / 56 sec. Gifford Catalogue 01055. www.imdb.com/title/tt2223268/?ref_=nm_flmg_slf_37. Accessed 11 December 2017.

Possibly the same as Warwick Trading Co. catalogue number 5483a. In this film, Queen Victoria reviews the troops and officers of the 1st and 2nd Life Guards at Spital Barracks, Windsor on 11 November 1899. The review took place prior to the Life Guards' departure for South Africa (Boer War). www.youtube.com/watch?v=18BNcasiMVw. Accessed 11 December 2017.

Queen Victoria with Horse Guards (1899). British Mutoscope & Biograph Co. (UK). 8.2 m. www.imdb.com/title/tt2212046/?ref_=nm_flmg_slf_36. Accessed 11 December 2017.

Possibly the same as Huntley Film Archives, film number 1407: *Visit by Queen Victoria, early 1900's*. www.youtube.com/watch?v=4qVTxN2U9xU. Accessed 11 December 2017.

Queen Victoria Reviewing the Life Guards (1899). British Mutoscope & Biograph Co. (UK). Unknown length. www.imdb.com/title/tt2316488/?ref_=nm_flmg_slf_35. Accessed 11 December 2017.

Queen Victoria Reviewing Household Cavalry (1899). British Mutoscope & Biograph Co. (UK). 10.1 m, 7.3 m. www.imdb.com/title/tt2228282/?ref_=nm_flmg_slf_34.. Accessed 12 December 2017.

Queen and Royal Family Entering Their Carriages (1899). Warwick Trading Co. (UK). 45.7 m. Gifford Catalogue 00815.1. www.imdb.com/title/tt2270974/?ref_=nm_flmg_slf_32. Accessed 12 December 2017.

Presentation of the New State Colours to the Scots Guards: Arrival of Her Majesty the Queen (1899). Warwick Trading Co. (UK). 30 m. Gifford Catalogue 00881.1. www.imdb.com/title/tt2223256/?ref_=nm_flmg_slf_30. Accessed 12 December 2017

Presentation of the New State Colours to the Scots Guards: Review of Scots Guards by Her Majesty the Queen (1899). Warwick Trading Co. (UK). 15.2 m. Gifford Catalogue 00881.2. www.imdb.com/title/tt2213530/?ref_=nm_flmg_slf_31. Accessed 12 December 2017.

Her Majesty the Queen Inspecting Life Guards (1899). Warwick Trading Co. (UK). 15.2 m. Gifford Catalogue 01054. www.imdb.com/title/tt2211764/?ref_=nm_flmg_slf_29. Accessed 12 December 2017.

Queen Victoria Laying Corner Stone aka ***The Queen Arriving at South Kensington*** (1899). British Mutoscope & Biograph Co. (UK). Unknown length. Gifford Catalogue 00754. www.imdb.com/title/tt2304496/?ref_=nm_flmg_slf_33. Accessed 12 December 2017.

Her Majesty the Queen Arriving at South Kensington on the Occasion of the Laying of the Foundation Stone of the Victoria &

Albert Museum (1899). British Mutoscope & Biograph Co. (UK). Unknown length. www.imdb.com/title/tt0345391/?ref_=nm_flmg_slf_28. Accessed 12 December 2017.

This film is listed in the *Daily Chronicle* 20 May 1898 and in the Palace Theatre program 12 June 1898 (Brown and Anthony 265).

Her Majesty Leaving Spittal Barracks Amid Cheers (1899). Warwick Trading Co. (UK). 15.2 m. www.imdb.com/title/tt2228318/?ref_=nm_flmg_slf_27. Accessed 12 December 2017.

Her Majesty, Queen Victoria, Reviewing the Household Cavalry at Spital Barracks (1899). British Mutoscope & Biograph Co. (UK). 7.32 m. www.imdb.com/title/tt0242518/?ref_=nm_flmg_slf_25. Accessed 12 December 2017.

This film is listed in the *Daily Chronicle* 15 November 1898 and in the Palace Theatre program 21 November 1898 (Brown and Anthony 274).

"This view shows the Queen in an open carriage reviewing the dismounted battalion of the Household Cavalry, just before its departure for South Africa, where the organization served with signal gallantry." *(Mutoscope & Biograph Co. Picture Catalogue 1902*, film #528, 104. rucore.libraries.rutgers.edu/rutgers-lib/24582/PDF/1/play/. Accessed 25 January 2018).

Her Majesty, Queen Victoria, Reviewing the Household Cavalry at Spital Barracks (No. 2) (1899). British Mutoscope & Biograph Co. (UK). 101.1 m. www.imdb.com/title/tt2308698/?ref_=nm_flmg_slf_26. Accessed 12 December 2017.

This film is listed in *Today* 23 November 1899 (Brown and Anthony 274).

"Showing the arrival of Queen Victoria at the parade grounds; the regiment being drawn up in dress parade formation to receive her." *(American Mutoscope & Biograph Co. Picture Catalogue 1902*, film #529,104. rucore.libraries.rutgers.edu/rutgers-lib/24582/PDF/1/play/. Accessed 25 January 2018).

Her Majesty, Queen Victoria, Reviewing the Honorable Artillery (1899). British Mutoscope & Biograph Co. (UK). 8.23 m. www.imdb.com/title/tt0242517/?ref_=nm_flmg_slf_24. Accessed 12 December 2017.

"Her Majesty, the Queen, with Princesses Christian and Louise in the royal carriage at Windsor reviewing the Honorable Artillery. The Prince of Wales rides at the head of the line. On this occasion, the Queen graciously dispensed with the use of a parasol, permitting the Biograph to secure an excellent portrait. This was one of the last occasions on which she appeared at a public function." *(American Mutoscope & Biograph Co. Picture Catalogue 1902*, film # 411, 103. rucore.libraries.rutgers.edu/rutgers-lib/24582/PDF/1/play/. Accessed 15 January 2018).

Her Majesty, Queen Victoria Part 1 (1899). British Mutoscope & Biograph Co. (UK). 21.34 m. www.imdb.com/title/tt0242515/?ref_=nm_flmg_slf_23. Accessed 12 December 2017.

This film is listed in the *Daily Chronicle* 5 July 1899 and in the Palace Theatre program 21 August 1899 (Brown and Anthony 267).

"The Honorable Artillery passing in review at Windsor before the Royal Carriage in which are Her Majesty, and the Princesses Christian and Louise. The Prince of Wales, now King Edward VII, rides at the head of the line." *(American Mutoscope & Biograph Co. Picture Catalogue 1902*, film #409, 103. rucore.libraries.rutgers.edu/rutgers-lib/24582/PDF/1/play/. Accessed 15 January 2018).

Her Majesty, Queen Victoria Part 2 (1899). British Mutoscope & Biograph Co. (UK). 8.23 m. www.imdb.com/title/tt0242516/?ref_=nm_flmg_slf_22. Accessed 12 December 2017.

This film received an uncredited review in the Graeme Cruickshank Theatre Collection (Brown and Anthony 267).

"The arrival of Her Majesty with escort of the Horse Guards. In the first carriage appears the Queen, Princesses Christian and Louise, and the Marchioness of Lorne. In the second carriage, The Duchess of Connaught, Princesses Margaret and Patricia of Connaught and Victoria of Schleswig-Holstein." *(American Mutoscope & Biograph Co. Picture Catalogue 1902*, film #410, 103. rucore.libraries.rutgers.edu/rutgers-lib/24582/PDF/1/play/. Accessed 15 January 2018).

Departure from Folkestone of the Queen (1899). British Mutoscope & Biograph Co. (UK). Unknown length. www.imdb.com/

Appendix: Select Filmography 157

title/tt2320496/?ref_=nm_flmg_slf_20. Accessed 12 December 2017.

God Save the Queen (1899). British Mutoscope & Biograph Co. (UK). 7.62 m. www.imdb.com/title/tt0241491/?ref_=nm_flmg_slf_21. Accessed 12 December 2017.

Queen Victoria appears at Windsor.

This film is listed in *Today* 23 November 1899 (Brown and Anthony 274).

"Showing officers and men of the Life Guards cheering Her Majesty, Queen Victoria, after wishing them God speed and safe return, as they were about to leave for Africa. The Queen is seen in an open carriage." *(American Mutoscope & Biograph Co. Picture Catalogue 1902,* film #533, 104. rucore.libraries.rutgers.edu/rutgers-lib/24582/PDF/1/play/. Accessed 25 January 2018.

Arrival of the Queen and Bodyguard (1899). Warwick Trading Co. (UK). 23 m. Gifford Catalogue 00880.1. www.imdb.com/title/tt2215738/?ref_=nm_flmg_slf_19. Accessed 12 December 2017.

This is the first part of a series noted in Gifford Catalogue as 00880: *Honourable Artillery Company.*

Lord Roberts Unveils Statue of Queen Victoria (1899). Hepworth (UK). 56 sec. www.imdb.com/title/tt2213484/?ref_=fn_al_tt_1. Accessed 26 March 2018.

Lord Frederick Sleigh Roberts pulls down curtain to unveil a statue of Queen Victoria at Manchester, UK. The sculptor is Edward Onslow Ford.

Queen's Visit to Dublin (1900). Hepworth (UK). 38 m. www.imdb.com/title/tt2415054/?ref_=nm_flmg_slf_13. Accessed 5 June 2019.

Queen Victoria in Dublin (1900). British Pathé (UK). 1:48 min. https://ifiplayer.ie/-queen-victoria-in-dublin-1900/. Accessed 29 April 2019

A man steps out from crowd at right side of screen and waves arms at the crown. It is not clear if he is protesting or encouraging the crowd to cheer.

Not in IMDB.

The Queen Reviewing the Guards (1900). British Mutoscope & Biograph Co. (UK). Unknown length. Gifford Catalogue 01237. www.imdb.com/title/tt2479626/?ref_=nm_flmg_slf_18. Accessed 12 December 2017.

The Queen Leaving Windsor Castle (1900). British Mutoscope & Biograph Co. (UK). Unknown length. Gifford Catalogue 01235. www.imdb.com/title/tt2440460/?ref_=nm_flmg_slf_17. Accessed 12 December 2017.

"A Windsor we were stationed about a hundred yards from the gates, the road from which ran straight down to us and only just as it reached us curved off to the right. We had a goodly number of Windsor subjects along the road to bear us company. First appeared an advance guard in the shape of a dog that, having glanced round and satisfied himself that all was in order, trotted quietly out of focus. Then the escorted carriage was seen to be at the gate, and shortly drove down the road towards us. Of its occupants little could be seen until it reached the curve, when a full but momentary glimpse of the Queen led to some of the loudest cheering of the evening" (Film review in the Graeme Cruickshank Theatre Collection 9 March 1900. Brown and Anthony 280).

Queen Victoria's Carriage Passing along the Thames Embankment (1900). British Mutoscope & Biograph Co. (UK).

This film is listed in the Graeme Cruickshank Theatre Collection 9 March 1900 (Brown and Anthony 280).

Not in IMDB.

The Queen Leaving Buckingham Palace (1900). British Mutoscope & Biograph Co. (UK). Unknown length. Gifford Catalogue 01236. www.imdb.com/title/tt2422568/?ref_=nm_flmg_slf_16. Accessed 12 December 2017.

This film is listed in the Palace Theatre program 2 April 1900 (Brown and Anthony 280).

The Queen Entering Phoenix Park (1900). British Mutoscope & Biograph Co. (UK). Unknown length. Gifford Catalogue 01275.2. www.imdb.com/title/tt2479624/?ref_=nm_flmg_slf_15. Accessed 12 December 2017.

The Queen's Visit to London (1900). Robert W. Paul (UK). 18.3 m. Gifford Catalogue 01231. www.imdb.com/title/tt2479938/?ref_=nm_flmg_slf_14. Accessed 12 December 2017.

Appendix: Select Filmography

The Queen's Visit to Dublin (1900) Warwick Trading Co (UK). 30 m. www.imdb.com/title/tt2439598/?ref_=nm_flmg_slf_12. Accessed 12 December 2017.

The Queen's Entry Into Dublin (1900). Northern Photographic Works (UK). 24.4 m. Gifford Catalogue 01258. www.imdb.com/title/tt2388676/?ref_=nm_flmg_slf_11. Accessed 12 December 2017.

Review of Berkshire Volunteers by the Queen (1900). Robert W. Paul (UK). 15.2 m. Gifford Catalogue 01257. www.imdb.com/title/tt2370840/?ref_=nm_flmg_slf_10. Accessed 12 December 2017.

Queen Victoria in Ireland (1900). Williamson Kinematograph Co. (UK). 23 m. Gifford Catalogue 01575 (series). www.imdb.com/title/tt2390134/?ref_=nm_flmg_slf_9. Accessed 12 December 2017.

Queen Victoria's Last Visit to Ireland aka ***H.M. The Queen Entering Phoenix Park*** (1900). British Mutoscope & Biograph Co. (UK). 16.76 m. www.imdb.com/title/tt0266871/?ref_=nm_flmg_slf_8. Accessed 12 December 2017.

This film is listed in the Palace Theatre program 23 April 1900 (Brown and Anthony 281).

"This is the last ceremonious public appearance of Her Majesty, Queen Victoria. The picture was taken in Phoenix Park, Dublin, April 4th, 1900, and shows the Queen in an open carriage, being cheered by thousands of people, as she passes through an arch of welcome." *(American Mutoscope & Biograph Co. Picture Catalogue 1902,* film #603,104. rucore.libraries.rutgers.edu/-rutgers-lib/24582/PDF/1/play/. Accessed 25 January 2018).

Presenting Bouquet to Queen in Phoenix Park aka ***Queen Victoria's Last Visit to Ireland*** (1900). British Mutoscope & Biograph Co. (UK). Unknown length. Gifford Catalogue 01275.3. www.imdb.com/title/tt2415008/?ref_=nm_flmg_slf_7. Accessed 12 December 2017.

"This picture was taken in Phoenix Park, Dublin, on the same day as the one above described, but in this negative a very close view of the Queen is given. The occasion was the presentation of flowers to Her Majesty by a deputation of little girls, and our camera was placed so near to the spot where the ceremony occurred, that the most minute details are shown. The carriage drives up, stops, the little girls are presented to the Queen, to whom they courtesy. The Queen addresses a few pleasant remarks to the children, and smiles happily, and they in turn give her a huge basket of flowers with which she is apparently very much pleased. The ceremony is then concluded, and the carriage drives off." *(American Mutoscope & Biograph Co. Picture Catalogue 1902,* film #605, 105. rucore.libraries.rutgers.edu/-rutgers-lib/24582/PDF/1/play/. Accessed 25 January 2018.

Great Review by the Queen in Phoenix Park (1900). Robert W. Paul (UK). 36.6 m. Gifford Catalogue 01285. www.imdb.com/title/tt2405836/?ref_=nm_flmg_slf_6. Accessed 12 December 2017.

The Queen Leaving Netley Hospital (1901). Haydon & Urry (UK). 21.3 m. Gifford Catalogue 01598. www.imdb.com/title/tt2604174/?ref_=nm_flmg_slf_2. Accessed 14 December 2017.

Queen Victoria leaves Netley Hospital after her last public appearance.

The Queen in Her State Carriage (1901). Haydon & Urry (UK). Gifford Catalogue 01599. www.imdb.com/title/tt2539604/?ref_=nm_flmg_slf_1. Accessed 14 December 2017.

This film shows Queen Victoria's last public appearance.

Royal Proclamation of the Death of Queen Victoria, Blackburn (1901). Mitchell & Kenyon (UK). 2 min. www.imdb.com/title/tt1090263/?ref_=fn_al_tt_1. Accessed 27 March 2018. www.youtube.com/watch?v=e3JsDyD9Rng. Accessed 27 March 2018.

This film shows the official proclamation of Queen Victoria's death.

Queen Victoria's Funeral [Number 1] aka ***The Funeral of the Queen:–"Alberta" Leaving Trinity Pier*** (1901). British Mutoscope & Biograph Co. (UK). 16.15 m. www.imdb.com/title/tt0345833/?ref_=nm_flmg_slf_3. Accessed 14 December 2017.

Taken at East Clowes, this film shows Queen Victoria's funeral, including Kaiser Wilhelm II and King Edward VII.

It is listed in the *Daily Chronicle* 6 February 1901 and in the Palace Theatre program 18 February 1901 (Brown and Anthony 289).

"Scene at Trinity Pier, showing the coffin arriving on gun-carriage, which is stopped at the landing stage. The pall with the crown and sceptre being taken off, the coffin is carried through to the boat. King Edward VII and Emperor William, with the ladies of the court in deep mourning, walk behind the gun carriage. A very fine picture is afforded of the entire party." (*American Mutoscope & Biograph Co. Picture Catalogue 1902*, film #750, 106. rucore.libraries.rutgers.edu/rutgers-lib/24582/PDF/1/play/. Accessed 15 January 2018).

Queen Victoria's Funeral [Number 2] (1901). British Mutoscope & Biograph Co. (UK). 24.38 m. www.imdb.com/title/tt0345834/?ref_=nm_flmg_slf_4. Accessed 14 December 2017.

It is listed in the Palace Theatre program 18 February 1901(Brown and Anthony 290).

"This scene, taken from Earl Gray's Gardens, London, with the Marble Arch in background, shows the funeral processing passing Lord Brassey's house, in the following order: Earl Marshal Roberts and staff, Heraldic Offices, Household Officers, Gun carriage bearing coffin, the Royal Standard, His Majesty, King Edward VII, His Royal Highness, the Duke of Connaught, His Imperial Majesty, Emperor William of Germany, Monarchs and Foreign Princes, carriages containing Ladies of the Royal Family." (*American Mutoscope & Biograph Co. Picture Catalogue 1902*, film #753, 106. rucore.libraries.rutgers.edu/rutgers-lib/24582/PDF/1/play/. Accessed 15 January 2018).

Queen Victoria's Funeral [Number 3] (1901). British Mutoscope & Biograph Co. (UK). 15.85 m. www.imdb.com/title/tt0345835/?ref_=nm_flmg_slf_5. Accessed 14 December 2017.

It is listed in the *Daily Chronicle* 6 February and in the Palace Theatre program 18 February 1901 (Brown and Anthony 290).

"A close view of the funeral procession coming toward the camera. This view is of particular interest, as it shows the naval brigade drawing the gun carriage, after it became impossible to control the horses. King Edward VII, and Emperor William walk in the military escort at the rear of the carriage." (*American Mutoscope & Biograph Co. Picture Catalogue 1902*, film #762, 106. rucore.libraries.rutgers.edu/rutgers-lib/24582/PDF/1/play/. Accessed 15 January 2018).

Alberta Conveying Royal Bier aka ***The Funeral of the Queen—The "Alberta" Conveying the Royal Bier and "Victoria and Albert," with Royal Mourners Aboard, Passing through Line of Battleships*** (1901). British Mutoscope & Biograph Co. (UK). Unknown length. Gifford Catalogue 01623.4. www.imdb.com/title/tt2604074/?ref_=fn_tt_tt_3. Accessed 6 March 2018.

This film of Queen Victoria's funeral is listed in the *Daily Chronicle* 6 February and in the Palace Theatre program 18 February 1901 (Brown and Anthony 290).

The Cortege on its Way from Osborne to Trinity Pier aka ***The Funeral of the Queen—The Cortege on its Way from Osborne to Trinity Pier*** (1901). British Mutoscope & Biograph Co. (UK). Unknown length. Gifford Catalogue 01623.1. www.imdb.com/title/tt2596756/?ref_=fn_tt_tt_1. Accessed 6 March 2018.

This film of Queen Victoria's funeral is listed in the *Daily Chronicle* 6 February 1901 and in the Palace Theatre program 18 February 1901 (Brown and Anthony 290).

Funeral of Queen Victoria A (1901). British Pathé (UK), film #1692.07, canister UN 1 B (F) 15:00 min. Gifford Catalogue 01606 series. www.britishpathe.com/video/funeral-of-queen-victoria/query/funeral+of+queen+victoria. Accessed 15 January 2018.

According to the *British Pathé Catalog*, the *Funeral of Queen Victoria A* film is a duplicate of the *Funeral of Queen Victoria B.*, marked as unused/unissued material. Also, the *Funeral of Queen Victoria D* film appears to be a duplicate of the *A* and *B* films.

Subtle differences in timings between the *A*, *B*, and *C* films, suggest that that Pathé created three different prints, but shorter *B* film was put into use and, through use, lost a few seconds of frames. The *D* film is the longest by one second. Also a few shots are reversed, flipped right vs. left, but they are the same content. The scenes of the coffin and dignitaries ascending the steps of St.

George's Chapel at Windsor were taken with two separate cameras, and the prints mix and match shots. The differences are trivial, so it is best to consider this as three slightly different prints of the same film:

In the *A* and *B* films, the first shots up to about 2:45 minutes are reversed; medals and swords are presented as worn on the person's right side, when it should be on the left. The *D* film is not reversed; it shows medals and swords on the left side.

The stray dog shot appears at 2:43 minutes in the *A* film and at 2:45 minutes in the *B* film; in both *A* and *B* films, the dog runs from the left side of the procession. In the *D* film the dog runs from the right side of the procession at 2:45 minutes.

In the *A* and *B* films, the royal yacht moves left to right across the frame. In the *D* film, it moves right to left.

In the *A* and *B* films, the procession moves from left to center of the frame. The hugging woman, who breaks rank in the procession up the chapel steps to hug a bystander on the left, occurs at 10:21 minutes in the *A* film and at 10:17 minutes in the *B* film. In the *D* film, the shot is taken on a different camera showing the coffin going up the steps from right to center of the frame; the hugging woman is barely visible.

Funeral of Queen Victoria B (1901). British Pathé (UK), film # 3276.05, canister DOCS. 14:56 min. www.britishpathe.com/video/queen-victorias-funeral-2/query/funeral+of+queen+victoria. Accessed 13 December 2017.

Queen Victoria's funeral procession goes through the streets of Cowes, Isle of Wight. A clear shot of coffin shows that it is covered by three crowns. From 0:29 to 2:40 minutes, the images appear to be reversed: soldiers' medals, rifles and swords are on the wrong side, and the drummers are wearing their drums on the wrong side.

At 2:45 minutes, a dog runs out in front of the marchers.

Royal Yacht sails between Isle of Wight and mainland. A puff of smoke from a booming cannon is visible.

At 5:37 minutes, the funeral procession moves through the streets of London. King Edward VII and Kaiser Wilhelm appear on horseback at the Marble Arch and take a left turn. The procession moves from right to left across the frame in this shot.

The coffin arrives at Windsor, and procession moves toward Windsor Castle. The gun carriage is pulled by seamen from right to left across the frame. They are followed by military groups, the Yeomen Warders (Beefeaters), and a group of Scotsmen in kilts.

At 8:13 minutes, the shot shows the procession arriving at St. George's Chapel. The gun carriage moves from left to right into the center of the frame. The coffin's cover and three crowns are removed, and the coffin is carried up the steps toward the right of the frame. Long line of dignitaries follows the coffin. This shot is rather dark and fuzzy.

At 10:17 minutes, a woman in the procession moves out of formation and goes to left to hug a bystander on the steps. A uniformed man intervenes.

At 10:40 minutes, a reverse angle shot shows the arrival of the coffin, which moves right to left. The coffin is drawn by sailors, first seen with backs to camera, and then they turn around to face the coffin. This shot shows the removal of the three-crown covering and then removal of the coffin from the gun carriage. Sailors stand bareheaded in background; then they turn around, replace their caps, and pull the gun carriage from center to left of the frame, while the coffin is moved up the steps into the Chapel from center to right of frame. This shot is a much brighter and sharper image.

Funeral of Queen Victoria C (1901). British Pathé (UK), film #2309, canister UN 1396 D. 5:12 min. www.britishpathe.com/video/queen-victorias-funeral-1/query/funeral+of+queen+victoria. Accessed 15 January 2018.

Filmed in London and Windsor, this print shows Queen Victoria's coffin with three crowns, King Edward VII, Duke of Connaught (Victoria's son Prince Arthur), and Kaiser Wilhelm on horseback.

Sailors wait at Windsor train station as train pulls in. The white funeral drapery on the engine is barely visible.

Sailors pull the coffin. King Edward VII,

Appendix: Select Filmography 161

Duke of Connaught (Victoria's son Prince Arthur) and Kaiser Wilhelm march on foot behind coffin, followed by military dignitaries.

This print shows a shot of man who appears to be Sir James Reid, the royal physician.

Funeral of Queen Victoria D (1901). British Pathé (UK), film #1702.14, canister UN 1 D (N). 15:01 min. www.britishpathe.com/video/funeral-of-edward-vii/query/funeral+of+queen+victoria. Accessed 19 January 2018.

This compilation of various shots from Queen Victoria's funeral procession through London includes a good shot of the coffin going past on gun carriage.

Funeral of Queen Victoria—The Marble Arch (1901). Unknown production company. 30 sec. www.youtube.com/watch?v=oix00dgAcyI. Accessed 6 November 2017

Queen Victoria's coffin passes in front of the Marble Arch. The image is poor quality and fuzzy.

Queen Victoria Funeral Procession (1901). Cecil Hepworth. Huntley Film Archives, film number 11019. 43 sec. www.youtube.com/watch?v=cYMcUD8vqhw. Accessed 15 December 2017. www.huntleyarchives.com/preview.asp?image=1011019. Accessed 5 June 2019.

This film shows the departure of Queen Victoria's coffin from the Isle of Wight on 1 February 1901.

Taken from a lower, closer angled position than those seen in the Pathé "A" and "B" films, it has a more personal, dramatic touch.

At 0:16 minutes there is a medium shot of royal physician Sir James Reid marching on the left side of the procession.

Hepworth's film shows the soldiers medals correctly (on their left side), indicating that this print was not take by Pathé, which has the reversed shots of the soldiers and their medals.

Victoria's Funeral, 1900's (1901). Unknown production company. Huntley Film Archives, film number 33496. 2:32 min. www.youtube.com/watch?v=GprvcnqTY2Q. Accessed 15 December 2017. www.huntleyarchives.com/preview.asp?image=1033496. Accessed 5 June 2019.

This compilation of several different shots of Queen Victoria's funeral procession is presented in random order, not in the order in which they actually occurred. The image quality is poor.

The first shot shows the sailors pulling the gun carriage up to the steps of St. George's Chapel at Windsor. The pallbearers and honor guard carry the coffin up the steps left to right, as the sailors pull the empty gun carriage away from center to left.

At 1:08 minutes, the scene shows the procession in London at the Marble Arch, moving left to right. The next shot at 1:17 minutes shows a military band moving right to left followed by the coffin on gun carriage. King Edward VII and Kaiser Wilhelm ride on horseback, pausing briefly in front of the camera.

At 2:02 minutes, sailors are shown close to the camera pulling the gun carriage at Windsor, right to left across the frame.

Queen Victoria's Funeral (1901). Unknown production Company. Huntley Film Archives, film number 32373. 5:10 min. www.huntleyarchives.com/preview.asp?image=1032373 Accessed 17 December 2018.

Queen Victoria's funeral procession at Cowes is shot at medium height and at middle distance, showing mounted soldiers, marching soldiers, a military band, and the gun carriage.

At 1:48 minutes, the film shows royal physician Sir James Reid.

At 2:37 minutes, a stray dog runs from the right side of the procession.

In London, the film shows the gun carriage going past the Marble Arch. Edward VII rides past camera with Kaiser Wilhelm, followed by policemen.

At 3:38 minutes, the film includes a repetition of the gun carriage moving past the Marble Arch.

It ends with carriages going past the Marble Arch; it is not possible to distinguish who is riding in the carriages.

Early Films, 1900's (1901). Unknown production company. Huntley Film Archives, film number 32212. 4 sec. www.huntleyarchives.com/searchresult.php?keywords=&option=all&filmCategory=&filmDecade=&film

Sound=&filmColour=&filmNumber=32212. Accessed 18 January 2018.
This film is a compilation for several unrelated topics.

A four second clip from 0:27 to 0:31 shows Queen Victoria's funeral procession marching past the Marble Arch.

Other clips on this compilation are Edison's *The Burning Stable* and a shot of lightning sketch artist drawing a cartoon. The motive behind such a compilation is baffling.

Her Late Majesty the Queen's Funeral (1901). Harrison and Company (UK). Gifford Catalogue 01627. 45.7 m. www.imdb.com/title/tt2604168/?ref_=fn_tt_tt_7. Accessed 5 March 2018.

In this film, Queen Victoria's funeral was photographed in London Street, Paddington.

The Queen's Funeral Pageant Enters Hyde Park (1901). Warwick Trading Company (UK). Gifford Catalogue 01618.3. 45.7 m. www.imdb.com/title/tt2613156/?ref_=fn_tt_tt_9. Accessed 5 March 2018.

Queen Victoria's funeral procession reaches Hyde Park.

Funeral of Her Late Majesty Queen Victoria (1901). Robert W. Paul (UK). 45.7 m. www.imdb.com/title/tt2561074/?ref_=fn_tt_tt_10. Accessed 5 March 2018.

Queen Victoria's funeral procession moves through the streets of London.

The Queen's Funeral (1901). Siegmund Lubin (USA). 91.44 m. www.imdb.com/title/tt0350019/?ref_=fn_tt_tt_2. Accessed 6 March 2018.

Queen Victoria's funeral procession moves through the streets of London.

"Showing the funeral procession of England's queen. A gorgeous spectacle. Will be furnished at any length desired." (IMDB).

Queen's Funeral Procession at Cowes (1901). Hepworth (UK). Gifford Catalogue 01606.1. 53.3 m. www.imdb.com/title/tt2539624/?ref_=fn_al_tt_1. Accessed 6 March 2018.

Queen Victoria's Funeral: Ships Fire a Salute in the Solent (1901). Unknown production company. BFI Catalog N-457414. collections-search.bfi.org.uk/web/Details/ChoiceFilmWorks/154381241. Accessed 6 March 2018.

Life and Death of Queen Victoria (1901). Walturdaw (UK). Gifford Catalogue 018 54. 30 min. www.imdb.com/title/tt25748 14/?ref_=fn_tt_tt_1. Accessed 6 March 2018.

This half-hour film compiles various companies' shots of Queen Victoria's funeral procession.

Silent Films Featuring Queen Victoria as a Character

These silent films are dramas in which Queen Victoria appears as a character, played by an actress. The films are listed alphabetically by title.

Balaclava aka *The Jaws of Hell* aka *The Valley of Death* aka *Charge of the Light Brigade* (1928/1930). Gainsborough Pictures (UK). Director: Maurice Elvey (silent version), Milton Rosmer (sound version). Writers: Boyd Cable (story), Gareth Gundrey (story), W.P. Lipscomb (story), Alfred Lord Tennyson (poem), Angus MacPhail, Milton Rosmer and Robert Stevenson (scenario). 72 min. www.imdb.com/title/tt0018671/?ref_=fn_al_tt_1. Accessed 10 February 2018.

Principal cast: Marian Drada—Queen Victoria; Cyril McLaglen—John Kennedy; Benita Hume—Jean McDonald; Alf Goddard—Nobby; Miles Mander—Lord Raglan; Wallace Bosco—Lord Palmerston; Betty Bolton—Natasha; Boris Ranevsky—Tsar; Eugene Leahy—Prince Albert

A British army office is cashiered and re-enlists as a private in the Crimean War. He serves at the siege of Sebastopol and unmasks a spy. The film ends with the Charge of the Light Brigade.

This film was originally shot by Maurice Elvey in 1928 as a silent film, including a reconstruction of the Charge of the Light Brigade. Gainsborough Pictures withheld release in 1929 when their distribution partner Gaumont announced that they were installing sound systems in their entire circuit. In 1930 a new director Milton Rosmer completed the sound scenes, after a brief delay due to a fire at the studio. The silent / sound version was released in April 1930 in London.

The Campbells Are Coming (1915). Universal (USA). Director: Francis Ford. Writers: Grace Cunard, Emerson Hough. 40 min. www.imdb.com/title/tt0005050/?ref_=ttfc_fc_tt. Accessed 30 March 2018.

Principal cast: Francis Ford—Nana Sahib; Grace Cunard—Mary McLean; Ervin Denecke—Colin Campbell; Duke Worne—Azimooah; John Ford (as Jack Ford)—uncredited role

Queen Victoria is not listed as a character in the film credits; however, the AFI Catalog provides a plot synopsis that implies she is an active character: "In India, the new Sepoy leader, Nana Sahib, sends his agent Azimooah to appeal to Queen Victoria to restore the pension given during his father's reign, but the Queen refuses because Nana Sahib is an adopted son." (catalog.afi.com/Catalog/moviedetails/18082. Accessed 26 April 2018). This film is presumed lost according to IMDB and Library of Congress, so it is not possible to determine the amount of screen time, if any, given to Queen Victoria character.

Queen Victoria's refusal to restore a pension to the new Sepoy leader Nana Sahib results in a Sepoy attack on an English town. The heroine Mary McLean is captured, escapes from the Sepoy, is recaptured at the siege of Lucknow, and is rescued by Colin Campbell and his Scottish brigade.

Universal Weekly reported "'The Campbells Are Coming' is quite the most expensive and extensive photo-drama yet staged at Universal City.... Wild animals roam and kill in the Indian jungle, while crafty natives burn the homes of British soldiers and their wives in any attempt to drive their conquerors into the Indian ocean. [It] will tell again the Victorian epic of the relief of Lucknow and the massacre at Cawnpore." (*Universal Weekly*, 26 December 1914, 16. sensesofcinema.com/2009/feature-articles/-brother-feeney-francis-ford/. Accessed 30 March 2018).

Reportedly, director Francis Ford used 7,000 extras, plus 11,000 pounds of powder, and 550 ammo rounds. (*Universal Weekly*, 16 October 1915. sensesofcinema.com/2009/-feature-articles/brother-feeney-francis-ford/. Accessed 30 March 2018).

Disraeli (1916). NB Films (UK). Director: Charles Calvert, Percy Nash. Writers: Louis N. Parker (play and scenario). Producer: Arrigo Bocchi. 60 min. Gifford Catalogue 06166. www.imdb.com/title/tt0322038/?ref_=nv_sr_5. Accessed 10 February 2018.

Principal cast: Mrs. Henry Lytton—Queen Victoria; Dennis Eadie—Benjamin Disraeli; Mary Jerrold—Lady Beaconsfield; Daisy Cordell—Mrs. Travers; Cecil Morton York—Duke of Glastonbury; Evelyn Harding—Duchess of Glastonbury

Disraeli's wife helps the Prime Minister obtain British shares in the Suez Canal.

This film is based on the play *Disraeli* by Louis N. Parker, which premiered at the Wallack's Theatre on 18 September 1911. The play's cast listing does not include a role for Queen Victoria (www.ibdb.com/broadway-production/disraeli-7345. Accessed 27 April 2018).

Since prints of this film are lost, it is not possible to verify how much of a role the Queen Victoria character had.

In 1921 George Arliss was negotiating to the purchase rights to the Parker play in order to make his 1921 silent film *Disraeli*. Part of the deal with producer Arrigo Bocchi was his agreement to cease exhibition of the 1916 film and to destroy all negatives (Fells 66).

Disraeli (1921). Distinctive Productions (USA). Director: Henry Kolker. Writers: Forest Halsey, Louis N. Parker (play). 90 min. www.imdb.com/title/tt0012111/?ref_=nv_sr_4. Accessed 10 February 2018.

Principal cast: George Arliss—Benjamin Disraeli; Florence Arliss—Lady Beaconsfield; Margaret Dale—Mrs. Noel Travers (the Russian spy); Louise Huff—Clarissa

Based on the play by Louis N. Parker, this film tells the story of the Suez Canal's purchase by Prime Minister Disraeli.

The Queen Victoria character is not included in the cast list, although the 1916 film version of the Parker play includes a Queen Victoria character. Since only incomplete copies exist, it is impossible to verify if the Queen Victoria character appears in this 1921 film.

Library of Congress lists incomplete copies: one reel at George Eastman House and seven reels at Cinematheque Royale de Belgique and Gosfilmofond of Russia (memory.loc.gov/diglib/ihas/loc.mbrs.sfdb.695/default.html. Accessed 6 February 2019).

Livingstone (1925). Hero Films (UK). Director: M.A. Wetherell. Writer: M.A. Wetherell. Cinematographer: Gustav Pauli. 90 min. www.imdb.com/title/tt0226975/?ref_=fn_tt_tt_3. Accessed 19 February 2018. www.bfi.org.uk/films-tv-people/4ce2b6af0e8ce. Accessed 2 May 2018.

Principal cast: Blanche Graham—Queen Victoria; M.A. Wetherell—David Livingstone; Molly Rogers—Mary Moffatt; Henry Walton—H.M. Stanley

This film tells the story of Dr. David Livingstone's work to stop slavery and bring education to people in Africa. It includes a scene of his audience with Queen Victoria. Its use of African safari footage shot in 1923 predates the better-known MGM film *Trader Horn* (1931), which has been incorrectly touted as the first non-documentary film shot on location in Africa.

Sixty Years a Queen **aka** ***The Life and Times of Queen Victoria*** (1913). Barker Motion Photography Ltd. (UK). Director: Bert Haldane. Writers: Harry Engholm, George Berthold Samuelson, Arthur Shirley (scenario), Herbert Maxwell (book). 7 reels, 2,926 m. www.imdb.com/title/tt0003379/?ref_=nv_sr_1. Accessed 11 January 2018.

Principal cast: Blanche Forsythe—Queen Victoria (younger); Mrs. Henry Lytton—Queen Victoria (older); Fred Paul—Archbishop of Canterbury; Roy Travers—Prince Albert; Gilbert Esmond—Duke of Wellington; E. Story Gofton—W.E. Gladstone; Rolf Leslie—27 different roles

This biopic of the life of Queen Victoria was produced by Barker Motion Photography Ltd. at Ealing Green, predecessor to Ealing Studios.

Only a few seconds of this film survive. A brief clip where the young Victoria is informed of her accession can be seen in the 2002 television documentary *Forever Ealing* (www.imdb.com/title/tt0343675/?ref_=nv_sr_1. Accessed 10 February 2018).

A still from this film, showing Disraeli asking Victoria to assume the title of Empress of India, was published in the Kinematograph Year Book 1914. www.bfi.org.uk/sites/bfi.org.uk/files/downloads/-kinematograph-year-book-program-diary-and-directory-1914-2014-09-18.pdf. Accessed 22 December 2018.

The Victoria Cross. A Story of the Charge of the Light Brigade (1912). Vitagraph Company (USA). Director: Hal Reid. Writer: Hal Reid. 15 min. www.imdb.com/title/tt0002562/?ref_=ttfc_fc_tt. Accessed 13 April 2018. Available for viewing on Amazon Prime: www.amazon.com/Victoria-Cross-Wallace-Reid/dp/B06XBTX5KN/ref=sr_1_1?ie=UTF8&qid=1515681519&sr=8-1&keywords=the+victoria+cross+1912. Accessed 11 January 2018.

Principal cast: Rose Tapley—Queen Victoria; Tefft Johnson—Col. Carson; Edith Storey—Ellen Carson; Wallace Reid—Lt. Cholmodeley; Julia Swayne Gordon—Florence Nightingale

Ellen's father refuses to allow her to marry Lt. Cholmo[n]deley until he has proved himself to be a brave soldier. When war breaks out between England and Russia, the Lieutenant is called to the Crimea, and Ellen follows as a nurse under Florence Nightingale. Ellen witnesses her lover into danger during the disastrous Charge of the Light Brigade. She is shown using binoculars to view the battle, with cross cutting of battle shots framed as two semicircles, as if seen through binoculars. The Lieutenant distinguishes himself for bravery in battle. Back in London, Queen Victoria awards him the Victoria Cross.

Queen Victoria has about two minutes of screen time. She arrives at a parade ground in a carriage drawn by four white horses. The next shot shows her walking to the soldiers, talking to them, and awarding the Victoria Cross to Lt. Cholmo[n]deley.

Yankee Clipper (1927). DeMille Pictures Corporation (USA). Director: Rupert Julian. Writers: Denison Clift (story), Garrett Fort (adaptation), John W. Krafft (titles), Garnett Weston (adaptation). 88 min. www.imdb.com/title/tt0018601/?ref_=nv_sr_1. Accessed 10 February 2018.

Principal cast: Julia Faye—Queen Victoria; William Boyd—Captain Hal Winslow; Elinor Fair—Lady Jocelyn Huntington; Frank Coghlan, Jr.—Mickey; Louis Payne—Lord Huntington; Nicholas Soussanin—Prince Consort

In this story of maritime rivalry between the United States and Great Britain, and American and English clipper ships race each other from China to Boston in pursuit of a tea trade contract. The American wins, hardly surprising in a DeMille film.

Theatrical Release Films

These feature films were intended for theatrical release and include Queen Victoria as a character, played by an actress or, in some cases, an actor. Films are listed alphabetically by title. Excluded from this list are films that include a passing reference to Queen Victoria, the Victorian age, or Victoria's Empire. For documentaries, see the "Miscellaneous and Select Documentaries" section in this filmography.

The Adventures of Sherlock Holmes' Smarter Brother (1975). Jouer Films, Twentieth Century–Fox (USA). Director and writer: Gene Wilder. 91 min. www.imdb.com/title/tt0072608/?ref_=nv_sr_3. Accessed 10 February 2018.

Principal cast: Susan Field—Queen Victoria; Gene Wilder—Sigerson Holmes; Madeline Kahn—Jenny Hill; Marty Feldman—Sgt. Orville Stanley Sacker; Dom DeLuise—Gambetti; Leo McKern—Moriarty; Douglas Wilmer—Sherlock Holmes

This musical comedy / spoof film opens with Queen Victoria giving an important document to her Foreign Secretary, whereupon it is promptly stolen. Holmes turns the case over to his younger brother Sigerson to recover the stolen document that could lead to war if it gets into the wrong hands.

Alice in Wonderland aka *Alice au pays des merveilles* (1949). Lou Bunin Productions, Rank, Union Générale (France). Director: Dallas Bower. Writers: Lewis Carroll (novel), Henry Myers (screenplay). 76 min. www.imdb.com/title/tt0042189/?ref_=fn_tt_tt_12. Accessed 19 February 2018.

Principal cast: Pamela Brown—Queen Victoria / The Queen of Hearts (voice); Carol Marsh—Alice; Stephen Murray—Lewis Carroll / The Knave of Hears (voice); Felix Aylmer—Dr. Liddle / The Cheshire Cat (voice); Ernest Milton—The Vice Chancellor / The White Rabbit (voice); David Reed—The Prince Consort / The King of Hearts (voice)

This live action and stop-motion puppetry film is a version of the Lewis Carroll 1865 novel *Alice in Wonderland*.

The film was kept out of Britain due to the perception that the Queen of Hearts character was too close to Queen Victoria. It was not widely seen in the U.S. because of a legal dispute with Walt Disney Productions, then making their animated *Alice* (1951).

Annie Get Your Gun (1950). MGM (USA). Directors: George Sidney, Busby Berkeley (uncredited). Writers: Sidney Sheldon (screenplay), Herbert Fields (book), Dorothy Fields (book). 107 min. www.imdb.com/title/tt0042200/?ref_=nv_sr_1. Accessed 14 February 2018.

Principal cast: Evelyn Beresford—Queen Victoria (uncredited); Betty Hutton—Annie Oakley; Howard Keel—Frank Butler; Louis Calhern—'Buffalo Bill' Cody; J. Carrol Naish—Chief Sitting Bull

This film presents the story of Annie Oakley the sharpshooter and Frank Butler, her lover and rival. Buffalo Bill's Wild West Show performs for Queen Victoria.

This film is notorious for the firing of Judy Garland from the lead role after two months of spotty attendance and clashes with Busby Berkeley over production numbers.

Around the World in 80 Days (1956). Directors: Michael Anderson, John Farrow (uncredited for Spanish sequences). Writers: James Poe, John Farrow, S.J. Perelman, Jules Verne (book). 175 min. www.imdb.com/title/tt0048960/?ref_=nv_sr_2. Accessed 6 February 2019.

Principal cast: Uncredited extra—Queen Victoria; David Niven—Phileas Fogg; Cantinflas—Passepartout; Shirley MacLaine—Princess Aouda

Immediately after the film's intermission, the scene shifts to a London street where the newspaper headline says "Fogg in America." Two Palace guards march towards each other and say "He's in America," followed by an exterior shot of Windsor Castle. A breakfast tray with newspaper headline "Fogg" is delivered to Queen Victoria, and the camera shows one hand reaching for the paper.

Around the World in 80 Days (2004). Walden Media, Spanknyce Films, Mostow/Lieberman Productions. Director: Frank Coraci. Writers: David Titcher (screenplay), David Benullo (screenplay), David Andres Goldstein (screenplay). Jules Verne (novel). 120 min. www.imdb.com/title/tt0327437/?ref_=nv_sr_1. Accessed 14 February 2018.

Principal cast: Kathy Bates—Queen Victoria; Jackie Chan—Passepartout/Lau Xing; Steve Coogan—Phileas Fogg; Cécile De France—Monique La Roche; Jim Broadbent—Lord Kelvin

This film's story begins with a bet to travel around the world in 80 days. When Phileas and Passepartout reach London, Lord Kelvin's plot against Phileas is revealed. Kelvin scoffs at them and insults the Queen ("inbred antiquated cow"), just as the Queen walks up behind him. Queen Victoria sends Lord Kelvin to jail for attempted murder and tells Fogg that he has won and that she had 20 quid riding on him. The Queen appoints Fogg as the new Minister of Science.

Note costuming goof: Queen Victoria is shown wearing a purple dress with black lace, instead of widow black, despite the film's setting towards the end of the nineteenth century.

Barnum (1986 television movie). Robert Halmi, Filmline International and CBS (USA). Director: Lee Phillips. Writer: Michael Norell. 90 min. www.imdb.com/title/tt0090701/?ref_=fn_al_tt_2. Accessed 14 March 2018.

Principal cast: Bronwen Mantel—Queen Victoria; Burt Lancaster—Phineas Taylor Barnum; Hanna Schygulla—Jenny Lind; Laura Press—Charity Barnum; Sando Raski and Patty Maloney—Tom Thumb

P.T. Barnum looks back on his life, including an audience with Queen Victoria.

Black Butler: Book of the Atlantic (2017). A-Pictures, Aniplex, Square Enix Company (Japan). Directors: Noriyuke Abe, Stephen Hoff. Writers: Yana Toboso (manga), Hiroyuki Yoshino (screenplay). 101 min. www.imdb.com/title/tt5476944/?ref_=nv_sr_2. Accessed 16 February 2018.

Principal cast (English dub): Julie Mayfield—Queen Victoria (English voice); Brina Palencia—Ciel Phantomhive (voice); Daisuke Ono—Sebastian Michaelis (voice); Spike Spencer—Snake (voice); Jun'ichi Suwabe—Undertaker (voice)

Based on the *Black Butler* manga series, this film begins with Ciel Phantomhive and Sebastian Michaelis, his demon butler, boarding a luxury cruise ship to investigate claims of the dead being returned to life by the Aurora Society. They foil the plot and kill all the animated corpses.

Queen Victoria appears in a scene where she invests Ciel as Earl Phantomhive.

The Black Prince (2017). Brillstein Entertainment Partners, Firdaus Production (India). Director: Kavi Raz. Writer: Kavi Raz. 118 min. www.imdb.com/title/tt3962984/?ref_=ttco_co_tt. Accessed 18 Sept 2018.

Principal cast: Amanda Root—Queen Victoria; Satinder Sartaaj—Duleep Singh; Shabana Azmi—Maharani Jindan

This film tells the story of Duleep Singh, the last Maharajah of the Sikh Empire and Punjab, and his relationship with Queen Victoria.

Buffalo Bill (1944). Twentieth Century–Fox (USA). Director: William A. Wellman. Writers: Aeneas MacKenzie, Clements Ripley, Cecile Kramer, Frank Winch. 90 min. www.imdb.com/title/tt0036677/?ref_=nv_sr_3. Accessed 16 February 2018.

Principal cast: Evelyn Beresford—Queen Victoria (uncredited); Joel McCrea—William Frederick "Buffalo Bill" Cody; Maureen O'Hara—Louisa Frederici Cody; Linda Darnell—Dawn Starlight

In this biopic, William "Buffalo Bill" Cody and his Wild West Show create an international sensation and appear before Queen Victoria.

Court Waltzes aka ***La guerre des valses*** (1933). Universum Film (UFA) (Germany), L'Alliance Cinématographique Européenne. Directors: Ludwig Berger, Raoul Ploquin. Writers: Robert Liebmann, Hans Müller (story), Jacques Bousquet (dialog). 85 min. www.imdb.com/title/tt0169978/?ref_=fn_al_tt_1. Accessed 6 February 2019.

Principal cast: Madeleine Ozeray—Queen Victoria; Fernand Gravey—Franz; Pierre Mingand—Johann Strauss

This film is the French version of the *Waltz War* aka *Walzerkrieg* (1933).

David Livingstone (1936). FitzPatrick Pictures (UK). Director: James A. FitzPatrick. Writer: W.K. Williamson. 71 min. www.imdb.com/title/tt0028771/?ref_=fn_al_tt_1. Accessed 22 February 2018.

Principal cast: Pamela Stanley—Queen Victoria; Percy Marmont—David Livingstone; Marian Spencer—Mary Moffatt; Hugh McDermott—H.M. Stanley

Livingstone's explorations in Africa are presented in episodes similar to the silent *Livingstone* (1925).

Disraeli (1929). Warner Bros. (USA). Director: Alfred E. Green. Writer: Julien Josephson (screenplay). 90 min. www.imdb.com/title/tt0019823/. Accessed 2 January 2017.
Principal cast: Margaret Mann—Queen Victoria (uncredited, not a speaking role); George Arliss—Disraeli (Arliss won the Oscar for Best Actor for this role); Florence Arliss—Lady Beaconsfield; Doris Lloyd—Mrs. Travers (the Russian spy); Joan Bennett—Clarissa

Prime Minister Disraeli manages the purchase of the Suez Canal, despite Russian plotting and opposition at home. Queen Victoria is declared Empress of India and appears in an extreme long shot at a reception honoring Disraeli.

This film is a remake of Arliss' 1921 silent film version based on the play *Disraeli* (1911) by Louis N. Parker.

Dolittle (2020). Team Downey, Roth Films, Perfect World Pictures (USA). Director: Stephen Gaghan. Writers: Stephen Gaghan, Dan Gregor, Doug Mand, Chris McKay, Thomas Shepherd (story), Hugh Lofting (character). 101 min. www.imdb.com/title/tt6673612/?ref_=fn_al_tt_1. Accessed 20 January 2020. **Principal cast:** Jessie Buckley—Queen Victoria; Robert Downey Jr.—Dr. John Dolittle; Antonio Banderas—King Rassouli; Michael Sheen—Dr. Blair Müdfly; Jim Broadbent—Lord Thomas Badgley; Emma Thompson—Polynesia the macaw (voice); Octavia Spencer—the duck (voice); Rami Malek—the gorilla (voice)

Dr. Dolittle is recruited to find a cure for an ailing young Queen Victoria. After many adventures with his coterie of animal assistants, Dolittle returns to save the Queen from Lord Badgley and Dr. Müdfly's plot against her life.

Entente cordiale (1939). Arcadia Films, Flora Film (France). Director: Marcel L'Herbier. Writers: Max Glass (scenario), Abel Hermant (dialogue). 110 min. www.imdb.com/title/tt0031273/. Accessed 7 November 2018.
Principal cast: Gaby Morlay—Queen Victoria; Victor Francen—King Edward VII; Pierre Richard-Willm—Captain Charles Roussel; Arlette Marchal—Queen Alexandra

This film presents the history of the 1904 Entente Cordiale between England and France, the turnaround in public opinion in both countries, and the parallel evolution of two families, resulting in the marriage of a French heir to an English daughter. It is based on Andre Maurois' novel *Life of Edward VII.*

From Hell (2001). Twentieth Century–Fox, Underworld Entertainment (USA). Directors: Albert Hughes, Allen Hughes (as The Hughes Brothers). Writers: Alan Moore (graphic novel), Eddie Campbell (graphic novel), Terry Hayes (screenplay), Rafael Yglesias (screenplay). 122 min. www.imdb.com/title/tt0120681/?ref_=nv_sr_1. Accessed 19 February 2018.
Principal cast: Liz Moscrop—Queen Victoria; Johnny Depp—Inspector Frederick Abberline; Heather Graham—Mary Kelly; Ian Holm—Sir William Gull; Robbie Coltrane—Sergeant Peter Godley; Joanna Page—Ann Crook; Peter Eyre—Lord Hallsham; Mark Dexter—Albert Sickert / Prince Edward Albert Victor

Prince Albert Victor, grandson of Queen Victoria, marries a prostitute in a clandestine marriage and fathers a daughter. The Queen enlists Sir William Gull to cover up the affair, and Gull goes on a murderous rampage as Jack the Ripper to eliminate all witnesses to the marriage. Inspector Abberline investigates these Jack the Ripper murders and discovers Gull's guilt. The Freemasons take revenge on their murderous member Gull by lobotomizing him, while Abberline dies of an overdose.

Gilbert and Sullivan aka ***The Story of Gilbert and Sullivan*** (1953). London Film Productions (UK). Director: Sidney Gilliat. Writer: Leslie Bailey. 109 min. www.imdb.com/title/tt0045839/?ref_=fn_al_tt_1. Accessed 19 February 2018.
Principal cast: Muriel Aked—Queen Victoria; Robert Morley—William S. Gilbert; Maurice Evans—Arthur Sullivan; Eileen Herlie—Helen D'Oyly Carte; Martyn Green—George Grossmith; Peter Finch—Richard D'Oyly Carte

This film tells the story of W.S. Gilbert and Arthur Sullivan's collaboration on fourteen operettas between 1871 and 1896. Queen

Victoria attends their production of *The Golden Legend* and knights Sullivan.

The Great McGonagall (1975). Darlton, Oppidan Film Productions. Director: Joseph McGrath. Writers: Joseph McGrath, Spike Milligan. 95 min. www.imdb.com/title/tt0071579/?ref_=nv_sr_1. Accessed 14 February 2018.

Principal cast: Peter Sellers—Queen Victoria; Spike Milligan—William McGonagall

Scottish poet William McGonagall wants to become England's Poet Laureate, but his poetry is terrible.

The Great Mouse Detective (1986). Walt Disney Pictures (USA). Directors: Ron Clements, Burny Mattison, Dave Michener, John Musker. Writers: Eve Titus (book), Pete Young, Vance Gerry, Steve Hulett, John Musker, Ron Clements, Bruce Morris, Matthew O'Callaghan, Burny Mattinson, Dave Michener. 74 min. www.imdb.com/title/tt0091149/. Accessed 10 July 2018.

Principal cast: Eve Brenner—The Mouse Queen (voice); Vincent Price—Professor Ratigan (voice); Barrie Ingham—Basil of Baker Street (voice); Val Bettin—Dr. David Q. Dawson / Thug Guard (voice); Susanne Pollatschek—Olivia Flaversham (voice); Candy Candido—Fidget (voice); Alan Young—Hiram Flaversham (voice); Basil Rathbone—Sherlock Holmes (archive voice)

Basil of Baker Street investigates the disappearance of toy-maker Flaversham and uncovers a plot by arch-villain Professor Ratigan to seize control of the mouse monarchy by using a mechanical toy Queen Victoria that is under his control.

This film is noteworthy for its combination of computer animation with traditional hand-drawn 2D animation in the clock scene.

The Greatest Showman (2017). Chernin Entertainment, TSG Entertainment, Twentieth Century-Fox (USA). Director: Michael Gracey. Writers: Jenny Bicks, Bill Condon. 105 min. www.imdb.com/title/tt1485796/?ref_=nv_sr_1. Accessed 7 February, 2019.

Principal cast: Gayle Rankin—Queen Victoria; Hugh Jackman—P.T. Barnum; Michelle Williams—Charity Barnum; Zac Efron—Phillip Carlyle; Rebecca Ferguson—Jenny Lind; Sam Humphrey—Tom Thumb

In 1844 Queen Victoria meets P.T. Barnum and company and is very amused. She laughs heartily at Tom Thumb's jests.

Holmes & Watson (2018). Columbia Pictures (USA). Director: Etan Cohen. Writers: Etan Cohen, Arthur Conan Doyle (characters created by). 90 min. www.imdb.com/title/tt1255919/. Accessed 23 December 2018.

Principal cast: Pam Ferris—Queen Victoria; Will Ferrell—Holmes; John C. Reilly—Watson; Ralph Fiennes—Moriarty; Kelly Macdonald—Mrs. Hudson; Hugh Laurie—Mycroft (uncredited); Rebecca Hall—Dr. Grace Hart

Moriarty threatens to kill Queen Victoria unless Holmes and Watson solve a case in four days.

This film is considered a parody of the most recent Sherlock Holmes interpretations, especially of Benedict Cumberbatch and Robert Downey, Jr.

Watch closely for a cameo of the Elephant Man.

Hysteria (2011). Informant Media, Forthcoming Productions (UK). Director: Tanya Wexler. Writer: Stephen Dyer, Jonah Lisa Dyer, Stephen Dyer, Jonah Lisa Dyer, Howard Gensler. 100 min. www.imdb.com/title/tt1435513/?ref_=ttfc_fc_tt. Accessed 29 March 2018.

Principal cast: Sylvia Strange—Queen Victoria; Hugh Dancy—Dr. Mortimer Granville; Jonathan Pryce—Dr. Robert Dalrymple; Maggie Gyllenhaal—Charlotte Dalrymple

Mortimer Granville invents the vibrator. Queen Victoria receives a sample.

Jules Verne's Rocket to the Moon aka *Those Fantastic Flying Fools* aka *Blast Off!* (1967). Jules Verne Films Ltd. Director: Don Sharp. Writers: Harry Alan Towers, Dave Freeman, Jules Verne (inspired by the writings of). 95 min. www.imdb.com/title/tt0062363/?ref_=ttfc_fc_tt. Accessed 29 March 2018.

Principal cast: Joan Sterndale Bennett—Queen Victoria (screen credit includes "God Bless her!"); Burl Ives—Phineas T. Barnum; Troy Donahue—Gaylord Sullivan; Jimmy Clitheroe—General Tom Thumb;

Appendix: Select Filmography

Terry-Thomas—Captain Sir Harry Washington Smythe

Phineas Barnum builds a giant cannon designed to fire a people filled projectile to the moon. Queen Victoria's enthusiasm for scientific progress leads her to witness the rocket launch.

This film was originally released in UK as *Jules Verne's Rocket to the Moon*. The US title was changed to *Those Fantastic Flying Fools* to capitalize on the successful 1965 film *Those Magnificent Men in Their Flying Machines*.

The Lady with a Lamp (1951). Herbert Wilcox Productions (UK). Director: Herbert Wilcox. Writers: Reginald Berkeley (play), Warren Chetham Strode. 110 min. www.imdb.com/title/tt0043724/?ref_=fn_al_tt_1. Accessed 10 February 2018.

Principal cast: Helena Pickard—Queen Victoria; Anna Neagle—Florence Nightingale; Michael Wilding—Sidney Herbert; Felix Aylmer—Lord Palmerston; Arthur Young—W.E. Gladstone; Gordon Jackson—Dr. Anson; Peter Graves—Prince Albert

Based on a play by Reginald Berkeley, this biopic follows Florence Nightingale and her nursing in the Crimean War. She gains a reputation for being devoted to the care of wounded soldiers and for pioneering higher standards for hospital sanitation. Queen Victoria receives Nightingale and backs her request for improvements to troop living conditions in India.

Let's Make Up aka Lilacs in the Spring! (1954). Herbert Wilcox Productions (UK). Director: Herbert Wilcox. Writers: Robert Nesbitt, Harold Purcell. 72 min. www.imdb.com/title/tt0048294/?ref_=nv_sr_4. Accessed 30 March 2018.

Principal cast: Anna Neagle—Carole Beaumont / Lillian Grey / Nell Gwynn / Queen Victoria; Errol Flynn—John 'Beau' Beaumont; David Farrar—Charles King / King Charles II; Peter Graves—Albert Gutman / Prince Albert

A young actress tries to decide between two suitors. Injured in an air raid, she has several dreams, including seeing herself as young Queen Victoria with Prince Albert at Windsor Castle.

This film is also notable for an aging Errol Flynn (playing Neagle's father) in a singing number, done in his own voice.

The Little Princess (1939). Twentieth Century-Fox (USA). Directors: Walter Lang, William A. Seiter (uncredited). Writers: Ethel Hill (screenplay), Walter Ferris (screenplay), Frances Hodgson Burnett (novel). 93 min. www.imdb.com/title/tt0031580/?ref_=nv_sr_3. Accessed 10 February 2018.

Principal cast: Beryl Mercer—Queen Victoria; Shirley Temple—Sara Crewe; Richard Greene—Geoffrey Hamilton; Anita Louise—Rose; Ian Hunter—Capt. Crewe; Cesar Romero—Ram Dass; Arthur Treacher—Bertie Minchin; Mary Nash—Amanda Minchin

After Sara's father goes off to fight in the Second Boer War, she is mistreated at Miss Minchin's School for Girls. Hearing that her father is in hospital, Sara sneaks into the facility and encounters Queen Victoria, who gives her permission to search for her father. After some setbacks, Sara finds her father and helps him stand as Queen Victoria departs.

Marigold (1938). Associated British Picture Corporation (UK). Director: Thomas Bentley. Writers: Charles Garvice (play), Dudley Leslie, Lizzie Allen Harker (play), F.R. Pryor. Unknown length. www.imdb.com/title/tt0160514/?ref_=ttfc_fc_tt. Accessed 26 February 2018.

Principal cast: Pamela Stanley—Queen Victoria; Sophie Steward—Marigold Sellar; Patrick Barr—Lt. Archie Forsyth; Nicholas Hannen—Major Sellar

A young girl runs away from home to see Queen Victoria in Edinburgh and discovers that her mother was an actress.

Melba (1953). Horizon Pictures. Director: Lewis Milestone. Writer: Harry Kurnitz. 112 min. www.imdb.com/title/tt0046062/?ref_=fn_al_tt_1. Accessed 19 February 2018.

Principal cast: Sybil Thorndike—Queen Victoria; Patrice Munsel—Nellie Melba; Robert Morley—Oscar Hammerstein I

This biopic follows the career of soprano Nellie Melba, including a meeting with Queen Victoria.

Mr. Turner (2014). Amusement Park Films, BFI (UK). Director: Mike Leigh. Writer: Mike Leigh. 150 min. www.imdb.com/title/tt2473794/?ref_=ttfc_fc_tt. Accessed 29 March 2017.

Principal cast: Sinead Matthews—

Queen Victoria; Timothy Small—J.M.W. Turner; Tom Wlaschiha—Prince Albert

This film covers the last quarter century of British painter J.M.W. Turner's life. Young Queen Victoria sneers at Turner's later paintings.

Mrs Brown (1997). BBC Scotland (UK). Ecosse Films, Irish Screen, WGBH. Director: John Madden. Writer: Jeremy Brock. 101 min. www.imdb.com/title/tt0119280/?ref_=nv_sr_2. Accessed 14 February 2018.

Principal cast: Judi Dench—Queen Victoria; Billy Connolly—John Brown; Geoffrey Palmer—Henry Ponsonby; Antony Sher—Disraeli; Richard Pasco—Dr. Jenner; David Westhead—Bertie, Prince of Wales

The relationship between widowed Queen Victoria and her Scottish servant John Brown causes a scandal at court.

The Mudlark (1950). Twentieth-Century Fox (USA). Director: Jean Negulesco. Writers: Nunnally Johnson (screenplay), Theodore Bonnet (based on the novel by). 99 min. www.imdb.com/title/tt0042757/?ref_=nv_sr_1. Accessed 14 February 2018.

Principal cast: Irene Dunne—Queen Victoria; Alec Guinness—Benjamin Disraeli; Andrew Ray—Wheeler, the mudlark; Finlay Currie—John Brown; Ronan O'Casey—Slattery

Set in 1875, a mudlark (street child who scavenges on the banks of the Thames) wants to see Queen Victoria and slips into Windsor Castle. Disraeli and the mudlark persuade the Queen to end her long seclusion and return to public life.

The *Mudlark* had different credits in the American and British releases. Alec Guinness' contract stipulated co-star billing in the UK, so in the English print the names of Dunne and Guinness appear before the title. In the US print, Guinness comes after the title.

Dunne's makeup sessions to transform her into Queen Victoria were featured in *Life Magazine* on 11 September 1950. books.google.com/books?id=9U0EAAAAMBAJ&q=mudlark#v=snippet&q=mudlark&f=false. Accessed 7 January 2019.

Mystery of the Wax Museum (1933). Warner Bros. (USA). Director: Michael Curtiz. Writers: Don Mullaly, Carl Erickson, Charles Belden (from the story by). 77 min. www.imdb.com/title/tt0024368/?ref_=ttfc_fc_tt. Accessed 29 March 2018.

Principal cast: Margaret Mann—Wax figure of Queen Victoria (uncredited); Lionel Atwill—Ivan Igor; Fay Wray—Charlotte Duncan; Glenda Farrell—Florence Dempsey

A reporter's investigation of the disappearances of people leads to a wax museum. Several of the "wax" figures, including Queen Victoria, are actually live actors. In the scene where Victoria is most clearly shown, the actress, Margaret Mann, blinks once.

The Opium War aka *Yapian zhanzheng* (1997). Emei Film Studio, Jin Xie—Heng Tong Film and TV Company (China). Director: Jin Xie. Writers: Ann Hui, Mai Tianshu, Ni Zhen, Sujin Zhu, Fuxian Zong. 153 min. www.imdb.com/title/tt0120538/?ref_=fn_al_tt_1. Accessed 10 February 2018.

Principal cast: Debra Beaumont—Queen Victoria; Guoan Bao—Lin Zexu; Rob Freeman—Hill; Emma Griffiths Malin—Mary Denton; Jiang Hua—Guan Tianpei; Philip Jackson—Captain White; Bob Peck—Denton; Simon Williams—Captain Charles Elliot; Gao Yuan—Rong'er; James Innes-Smith—Prince Albert; Benjamin Whitrow—Lord Palmerston; Corin Redgrave—Lord Melbourne

This Chinese historical epic depicts the First Opium War (1839–1842) between the Qing Empire of China and the British Empire. After the Chinese ban opium and destroy 20,000 boxes of opium, England declares war, with Queen Victoria's concurrence. The British navy defeats the Chinese, and in the Treaty of Nanking, Britain gets Hong Kong as a colony.

Pearls of the Crown aka *Les perles de la couronne* (1937). Cinéas (France). Director: Sacha Guitry. Writers: Sacha Guitry, Christian-Jaque. 105 min. www.imdb.com/title/tt0029394/?ref_=nv_sr_1. Accessed 19 February 2018.

Principal cast: Yvette Pienne—Queen Marie Tudor / Queen Elizabeth I / Queen Victoria; Jacqueline Delubac—Françoise Martin / Marie Stuart / Joséphine de Beauharnais; Sacha Guitry—Jean Martin / François Ier / Barras / Napoléon III; Barbara Shaw—Anne Boleyn

This film tells the story of seven matched

pearls, four of which ended up in the British Crown. The timeline covers from 1587 to 1937.

The Pirates! Band of Misfits aka ***The Pirates! In an Adventure with Scientists!*** (2012). Aardman Animations (UK). Directors: Peter Lord, Jeff Newitt. Writer: Gideon Defoe. 88 min. www.imdb.com/title/tt1430626/?ref_=fn_tt_tt_1. Accessed 10 December 2018.
Principal cast: Imelda Staunton—Queen Victoria (voice); Hugh Grant—The Pirate Captain (voice); Martin Freeman—The Pirate with a Scarf (voice); David Tennant—Charles Darwin (voice); Brian Blessed—The Pirate King (voice)

Pirates capture Charles Darwin, who has a crush on Queen Victoria. To impress her, he stages a show with the pirates' pet bird. Victoria steals the bird and takes it to her dining club where the members eat rare animals. The Pirate Captain defeats the Queen rescues Polly the pet bird, and leaves the Queen to the mercy of several rare animals escaped from the dining club.

The Prime Minister (1941). Warner Brothers–First National Productions (UK). Director: Thorold Dickinson. Writers: Michael Hogan, Brock Williams. 94 min. (US), 109 min (UK). www.imdb.com/title/tt0034065/?ref_=ttspec_spec_tt. Accessed 11 February 2018.
Principal cast: Fay Compton—Queen Victoria; John Gielgud—Benjamin Disraeli; Diana Wynyard—Mary Disraeli; Lyn Harding—Bismarck; Pamela Standish—young Princess Victoria

This biopic of Benjamin Disraeli covers his rise to become the confidante of Queen Victoria, the purchase of shares in the Suez Canal, and Disraeli's attendance at the 1878 Congress of Berlin.

The Private Life of Sherlock Holmes (1970). Mirisch Films, Sir Nigel Films, Phalanx Productions (USA). Director: Billy Wilder. Writers: Billy Wilder, I.A.L. Diamond, Arthur Conan Doyle (characters). 125 min. www.imdb.com/title/tt0066249/?ref_=nv_sr_2. Accessed 27 February 2018.
Principal cast: Mollie Maureen—Queen Victoria; Robert Stephens—Sherlock Holmes; Colin Blakely—Dr. Watson; Geneviève Page—Gabrielle Valladon; Christopher Lee—Mycroft Holmes; Irene Handl—Mrs. Hudson

Sherlock's search for a woman's missing husband leads to midgets, monks, covert naval experiments for a pre–World War I submarine, a Scottish castle, the Loch Ness monster, and Queen Victoria.

Queen Victoria (1942). Imperator Film Productions (UK). Director: Herbert Wilcox. 84 mins. www.bfi.org.uk/films-tv-people/4ce2b75e21b16. Accessed 26 April 2018.

In 1942, Wilcox "released an edited compilation of both films [*Victoria the Great* and *Sixty Glorious Years*] under the title *Queen Victoria*" (Chapman 64). This compilation film covers Victoria's accession in 1837 to her death in 1901.

See entries for *Victoria the Great* and *Sixty Glorious Years* for more details.

Shanghai Knights (2003). Birnbaum / Barber Productions, Jackie Chan Films Ltd, All Knight Productions. (USA). Director: David Dobkin. Writers: Alfred Gough, Miles Millar. 114 min. www.imdb.com/title/tt0300471/?ref_=nv_sr_2. Accessed 10 February 2018.
Principal cast: Gemma Jones—Queen Victoria; Jackie Chan—Chon Wang; Owen Wilson—Roy O'Bannon; Aidan Gillen—Rathbone; Fann Wong—Chon Lin; Oliver Cotton—Jack the Ripper

When a Chinese Boxer rebel murders Chon Wang's estranged father and escapes to England, Wang and Roy make their way to London with revenge on their minds. Wang's sister, Lin, has the same idea and uncovers a worldwide conspiracy to murder Queen Victoria and the royal family. Wang and Roy foil the assassination attempt and receive knighthoods.

This film is notable for the image of Jackie Chan dangling from the clock arm of Big Ben, an homage to Harold Lloyd's *Safety Last* (1923).

Sixty Glorious Years aka ***Queen of Destiny*** (1938). Herbert Wilcox Productions (UK). Director: Herbert Wilcox. Writers: Miles Malleson, Robert Vansittart, Charles de Grandcourt. 95 min. www.imdb.com/title/tt0206302/?ref_=nv_sr_1. Accessed 10 February 2018.
Principal cast: Anna Neagle—Queen

Victoria; Anton Walbrook—Prince Albert; C. Aubrey Smith—Duke of Wellington; Charles Carson—Sir Robert Peel; Felix Aylmer—Lord Palmerston; Gordon McLeod—John Brown; Malcolm Keen—William E. Gladstone; Derrick De Marney—Benjamin Disraeli; Pamela Standish—Princess Royal; Laidman Browne—General Gordon; Olaf Olsen—Prince Frederick

This sequel to *Victoria the Great* (1937) covers Victoria's marriage, the birth of her first daughter, Albert's efforts to repeal the Corn Laws, the Great Exhibition of 1851, accusations against Albert as a traitor, the Crimean War, Albert's death, Victoria's long withdrawal from public life, the purchase of the Suez Canal, the death of General Gordon at the fall of Khartoum, the later victory in the Sudan, the Diamond Jubilee, and Victoria's death.

Content from this film was included in the 1942 *Queen Victoria*, which was Wilcox's compilation of *Victoria the Great* and *Sixty Glorious Years*.

Souls at Sea (1937). Paramount Pictures (USA). Director: Henry Hathaway. Writers: Grover Jones, Dave Van Every, Ted Lesser (based on a story by). 92 min. www.imdb.com/title/tt0029593/?ref_=fn_al_tt_1. Accessed 6 February 2019.

Principal cast: Viva Tattersall—Queen Victoria (uncredited, not in final cut); Gary Cooper—Michael "Nuggin" Taylor; George Raft—Powdah; Frances Dee—Margaret Tarryton; Virginia Weidler—Tina

The film presents the story of a sea tragedy and of abolitionists who try to stop the slave trade in 1842.

According to John Howard Reid, "before *Souls at Sea* was released in September of 1937, it had undergone many major cuts, including Queen Victoria's court … and several other sequences" (Reid 83).

The Story of Alexander Graham Bell (1939). Twentieth Century–Fox (USA). Director: Irving Cummings. Writers: Ray Harris, Lamar Trotti, Boris Ingster (uncredited), Milton Sperling (uncredited). 98 min. www.imdb.com/title/tt0031981/?ref_=ttfc_fc_tt. Accessed 29 March 2018.

Principal cast: Beryl Mercer—Queen Victoria; Don Ameche—Alexander Graham Bell; Loretta Young—Mrs. Mabel Hubbard Bell; Henry Fonda—Thomas Watson

In this story of Alexander Graham Bell's invention of the telephone, Queen Victoria tries out the new invention.

Stories from a Flying Trunk aka ***Tales from a Flying Trunk*** (1979). Sands Films (UK). Director: Christine Edzard. Writers: Christine Edzard, Hans Christian Andersen (stories). 88 min. www.imdb.com/title/tt0253761/?ref_=nv_sr_1. Accessed 19 February 2018.

Principal cast: John Dalby—Queen Victoria; Murray Melvin—Hans Christian Andersen; Ann Firbank—Mother; Tasneem Maqsood—Little Match Girl; John Tordoff—Tramp

In this stop-motion and live action film, a little matchstick girl wanders the streets of London searching for Queen Victoria and finds a living statue of the Queen. It is based on an 1839 story by Hans Christian Andersen.

Uncle Kruger aka ***Ohm Kruger*** (1941). Tobis Filmkunst (Germany). Directors: Hans Steinhoff, Karl Anton (uncredited), Herbert Maisch (uncredited). Writers: Harald Bratt, Kurt Heuser, Arnold Krieger (novel). 135 min (Germany), 124 min (USA). www.imdb.com/title/tt0033973/?ref_=fn_al_tt_1. Accessed 10 February 2018.

Principal cast: Hedwig Wangel—Queen Victoria; Emil Jannings—Ohm Krüger; Lucie Höflich—Sanna Krüger; Werner Hinz—Jan Krüger; Ernst Schröder—Adrian Krüger; Elisabeth Flickenschildt—Frau Kock; Gisela Uhlen—Petra Krüger; Ferdinand Marian—Cecil Rhodes; Gustaf Gründgens—Chamberlain; Alfred Bernau—Prince of Wales

This biopic of Paul Krüger, the Boer guerilla fighter turned statesman and first president of South Africa, is one of the most notorious of Nazi Germany's anti-British propaganda films. Queen Victoria is presented in a highly negative light.

For his performance as Paul Krüger, President of the Transvaal Free State, Emil Jannings was presented by Josef Goebbels with the "Ring of Honour of the German Cinema."

Van Helsing: The London Assignment (2004 video release). Universal Cartoon Studios (USA), Universal Home Video (USA), Universal Pictures (USA). Director: Sharon

Appendix: Select Filmography

Bridgeman. Writers: Garfield Reeves-Stevens, Judith Reeves-Stevens. 30 min. www.imdb.com/title/tt0406310/?ref_=nv_sr_5. Accessed 14 February 2018.
 Principal cast: Tress MacNeille—Queen Victoria (voice); Hugh Jackman—Gabriel Van Helsing (voice); Robbie Coltrane—Mr. Hyde (voice); Dwight Schultz—Dr. Jekyll (voice); Tara Strong—young Victoria (voice)
 In this animated prequel to the *Van Helsing* movie, Dr. Jekyll is in love with Queen Victoria. He turns her into a young woman for one night and kidnaps her. Monster-hunter Van Helsing rescues Victoria, who returns to her old self at day break.

Victoria & Abdul (2017). BBC Films (UK), Cross Street Films, Perfect World Pictures, Working Title Films, Isobel Griffith Ltd (orchestra contractor). Director: Stephen Frears. Writers: Lee Hall (screenplay), Shrabani Basu (book). 111 min. www.imdb.com/title/tt5816682/?ref_=nv_sr_2. Accessed 14 February 2018.
 Principal cast: Judi Dench—Queen Victoria; Ali Fazal—Abdul Karim; Tim Pigott-Smith—Sir Henry Ponsonby; Eddie Izzard—Bertie, Prince of Wales; Adeel Akhtar—Mohammed; Michael Gambon—Lord Salisbury; Paul Higgins—Dr. Reid; Olivia Williams—Lady Churchill; Fenella Woolgar—Harriet Phipps
 This film details the friendship between Queen Victoria and Indian clerk Abdul Karim and the British court's negative reaction to their relationship.

Victoria in Dover aka *Girlhood of a Queen* aka *Mädchenjahre einer Königen* (1936). Klagemann-Film GmbH (Germany). Unknown length. Director: Erich Engel Writers: Ernst Marischka, Geza Silberer under the pen name Sil-Vara (play). 96 min. www.imdb.com/title/tt0028016/?ref_=nm_flmg_act_15. Accessed 26 February 2018.
 Principal cast: Jenny Jugo—Queen Victoria; Friedrich Benfer—Prince Albert; Olga Limburg—Duchess of Kent; Renée Stobrawa—Baroness Lehzen; Gustav Waldau—Professor Lenkmann; Paul Henckels—King Leopold; Otto Tressler—Lord Melbourne
 After Lord Melbourne arranges a marriage with her cousin, young Queen Victoria leaves London to spend some time in Kent. She meets and falls in love with a young German, unaware that he is her intended husband Albert.

Victoria in Dover aka *The Story of Vickie* aka *Mädchenjahre einer Königen* (1954). Erma-Film, Sie Verling (Austria). Director: Ernst Marischka. Writers: Ernst Marischka (screenplay), Sil Vara (play). 108 min. www.imdb.com/title/tt0047259/?ref_=fn_tt_tt_1. Accessed 26 February 2018.
 Principal cast: Romy Schneider—Princess Victoria / Queen Victoria; Adrian Hoven—Prince Albert; Magda Schneider—Baroness Lehzen; Karl Ludwig Diehl—Lord Melbourne; Cristl Mardayn—Duchess of Kent; Paul Höbiger—Prof. Landmann; Rudolf Vogel—George, a lackey; Fred Liewehr—King Leopold of the Belgians; Stefan Skodler—Sir John Conroy
 After Lord Melbourne arranges a marriage with her cousin, young Queen Victoria leaves London to spend some time in Paris but is delayed in Dover due to a storm. She meets and falls in love with a young German, unaware that he is her intended husband Albert.
 This is a remake of the 1936 film *Mädchenjahre einer Königen*.

Victoria the Great (1937). Herbert Wilcox Productions (UK). Director: Herbert Wilcox Writers: Miles Malleson, Charles de Grandcourt, Laurence Housman (play, uncredited). 112 min. www.imdb.com/title/tt0029734/?ref_=nv_sr_1. Accessed 10 February 2018.
 Principal cast: Anna Neagle—Queen Victoria; Anton Walbrook—Prince Albert; Walter Rilla—Prince Ernest; H.B. Warner—Lord Melbourne; Mary Morris—Duchess of Kent; James Dale—Duke of Wellington; Felix Aylmer—Lord Palmerston; Charles Carson—Sir Robert Peel; Gordon McLeod—John Brown; Greta Schröder—Baroness Lehzen; Hugh Miller—older Disraeli; Derrick De Marney—young Disraeli
 This biopic covers Victoria's accession to the throne, her marriage to Albert, the Chartist movement, the repeal of the Corn Laws, the Trent affair, Prince Albert's death, and the Diamond Jubilee in 1897.
 Content from this film was included in the 1942 *Queen Victoria*, which was Wilcox's compilation of *Victoria the Great* and *Sixty Glorious Years*.
 A recently completed restoration of this

film has recovered nine minutes including scenes with the Duchess of Kent, Wellington, Albert singing with brother Ernest and would-be assassin Edward Oxford (Stanborough np).

***Waltz War* aka *Walzerkrieg* aka *Waltz Time in Vienna*.** (1933). Universum Film (UFA) (Germany). Director: Ludwig Berger. Writers: Robert Liebmann, Hans Müller. 93 min. www.imdb.com/title/ tt0024749/?ref_=nv_sr_1. Accessed 11 February 2018.

Principal cast: Hanna Waag—Queen Victoria; Renate Müller—Katti Länner; Willy Fritsch—Pauker Gustl; Paul Höbiger—Joseph Länner; Anton Walbrook—Johann Strauss

This film presents the musical rivalry between Joseph Länner and Johann Strauss and their respective waltz orchestras during Queen Victoria's reign.

Queen Victoria's role is limited to inviting Strauss to play in England.

A French version was distributed as *Court Waltzes* aka *La guerre des valses* (1933).

The White Angel (1936). Warner Bros.-First National Pictures (USA). Director: William Dieterle. Writers: Mordaunt Shairp (screenplay), Henry Wadsworth Longfellow (poem). 92 min. www.imdb.com/ title/tt0028499/?ref_=nv_sr_2. Accessed 10 February 2018.

Principal cast: Fay Holden—Queen Victoria (uncredited); Kay Francis—Florence Nightingale; Ian Hunter—Reporter Fuller of the *London Times*; Donald Crisp—Dr. Hunt; Montagu Love—Mr. Bullock, Under Secretary of War

Florence Nightingale pursues nursing training in Germany and a nursing assignment in the Crimean War despite opposition from Dr. Hunt. Undersecretary of War Bullock tries to turn Queen Victoria against Florence, but the monarch approves of Florence and presents her with a brooch.

In the brooch award scene, only the Queen's hand is visible, giving the commemorative brooch over to an official who pins it on Nightingale. The film ends with a close-up of the Nightingale brooch.

The Wrong Box (1966). Salamander Film Productions (UK). Director: Bryan Forbes. Writers: Larry Belbart (screenplay), Burt Shevelove (screenplay), Robert Louis Stevenson (suggested by a novel by), Lloyd Osborne (suggested by a novel by). 105 min. www.imdb.com/title/tt0061204/?ref_=nv_ sr_1. Accessed 19 February 2018.

Principal cast: Avis Bunnage—Queen Victoria; Michael Caine—Michael Finsbury; John Mills—Masterman Finsbury; Ralph Richardson—Joseph Finsbury; Peter Sellers—Doctor Pratt; Peter Cook—Morris Finsbury; Dudley Moore—John Finsbury

In 1882, two brothers compete to outlive each other and win a tontine prize worth over a hundred thousand pounds. Queen Victoria appears in a scene where she accidentally decapitates one of the tontine beneficiaries during a knighting ceremony ("We are frightfully sorry, Sir Robert").

The Young Victoria (2009). GK Films (UK). Director: Jean-Marc Vallée. Writer: Julian Fellowes. 105 min. www.imdb.com/title/ tt0962736/?ref_=nv_sr_1. Accessed 14 February 2018.

Principal cast: Emily Blunt—Queen Victoria; Rupert Friend—Prince Albert; Paul Bettany—Lord Melbourne; Miranda Richardson—Duchess of Kent; Jim Broadbent—King William; Thomas Kretschmann—King Leopold; Mark Strong—Sir John Conroy; Harriet Walter—Queen Adelaide; Jeanette Hain—Baroness Lehzen; Michaela Brooks—Princess Victoria, age 11; Grace Smith—Princess Victoria, age 5

This biopic covers Victoria life from childhood to ascension, courtship, marriage to Albert, and the birth of her first child.

Zorro in the Court of England* aka *Zorro alla corte d'Inghilterra (1969). Romana Film (Italy). Director: Franco Montemurro. Writers: Arpad DeRiso, Franco Montemurro. 90 min. www.imdb.com/title/ tt0065247/?ref_=nm_ov_bio_lk2. Accessed 26 February 2018.

Principal cast: Barbara Carroll—Queen Victoria; Spiros Focás—Pedro Suarez / Zorro; Dada Gallotti—Rosanna Gonzales; Franco Ressel—Lord Percy Moore

Zorro fights against the tyrannical governor of Bermuda and travels to England to reveal the truth to Queen Victoria, who knights him after he defeats the corrupt politicians.

Appendix: Select Filmography 175

Television

This section includes made-for television movies, television series, or episodes in television shows that include Queen Victoria as a character. Titles are listed in alphabetical order. Italics indicate the titles of series or made-for television movies, and quotation marks indicate episodes within a television series.

Albert: The Power Behind Victoria (29 September 2018). Elephant House Studios (UK). Director: Paul Olding. Writer: Paul Olding. 120 min. www.imdb.com/title/tt9050312/?ref_=fn_tt_tt_7. Accessed 20 January 2019.
Principal cast: Olivia Hallinan—Queen Victoria; Gareth David-Lloyd—Prince Albert; Angela Bull—Baroness Lehzen; Paul Antony-Barber—Baron Stockmar; Jeremy Clyde—Lord Melbourne; Drew Cain—Sir Robert Peel; Alex Bartram—George Edward Anson; Samantha Bond—Narrator
This scripted docu-drama tells the story of how the 20-year-old 'Pauper Prince' rose from obscurity in Germany to be one of the most powerful men in the world as a driving force behind the industrial revolution and a campaigner for the welfare of the working class. It draws heavily from private letters, historical accounts and analysis by historians.

"Annie Oakley" (24 December 1985), Episode 1.9 of *Tall Tales & Legends* (1985–1988). Showtime (USA). Director: Michael Lindsay-Hogg. Writer: Pamela Pettler. Unknown length. www.imdb.com/title/tt0088728/?ref_=ttfc_fc_cl_i48. Accessed 31 January 2019.
Principal cast: Lu Leonard—Queen Victoria; Shelley Duvall—Host; Jamie Lee Curtis—Annie Oakley; Brian Dennehy—Buffalo Bill; Cliff De Young—Frank Butler
In this American folklore anthology series, this episode covers the story of Annie Oakley's career, including her presentation to Queen Victoria.

Around the World in 80 Days (1989). Avala Film, Harmony Gold, Rete Europa (Italy). Director: Buzz Kulik. Writers: John Gay (written for television), Jules Verne (novel). www.imdb.com/title/tt0096535/?ref_=nv_sr_4. Accessed 21 March 2018.

Principal cast: Anna Massey—Queen Victoria; Pierce Brosnan—Phileas Fogg; Eric Idle—Passepartout; Julia Nickson—Princess Aouda; Peter Ustinov—Detective Wilbur Fix; Lee Remick—Sarah Bernhardt

Episodes:
"Episode 1.1" (16 April 1989). 90 min. www.imdb.com/title/tt1792865/?ref_=tt_cl_i53. Accessed 21 March 2018. Fogg and Passepartout are delayed as the boat to France is waiting for Sarah Bernhardt.
"Episode 1.2" (17 April 1989). 90 min. www.imdb.com/title/tt1881197/?ref_=tt_ep_nx. Accessed 21 March 2018. Fogg encounters delays in Burma and Hong Kong and gains Princess Aouda as a companion.
"Episode 1.3" (18 April 1989). 90 min. www.imdb.com/title/tt1881198/?ref_=tt_ep_nx. Accessed 21 March 2018. Queen Victoria is informed of Fogg's help with Burmese-UK relations and that he is suspected of being a bank thief. She thinks it as a "great pity" that he has been lost at sea. Fogg reaches England and is arrested by Fix.

"Aunt Clara's Victoria Victory" (9 March 1967), Episode 3.26 of *Bewitched* (1964–1972). Screen Gems (USA). Director: William Asher. Writers: Robert Riley Crutcher, Sol Saks (created by). 25 min. www.imdb.com/title/tt0523057/?ref_=nm_flmg_act_26. Accessed 27 February 2018.
Principal cast: Jane Connell—Queen Victoria; Elizabeth Montgomery—Samantha Stephens; David White—Larry Tate; Marion Lorne—Aunt Clara
Aunt Clara bumbles a time-travel spell; as a result, Queen Victoria appears in Samantha's house. Victoria is dictatorial and expected to clash with the client who is coming to dinner to meet Samantha.

"Baby Blues" (3 January 1994), Episode 5.11 of *Northern Exposure* (1990–1995). Finnegan / Pinchuk Productions, Brand / Falsey Productions, Universal Television (USA). Director: Jim Charleston. Writers: Joshua Brand, John Falsey, Barbara Hall. 46 min. www.imdb.com/title/tt0662323/?ref_=ttfc_fc_tt. Accessed 31 January 2019.
Principal cast: Pamela Kosh—Queen Victoria
This comedy focuses on women about to

become mothers. The Queen Victoria character has a small role.

Black Butler aka ***Kuroshitsuji*** (2008–2010). A-1 Pictures, Aniplex, Mainichi Broadcasting System (Japan). Director: Toshiya Shinohara. Writers: Yana Toboso, Mari Okada, John Burgmeier, Bonny Clinkenbeard, Yuka Yamada, Hirouki Yoshino. www.imdb.com/title/tt1316554/?ref_=ttco_co_tt. Accessed 23 October 2018.

Principal cast: Queen Victoria, old—Sayuri Sadaoka (Japanese voice); Queen Victoria, old—Bridgett Dahl (English voice in Episode 24); Queen Victoria, young—Alexis Tipton (English voice); Queen Victoria—Ayako Kawasumi (Japanese voice); Daisuke Ono—Sebastian Michaelis (Japanese voice); J. Michael Tatum—Sebastian Michaelis (English voice); Maaya Sakamoto—Ciel Phantomhive (Japanese voice); Brina Palencia—Ciel Phantomhive (English voice); Gloria Ansell—Ciel Phantomhive (English voice)

A boy sells his soul to a demon in a quest to avenge his family's death. The demon takes the form of a butler who is required to protect his master Ciel Phantomhive.

Episodes:

"His Butler, Merrymaking" aka "Sono shitsuji, yuukyou" (13 November 2008), Episode 1.7. 24 min. www.imdb.com/title/tt1369985/?ref_=ttep_ep7. Accessed 6 February 2019. Queen Victoria is mentioned as commanding Ciel to investigate the village of Houldsworth, but she does not actually appear in this episode.

"His Butler, Supremely Talented" aka "Sono shitsuji, inou" (15 January 2009), Episode 1.14. 24 min. www.imdb.com/title/tt1369977/?ref_=ttep_ep1. Accessed 6 February 2019. Queen Victoria arrives at a curry contest.

"His Butler, Competing" aka "Sono shitsuji, kyousou" (22 January 2009), Episode 1.15. www.imdb.com/title/tt1369980/?ref_=ttep_ep2. Accessed 6 February 2019. 24 min. Queen Victoria judges a curry contest that includes the Demon butler and Prince Soma's royal servant.

"His Butler, Dissolution" aka "Sono shitsuji, kaishou" (12 March 2009), Episode 1.22. www.imdb.com/title/tt1369214/?ref_=ttep_ep9. Accessed 6 February 2019. 24 min. The Young Master's journey to Paris results in a showdown with a manic Queen, who commands her aide Ash Landers to kill Ciel.

"His Butler, Up in Flames" aka "Sono shitsuji, enjou" (19 March 2009), Episode 1.23. www.imdb.com/title/tt1369214/?ref_=ttep_ep9. Accessed 6 February 2019. 24 min. Ciel returns to find London aflame, his Phantomhive estate burned down, and a dead Queen Victoria.

"His Butler, Fluent" aka "Sono shitsuji, toutou" (26 March 2009), Episode 1.24. www.imdb.com/title/tt1369214/?ref_=ttep_ep9. Accessed 6 February 2019. 24 min. A false Queen Victoria appears and urges London to rebuild after the fire.

Black Butler: Book of Circus aka ***Kuroshitsuji: Book of Circus*** (2014). A-1 Pictures (Japan). Director: Noriyuki Abe. Writers: Yana Toboso, Yuka Miyata, Hiroyuki Yoshino, Ichiro Okouchi. www.imdb.com/title/tt3639888/?ref_=ttfc_fc_tt. Accessed 9 October 2018.

Principal cast: Hiromi Seta—Queen Victoria (Japanese voice); Julie Mayfield—Queen Victoria (English voice); Daisuke Ono—Sebastian Michaelis (Japanese voice); J. Michael Tatum—Sebastian Michaelis (English voice); Maaya Sakamoto—Ciel Phantomhive (Japanese voice); Brina Palencia—Ciel Phantomhive (English voice)

Ciel Phantomhive, Queen Victoria's watch dog, and his demon butler Sebastian Michaelis enter a travelling circus to search for abducted children and uncover sinister plots.

Episodes:

"His Butler, Taking the Stage" (18 July 2014), Episode 1.2. Unknown length. www.imdb.com/title/tt4897826/?ref_=ttfc_fc_tt. Accessed 6 February 2019. The Queen orders Ciel to investigate the Noah's Ark Circus and its possible role in abduction of children. The Queen Victoria character is mentioned occasionally in the remaining nine episodes, but does not actually appear.

Black Butler: Book of Murder (2014 OVA). A-1 Pictures (Japan). Director: Noriyuki Abe,

Ian Sinclair. Writer: Yana Toboso. 116 min. www.imdb.com/title/tt5714216/?ref_=fn_al_tt_5. Accessed 6 February 2019.
Principal cast: Non-speaking role—Queen Victoria; Daisuke Onon—Sebastian Michaelis (voice); J. Michael Tatum—Sebastian Michaelis (English voice); Maaya Sakamoto—Ciel Phantomhive (voice); Brina Palencia—Ciel Phantomhive (English voice)

The Queen decides to test Ciel's loyalty and orders the Phantomhive family to host a banquet for German banker Siemens, who is murdered. The Queen communicates to Ciel through two emissary butlers and attempts to frame Ciel for the murder.

Blackadder (1982–89). BBC (UK). Writers: Richard Curtis, Rowan Atkinson.

Episodes:

Blackadder's Christmas Carol (23 December 1988). BBC (UK). Director: Richard Boden. Writers: Richard Curtis, Ben Elton. 43 min. www.imdb.com/title/tt0094754/?ref_=nv_sr_1. Accessed 14 March 2018. **Principal cast:** Miriam Margolyes—Queen Victoria; Rowan Atkinson—Blackadder; Tony Robinson—Baldrick; Miranda Richardson—Queen Elizabeth I / Asphyxia XIX; Robbie Coltrane—Spirit of Christmas; Jim Broadbent—Prince Albert. Queen Victoria and Prince Albert visit Blackadder and attempt to give him an award.

"General Hospital" (26 October 1989), Episode 1.5 of *Blackadder Goes Forth* (1989). BBC (UK). Director: Richard Boden. Writers: Richard Curtis, Ben Elton. 28 min. www.imdb.com/title/tt0526711/?ref_=ttep_ep5. Accessed 23 March 2018. **Principal cast:** Rowan Atkinson—Captain Edmund Blackadder; Tony Robinson—Private Baldrick; Tim McInnery—Captain Kevin Darling. Blackadder confronts Darling thinking he is a German spy. Darling claims he is "as British as Queen Victoria." Blackadder replies "So your father's German, you're half German and you married a German?"

"Buffalo Bill and Annie Play the Palace" (9 January 1983), Episode 1.12 of *Voyagers!* (1982–1983). NBC (USA). Director: Alan J. Levi. Writers: James D. Parriott (creator), Jill Donner (as Jill Sherman), Nick Thiel. 49 min. www.imdb.com/title/tt0742356/?ref_=ttfc_fc_cl_i141. Accessed 14 March 2018.
Principal cast: Lurene Tuttle—Queen Victoria; Jon-Erik Hexum—Phineas Bogg; Meeno Peluce—Jeffrey Jones; Diana Cary (as Diane Civita)—Annie Oakley; Robert Donner—Buffalo Bill Cody; Robin Eisenman—Princess Victoria

Time travelers Phineas Bogg and Jeffrey Jones correct errors in world history, in this episode the betrothal of Queen Victoria's granddaughter to a Russia duke. During a performance of Annie Oakley and Buffalo Bill's Wild West show, Queen Victoria uncovers a Russian plot and cancels the marriage alliance.

"Christmas with Morecambe & Wise" aka **"1972 Christmas Show"** (25 December 1972), Episode 7.0 of *The Morecambe & Wise Show* (1968–1977). BBC (UK). Director: Ed Stuart. Writers: Barry Cryer, John Junkin. 67 min. www.imdb.com/title/tt1186351/?ref_=ttep_ep1. Accessed 31 January 2019.
Principal cast: Glenda Jackson—Queen Victoria

In this comedy skit show, Ernie Wise presents his play called "Victoria and Albert."

"The Consort" (27 January 1957), Episode 2.19 of *Telephone Time* (1956–1958). Hal Roach Studios (USA). Director: Owen Crump. Writer: David Evans. 30 min. www.imdb.com/title/tt0719278/?ref_=fn_al_tt_3. Accessed 27 February 2018. **Principal cast:** Judi Meredith (as Judi Boutin)—Queen Victoria; Robert Vaughn—Prince Albert

This episode tells the story of Prince Albert and Queen Victoria.

A Curse on the House of Windsor (26 April 1994). The Drama House (UK). Director: David Giles. 39 min. collections-search.bfi.org.uk/web/Details/ChoiceFilmWorks/150411989. Accessed 31 March 2018.
Principal cast: Miriam Margolyes—Queen Victoria; Michael Kilgarriff—John Brown

Queen Victoria returns to 1992 to discover the restoration work on the Albert Memorial at Kensington. She interviews a series of art experts, politicians, historians, biographers, and journalists, only to discover that the monarchy is under threat.

During a telephone call with Queen Eliz-

abeth II, Victoria consoles her great-great granddaughter.
Not in IMDB.

"Daisy" (2 January 1973), Episode 1.7 of *The Edwardians* (1972–73). BBC (UK). Director: James Cellan Jones. Writer: David Turner. 50 min. www.imdb.com/title/tt1265366/?ref_=ttfc_fc_cl_i30. Accessed 8 March 2018.

Principal cast: Mollie Maureen—Queen Victoria; Virginia McKenna—Daisy; Thorley Walters—King Edward VII; Vernon Dobtcheff—Disraeli

Daisy, the mistress of King Edward VII, dictates her memoirs to a writer. Queen Victoria disapproves of her son's philandering.

Queen Victoria does not appear in the other episodes of this series.

Disraeli: Portrait of a Romantic (1978 UK, 1980 USA). Associated Television (ATV) (UK). Director: Claude Whatham. Writer: David Butler. www.imdb.com/title/tt0078601/?ref_=kw_li_tt. Accessed 13 February 2018.

Principal cast: Rosemary Leach—Queen Victoria; Ian McShane—Benjamin Disraeli; Mary Peach—Mary Anne Disraeli; Brett Usher—Edward Lytton Bulwer; John Carlisle—W.E. Gladstone; Brewster Mason—Chancellor Bismarck; John Gregg—Lord Salisbury; Frances Bennett—Lady Chesterfield; Anthony Brown—Sir Robert Peel; Jeremy Longhurst—Prince Albert

Episodes:

"Dizzy" (1 June 1980), Episode 1.1. 60 min. www.imdb.com/title/tt1259272/?ref_=ttep_ep1. Accessed 6 February 2019. Disraeli writes novels, pursues affairs with women, and attempts to get elected to Parliament. Queen Victoria disapproves.

"Mary Anne" (8 June 1980), Episode 1.2. 60 min. www.imdb.com/title/tt1259273/?ref_=ttep_ep2. Accessed 6 February 2019. Disraeli marries Mary Anne and pursues a political career. Queen Victoria continues her cool attitude towards him.

"The Great Game 1858–1872" (15 June 1980), Episode 1.3. 60 min. www.imdb.com/title/tt1259275/?ref_=ttep_ep3. Accessed 6 February 2019. Disraeli rises to power and improves his relationship with Queen Victoria.

"The Chief 1872–1881" (22 June 1980), Episode 1.4. 60 min. www.imdb.com/title/tt1259274/?ref_=ttep_ep4. Accessed 6 February 2019. Disraeli becomes Prime Minister and deals with the Suez Canal and the Balkans. Queen Victoria mourns his death.

"Dizzy" (20 March 1983), Episode 1.6 of *Number 10* (1983). Yorkshire Television (YTV) (UK). Director: David Cunliffe, John Glenister, Alvin Rakoff, David Reynolds Writer: Terence Feely. 52 min. www.imdb.com/title/tt0897946/?ref_=ttep_ep6. Accessed 7 February 2019.

Principal cast: Zena Walker—Queen Victoria; Richard Pasco—Benjamin Disraeli; Sheridan Fitzgerald—Princess Beatrice

This episode covers the political and personal life of Disraeli.

East Lynne (21 December 1976). BBC Manchester (UK). Directors: Barney Colehan as Barney Coleman, Phillip Grout. Writers: Patrick Bond (adaptation), Mrs. Henry Wood (novel). 60 min. www.imdb.com/title/tt0272378/?ref_=fn_tt_tt_7. Accessed 12 March 2018.

Principal cast: Shirley Steedman—Queen Victoria; Polly James—Lady Isabel Vane; Philip Lowrie—Archibald Carlyle; Annette Crosbie—Cornelia Carlyle

This television movie is based on the 1861 sensation novel by Ellen Wood, broadcast from the City Varieties Theatre in Leeds. Queen Victoria and a Victorian-clad audience appear in a theater frame around a play based on the Wood novel.

The play's plot revolves around a run-away wife, who returns in disguise to become the governess in her ex-husband's house, in order to be near her children.

Edward the Seventh aka ***Edward the King*** (1975). ATV (UK). Director: John Gorrie. Writers: David Butler, John Gorrie, Philip Magnus. www.imdb.com/title/tt0072925/?ref_=fn_al_tt_1. Accessed 7 February 2019.

Principal cast: Annette Crosbie—Queen Victoria; Timothy West—Prince of Wales/King Edward; Helen Ryan—Princess Alexandra; Felicity Kendal—Princess Vicky; Michael Hordern—W.E. Gladstone; John

Gielgud—Benjamin Disraeli; Francesca Annis—Lillie Langtry; William Dysart—John Brown; Joseph O'Connor—Viscount Melbourne; Robert Hardy—Prince Albert

Life of Edward VII, his years as a playboy as well as his modernizations and reforms during his reign. Queen Victoria appears in 10 of the 13 episodes.

Episodes:

"The Boy" (1 April 1975), Episode 1.1. 50 min. www.imdb.com/title/tt1191376/?ref_=ttep_ep1. Accessed 7 February 2019. Prince Albert Edward is born.

"An Experiment in Education (8 April 1975), Episode 1.2. 50 min. www.imdb.com/title/tt1191375/?ref_=ttep_ep2. Accessed 7 February 2019. Bertie rebels against the strict discipline and education dictated by his father. Vicky's marriage absorbs both parents' time.

"The New World" (15 April 1975), Episode 1.3. 50 min. www.imdb.com/title/tt1191377/?ref_=ttep_ep3. Accessed 7 February 2019. Bertie returns from a tour of America, goes to Ireland for military training, and has an affair with a music hall performer.

"Alix" (22 April 1975), Episode 1.4. 50 min. www.imdb.com/title/tt1191374/?ref_=ttep_ep4. Accessed 7 February 2019. Bertie continues his affair, while his parents arrange a marriage with Princess of Alexandra of Denmark. After learning of Bertie's affair, Prince Albert falls ill and dies.

"A Hundred Thousand Welcomes" (29 April 1975), Episode 1.5. 50 min. www.imdb.com/title/tt1193717/?ref_=ttep_ep5. Accessed 7 February 2019. While in mourning, the Queen allows Bertie to perform public duties but refuses to involve him in political decisions. Bertie and Alix are married.

"The Invisible Queen" (6 May 1975), Episode 1.6. 50 min. www.imdb.com/title/tt1203664/?ref_=ttep_ep6. Accessed 7 February 2019. Princess Alix refuses to meet the King of Prussia after Germany annexes parts of Denmark. Queen Victoria is still in seclusion. Bertie is forced to appear in court for a divorce case involving one of his mistresses. Later, Bertie falls ill with typhoid.

"Dearest Prince" (13 May 1975), Episode 1.7. 50 min. www.imdb.com/title/tt1216373/?ref_=ttep_ep7. Accessed 7 February 2019. Bertie goes on official trip to India without Alix, who is bitter about being left at home. Bertie is involved in a scandal involving Lord Aylesford's wife.

"The Royal Quadrille" (20 May 1975), Episode 1.8. 50 min. www.imdb.com/title/tt1225435/?ref_=ttep_ep8. Accessed 7 February 2019. Bertie visits Denmark and Prussia, where he and sister Vicky are concerned about Bismarck's influence over Vicky's son Prince Wilhelm. Refused permission for military service in Egypt, Bertie continues his affair with Lillie Langtry and also tours poor working-class districts.

"Scandal" (27 May 1975), Episode 1.9. 50 min. www.imdb.com/title/tt1232916/?ref_=ttep_ep9. Accessed 7 February 2019. Bertie is involved in multiple scandals involving Lady Brooke and a card cheat. His son Prince Eddy becomes engages but dies before the marriage takes place.

"The Years of Waiting" (3 June 1975), Episode 1.10. 50 min. www.imdb.com/title/tt1241821/?ref_=ttep_ep10. Accessed 7 February 2019. During the Boer War, Queen Victoria refuses to let Bertie have a political role. The Queen celebrates her Diamond Jubilee, and Bertie is the subject of an assassination attempt in Brussels. Queen Victoria dies in 1901, and Bertie becomes King Edward VII.

Queen Victoria does not appear in Episodes 1.11 "King at Last," 1.12 "The Peacemaker," and 1.13 "Good Old Teddy!"

"1854: The Dog" (28 September 1969), Episode 1.2 of drama series *The Flaxton Boys* (1969–1973). Yorkshire Television (YTV) (UK). Director: Robert D. Cardona. Writers: Don Houghton, Sid Waddell (originator). 30 min. www.imdb.com/title/tt0947245/?ref_=ttfc_fc_cl_i57. Accessed 8 March 2018.

Principal cast: Christine Ozanne—Queen Victoria; Gerry Cowan—Narrator; Peter Firth—Archie Weekes; David Smith—Jonathan Flaxton; Simon Taylor—Martin, the Deserter

In 1854, the Flaxton Hall boys meet Martin, a deserter, who effects a rescue in sight of Queen Victoria.

The Empress and the Munshi (6 November 1984). Central Independent Television

(UK). Director: Michael Hayes. Writer: Farrukh Dhondy www.bfi.org.uk/films-tv-people/4ce2b72563ded. Accessed 7 February 2019.

Principal cast: Zia Mohyeddin—Abdul Karim

This televised version of play by Farrukh Dhondy focuses on the relationship between Munshi Abdul Karim and Queen Victoria. Not in IMDB.

"Enemy of the Bane, Part 1" (1 December 2008), Episode 2.11 of *The Sarah Jane Adventures* (2007-2011). BBC Wales (UK). Director: Graeme Harper. Writers: Russell T. Davies (creator), Phil Ford. 28 min. www.imdb.com/title/tt1285085/?ref_=ttep_ep11. Accessed 7 February 2019.

Principal cast: Elisabeth Sladen—Sarah Jane Smith; Anjli Mohindra—Rani Chandra

In a reference to the "Tooth and Claw" episode of *Doctor Who*, Sarah Jane mentions Queen Victoria's awareness of aliens, to which Rani (echoing Rose Tyler) replies "I'll bet she wasn't amused."

"Episode 1.2" (8 May 1983) of *Alfresco* (1983-1984). Granada Television (UK). Director: Stuart Orme. Writers: Ben Elton, Stephen Fry, Hugh Laurie, Paul Shearer, Nicky Symons, Emma Thompson. 24 min. www.imdb.com/title/tt1144959/?ref_=tt_cl_i1. Accessed 14 March 2018.

Principal cast: Siobhan Redmond—Queen Victoria (and other characters); Hugh Laurie—Duke of Wellington (and other characters); Emma Thompson—Florence Nightingale (and other characters)

In this comic variety show episode, Florence Nightingale seeks permission to go to war and demonstrates her lamp to the Duke of Wellington (who sells boots). Florence arrives at the Crimea in 1854, goes though the wards to see unappreciative patients, and returns to Windsor Castle to meet Queen Victoria, who makes nonsensical replies to Florence's earnest pleas.

"The Eye of the Peacock" (19 December 1982), Episode 1.8 of *Young Sherlock: The Mystery of the Manor House* (1982). Granada Television (UK). Director: Nicholas Ferguson. Writer: Gerald Frow. 30 min. www.imdb.com/title/tt1400310/?ref_=ttfc_fc_cl_i23. Accessed 12 March 2018. en.wikipedia.org/wiki/Young_Sherlock:_The_Mystery_of_the_Manor_House. Accessed 12 March 2018.

Principal cast: Marina McConnell—Queen Victoria; Guy Henry—Sherlock Holmes

A priceless diamond will vanish unless teenage Sherlock Holmes can foil a conspiracy against Queen Victoria.

Fall of Eagles (1974). BBC (UK). Creator: John Elliot. www.imdb.com/title/tt0207885/?ref_=tt_ov_inf. Accessed 23 March 2018.

Drama series about the collapse of the Romanov, Hapsburg, and Hohenzollern dynasties.

Episodes:

"The English Princess" (22 March 1974), Episode 1.2. Director: David Cunliffe. Writers: John Elliot, Elizabeth Holford. 50 min. www.imdb.com/title/tt1269830/?ref_=ttep_ep2. Accessed 7 February 2019. **Principal cast:** Perlita Neilson—Queen Victoria; Curd Jürgens—Otto von Bismarck; Denis Lill—Prince Frederick William / Frederick III; Gemma Jones—Princess Vicky; Bertie—Mike Elles; Frank Thornton—Prince Albert. Princess Victoria of England, daughter of Queen Victoria and Prince Albert, marries Crown Prince Frederick William of Prussia. They later come into conflict with Otto von Bismarck.

"The Last Tsar" (12 April 1974), Episode 1.5. Director: Bill Hays. Writer: John Elliot. 50 min. www.imdb.com/title/tt1269832/?ref_=ttep_ep5. Accessed 7 February 2019. **Principal cast:** Mavis Edwards—Older Queen Victoria; Charles Kay—Nicholas II; Gayle Hunnicutt—Alexandra; Patrick Stewart—Lenin. Queen Victoria approves of the marriage between Tsarevich Nicholas of Russia and Princess Alexandra of Hesse-Darmstadt.

"Gordon of Khartoum" (18 January 1966), Episode 1.4 of *BBC Play of the Month* (1965-1983). BBC (UK). Director: Rudolph Cartier. Writers: David Benedictus (adaptation), Robin Maugham. 120 min. www.imdb.com/title/tt0060470/?ref_=fn_al_tt_1. Accessed 7 February 2019.

Principal cast: Gladys Spencer—Queen Victoria; Alan Badel—General Gordon;

Charles Carson—Gladstone. This now-lost episode gives the story of General Charles Gordon and his death at Khartoum in 1885, not to be confused with the 1966 film *Khartoum* staring Charlton Heston.

"**The Hand That Rocks the Cradle**" (12 April 1981), Episode 2.3 of *Cribb* (1980–1981). Granada Television (UK). Director: George Spenton-Foster. Writers: Peter Lovesey, Jacqueline Lovesey. 90 min. www.imdb.com/title/tt0550298/?ref_=ttfc_fc_cl_i43. Accessed 12 March 2018.
Principal cast: Jessica Spencer—Queen Victoria; Alan Dobie—Sergeant Cribb; David Waller—Inspector Jowett; Irene Richard—Princess Beatrice; Scott Fredericks—Prince Henry; Rosalie Crutchley—Mrs. Innocent; Sarah Neville—Jane Temple.

Princess Beatrice and Prince Henry disagree with the Queen over the appointment of a nursemaid for their baby. At the Prince's request, Cribb investigates and discovers that one of the candidates, young Miss Temple, is an anarchist. Queen Victoria approves of the other candidate, old Mrs. Innocent, particularly her use of Gregory Powder (an herbal laxative).

The Hands of a Murderer (16 May 1990). Green Pond Productions, Storke Enterprises, Yorkshire International Films (UK). Director: Stuart Orme. Writer: Charles Edward Pogue. 90 min. www.imdb.com/title/tt0099732/?ref_=ttco_co_tt. Accessed 21 March 2018.
Principal cast: Honora Burke—Queen Victoria; Edward Woodward—Sherlock Holmes; John Hillerman—Dr. John Watson; Anthony Andrews—Prof. James Moriarty; Peter Jeffrey—Mycroft Holmes

Moriarty steals state secrets and kidnaps Mycroft to force him to decode the message. Sherlock comes to the rescue to recover the state secrets and is presented to Queen Victoria, who is "his biggest fan."

Happy and Glorious (1952). BBC (UK). Director: Desmond Davis. Writers: Desmond Davis, Laurence Housman. www.imdb.com/title/tt0423665/?ref_=ttfc_fc_tt. Accessed 16 February 2018.
Principal cast: Renée Asherson—Queen Victoria; Michael Aldridge—Prince Albert; Laidman Browne—Lord Palmerston; Dorothea Alexander—Baroness Lehzen; Hilda Fenemore—Princess Beatrice; Wyndham Goldie—Baron Stockmar

This biopic series about Queen Victoria was aired live, without any recordings.

Episodes:

"1837" (13 September 1952), Episode 1.1. 30 min.
"1838–1841" (20 September 1952), Episode 1.2. 30 min.
"1842–1853" (27 September 1952), Episode 1.3. 30 min.
"1861–1862" (4 October 1952), Episode 1.4. 30 min.
"1875–1887" (11 October 1952), Episode 1.5. 30 min.
"1891–1900" (18 October 1952), Episode 1.6. 30 min.

Horrible Histories (2009–2019). Lion Television (UK). www.imdb.com/title/tt1400819/?ref_=nv_sr_1. Accessed 7 February 2019. See also horriblehistoriestv.wixsite.com/horriblehistoriestv. Accessed 7 February 2019.
Principal cast: Martha Howe-Douglas—various including Queen Victoria; Sarah Hadland—various including Queen Victoria; Jim Howick—various; Simon Farnaby—various; Matthew Baynton—various

These comic skits of the history that isn't taught in school feature Queen Victoria in segments titled "Vile Victorians."

Episodes:

"Episode 1.12" (2 July 2009). 28 min. Director: Chloe Thomas. Writers: Terry Deary, George Poles, Laurence Rickard, Arnold Widdowson. www.imdb.com/title/tt1510026/?ref_=ttep_ep12. Accessed 7 February 2019. In the "Work Out With Queen Victoria" skit, viewers are advised on how to keep wider than you are tall. Exercises include: Sit and Rule, Sit and Mourn, and Dip Away from Assassin.

"Episode 4.2"(10 April 2012). 28 min. Director unknown. Writer: Laurence Rickard. www.imdb.com/title/tt2360195/?ref_=ttep_ep2. Accessed 23 March 2018. In the "Victoria and Albert's Love Story" skit, Queen Victoria reviews the Crystal Palace, which is infested with sparrows, and the Duke of Wellington suggests releasing sparrow hawks. The episode concludes with a love ballad, summarizing the royal marriage, with a montage of images of Albert and old and young Victoria.

"Episode 5.6" (4 June 2013). 28 min. Directors: Dominic Brigstocke, Steve Connelly. Writers: Laurence Rickard, Ben Ward. www.imdb.com/title/tt3682472/?ref_=ttep_ep6. Accessed 23 March 2018. **Principal cast:** Martha Howe-Douglas—Queen Victoria. In the "Queen Victoria's Coronation" skit, undignified snags occur during Queen Victoria's coronation, such as the placement of a ring on the wrong finger. Prince Albert's moustache becomes fashionable.

"Episode 6.11" (27 July 2015). 28 min. Director: Simon Gibney, Ian Curtis. Writers: Lucy Clark, David Cohen, Justin Edwards, Greg Jenner, Benjamin Partridge, Howard Read, George Sawyer, Ben Ward, Daniel Maier. www.imdb.com/title/tt5573364/?ref_=ttep_ep11. Accessed 7 February 2019. **Principal cast:** Sarah Hadland–Queen Victoria. In the "Tricky Queen Vicky" skit, young Vicky becomes queen at age 18, marries her true love Albert, and endures the open sewers at a not-so-luxurious Buckingham Palace. In the Bollywood-style song "Empress of India," Victoria refuses Disraeli's request for her to visit India. Sample of the lyrics to "Empress of India" song: "It's good to be boss and Queen Victoria, But what if all the world's other leaders ignore ya? Rule the world's biggest empire, but who does that impress, When even my own subjects don't know me as Empress? Sort it, Disraeli, you're PM in charge."

In Court with Queen Victoria (18 February 2012). Talking Pictures (UK). Director: Sati Sohal. Writer: Sati Sohal. Unknown length. www.imdb.com/title/tt7333894/?ref_=ttspec_spec_tt. Accessed 26 March 2018.

Principal cast: Tina Rath—Queen Victoria; David Aldridge—Prince Albert; Kushalpal Singh—Abdul Karim

This television short dramatizes Queen Victoria's romance with India and her relationships with Maharajah Duleep Singh and servant Abdul Karim.

"The Invincible Mr. Disraeli" (4 April 1963), Episode 12.4 of *Hallmark Hall of Fame*. Compass Productions (USA). Director: George Schaefer. Writer: James Lee. 76 min. www.imdb.com/title/tt0057186/?ref_=fn_al_tt_1. Accessed 27 February 2018.

Principal cast: Kate Reid—Queen Victoria; Trevor Howard—Benjamin Disraeli; Greer Garson—Mary Anne Disraeli; Eric Berry—Sir Robert Peel

This episode spans 30 years of Disraeli's career as politician and prime minister, including the purchase of the Suez Canal.

Lillie (1978). London Weekend Television (UK). www.imdb.com/title/tt0077042/?ref_=tt_ov_inf. Accessed 12 March 2018.

This miniseries features Lillie Langtry, her love affair with the Prince of Wales, and her acting career.

Principal cast: Sheila Reid—Queen Victoria; Francesca Annis—Lillie; Denis Lill—Prince of Wales

Episodes:

"Bertie" (22 October 1978), Episode 1.5. Director: Christopher Hodson. Writers: David Butler, James Brough (novel). 51 min. www.imdb.com/title/tt1313396/?ref_=ttep_ep5. Accessed 7 February 2019. After a season in London, Lillie Langtry has an affair with the Prince of Wales.

"Let Them Say" (29 October 1978), Episode 1.6. www.imdb.com/title/tt1313400/?ref_=ttep_ep6. Accessed 7 February 2019. Bertie builds a seaside house for Lillie and arranges for her to be presented to Queen Victoria. After the Prince of Wales pursues Sara Bernhardt, Lillie ends the relationship. Queen Victoria does not appear in the other episodes of this series.

"Melt Down" (21 March 1991), Episode 4.6 of *Red Dwarf*. BBC (UK). Director: Ed Bye. Writers: Rob Grant, Doug Naylor. 27 min. www.imdb.com/title/tt0684164/?ref_=ttfc_fc_tt. Accessed 25 March 2018. **Principal cast:** Alice De Mallet De Donas—Queen Victoria (uncredited); Chris Barrie—Rimmer; Craig Charles—Lister; Danny John-Jules—Cat; Robert Llewellyn—Kryten; Clayton Mark—Elvis; Kenneth Hadley—Hitler

In an android theme park called Waxworld, the Red Dwarf crew battle on the side of the good droids (Marilyn Monroe,

Albert Einstein, Gandhi, Santa Claus, St. Francis of Assisi, the Dalai Lama, Mother Theresa, Queen Victoria) against the evil droids (Hitler, Caligula, Al Capone, Benito Mussolini, Napoleon, Richard III). Kryten smuggles Queen Victoria into the villains' headquarters, where she shoots down Hitler and is killed herself.

Monty Python's Flying Circus. BBC (UK). Creators: Graham Chapman, Eric Idle, Terry Jones, Michael Palin, Terry Gilliam, John Cleese, Neil Innes, Douglas Adams. www.imdb.com/title/tt0063929/?ref_=tt_ov_inf. Accessed 23 March 2018.

Episodes:

"The Wacky Queen" skit in "Sex and Violence" (12 October 1969), Episode 1.2 of *Monty Python's Flying Circus.* BBC (UK). Director: John Howard Davies, Ian MacNaughton. Writers: John Cleese, Graham Chapman, Terry Jones, Eric Idle, Michael Palin, Terry Gilliam. 34 min. www.imdb.com/title/tt0758094/?ref_=ttep_ep2. Accessed 7 February 2019. **Principal cast:** Terry Jones—Queen Victoria; Graham Chapman—Gladstone

"The Wacky Queen" skit is set in "1880" and features a voice-over narrative and silent footage of the Queen walking with Gladstone, playing with a garden hose, hiking up her skirts, running around on the lawn, painting the Prime Minister's face, and shoving a pie into the Prime Minister's face.

"Tax on Thingy" skit in "The Spanish Inquisition" (22 September 1970), Episode 2.2. Director: Ian MacNaughton. Writers: Graham Chapman, John Cleese, Eric Idle, Terry Jones, Michael Palin, Terry Gilliam. 31 min. www.imdb.com/title/tt0651001/?ref_=ttep_ep4. Accessed 7 February 2019. An animation of Queen Victoria says "we are not amused" as a bullet goes into her forehead. Tag line: "Nobody expects the Spanish Inquisition."

"Poetry Reading" skit in "Michael Ellis" (11 November 1974), Episode 4.2. Director: Ian MacNaughton. Writers: John Cleese, Graham Chapman, Terry Jones, Eric Idle, Michael Palin, Terry Gilliam. 57 min. www.imdb.com/title/tt0650983/?ref_=ttep_ep21. Accessed 7 February 2019. **Principal cast:** Michael Palin—Queen Victoria; Terry Jones—William Wordsworth; Eric Idle—John Keats; Terry Gilliam—Percy Bysshe Shelley. During a poetry reading about ants by Wordsworth, Shelley, Keats, and Tennyson ("The Charge of the Ant Brigade"—"half an inch onward"), Queen Victoria enters with Albert's coffin and forbids poetry about ants "in Germany—er England."

"Queen Victoria Handicap" skit in "Hamlet" (21 November 1974), Episode 4.4. Director: Ian MacNaughton. Writers: Terry Jones, Michael Palin, Terry Gilliam. 27 min. www.imdb.com/title/tt0650975/?ref_=ttep_ep4. Accessed 7 February 2019. **Principal cast:** Uncredited—Queen Victoria runners; Eric Idle—narrator. This skit features a footrace where all contestants are dressed as Queen Victoria, and the race narrator repeats "Queen Victoria" numerous times.

My Father Knew Lloyd George (18 December 1965). BBC (UK). Director: Jack Gold. Writers: John Bird, Alan Bennett. 70 min. www.imdb.com/title/tt0390280/?ref_=ttfc_fc_tt. Accessed 30 March 2018. **Principal cast:** John Bird—Queen Victoria and various roles; John Fortune—various roles

A young aristocrat (John Fortune) tries to distance his grandfather from a scandal involving the Prime Minister's wife.

Orson & Olivia (1995). Ellipse Animation, TF1, RAI Radiotelevisione Italiana (France, Italy). Director: Arthur Qwak. Writers: Jean-Louis Bachellier, Sylvie Dervin, Edith, Gilles Gonord, Véronique Herbaut, Yann. www.imdb.com/title/tt0106092/?ref_=ttfc_fc_tt. Accessed 30 March 2018.

Principal cast: Uncredited recurring role—Queen Victoria (voice); Gay Marshall—Orson (English voice); Karen Strassman—Olivia (English voice)

This animated comedy-drama series concerns two orphans living on a boat in nineteenth-century London. At various times, they encounter Sherlock Holmes, Charles Dickens, and Queen Victoria.

Episodes:

"The Crown Jewels" aka "Les Joyaux

de la couronne" (29 March 1995), Episode 1.3. 25 min. imdb.com/title/tt0885336/?ref_=ttep_ep3. Accessed 7 February 2019. Days before Queen Victoria's Golden Jubilee, a master thief steals the crown jewels, which are recovered by Orson and Olivia. Note: Queen is dressed in blue, gold and purple in one scene, and in red with ermine in another scene, instead of her usual black and white attire.

"The Bomb" aka "La bombe" (3 May 1995), Episode 1.10. 25 min. www.imdb.com/title/tt0885323/?ref_=ttep_ep8. Accessed 7 February 2019. A plot to assassinate the Queen is thwarted by Orson and Olivia.

"The Phantom Raspberry Blower of Old London Town" (1971/1976). BBC (UK). Director: Maurice Murphy. Writer: Spike Milligan. 30 min. www.imdb.com/title/tt0066721/?ref_=ttfc_fc_tt. Accessed 29 May 2019.

A version of the "The Phantom Raspberry Blower of Old London Town" was originally broadcast on 15 January 1971, as Episode 1.2 of *Six Dates with Barker* (1971). The story features a Jack the Ripper madman stalking Victorian London and killing or stunning his victims by blowing a raspberry on them.

It was later serialized on *The Two Ronnies*, a British sketch show (1971–1987). www.imdb.com/title/tt0066721/?ref_=ttfc_fc_tt. Accessed 10 June 2019.

Episodes:

Episode 5.3 (18 September 1976). Director: unknown. Writers: Spike Mullins, David Nobbs. Length unknown. www.imdb.com/title/tt0798323/?ref_=ttep_ep3. Accessed 7 February 2019. **Principal cast:** Ronnie Corbett—various characters including Queen Victoria; Ronnie Barker—various characters including Edward Prince of Wales. Domineering Queen Victoria and browbeaten son appear in a parody of the Edward the Seventh television series starring Timothy West. The Prince argues with Queen, who tells him to stay at home. The Queen thinks Edward is the Phantom Raspberry Blower.

Episode 5.5 (2 October 1976). Director: unknown. Writers: Ian Davidson, Spike Mullins. Length unknown. www.imdb.com/title/tt0798325/?ref_=ttep_ep5. Accessed 7 February 2019. **Principal cast:** Alec Bergonzi—Queen Victoria; Ronnie Barker—various characters; Ronnie Corbett—various characters. The two Ronnies dress up a squad of police as Queen Victoria for protection from the Phantom Raspberry Blower.

"Pocket Watch Full of Miracles" (10 November 1990), Episode 1.8 of *Bill & Ted's Excellent Adventures*. Hanna-Barbera Productions, Nelson Entertainment, Orion Television (USA). Directors: Robert Alvarez, Don Lusk. Writer: Doug Molitor. 30 min. www.imdb.com/title/tt1356309/?ref_=ttep_ep8. Accessed 3 April 2018.

Principal cast: Queen Victoria—uncredited (voice); George Carlin—Rufus (voice); Keanu Reeves—Ted Logan (voice); Alex Winter—Bill S. Preston, Esq. (voice)

Slackers Bill and Ted use time travel to get birthday presents for Mr. Preston, including a watch from Queen Victoria. The Queen is shown in her carriage, comparing her watch to Big Ben and discovering she is late for being crowned Empress of India. Bill and Ted help her get crowned in time, and she gives them her broken watch.

This 1990 animation is a spin-off from the 1989 film *Bill & Ted's Excellent Adventures*.

"Poor Butterfly" (9 January 1968), Episode 1.6 of *Journey to the Unknown*. Hammer Films (UK). Director: Alan Gibson. Writers: William Abney, Jeremy Paul. 60 min. www.imdb.com/title/tt0617041/?ref_=ttep_ep6. Accessed 7 February 2019.

Principal cast: Fay Compton—Queen Victoria / Lady Sawyer; Chad Everett—Steven Miller; Susan Brodrick—Rose, the butterfly girl

In this ghost story, Steve Miller attends a costume party where everything looks as it did the 1920s. Everyone seems to know him, although he has never met them. One of the party goers is dressed as Queen Victoria. He meets a woman in a butterfly costume, who is anxious to leave the party. Steve goes off to get gas in his car, and when he returns, he can't find the house. A local couple tell him that a disastrous fire killed everyone at the party.

Edited together with another episode "The Indian Spirit Guide" for theatrical release as *Journey to Midnight* (November 1971). www.imdb.com/title/tt0230379/?ref_=ttco_co_tt. Accessed 7 February 2019.

"**The Price of My Blood**" (6 October 1996), Episode 1.4 of *Rhodes*. WGBH, Zenith Entertainment (UK). Director: David Drury. Writer: Antony Thomas. 58 min. www.imdb.com/title/tt1475995/?ref_=ttfc_fc_cl_i57. Accessed 21 March 2018).
Principal cast: Margaret Heale—Queen Victoria; Martin Shaw—Cecil John Rhodes; Frances Barber—Princess Catherine Radziwill; David Butler—Charles Rudd

This episode tells the story of Cecil Rhodes, who founded the nation of Rhodesia (now called Zimbabwe). Queen Victoria meets King Lobengula's emissaries to discuss a mining concession and gives them honest advice against the gold mining concession. The British government overrides the Queen and decides to grant Rhodes a royal charter to create the British South Africa Company.

"**Queen Victoria**" (1995), Episode 1.30 of *A.J.'s Time Travelers*. DNA Productions, Gold Coast Television Entertainment (USA). Director: Mike Finney. Writer: Barry Friedman. 30 min. www.imdb.com/title/tt1119736/?ref_=ttep_ep30. Accessed 7 February 2019.
Principal cast: Uncredited—Queen Victoria; John Patrick White—A.J. Malloy; Jeremiah Birkett—Pulse

A.J. Malloy, a teen-age time traveler, meets with Queen Victoria in one of his adventures in the time travelling ship Kryos.

"**Responsible Government**" (31 March 1991), Episode 1.7 of *Heritage Minutes*. Historica Canada (Canada). Director: Richard Ciupka. Writer: unknown. 1 min. www.imdb.com/title/tt4769870/?ref_=nm_flmg_act_46. Accessed 14 March 2018.
Principal cast: Bronwen Mantel—Queen Victoria; Harry Hill—Lord Melbourne

Queen Victoria discusses the Canadian Rebellions of 1837 with Lord Melbourne and decides to grant Canada responsible government, meaning the Governor General is responsible to Canada's elected assembly.

"**Saving Mr. Lincoln**" (19 October 1998), Episode 1.3 of *The Secret Diary of Desmond Pfeiffer*. Paramount Network Television (USA). Director: Matthew Diamond. Writers: Brian Pollack, Mert Rich. 30 min. www.imdb.com/title/tt0697343/?ref_=ttep_ep3. Accessed 7 February 2019.
Principal cast: Wendy Worthington—Queen Victoria; Chi McBride—Desmond Pfeiffer; Dann Florek—Abraham Lincoln; Christine Estabrook—Mary Todd Lincoln

In Episode 1.3, Lincoln falls ill before a scheduled meeting with Queen Victoria, so Mrs. Lincoln hires a body double. She has other plans for this double (hint: sex).

This comedy series of a loony Abraham Lincoln, his loony associates and the only sane person, his black butler Desmond, was cancelled after four episodes in response to protests against its comic handling of slavery.

The Secret Adventures of Jules Verne (2000). Talisman Films (UK). www.imdb.com/title/tt0178161/?ref_=nv_sr_1. Accessed 11 December 2018.
Principal cast: Patti Allan (as "Patti Allen" in Episodes 1.1 and 1.2)—Queen Victoria; Francesca Hunt—Rebecca Fogg; Michel Courtemanche—Passepartout; Chris Demetral—Jules Verne; Michael Praed—Phileas Fogg

These fantastic steampunk adventures are based on the premise that Verne actually experienced the adventures he writes about in his books *Twenty Thousand Leagues Under the Sea*, *Journey to the Center of the Earth*, and *Around the World in Eighty Days*.

Episodes:

"In the Beginning" (18 June 2000), Episode 1.1. 60 min. www.imdb.com/title/tt0697261/?ref_=ttep_ep1. Accessed 7 February 2019. Director: Mark Roper. Writers: Gavin Scott (creator), Gregory Elmont (as Gregory de la Doucette). Verne fights against the League of Darkness and meets Phileas Fogg and his cousin Rebecca Fogg, a British spy. Queen Victoria intervenes to bring Verne back into the Secret Service.

"Queen Victoria and the Giant Mole" (25 June 2000), Episode 1.2. 60 min. www.imdb.com/title/tt0697264/?ref_=ttep_ep2. Accessed 7 February 2019. Director: Pierre de Lespinois. Writers: Gavin Scott (creator). The League of Darkness plots to kill Queen Victoria by constructing a giant tunneling machine called the Mole, based on an idea stolen from Verne's mind in episode 1.1. Phileas, Jules, Passepartout, and Rebecca defeat the League and receive the Queen's gratitude.

"Secret of the Realm" (7 April 2000), Episode 1.20. 60 min. www.imdb.com/title/tt0697268/?ref_=ttep_ep20. Accessed 7 February 2019. Director: Mark Roper. Writers: Gavin Scott (creator), Alan Drury. The League of Darkness creates evil clones ("similars") of Phileas, Rebecca, and a Peruvian ambassador, who is the keeper of the Holy Grail. The League sends the clones to trick Queen Victoria into revealing the secret code to unlock the Holy Grail, so they can use it to dominate the world.

"The Victorian Candidate" (9 December 2000), Episode 1.21. 60 min. www.imdb.com/title/tt0697280/?ref_=ttep_ep21. Accessed 7 February 2019. Director: Ian Sharp. Writers: Gavin Scott (creator), John Brown. The League of Darkness kidnaps Phileas and brainwashes him into killing the now-widowed Queen Victoria at Balmoral Castle. Rebecca breaks the brainwashing and foils the plot against the Queen's life.

Shadow Play (2004). BBC (UK). Director: Dirk Campbell. Writer: unknown. www.imdb.com/title/tt0463835/?ref_=nv_sr_2. Accessed 23 March 2018.

Principal cast: Doreen Mantle—Queen Victoria; Anabel Barnston—Hester; Angellica Bell—herself—Presenter; Laura Davenport—Aunt Sophie; Jack Bannon—Ben; Janine Duvitski—Katie; Faye Jackson—Girl in Blue; Cameron Crighton—Nathan; Tim Bentinck—Uncle Augustus.

When Ben's family takes refuge in an abandoned manor house, he starts filming the house and finds he can see into the Victorian world, in which a child's life is very different from that of the twenty-first century. Queen Victoria appears in all episodes except 1.2.

Episodes:

"A Light at the Window" (1 March 2004), Episode 1.1. Length unknown. www.imdb.com/title/tt0836469/?ref_=ttep_ep1. Accessed 7 February 2019. Ben's camcorder allows him to see into the Victorian world.

"A Flicker at the Fairground" (15 March 2004), Episode 1.3. Length unknown. www.imdb.com/title/tt0865817/?ref_=ttep_ep3. 7 February 2019. Ben follows Hester and Katie to a fair and talks about the girl in blue.

"Phantoms and Photographs" (22 March 2004), Episode 1.4. Length unknown. www.imdb.com/title/tt0874673/?ref_=ttep_ep4. 7 February 2019. Ben helps Hester escape.

"A Secret Comes to Light" (29 March 2004), Episode 1.5. Length unknown. www.imdb.com/title/tt0874672/?ref_=ttep_ep5. Accessed 7 February 2019. Uncle Augustus recues Nathan.

Shaka Zulu (1986). South African Broadcasting Company (SA). www.imdb.com/title/tt0086798/?ref_=nv_sr_1. Accessed 14 March 2018.

Principal cast: Erica Rogers—Queen Victoria; Henry Cele—Shaka; Edward Fox—Lt. Francis Farewell; Christopher Lee—Lord Bathurst; Sokesimbone Kubheka—King Cetshwayo

"Episode 1.1" (24 November 1986). Director: William C. Faure. Writers: Joshua Sinclair, William C. Faure. 52 min. www.imdb.com/title/tt0086798/?ref_=nv_sr_1. Accessed 14 March 2018.

In this series about the life of King Shaka Zulu, Queen Victoria meets with defeated King Cetshwayo, a half-nephew of Shaka Zulu, and refuses to help him regain this lost throne.

Station Jim (2001). BBC (UK). Director: John Roberts. Writers: Joanne Reay (idea), Mark Wallington. 90 min. Accessed 21 March 2018.

Principal cast: Prunella Scales—Queen Victoria; George Cole—Stationmaster Pope; Charlies Creed-Miles—Bob Gregson; Celia Imrie—Miss Frazier; Timothy West—Sir Christopher Ellis. A young porter in a railway station befriends a stray dog called "Station Jim," who becomes famous for his tricks. The dog foils an assassination attempt on Queen Victoria.

Timekeepers of the Millennium, **aka *Queen Victoria*** (12 December 1999). Foundation TV Productions, New Millennium Expe-

rience Company, Carlton Television (UK). Director: Graham C. Williams. Writers: Ged Allen, Steve Kidgell. 14:30 min. www.imdb.com/title/tt3638224/?ref_=ttpl_pl_tt. Accessed 31 March 2018. collections-search.bfi.org.uk/web/Details/ChoiceFilm-Works/150561133. Accessed 31 March 2018.
Principal cast: June Whitfield—Queen Victoria (voice).

This animated time travel show involves two muppet-like workers who must travel back in time to retrieve key parts of the Great Clock before the end of the year 1999 or there will be no millennium. The twelve crystals are scattered through different parts of history, including Queen Victoria's era.

"Tooth and Claw" (6 October 2006), Episode 2.2 of *Doctor Who*. (BBC (UK). Director: Euros Lyn. Writer: Russell T. Davies. 45 min. www.imdb.com/title/tt0563002/?ref_=fn_al_tt_3. Accessed 7 February 2019. en.wikipedia.org/wiki/Tooth_and_Claw_(Doctor_Who). Accessed 16 February 2018.
Principal cast: Pauline Collins—Queen Victoria; Davie Tennant—the Tenth Doctor; Billie Piper—Rose Tyler (companion); Derrick Ridell—Sir Robert MacLeish; Ian Hanmore—Father Angelo.

The Doctor and Rose meet Queen Victoria and save her from death at the hands of the Torchwood monks, who want to turn her into a werewolf. Sir Robert, the owner of Torchwood estate, sacrifices himself to allow the Doctor to use a telescope and the Koh-i-Noor diamond to kill the werewolf. While the Queen is wounded (passing hemophilia to her children), she thanks the Doctor and Rose, then banishes them from her realm, and creates the Torchwood Institute to defend Britain against aliens, including the Doctor.

"Under the Linden Tree with Queen Victoria" skit in Episode 3.1 (11 June 2009) of *That Mitchell and Webb Look*. BBC (UK). Ben Gosling Fuller. Writers: David Mitchell, Robert Webb. 29 min. www.imdb.com/title/tt1453848/?ref_=ttfc_fc_tt.
Principal cast: Robert Webb—Queen Victoria; David Mitchell—Prime Minister.

Queen Victoria objects to a gift of 20,000 Linden trees as a gift from America because of their bad smell.

Victoria (2016–19). Mammoth Screen (UK), ITV Network (UK). Creator: Daisy Goodwin. www.imdb.com/title/tt5137338/?ref_=fn_al_tt_1. Accessed 7 February 2019.
Principal cast: Jenna Coleman—Queen Victoria; Tom Hughes—Prince Albert; Catherine Flemming—Duchess of Kent; Daniela Holtz—Baroness Lehzen; Margaret Clunie—Harriet, Duchess of Sutherland; David Oakes—Prince Ernest; Alex Jennings—King Leopold; Nigel Lindsay—Sir Robert Peel; Jordan Waller—Lord Alfred Paget; Leo Suter—Drummond; Nell Hudson—Nancy Skerrett; Ferdinand Kingsley—Francatelli; Adrian Schiller—Penge; Diana Rigg—Duchess of Buccleuch; Bebe Cave—Wilhelmina Coke; Peter Firth—Duke of Cumberland / King of Hanover; Laurence Fox—Lord Palmerston; Kate Fleetwood—Princess Feodora; John Sessions—Lord John Russell; Lily Travers—Sophie, Duchess of Monmouth; Abigail Turner—Sabrina Bartlett

Season 1 Episodes (Dates given are first the UK broadcast and the second the US broadcast):

"Doll 123" (28 August 2016 / 17 January 2017), Episode 1.1. Director: Tom Vaughan. Writer: Daisy Goodwin. 95 min. www.imdb.com/title/tt5267180/?ref_=ttep_ep1. Accessed 7 February 2019. Victoria inherits the throne. Lady Flora Hastings falls ill. Nancy Skerrett is appointed as assistant to the Queen's dresser.

"Ladies in Waiting" (29 August 2016 / 17 January 2017), Episode 1.2. Director: Tom Vaughan. Writer: Daisy Goodwin. 60 min. www.imdb.com/title/tt5351820/?ref_=ttep_ep2. Accessed 7 February 2019. Melbourne resigns, and Peel becomes Prime Minister. Victoria precipitates a crisis by refusing to appoint Tory ladies-in-waiting. Pence sells off candles, and chef Francatelli falls in love with dresser Skerrett.

"Brocket Hall" (4 September 2016 / 22 January 2017), Episode 1.3. Director: Tom Vaughan. Writer: Daisy Goodwin. 46 min. www.imdb.com/title/tt5351822/?ref_=ttep_ep3. Accessed 7 February 2019. King Leopold suggests Prince Albert as a husband, but Victoria is not favorably impressed. She banishes Conroy to Ireland and is lenient to the Chartists.

"The Clockwork Prince" (11 September 2016 / 29 January 2017), Episode 1.4. Director: Sandra Goldbacher. Writer: Daisy Goodwin. 46 min. www.imdb.com/title/tt5351826/?ref_=ttep_ep4. Accessed 7 February 2019. Victoria proposes to Albert. Skerrett commits a crime to help her poor cousin.

"An Ordinary Woman" (18 September 2016 / 4 February 2017), Episode 1.5. Director: Sandra Goldbacher. Writer: Daisy Goodwin. 47 min. www.imdb.com/title/tt5351824/?ref_=ttep_ep5. Accessed 7 February 2019. Albert receives a reduced income without a title, and the wedding occurs in February 1840. Francatelli proposes to Skerrett.

"The Queen's Husband" (25 September 2016 / 11 February 2017), Episode 1.6. Director: Oliver Blackburn (as Olly Blackburn). Writer: Daisy Goodwin. 46 min. www.imdb.com/title/tt5351830/?ref_=ttep_ep6. Accessed 7 February 2019. Albert champions the anti-slavery movement. Prince Ernest begins an affair with the Duchess of Sutherland. Francatelli helps Skerrett's cousin.

"Engine of Change" (2 October 2016 / 4 February 2017), Episode 1.7. Director: Oliver Blackburn (as Olly Blackburn). Writers: Daisy Goodwin, Guy Andrews. 47 min. www.imdb.com/title/tt5351828/?ref_=ttep_ep7. Accessed 7 February 2019. A pregnant Victoria appoints Albert as regent in the event of her death, which outrages the Tories. Peel and Albert convince Victoria of the benefits of the railway travel. Francatelli charms Skerrett with hot chocolate.

"Young England" (9 October 2016 / 5 March 2017), Episode 1.8. Director: Oliver Blackburn (as Olly Blackburn). Writer: Daisy Goodwin. 47 min. www.imdb.com/title/tt5351832/?ref_=ttep_ep8. Accessed 7 February 2019. Duke of Cumberland is suspected of engineering Edward Oxford's assassination attempt on Victoria. Princess Vicky is born. Francatelli leaves service to open a bakery.

Season 2 Episodes (Dates are given as UK date, then US date):

"A Soldier's Daughter" (27 August 2017 / 14 January 2018), Episode 2.1. Director: Lisa James Larsson. Writer: Daisy Goodwin. 49 min. www.imdb.com/title/tt6100074/?ref_=ttep_ep1. Accessed 7 February 2019. Albert and Peel conceal a military disaster in Afghanistan from Victoria. Annoyed with their condescending treatment, Victoria rallies the country with a public appearance. Skerrett is promoted to head dresser, and Francatelli returns. The Duchess of Buccleuch becomes Mistress of the Robes.

"The Green-Eyed Monster" (3 September 2017 / 14 January 2018), Episode 2.2. Director: Lisa James Larsson. Writer: Daisy Goodwin. 65 min. www.imdb.com/title/tt6327804/?ref_=ttep_ep2. Accessed 7 February 2019. Victoria is jealous of Albert's interest in a female scientist, but they reconcile when she tells him of her second pregnancy. A young thief invades the palace.

"Warp and Weft" (10 September 2017 / 21 January 2018), Episode 2.3. Director: Geoffrey Sax. Writer: Daisy Goodwin. 47 min. www.imdb.com/title/tt6327804/?ref_=ttep_ep2. Accessed 7 February 2019. Victoria's costume ball, intended to help the silk weavers of Spitalfields, is met with public outrage. Melbourne hides his terminal illness. The palace thief is caught.

"The Sins of the Father" (17 September 2017 / 21 January 2018), Episode 2.4. Director: Geoffrey Sax. Writers: Daisy Goodwin, Ottilie Wilford. 46 min. www.imdb.com/title/tt6327808/?ref_=ttep_ep4. Accessed 7 February 2019. Victoria cannot bond with her newborn son. Albert learns that Uncle Leopold may be his true father. Skerrett's cousin sells the story of the palace thief to the newspapers.

"Entente Cordiale" (24 September 2017 / 28 January 2018), Episode 2.5. Director: Jim Loach. Writer: Daisy Goodwin. 47 min. www.imdb.com/title/tt6327810/?ref_=ttep_ep5. Accessed 7 February 2019. Victoria and Albert visit the French court in a vain attempt to prevent the marriage of the French king's son to the Queen of Spain. Albert confesses the information about his paternity to Victoria, who tells him that it does not change their relationship. Paget and Drummond pursue their love affair.

"Faith, Hope & Charity" (1 October 2017 / 4 February 2018), Episode

2.6. Director: Jim Loach. Writer: Daisy Goodwin. 65 min. www.imdb.com/title/tt6327812/?ref_=ttep_ep6. Accessed 7 February 2019. Victoria presses Peel to arrange government help for Ireland, now suffering from potato blight. Ernest has health issues, while Albert takes on sanitation projects. Francatelli assists a family in Ireland.

"The King Over the Water" (8 October 2017 / 11 February 2018), Episode 2.7. Director: Daniel O'Hara. Writers: Daisy Goodwin, Ottilie Wilford. 46 min. www.imdb.com/title/tt6327816/?ref_=ttep_ep7. Accessed 7 February 2019. Victoria and Albert visit Scotland. After escaping from a boring poetic reading, they wander the country side and stay overnight with a crofter and his wife. Wilhelmina Coke sees Paget and Drummond kissing. Ernest pursues the widowed Duchess of Sutherland.

"The Luxury of Conscience" (15 October 2017 / 18 February 2018), Episode 2.8. Director: Daniel O'Hara. Writer: Daisy Goodwin. 46 min. www.imdb.com/title/tt6327814/?ref_=ttep_ep8. Accessed 7 February 2019. Peel succeeds in the repeal of the Corn Laws and is forced to resign. Albert demands the dismissal of Baroness Lehzen. Prince Ernest rejects a bride chosen by King Leopold, while Francatelli and Skerrett are in love. Drummond is murdered.

"Comfort and Joy" (25 December 2017 / 25 February 2018), Episode 2.9. Director: Jim Loach. Writer: Daisy Goodwin. 90 min. www.imdb.com/title/tt7234250/?ref_=ttep_ep9. Accessed 7 February 2019. Albert introduces German-style Christmas trees to the palace. Victoria sponsors an African princess. Ernest hides his illness from the Duchess of Sutherland. Paget and Wilhelmina decide on a marriage of convenience. Penge loses money on a railway scheme, and Skerrett declines an inheritance based on the value of slaves.

Season 3 Episodes (Dates are given as US date, then UK date):

"Uneasy Lies the Head that Wears the Crown" (13 January 2019 / 24 March 2019), Episode 3.1. Director: Geoffrey Sax. Writer: Daisy Goodwin. 52 min. www.imdb.com/title/tt7745018/?ref_=ttep_ep1. Accessed 7 February 2019. Revolution in Europe drives exiled Louis Philippe to Victoria's palace. The Chartists are collecting signatures on their petition, but Abigail, who does embroidery for the Queen, has mixed loyalties. Victoria's half-sister Feodora arrives unexpectedly, and tension soon mounts between the sisters.

"London Bridge is Falling Down" (20 January 2019 / 31 March 2019), Episode 3.2. Director: Geoffrey Sax. Writer: Daisy Goodwin. 52 min. www.imdb.com/title/tt8098850/?ref_=ttep_ep2. Accessed 7 February 2019. Palmerston plants rifles in the Chartists workroom (historical inaccuracy), but Abigail uncovers the plot and informs the Queen. Victoria decides to accept the Chartists' petition. Francatelli and Skerrett secretly marry. Victoria informs a reluctant Bertie that he will be King one day.

"Et in Arcadia" (27 January 2019 / 7 April 2019), Episode 3.3. Director: Geoffrey Sax. Writers: Daisy Goodwin, Guy Andrews. 52 min. www.imdb.com/title/tt9280044/?ref_=ttep_ep3. Accessed 7 February 2019. Albert enjoys family time at Osborne house, but Victoria wants to return to Buckingham Palace and politics. Feodora sows more discord between Victoria and Albert. Francatelli and Skerrett resign their positions in the royal household. Joseph the footman and Lord Palmerston flirt with the Duchess of Monmouth. Victoria and Albert quarrel over foreign policy, and they return to London, not speaking to each other.

"Foreign Bodies" (3 February 2019 / 14 April 2019), Episode 3.4. Director: Chloe Thomas. Writers: Daisy Goodwin, Ottilie Wilford. 52 min. www.imdb.com/title/tt9280046/?ref_=ttep_ep4. Accessed 7 February 2019. Albert is elected Chancellor of Cambridge. A cholera epidemic sweeps through London. Victoria meets Florence Nightingale and lends support to Dr. John Snow in his campaign to turn off a contaminated pump in Soho. Nancy Skerrett Francatelli dies from cholera.

"A Show of Unity" (10 February 2019 / 21 April 2019), Episode 3.5. Director: Chloe Thomas. Writers: Daisy Goodwin, Guy Andrews. 52 min. www.imdb.com/title/tt9139182/?ref_=ttep_ep5. Accessed 7 February 2019. After an assassination attempt by Irish nationalist William Hamilton, Victoria decides to visit Ireland. During a stay at Lord Palmerston's estate, romance builds between Duchess Sophie and footman Joseph, and her husband mistakenly accuses Lord Palmerston. Albert discovers that Palmerston had sent all his villagers abroad after the potato blight. Back in London, Feodora accepts bribes for her influence and fails to see that Bertie's new tutor Mr. Caine is brutal; Victoria dismisses Caine when she finds out. Victoria informs Albert that their seventh child is on the way.

"A Coburn Quartet" (17 February 2019 / 28 April 2019), Episode 3.6. Director: Chloe Thomas. Writer: Daisy Goodwin. 52 min. www.imdb.com/title/tt9280054/?ref_=ttep_ep6. Accessed 7 February 2019. Private sketches of the royal family become public. Albert designs the new florin coin. Victoria objects to a phrenologist's examination of Bertie. Sister Feodora continues to sow discord, and during the Georgian costume ball the sisters have a confrontation. The Duchess of Monmouth continues her affair with footman Joseph.

"A Public Inconvenience" (24 February 2019 / 5 May 2019), Episode 3.7. Director: Delyth Thomas. Writers: Daisy Goodwin, Ottilie Wilford. 52 min. www.imdb.com/title/tt9074890/?ref_=ttep_ep7. Accessed 7 February 2019. Palmerston leads the effort to blockade Greece on behalf of a Jewish British subject. Victoria and Albert clash over Feodora, but Victoria distracts her sister by hosting her niece Heidi at court. Albert begins work on the Great Exhibition. The Duchess of Monmouth is committed to a madhouse by her sadistic husband.

"The White Elephant" (3 March 2019 / 12 May 2019), Episode 3.8. Director: Delyth Thomas. Writer: Daisy Goodwin. 52 min. www.imdb.com/title/tt9198344/?ref_=ttep_ep8. Accessed 7 February 2019. Young Bertie is enamored of his cousin Heidi. Palmerston loses his position as Foreign Secretary over his support for new French emperor Louis Napoleon. The Duchess of Monmouth is released from confinement after the Queen intervenes. Albert accuses Feodora of betrayal, and Victoria effectively disowns her sister. Victoria and Albert open the Great Exhibition, and Albert collapses from exhaustion.

Victoria & Albert (26 August 2001). A&E Television (USA), BBC (UK). Director: John Erman. Writer: John Goldsmith. 200 min. www.imdb.com/title/tt0262995/?ref_=ttpl_pl_tt. Accessed 21 March 2018.
Principal cast: Victoria Hamilton—Victoria; Joyce Redman—Old Queen Victoria; Jonathan Firth—Prince Albert; James Callis—Ernest; Diana Rigg—Baroness Lehzen; Patrick Malahide—Sir John Conroy; Penelope Wilton—Duchess of Kent; Peter Ustinov—King William IV; Nigel Hawthorne—Lord Melbourne; Rachel Pickup–Lady Henrietta Standish
This television film covers the love story of Victoria and Albert and the birth of their nine children.

Victoria Regina (20 November 1947). BBC (UK). Producer: Ian Atkins. Writer: Laurence Housman (play). 100 min. www.imdb.com/title/tt4365354/?ref_=nv_sr_6. Accessed 27 February 2018.
Principal cast: Sheila Beckett—Queen Victoria. This television film, based on the Houseman play, covers the life of Queen Victoria from age 18 to her Diamond Jubilee.

Victoria Regina (1948). Electric Radio Theater (USA). 25 min. www.youtube.com/watch?v=uj5l8EPwSx8. Accessed 11 December 2018.
Principal cast: Helen Hayes—Queen Victoria. This is a highly condensed radio version of the Laurence Housman play.

"Victoria Regina" (15 January 1951), Episode 2.10 of *Robert Montgomery Presents*. Neptune Productions (US). Director: Norman Felton. Writers: Thomas Phipps, Laurence Housman (play). 60 min. www.imdb.com/title/tt0687639/?ref_=fn_tt_tt_7. Accessed 27 February 2018.
Principal cast: Helen Hayes—Queen Victoria; Robert Harris—Benjamin Disraeli; Kent Smith—Prince Albert. This recreation of Helen Hayes' Broadway role covers the life of Queen Victoria from age 18 to her Diamond Jubilee and is based on Laurence Housman's play.

"Victoria Regina" (26 June 1957), Episode 2.43 of *ITV Play of the Week*. ITV (UK).

Appendix: Select Filmography

Director: unknown. Writers: William Redmond (adapted by), Laurence Housman (play). 90 min. www.imdb.com/title/tt1282904/?ref_=ttfc_fc_tt. Accessed 11 June 2019.
Principal cast: Dorothy Tutin—Princess Victoria; Harry Lockart—Prince Albert
This television version of the Housman play covers Queen Victoria's life from age 18 to her Diamond Jubilee, in 1897.

"**Victoria Regina**" (8 April 1957), Episode 8.31 of *Robert Montgomery Presents*. Neptune Productions (US). Director: unknown. Writer: Laurence Housman (play). 60 min. www.imdb.com/title/tt0687640/?ref_=ttfc_fc_tt. Accessed 11 June 2019.
Principal cast: Clair Bloom —Queen Victoria; Paul Stevens—Prince Albert
This television version of the Housman play covers Queen Victoria's life from age 18 to her Diamond Jubilee, in 1897.

"**Victoria Regina**" (30 November 1961), Episode 11.2 of *Hallmark Hall of Fame*. Compass Productions, Hallmark Hall of Fame Productions (US). Director: George Schaefer. Writers: Robert Hartung (adaptation), Laurence Housman (play). 77 min. www.imdb.com/title/tt0055598/?ref_=nv_sr_1. Accessed 27 February 2018.
Principal cast: Julie Harris—Queen Victoria; James Donald—Prince Albert; Basil Rathbone—Prime Minister Benjamin Disraeli; Pamela Brown—Duchess of Kent; Felix Aylmer—Lord Melbourne
This episode covers the life of Queen Victoria from age 18 to her Diamond Jubilee and is based on Laurence Housman's play.

Victoria Regina (1964). Granada Television (UK) and NET Playhouse. Director: Stuart Latham. Writers: Peter Wildeblood (adaptation), Laurence Houseman (play). www.imdb.com/title/tt0423478/?ref_=fn_al_tt_2. Accessed 7 February 2019.
Principal cast: Patricia Routledge—Queen Victoria; Joachim Hansen—Prince Albert; Marianne Deeming—Duchess of Kent; Cyril Luckham—Lord Melbourne; Max Adrian—Benjamin Disraeli; Kevin Brennan—Prince of Wales; Jameson Clark—John Brown

Episodes:
"Spring" (13 November 1964), Episode 1.1. www.imdb.com/title/tt1296777/?ref_=ttep_ep1. Accessed 7 February 2019.
"Summer" (20 November 1964), Episode 1.2. www.imdb.com/title/tt1296778/?ref_=ttep_ep2. Accessed 7 February 2019.
"Autumn" (27 November 1964), Episode 1.3. www.imdb.com/title/tt1296776/?ref_=ttep_ep3. Accessed 7 February 2019.
"Winter" (4 December 1964), Episode 1.4. Accessed 7 February 2019. www.imdb.com/title/tt1296779/?ref_=ttep_ep4. Accessed 7 February 2019.

"**We Are Not Amused**" (14 December 1976), Episode 4.7 of *It Ain't Half Hot Mum*. BBC (UK). Director: Bob Spiers. Writers: Jimmy Perry, David Croft. 29 min. www.imdb.com/title/tt0612702/?ref_=ttpl_pl_tt. Accessed 31 March 2018.
Principal cast: Melvyn Hayes—Bombardier Beaumont / Queen Victoria; Michael Bates—Rangi Ram; Windsor Davies—BSM Williams
A party for a new district officer includes a patriotic show featuring Bombardier Beaumont as Queen Victoria.

The Young Victoria (27 March 1963). Australian Broadcasting Company. Director: Alan Burke. Writer: Laurence Housman (play). 60 min. www.imdb.com/title/tt4062776/?ref_=nv_sr_2. Accessed 8 March 2018.
Principal cast: Lola Brooks—Victoria; Ric Hutton—Albert
This version of the Housman play *Victoria Regina* focuses on the courtship and marriage of Victoria and Albert.

The Young Visitors (26 December 2003). BBC (UK). Director: David Yates. Writers: Patrick Barlow (screenplay), Daisy Ashford (story). 90 min. www.imdb.com/title/tt0379053/?ref_=nv_sr_1. Accessed 21 March 2018.
Principal cast: Janine Duvitski—Queen Victoria; Jim Broadbent—Alfred Salteena; Lyndsey Marshal—Ethel Monticue; Hugh Laurie—Lord Bernard Clark; Bill Nighy—Earl of Clincham; Simon Russell Beale—Prince of Wales
A middle-aged man tries to impress a social climbing woman by improving his manners at a gentleman's training school.

The Wild Wild West Revisited (9 May 1979). CBS (USA). Director: Burt Kennedy. Writer: William Bowers. 96 min. www.imdb.com/title/tt0080132/?ref_=fn_al_tt_1. Accessed 12 March 2018.

Principal cast: Jacquelyn Hyde—Queen Victoria; Robert Conrad—Jim West; Ross Martin—Artemus Gordon; Paul Williams—Dr. Miguelito Loveless, Jr.; Rene Auberjonois—Capt. Sir David Edney

West and Gordon come out of retirement to battle a mad scientist who has replaced the crowned heads of England, Spain and Russia with clones he controls, in an attempt to take over the world. Clapped in jail with other world leaders, Queen Victoria insists that she is the real queen and demands release.

Miscellaneous

The section includes miscellaneous appearances of the Queen Victoria character in video games, animation, and internet comics, as well as some audio or radio productions. It excludes documentaries, histories, and docudramas about Queen Victoria as this type of production ultimately takes an historical-based approach rather than presenting Queen Victoria as a character.

Assassin's Creed: Syndicate (2015). Ubisoft Quebec (Canada). Director: Ramiro Bélanger. www.imdb.com/title/tt4332798/?ref_=fn_al_tt_1. Accessed 7 February 2019. en.wikipedia.org/wiki/Assassin%27s_Creed_Syndicate. Accessed 23 March 2018.

Principal cast: Ellen David—Queen Victoria (voice); Victoria Atkin—Evie Frye (voice); Paul Amos—Jacob Frye (voice)

Jacob and Evie Frye work to take back London from Templar control, aided by historical figures including Charles Dickens, Charles Darwin, Florence Nightingale, and Queen Victoria, who is a recurring character in this action-adventure game.

Civilization VI (2016). Firaxis Games (USA). www.imdb.com/title/tt5989308/?ref_=nv_sr_1. Accessed 7 February 2019. en.wikipedia.org/wiki/Civilization_VI. Accessed 7 February 2019.

Principal cast: Lucy Briggs-Owen—Queen Victoria (voice); Sean Bean—Narrator

In this computer game, the player builds a civilization from prehistory to near future. Queen Victoria appears as the leader of the English civilization.

An Evening with Queen Victoria aka *Evening at Osborne*. (2003). Play. 60 min. en.wikipedia.org/wiki/Prunella_Scales. Accessed 18 February 2018. Audio only version: archive.org/details/ANEVENINGWITHQUEENVICTORIA. Accessed 18 February 2018.

Principal cast: Prunella Scales—Queen Victoria; Ian Partridge (tenor) singing songs written by Prince Albert.

In this one-woman radio play, the old Queen reminisces about her life, using extensive quotations from Victoria's journal and letters.

A documentary *Looking for Victoria* (27 October 2003) covers Scales' research for her role in *An Evening with Queen Victoria*. www.imdb.com/title/tt0384747/?ref_=ttpl_pl_tt.

The Great Turnabout Trial: The Adventures of Ryūnosuke Naruhodō aka *Dai Gyakuten Saiban: Naruhodō Ryūnosuke no Bōken* (9 July 2015). Capcom (Japan). Nintendo 3DS game in the *Ace Attorney* series. Director and Writer: Shu Takumi. www.imdb.com/title/tt6290906/?ref_=nv_sr_1. Accessed 7 February 2019. en.wikipedia.org/wiki/Dai_Gyakuten_Saiban:_Naruhod%C5%8D_Ry%C5%ABnosuke_no_B%C5%8Dken. Accessed 7 February 2019.

In this courtroom style game, the game is divided between investigation and courtroom. This game is set in the Meiji Period (in Britain the Victorian era). Ryūnosuke Naruhodō and his assistant Susato Mikotoba, travel to England to further their legal studies and work with Sherlock Holmes and his assistant Iris Watson, daughter of Dr. John Watson (deceased).

Queen Victoria watches a climactic trial via a two-way hologram. She strips the main villain of his position as chief justice. The Queen does not appear in court; instead, another character reads her decree to the court.

As of June 2018, Capcom USA has not released an English language version of this game.

"The New Adventures of Queen Victoria." Internet web comic strip by Pab Sungenis.

Appendix: Select Filmography 193

www.gocomics.com/thenewadventuresofqueenvictoria. Accessed 20 November 2018.

This internet cartoon strip uses Queen Victoria and Bertie to comment on current cultural topics and aspects of Victoria's character.

Example: for 8 February 2019, the strip shows Queen Victoria meeting Governor Northam (Virginia) depicted as a black-face doll and explains to Bertie that blackface is inherently racist with one exception: "when you use it to mock racists who say that blackface isn't racist."

Post card of Smiling Queen Victoria (about 15 February 1898). By Charles Knight. www.loc.gov/resource/cph.3b39605/. Accessed 7 February 2019.

Queen Victoria smiles in this still image from about 1898.

Restoring the Queen Victoria Recording of 1888 (2017). Nick Bellow. 1 min. www.youtube.com/watch?v=TNsQRkHjoGQ. Accessed 25 July 2018.

This audio-only recording is supposedly based on a few words that Queen Victoria spoke into Sydney Morse's Bell Graphophone during a demonstration at Balmoral in 1888.

For more background, see Mike Dash, "In Search of Queen Victoria's Voice" www.smithsonianmag.com/history/in-search-of-queen-victorias-voice-98809025/.

Victoria: An Empire Under the Sun (2003). Paradox Interactive. en.wikipedia.org/wiki/Victoria:_An_Empire_Under_The_Sun. Accessed 7 February 2019. www.gamespot.com/reviews/victoria-an-empire-under-the-sun-review/1900-6085089/. Accessed 23 March 2018.

Principal cast: Lucy Briggs-Owen—Queen Victoria

In this grand strategy computer game, the player guides a nineteenth century country through colonization, industrialization, and various historical events. Queen Victoria lends her name only to this game, but appears on the cover of the game's box.

Victoria, Queen and Empress—The Princess Alice Interview (1977). BBC (UK). Unknown length. www.bfi.org.uk/films-tv-people/4ce2b88629eda. Accessed 20 July 2018.

In this interview, Princess Alice, Countess of Athlone, Queen Victoria's granddaughter, states that Queen Victoria denied using the phrase "We are not amused."

Victoria II (2009). Paradox Development Studio. en.wikipedia.org/wiki/Victoria_II. Accessed 7 February 2019.

This computer game is a follow up to *Victoria: An Empire Under the Sun*.

In this grand strategy game, the player controls and manages a nineteenth-century state.

Your Friend the Rat (2007). Walt Disney Pictures (USA). Director: Jim Capobianco. Writers: Jim Capobianco, Jeff Pidgeon, Alexander Woo. 11 min. www.imdb.com/title/tt1134859/?ref_=fn_al_tt_1. Accessed 11 December 2018.

Principal cast: Uncredited—Queen Victoria (image only); Patton Oswalt—Remy (voice); Peter Sohn—Emile (voice); Lou Romano—Linguini (voice); Tony Russel—Disclaimer guy (voice)

Remy and Emile discuss the history of the rat's relationship with humans. Queen Victoria receives a pet rat from catcher Jack Black and kisses it.

This animated short is included on the DVD of *Ratatouille* (2007)

Chapter Notes

Introduction

1. See Marieke Dubbelboes for a discussion of the Victoria caricatures that appeared in the French journal *La Caricature* in 1900. One particularly pointed example is titled "Le Spectre De Banquo" showing an obese Queen frightened by a figure labelled "Transvaal Independent," a reference to the Second Boer War.
2. Pab Sungenis has syndicated his Victoria strip, and panels back to 2006 are available at www.gocomics.com/thenewadventuresofqueenvictoria. Accessed 19 November 2018.

Chapter 1

1. For a history and interactive map of early cinemas in London, see Chris O'Rourke, "London's Silent Cinemas." One theatre, the Palace, showed American Biograph Company films in 70 mm format, including William Kenney Laurie Dickson's newsreel film of the Anglo-Boer War on 1900 (*Wikipedia*, "Palace Theatre").
2. The amount of film content available was staggering. For example, the Georges Méliès studio alone turned out 500 films between 1896 and 1914, of which approximately 200 survive today. During the last years of the Queen Victoria's reign, Méliès turned out an estimated 78 films in 1896, 52 in 1897, 27 in 1898, and 48 in 1899 (M. Rosen 751–53). In 1900, he released more ambitious works including a 13-minute *Joan of Arc*, *The One-Man Band* (Méliès playing seven instruments), and *The Christmas Dream* (M. Rosen, 754). See Ezra for a filmography of surviving Méliès prints.
3. The period between 1838 and 1896 saw the emergence of a highly commercialized distribution of royal engravings, resulting in a boom business for print sellers. For example, in the last six weeks of 1838, these firms sold 374 prints of Victoria, compared to 165 engravings of other subjects, indicating the overwhelming popularity of the monarch's print image (Plunkett 72).
4. Not all royal photographs were dowdy, and, in some cases, visual glamour was required. For example, in 1863, the royal family wished to project a more beautiful image for photographs of the Prince and Princess of Wales' wedding. Victoria's daughters the Princess Royal and Princess Alice were personally involved in retouching photos by "lightening the local colour, and taking off that affect of age" resulting from photography in full sun (Plunkett 189).
5. If the Czar of Russia looks rather glum in this film, he had good reason. During this visit, the Czar consulted the Queen's personal physician Sir James Reid about a painful decayed tooth. Reid applied a treatment of iodine to reduced swelling (Reid, *Ask Sir James* 120).
6. In 1897 several other cinematographers captured garden parties: *Queen Victoria and Royal Family at State Garden Party* (Velograph) and *Queen at State Garden Party* (Watson & Son). The 1900 film *The Queen Reviewing the Guards* (British Mutoscope & Biograph Co.) includes a shot of Queen Victoria at Buckingham Palace's gardens.
7. Reviewing the troops films include: *Gordon Highlanders* (1897, Walker), *The Coldstream Guards* (1897, British Mutoscope & Biograph Co.), *Queen Victoria Reviewing Troops at Aldershot* (1898, C. Goodwin Norton), *Queen Victoria Driving to Laffans*

Plain (1898), *Queen Victoria at Aldershot* (1898, British Mutoscope & Biograph Co.), *Queen Victoria Reviewing the Life Guards* (1899, British Mutoscope & Biograph Co), *Queen Victoria Reviewing Household Cavalry* (1899, British Mutoscope & Biograph Co., Presentation of the New State Colours to the Scots Guards: Arrival of Her Majesty* (1899, Warwick Trading Co.), *Presentation of the New State Colours to the Scots Guards: Review of Scots Guards by Her Majesty the Queen* (1899, Warwick Trading Co.), *Her Majesty the Queen Inspecting Life Guards* (1899, Warwick Trading Co), *Her Majesty Leaving Spital Barracks Amid Cheers* (1899, Warwick Trading Co), *Her Majesty, Queen Victoria, Reviewing the Household Cavalry at Spital Barracks* (1899, British Mutoscope & Biograph Co), *Her Majesty, Queen Victoria, Reviewing the Honorable Artillery* (1899, British Mutoscope & Biograph Co.), *Her Majesty, Queen Victoria Part 1 and 2* (1899, British Mutoscope & Biograph Co), *God Save the Queen* (1899, British Mutoscope & Biograph Co.), *Review of Berkshire Volunteers by the Queen* (1900, Robert W. Paul), and *The Queen Reviewing the Guards* (1900, British Mutoscope & Biograph Co.)

8. See Anthony and Brown 278–284 for listing of the Boer War films by the British Mutoscope and Biograph Company. Cinematographer William Dickson kept a diary and later published it as *The Biograph in Battle: Its Story in the South African War Related with Personal Experiences* (1901). "It is a unique and valuable account—the first book published by a film cameraman, and of exceptional interest and veracity from having been compiled on the spot while the events it records were taking place... Dickson was a brave man who took many risks and was nearly killed on a couple of occasions in his anxiety to remain close to the action" (Anthony and Brown 128). Despite having a telephoto lens on hand, Dickson was not able to capture actual battle footage. Of the various Biograph films of the Boer War, the closest to actual battle footage is *Bombardment of Colenso by 4.7 Guns of HMS "Terrible" / Battle of Colenso* (13–15 December 1899).

9. Sir James Reid estimated the school children at 40,000. He also noted that during this visit, the Queen's health improved. "The Queen, buoyed up by the excitement and novelty of the Irish visit, was in remarkably good health throughout although, hardly surprising at her age, she did get tired from time to time" (Reid, *Ask Sir James* 194).

10. After this first visit to Netley Hospital in 1863, Victoria reported her visit in a letter to her uncle King Leopold: "I made the effort to go and visit the truly magnificent Military Hospital at Netley...I felt it a duty... to walk alone and see those poor men, some dying—without Albert—was dreadful! I went through it all, but I have been ill ever since" (Hibbert 176).

11. The *Indian Medical Gazette* of February 1899 also mentions that during visit to Netley in December 1898, the Queen showed interest in a technological advance: x-rays. "Her Majesty also witnessed a demonstration of the Roentgen rays which were passed through her august hand, the shadow being projected on a screen."

12. While not the first British royal to travel by rail (that was Dowager Queen Adelaide in 1840), Queen Victoria was the first British monarch to do so. On 13 June 1842, Queen Victoria, at Prince Albert's urging, took her first rail ride, a 30-minute excursion on the Great Western Railroad from Slough to Paddington. Her journal recorded the impression "the motion was very slight, & much easier than a carriage, also no dust or great heat,—in fact, it was delightful, & so quick" (*QVJ*, cited by B. Rosen). Thirty years later, the railroad became so essential to Victoria's monarchy that she wrote a letter to Prime Minister Gladstone on 22 October 1872 deploring the government's inability to maintain this key industrial infrastructure: "A subject which demands the most serious attention of the Government is the very alarming and increasing insecurity of the Railroads...In no other country except ours are there so many dreadful accidents, and for the poor people who have to travel constantly by rail, and who cannot even have the comparative security which those who travel in first-class can have, to be in perpetual danger of their lives is monstrous. Independent of this, the Queen's own family, not to speak of her servants and visitors, are in perpetual danger, and are put to the most serious inconveniences by the inexactitude of the trains" (Hibbert 229).

13. This town has not forgotten Victoria's frequent visits. The Ballater Victoria Week is held annually in August, beginning in 1987

to commemorate the 150th anniversary of Victoria's accession and continuing through today, including such festivities as a book fair, storytelling, music, duck race, pet show, and ghost tours.

14. Queen Victoria had at least five royal trains: 1869, two coaches by the London and North Western Railway; 1874, a royal saloon by the Great Western Railway; 1877, a royal saloon by the London and South Western railway; the 1897 Diamond Jubilee train; and 1899, a royal train of five cars by the London, Brighton and South Coast Railway, which was also used for Victoria's funeral.

15. Not unlike arrangements today for a royal or presidential visit, the railroads had to be shut down when Victoria traveled. In a letter to Prime Minister Gladstone on 11 June 1885 regarding his resignation from office, she uses the railroad as one reason not to travel south to meet him: "With respect to the Queen's return south, she must observe first, that the Railway authorities, unless previously warned, do not consider it safe for her to start without some days' notice" (Hibbert, *QV Letters and Journals* 293). At another time, Victoria shows that she was aware of public opinion and managed her railway travel accordingly. In 1848, after a holiday at Balmoral, bad weather prevented their return south by yacht, and the trip by railway involved travelling on Sunday. In her journal Victoria notes "it being Sunday we had decided to start at 6, in order to arrive in London before the Service as people are so very particular about travelling on a Sunday in England, in my opinion it is overdone" (B. Rosen np).

16. Twain also notes political advancement in an expanded British electorate, the benefits of public education via newspapers, establishment of international copyright, use of surgical anesthesia, advances in sanitation, women's political rights and college education, organization of trade unions, and the reduction of labor to eight hours per day (Twain 1047–48).

17. Queen Victoria's response to the Diamond Jubilee was recorded in her journal: "No one ever, I believe, has met with such an ovation was given to me, passing through those 6 miles of streets... The crowds were quite indescribable and their enthusiasm truly marvelous and deeply touching. The cheering was quite deafening and every face seemed to be filled with joy" (*QVJ*, cited by Sully np).

18. Henri Joly (1866–1945) was a French inventor, who was introduced to the motion picture camera by Georges Demenÿ. He held four patents for projectors and cameras including a film-in-depth process. After going into partnership with Ernest Normandid, his projector was exhibited in Britain as "Professor Jolly's Cinematograph" (*Who's Who of Victorian Cinema* np).

19. Another lost film is described as showing a smiling Victoria: *Queen Victoria's Last Visit to Ireland* (1900). "This picture was taken in Phoenix Park, Dublin, on the same day as the one above described, but in this negative a very close view of the Queen is given. The occasion was the presentation of flowers to Her Majesty by a deputation of little girls, and our camera was placed so near to the spot where the ceremony occurred, that the most minute details are shown. The carriage drives, up, stops, the little girls are presented to the Queen, to whom they courtesy. The Queen addresses a few pleasant remarks to the children, and smiles happily, and they in turn give her a huge basket of flowers with which she is apparently very much pleased. The ceremony is then concluded, and the carriage drives off." (*AMB Picture Catalogue 1902*, film #605).

20. Another technological souvenir was produced by the London Stereoscopic Company which produced both still stereoscopic cards of the Diamond Jubilee, and also is credited by the BFI Catalog with one film: *The Queen's Carriage* in 1897. The stereoscope, demonstrated at the 1851 Great Exhibition, was "so popular that it is said that every Victorian home—regardless of class—had a stereoscope and a collection of views sold in a range of prices" (Clayton). Despite the development of a stereoscope with a moving image capability (turning drum positioned on a wheel or on a spinning paddle) by the late 1860's and 1870's, the craze for stereoscopic photographs had faded. The London Stereoscopic Company's foray into film is a natural extension of the technology and clearly an attempt to expand its offerings and leverage the high level of public interest in the Diamond Jubilee.

21. The stray dog runs from the left side of the procession in the Pathé *Funeral of Queen Victoria* "A" and "B" films, while he

runs from the right side of the procession in the "D" film. An unknown production company caught the dog running from the right side (Huntley Film Archives #32373). Coincidentally, the funeral footage represents another instance where a stray dog appears in a film about Victoria. In *H.M. The Queen Leaving Windsor Castle* (8 March 1900), just before the royal carriage appears, a small dog wanders into camera range: "First appeared an advance guard in the shape of a dog that, having glanced round and satisfied himself that all was in order, trotted quietly out of focus" (Anthony and Brown 280).

22. A poem published at the end of Brunel Redivivus' 1901 article "The Funeral of Queen Victoria" in the *Railway Magazine* explicitly comments on Victoria's first and last railway rides: "This new enchantment science now had wrought, The seal of Royal favour fain besought, And thus the Sov'reign's pleasure 'twas to test The 'marvel of the age' at its behest...In fairest flow'r of youth She came to grace This latest triumph over time and space." And "Where the great casket, with its balzon'd pall, Is borne aloft, the cynosure of all, On this last journey; sad, eventful stage, A fun'ral bier for queenly equipage." (Redivivus 264).

23. A multimedia approach to the funeral event is evident, including a railroad souvenir: *Great Western Railway. Funeral of Her Late Most Gracious Majesty the Queen. Arrangement of Royal Train. Paddington to Windsor 1:32 p.m. Saturday 2nd February. 1901* (Reid, *Ask Sir James* 218). This card provides a mediated view of the funeral event; it is both a directive those who wished to witness it (telling when and where to show up to see the train in person) and a glossary-like information giving the name of the engine (Royal Sovereign), which railway saloon held the coffin, who was in the other cars, all details that would not have been apparent to observers during the event. The Great Western Railway also used a ticketing system to control crowds: at Paddington Station, the railway issued admission tickets to a reserved enclosure, via a staircase at the end of No. 1 platform.

24. Reid was Queen Victoria's personal physician for the last twenty years of her life, and her trust in him was so profound that she charged him with the sad task of placing her body in the coffin and putting in various memorial objects: her wedding veil, Albert's dressing gown and plaster cast of his hand, five rings from Albert, photographs of Albert, their children and grandchildren. At Queen Victoria's request, Reid discretely placed a picture of John Brown in the coffin, a lock of his hair in Victoria's hand and Brown's mother's wedding ring on her finger (Baird 487).

Chapter 2

1. The following wars fought by the British Empire during the nineteenth century are not the subject of *any* existing films, or Queen Victoria is *not* a character portrayed in a film: the Canadian Rebellion of 1937–38; the First Anglo-Afghan War of 1839–42, aka the Disaster in Afghanistan, notorious for loss of 4,500 British and Indian soldiers; the Second Opium War of 1856–1860; the Indian Rebellion of 1857–58, aka Sepoy Mutiny (mentioned in a title card in *Victoria the Great*, but the film does not include any scenes about this war); the Second Anglo-Afghan War of 1878–80; the Maori Wars of 1845–72, aka New Zealand Wars—three films on this war do not include Victoria as a character: *Rewi's Last Stand* (1925, remade 1940), *The Te Kooti Trail* (1927), and *Utu* (1983); the Cape Frontier Wars (1779–1879); the Anglo-Ashanti Wars of 1824–1901 (no films about these wars, with the exception of a school project noted in the Filmography); the Anglo-Zulu War of 1879; the First Boer War aka the Transvaal War of 1880–81; the Anglo-Egyptian War of 1882.

2. This chapter will not discuss a lost silent *Sixty Years a Queen* (1913), which has been analyzed by Jude Cowan Montague based on other primary materials, including a 46-foot segment of the scene of Victoria's accession, a book of the film, a souvenir program or press book that contained 55 illustrations (Montague 47). This film covered the following wars: the Indian Mutiny and the storming of the Cashmere Gate, the Crimean War and Sebastopol, War in Sudan and Khartoum, and the siege of Ladysmith (Montague 51–53).

3. In showing a Nightingale nurse witnessing the Charge of the Light Brigade, *Victoria Cross* presents a small historical inaccuracy. Nightingale's team of 38 women

nurses and 15 Catholic nuns arrived in Scutari, located across the Black Sea from Balaclava, in early November 1854, a couple of weeks *after* the Charge, which occurred 25 October 1854. Thus, from both a temporal and geographic perspective, this scene is historically inaccurate.

4. The British Acoustic sound process put the sound on separate film stock from the visual, thus creating challenges for presenting synchronized sound in theaters (Porter 91–92). As if that wasn't enough, additional challenges occurred due to the necessity of controlling background ambient sound on location shoots. As *Kine Weekly* for 8 November 1928 noted, the *Balaclava* production was complicated: Army airplanes "had to be warned off, on account of their noise, which, being unmistakable, was in danger of being recorded by the British Acoustic apparatus, even when they flew a mile or so away." (G. Brown 2).

5. The harsh treatment of the Queen Victoria character in *Balaclava* did not dim the overall positive critical reaction. The consensus was that the silent footage was excellent, and the later addition of sound did little or nothing to improve the film. *Variety* (30 April 1930) noted that *Balaclava* "suffers from the comparative slowness of the sound sequence against those made silent—a factor which seems to arise whenever this making over happens…Theme is strung, very lightly, on Tennyson's 'Charge of the Light Brigade.' This part, kept in from the first-made silent, is easily the meat of the film, and is a fine piece of work. Sound effects and music have been dubbed onto this with no very great success." (Brown 3). And the *Times* (19 May 1930) agreed: "The squadrons driving inflexibly through the barrage are a genuinely moving spectacle, but the effect is suddenly spoiled by the sound of a voice raised above the noise of battle in frantic declamation of Tennyson's too familiar lines." (Brown 3).

6. Out of over 390 British and American films released in 1938, the dozen or so filmed in three-strip Technicolor included all genres: adventure films (*The Adventures of Robin Hood* and *The Adventures of Tom Sawyer*); westerns (*Heart of the North* and *Valley of the Giants*); war films, *The Drum* (about rebellion in India during the Raj), and *Men with Wings* (a love story set against the aircraft industry up to WWII); musicals *Sweethearts* (Jeannette MacDonald and Nelson Eddy) and the *Goldwyn Follies*; romance films (*Gold Is Where You Find It* and *Kentucky*); a comedy *The Divorce of Lady X* (Merle Oberon and Laurence Olivier); and *Sixty Glorious Years*.

7. In a nearly throwaway line in the Crimean hospital scene of *Sixty Glorious Years*, Albert asks if the antiseptic principles of Dr. Joseph Lister had been followed, receiving a negative reply. Albert's comment is anachronistic. Lister's work on antiseptic surgical methods was based on Louis Pasteur's 1865 research on micro-organisms. Lister's papers on use of carbolic acid to prevent gangrene were published in 1867.

8. Critical reception for *Sixty Years A Queen* was politically inspired and, as a result, quite mixed. The *Sunday Times* thought the film is merited "exhibition as a historical and authentic document… in every school and educational institute in the United Kingdom." (Chapman 80). The *New Statesman* disagreed: "anybody who possesses even a small acquaintance with the history and personalities of the nineteenth century must recognize that the thing is a travesty of the truth," and *World Film News* summed it up as "a propaganda film" (Chapman 80–81). *Today's Cinema* recognized the timeliness of the film: "in addition to creating the past in fascinating detail it has a message for today that cannot be ignored" (Chapman 81).

9. Another film about political tension is the silent *Yankee Clipper* (1927). A DeMille Pictures Corporation production, it is a tale of a maritime rivalry between the United States and Great Britain dramatized as a race from China to Boston of American vs. English clipper ships in pursuit of a tea trade contract. Queen Victoria (Julia Faye) has a small role. At the start of the film she commissions a fast ship to compete with the Americans in this semi-friendly competition. The DeMille touch prevails throughout a plot crammed full with a love triangle, a spectacularly photographed typhoon, a mutiny, a heroine climbing up the rigging to escape a lustful sailor, her timely rescue by child star freckle-faced Frank Coghlan, Jr., and an animated map showing the progress of the race. Not surprisingly for a DeMille film, the American ship Yankee Clipper wins, and the English heroine falls in love with the Yankee captain.

10. While *Victoria the Great* does not give

the exact details of how Albert reworded the dispatch (the film shows him writing but not the contents), a letter to Palmerston dated 30 November outlines his solution " Her Majesty's Government are ... glad to believe that they [the United States government] would spontaneously offer such redress as alone could satisfy this country, viz: the restoration of the unfortunate passengers and a suitable apology" (Ferris 34), which is what happened, although the American apology was couched as disavowal, not a formal apology. Queen Victoria kept a copy of the final draft of the Trent Affair dispatch and on it noted: "This draft was the last the beloved Prince ever wrote. He was very unwell at the time & when he brought it to the Queen he said 'I could hardly hold my pen' " (Hibbert 277).

11. *Victoria the Great*, despite the amount of research done for the film, deliberately departs from historical accuracy regarding Prince Albert's deathbed, which was attended by both Queen Victoria and five of their children. Furthermore, the film implies a generic decline from overwork and makes no mention of other possible contributions to Prince Albert's early death: typhoid fever, chronic stomach issues (possibly Crohn's disease or cancer), ongoing depression and stress about his role as Prince Consort, and his outrage over his son's immoral affair with the actress Nellie Clifden. By having only Victoria present at Albert's death, the film maintains a tight focus the Victoria and Albert partnership and offers the audience a closeup of Victoria's reaction to his death.

12. The 1929 *Disraeli* film was well received. A *Variety* review of 9 October 1929 opined "Warners have done it right. Production is unstinted, sedate, and colorful, in the style of 1874. Small bits as well as principal roles are equally meritorious... Good taste and general excellence mark this apex picture which should be commercially successful. It deserves to be."

13. Another interesting casting note: In *The Prime Minister* (1941) the young Princess Victoria is played by Pamela Standish, who also appeared in *Sixty Glorious Years* (1938) as the Princess Royal, Vicky the daughter of Queen Victoria, evolving in three years from daughter to mother!

14. The history seems a bit distorted here. The year 1878 did see a mobilization of the Anglo-India army, but that was for the Second Afghan War. The Crown Princess of Germany, Victoria's daughter Vicky, had indeed been writing to her mother, but her warnings are about Russia, not Germany's plans to invade France; she had been duped by Bismarck mistaking his "policy of aggressive self-preservation for a new and healthy antipathy to Russia" (Pakula 347). Queen Victoria and her government trusted neither the Russians nor Bismarck.

15. A French propaganda film from 1939 was released in response to the Munich Agreement (1938) and unease about the possibility of a second world war. *Entente Cordiale*, directed by Marcel L'Herbier and based on Andre Maurois' novel *Life of Edward VII*, covers the history of the 1904 Entente Cordiale between England and France. The decision to use the life of Edward VII to demonstrate the affinities between France and England foregrounds the personal against the larger political world. The Queen Victoria role (Gaby Morlay) is limited to one scene where she and Prince of Wales (Victor Francen) debate the need for a diplomatic accord with the French. Victoria is skeptical as she points out the history of French-British tension and her reliance on the sea as Britain's ally. Bertie pushes for a formal alliance with France.

16. The political impact of *The Prime Minister* was evident to reviewers of the film. A *Variety* review on 9 April 1941 captured the political overtones: "Under present conditions...and influenced by the fervid patriotic line taken by scripters, [the] picture will content many and number few critics...'The Prime Minister' is aimed to cash in on the present-day European scene of conflicting emotions, intrigue and broken promises, to show that distrust is no new thing and that the perfidy of the 70s was met by a strong, powerful leader of an aroused nation."

17. This scene showing conflict between Victoria and Gladstone in *Sixty Glorious Years* has basis in historical fact. Queen Victoria bombarded her government with protests against the delay in sending support to General Gordon. For example, 9 February 1884 to Prime Minister Gladstone: "The Queen...feels very strongly about the Soudan [sic] and Egypt, and she must say she thinks a blow must be struck, or we shall never be able to convince the Mohammedans that they have not beaten us...We must make a demonstration of strength and show

determination, and we must not let this fine and fruitful country, with its peaceable inhabitants, be left a prey to murder and rapine and utter confusion. It would be a disgrace to the British name, and the country will not stand it. The Queen trembles for General Gordon's safety. If anything befalls him, the result will be awful" (Hibbert 284).

18. Chapman 87. The historical details of General Gordon's death are uncertain. The sacrificial version in *Sixty Glorious Years* was highly popular with the 1885 public. Other versions have Gordon fighting to the death with a revolver and a sword (Perry 192–93), and being beheaded afterwards (Neufeld 332–37).

19. Only a few other feature films focus on the Sudan Campaign: *Khartoum* (1966), with Charlton Heston playing General Gordon and Laurence Olivier playing the Mahdi; *The Four Feathers* (1939) with John Clements, Ralph Richardson, and C. Aubrey Smith; *East of Sudan* (1964), with Anthony Quayle. Queen Victoria is not a character in these films.

20. According to a post-war government report approximately 50 percent of the Boer child population and 12 percent of black Africans died in British concentration camps (Ferguson 235). While scorched earth was hardly a new military policy (e.g. the second and third Punic Wars, William the Conqueror's Harrying of the North, the Russian retreat from Napoleon's invasion, Sherman's March to the Sea, to name a few), the use of forced internment against an entire nation was a first, resulting in the depopulation of entire regions of South Africa.

21. Other Nazi propaganda films against Great Britain in the same period as *Uncle Kruger* included: *Der Fuchs von Glenarvaon* (1940) and *Mein Leben für Irland* (1941), showing brutal oppression of the Irish; *Carl Peters* (1941) showing the British driving the title character from German colonies. None of these films include Queen Victoria.

22. Not surprisingly for a propaganda film, historical inaccuracies abound in *Uncle Kruger*. For example, the scene with John Brown is set about 1900 which was impossible since Brown died in 1883, long before the Second Boer War. Paul Kruger and Queen Victoria never met, despite the scene in this film (Meintjes 87–88).

23. Victoria's deathbed speech in *Uncle Kruger* is totally fabricated. Sir James Reid, personal physician to Victoria for the last twenty years of her life, kept detailed notes of her condition in the days leading up to her death on 22 January 1901. No such speech was recorded in his notes (Reid, *Ask Sir James* 211–12).

24. The 1925 *Livingstone* location footage predates the better-known MGM film *Trader Horn* (1931), which has been incorrectly touted as the first non-documentary film shot on location in Africa. Director Weatherall raised nearly £12,000 to fund a one-year expedition to Africa beginning October 1923 and travelled about 25,000 miles in Rhodesia and Zanzibar mainly (Rice np). Gustav Pauli accompanied the safari as camera man (Lowe 225). Henry Walton, who played Stanley, published an account of the trip (*BFI*, "Livingstone" np). This British film was never released in the United States, which may account for the general but incorrect impression that *Trader Horn* was the first non-documentary film to use African safari footage.

25. Chapman compares *Victoria the Great* to a Gaumont-British newsreel "The World Today" 27 August 1936, "which had contrasted international strife (Spain, Abyssinia, Palestine) with the social and political stability of [Britain] and concluded with an unequivocal endorsement of the monarchy as the symbol of a united and prosperous nation: 'And above all we look to the head of this great nation whose example and courage have won the admiration and envious respect of other nations less happy...' The similarity in language and tone to *Victoria the Great* is quite apparent: Beaconsfield's speech of 1877 seems to have been written with audiences of 1937 in mind" (Chapman 74–75).

26. Use of Elgar's "Pomp and Circumstance" in the 1897 Jubilee scene is a deliberate anachronism in an otherwise historically accurate film. This piece was composed in 1901, premiered 19 October 1901 (after Victoria's death), and was re-used in part for Edward VII's coronation.

27. A few other films about war or social issues include small roles for Queen Victoria, without much substance, more of a plot device rather than a fully formed character. *Souls at Sea* (1937), starring Gary Cooper and Frances Dee, is the story of abolitionists who try to stop the slave trade in 1842; the scenes with Queen Victoria (Viva Tatter-

sall, uncredited) were edited out of the final release cut. *Zorro in the Court of England* (1969), an Italian action film, has Zorro (Spiros Focás) fighting against a tyrannical Bermuda governor and receiving a knighthood from Queen Victoria (Barbara Carroll). *The Private Life of Sherlock Holmes* (1970) includes a subplot involving Mycroft Holmes (Christopher Lee) who builds a pre–World War I submarine. Queen Victoria (Mollie Maureen), inspects the submarine and rejects the design as un-sporting. *The Adventure of Sherlock Holmes' Smarter Brother* (1975) is a Gene Wilder musical comedy where Queen Victoria (Susan Field) gives an important document to her Foreign Secretary, and, of course, it is promptly stolen. Sherlock Holmes turns the case over to Sigerson Holmes, the titular younger brother, to recover the stolen government document that could lead to war if it gets into the wrong hands (i.e. Moriarty). *Shanghai Knights* (2003), a comic marital arts film starring Jackie Chan as Chon Wang, is very loosely based on the Boxer Rebellion. The plot begins with the murder of Chon Wang's father by a band of rebels and ends with Jackie and partner Roy (Owen Wilson) foiling an attempt to kill the royal family and receiving knighthoods from Queen Victoria (Gemma Jones). This film is notable for an homage to Harold Lloyd's 1923 *Safety Last*: Chan dangling from the minute hand of the Big Ben clock.

Chapter 3

1. The lost 1913 biopic *Sixty Years A Queen* had apparently staked out much of the territory. Directed by Bert Haldane, researched and written by G.B. Samuelson, this two-hour epic covered Victoria's entire reign. Surviving footage, rediscovered by Luke McKernan, shows Victoria receiving the notice of her accession to the throne (Montague 48). Two books by May Wynne, a press book and film book with fifty-five illustrations, suggest the film's content. Three separate actresses played Victoria: Ina Kastner as the young Queen Victoria, Ida Heath as the middle-aged queen, and Mrs. Henry Lytton as the older Victoria (Montague 49). The film had a chronological narrative, alternating private and public events, some filmed in great detail such as the 20-minute coronation scene. A still image from the May Wynne film book captures the proposal scene. "Many were fascinated by its apparent gender reversal as it was understood that Victoria had proposed to Prince Albert...But the young Queen was portrayed as a romantic figure, and the lace, satin, pearls and velvet of her costume added spectacle to the scene. Victoria is shown in the off-shoulder fashion and flowers associated with 1840s women's fashion" (Montague 52).

2. Herbert Wilcox seemed to think of his two Victoria films as one. He spliced the first half of *Victoria the Great* (1937) with the last half of *Sixty Glorious Years* (1938) and released it in 1942 under the title *Queen Victoria*. The combined film covers her entire reign. The first film was highly publicized and so popular that "a whole number of *Film Weekly* was devoted to it on 22 December 1937" (Harper 54). Despite its popularity with audiences of its day, Harper takes a modern perspective in her assessment that *Victoria* has "a dated look, and its pace is ponderous. The tone of the film is unctuous, and the structure of the narrative, with the change-over to colour towards the end, throws positive emphasis on the theme of Empire," and *Sixty Glorious Years* is "turgid propagandism" informed by Vansittart's anti-German perspective and pro-rearmament views, though positively reviewed in *The Weekly Illustrated* (Harper 51–52).

3. The waltz scene is also an example of deliberate anachronism and will be discussed in chapter 4.

4. Actually, Walbrook was about two inches taller than Prince Albert, but since Anna Neagle was somewhat taller than Victoria, the comparative visuals worked out. He was roughly twice Albert's age for the courtship scenes, though this worked to the actor's advantage in filming Albert's later years and death scene (Downs 93). One of the more authentic aspects of Walbrook's casting was his limited command of the English language when he left Germany in 1936, and consequently he "kept a dialect coach with him on the set of *Victoria the Great*" (Downs 96).

5. The concept of a honeymoon was already common before Victoria and Albert's wedding. The term shows up in Dr. Samuel Johnson's Dictionary (1755) as "the

first month after marriage, when there is nothing by tenderness ...comparing mutual affection of newly-married persons to the changing moon which is no sooner full that it begins to wane." (Johnson Vol). Historian Ginger Strand notes that bridal tours were popular in early nineteenth century Britain (Strand 2008).

6. See Downs (96) for a discussion of Albert's use of music and his biographer Theodore Martin's comment that in music "he found a vent for all that world of deeper emotion" (Martin 85). Organ playing was in fact a more usual method for Albert to vent his feelings and shows up in *Sixty Glorious Years* after a quarrel about the appointment of a personal secretary for Albert. Louder seems better when you have frustrations to work off.

7. Gillian Gill's perceptive *We Two, Victoria and Albert: Rules, Partners, Rivals* provides a fascinating view of this volatile relationship. "The new feminine deference, the decision that Business was man's work, was both reality and pretense for Victoria. She had the luxury of appearing to wish to give up her power and prerogatives to her husband, confident that the English Constitution would never allow her to do so irrevocably...Victoria was a shrewd judge of men, and she recognized real ability in her husband. She and Albert had the same financial and political goals. In a man's world, Albert could help her realize those goals better than she could alone" (Gill 189–90).

8. From 1937 to 1941, Nazi propaganda films remained a staple of the German film industry, such as the well-known Riefenstahl films *Triumph of the Will* and *Olympia 1 and 2*. In 1936, the same year as *Mädchenjahre Einer Königen*, the German film industry released a number of Nazi propaganda films, despite the continuing emigration of many German film makers and actors from 1933 onward (including Anton Walbrook). These films included: *Traumulus, Verräter* (*The Traitor*), *Erbkrank*, a short documentary on the Nazi T-4 Euthanasia Program, *Ewiger Wald*, which linked National Socialism with a shared destiny of German forests, and *Kaufman, nicht Händler*, a partially animated short vilifying Jewish economic exploiters. See chapter 2 for a full discussion of the 1941 German propaganda film *Ohm Kruger* (*Uncle Kruger*).

9. Both Shakespeare's *Comedy of Errors* and *Twelfth Night* leverage the stage convention of mistaken identity, which can be traced back to Roman comedy especially Plautus' *Menaechmi*. The *Victoria in Dover* play and film are clearly in that tradition.

10. The crinoline with stiff hoops did not come into fashion until the mid-1850s and was the subject of much negative commentary in the press, such as the satirical *Punch*, which in 1859 praised Queen Victoria "Long Live our gracious Queen, who won't wear Crinoline" (Graves 103). Many women suffered burns from their wide skirts getting too close to fireplaces, and nearly 3,000 deaths were due to crinoline-related fires (Kingston np). In addition, crinolines posed space issues for crowded events, and the guests at the January 1858 wedding of Princess Royal Victoria were asked to leave their hoops at home (Gernsheim 44). According to biographer Lucy Worsley, Queen Victoria resisted the fad until July 1858 when a heatwave induced her to start wearing a "Cage" as she wrote to daughter Vicky (Worsley 214), despite the ridicule in the press.

11. This is an example of John Ford's advice to "print the legend" in films. The authenticity of the "I will be good" statement has long been in dispute. Vallone sums up this as a "dubious" story that "survives in a number of competing versions." Victoria's journal records that she cried at the news (Vallone 45).

12. The way that *The Young Victoria* presents the initial meetings between Victoria and Albert takes much dramatic license. Victoria and Albert had one meeting in 1836, set up by Uncle Leopold. The film simplifies the situation to focus on Albert and one rival—cousin George Cambridge—instead of a parade of suitors such as Hugo and Alfonso Mendsdorff, Alexander and Ernst Würtemberg, or Ferdinand and Augustus of Saxe-Coburg (Erickson 51). Unlike the stiff and awkward first meeting shown in *The Young Victoria*, the 1836 meeting with Albert went well, and Victoria liked Albert from the start, praising him in a letter to Uncle Leopold as "extremely handsome" and declaring that "he possesses every quality that could be desired to make me perfectly happy" (Erickson 54). Victoria wasn't ready to marry, and no formal engagement occurred in 1836. Albert did not attend the 28 June 1838 coronation, as shown in *The Young Victoria*.

13. The downplaying of Albert's urge to rule over Victoria, his helpfulness, and his acceptance of a supportive role, contradict all the biographies that show Victoria and Albert struggling for control during their 21-year marriage. Gillian Gill summarizes the push-pull in the marriage and Albert's blind spots: "in the lessons that Albert preached to his wife [crown above party], in the guilt he laid upon her for her ardent support of Lord Melbourne and the Whigs, there was a double standard of which the prince appears to have been unconscious. When Victoria came to the throne, she was inexperienced, isolated, and vulnerable. That she succeeded so brilliantly at first was to her credit. That she made some mistakes was to be expected. There is little sign that Albert understood Victoria's difficulties or appreciated her achievements before their marriage…As he saw it, Victoria was a woman, she made mistakes, and she needed a man to show her the way. He was a man, and a superior one, and men learned from experience. It was as simple as that" (Gill 174).

14. Historical sloppiness abounds in *The Young Victoria*, pushing the concept of artistic license to the brink. Albert wasn't injured during the 1840 assassination attempt by Edward Oxford, though arguably this departure from history makes the point that Albert has come to accept his secondary role. Other historical departures are harder to forgive. For instance, a title card gives 18 June 1837 as the death of King William, which actually occurred on 20 June 1837. In scenes where characters complain about the cold temperature in the palace, an electric baseboard heater is clearly visible in the background. Actress Miranda Richardson stands in front of an historical painting of the Duchess and toddler Victoria; in the painting Duchess has dark hair, and the actress is blonde. Some of the historical license is justified to avoid audience confusion. For example, the film's so-called "Liberal" party was really the "Whig" party, a label that likely would not resonate with twenty-first century audiences. In contrast *The Young Victoria* is historically correct to show Victoria wearing a black dress to her first Privy Council meeting (Plunkett 88), in contradiction to white dress shown in the 1838 painting by Sir David Wilkie "Victoria's First Privy Council." See www.royalcollection. org.uk/collection/404710/the-first-council-of-queen-victoria. Accessed 17 August 2018.

15. The critical reception for *The Young Victoria* was mixed. Manohla Dargis in The *New York Times* cites "sumptuous frocks, soaring music, a dash of intrigue and thunderous nonsense" (Dargis np). Peter Bradshaw for *The Guardian* labels it as too conventional, "a kind of red-carpet fever had settled in, and a tone of celebratory reverence for Victoria predominates" (Bradshaw np). Roger Ebert praised the "engaging approach to show Victoria at the center of a mighty struggle that also involves her adolescent emotions" (Ebert np). Kirk Honeycutt for *The Hollywood Reporter* liked the acting: "Emily Blunt…puts healthy vigor and sexuality into a woman not associated with either. Meanwhile, Rupert Friend catches just the right nuances to a man who must figure out how to be a second fiddle" (Honeycutt np).

16. Victoria's apolitical attitude shown in *Mrs Brown* is at odds with the historical record. For example, on 16 December 1867 foreign secretary Lord Stanley suffered Victoria's wrath, in a letter demanding that he "observe the constitutional practice of taking the Queen's pleasure before he forwards dispatches of any importance to their destination. But she cannot approve the irregular habit which has crept in, of sending off dispatches with her sanction having been previously obtained, trusting to the power of cancelling them by telegraph, if disapproved" (Hibbert, *QV Letters and Journals* 201). The Widow of Windsor was in effect "telecommuting," working from home and leveraging the available tools for fast communication.

17. Having Victoria call this thanksgiving ceremony a "Mass" is an historical mistake. She was determinedly low church and look askance at any "popish" trappings in church services. Other historical inaccuracies in *Mrs Brown* include: Sir Henry Ponsonby became Victoria's personal secretary in 1870, not in 1864, and more importantly, he was noted for his ability to get along with Brown, instead of the great antagonism shown in the film. Queen Victoria was not present at Brown's sickbed, a dramatically effective scene fabricated for the film; in fact, she was unaware that his final illness was serious, and when Brown died 27 March 1883, Prince Leopold had to break the news

to her (Wilson, *Victoria* 423). The Parliamentary vote in favor of the Irish Church Act (disestablishment) is shown in 1867 during Disraeli's government, when in fact this occurred 1869 under W.E. Gladstone's administration. The motive for this change is to simplify the film's narrative by having the Queen deal with only one Prime Minister—Disraeli.

18. The funniest line in *Mrs Brown* occurs in the hunting scene, where Brown coaches Disraeli on how to shoot a deer: "Imagine it's Gladstone." It's a throw-away line, evoking the political context (a rarity in *Mrs Brown*), and hilarious at the same time.

19. *Mrs Brown* glosses over the topic of whether there was a physical relationship or even marriage between Victoria and Brown. This "did they or didn't they" question has been a point of debate among historians and biographers. The film leaves it ambiguous. When the Queen returns from the jaunt to the Grants, she is smiling and flushed; Ponsonby cautions Dr. Jenner, "don't even think it," meaning a physical relationship. Biographer A.N. Wilson reports that 300 "compromising" letters that were delivered to King Edward VII and presumably destroyed, so that "the mysterious relationship between Queen Victoria and her Highland soldier will therefore remain mysterious. Whether it was a marriage, as the Ponsonbys, other courtiers and the Home Secretary believed, or whether it was merely an intense intimacy which embarrassed her children, will never fully be known" (Wilson, *Victoria* 421–22). Biographer Julia Baird points to an encounter recorded in Dr. Reid's diary of flirting between Brown and Victoria, where they were seen lifting kilt and skirts, suggesting "a level of intimacy between them that would have scandalized society. The extent or nature of their physical relationship we will never know" (Baird 359, 361). Baird also wrote about attempts by Royal archivists to censor her book's passages about Victoria's burial instructions involving Brown. The publication of diaries by Lewis Harcourt that claiming that Rev. Norman Macleod married Victoria and Brown were reported in the *Sunday Morning Herald*, 5 May 2002. Ultimately, this is all circumstantial evidence, nothing conclusive.

20. Other historical goofs in *Victoria & Abdul* include the scene where the Prince of Wales and Dr. Reid show insanity papers to Victoria, which is somewhat exaggerated. In fact, what Reid presented to Queen Victoria was a detailed report of the Munshi's lies, financial cheating, and high-handedness, ending with a blunt warning that "there are people in high places, who know Your Majesty well, who say to me that the only charitable explanation that can be given is that Your Majesty is not sane" (Reid, *Ask Sir James* 145). Sir Henry Ponsonby died in 1895 but in the film shows up at Victoria's deathbed in 1901. The film depicts Victoria's lack of interest in the Boer War, while in fact her journals and letters show quite the opposite. Also incorrect is the film's portrayal of Victoria's misunderstanding of the Indian Mutiny; her journals and letters show that she knew what was happening and deplored atrocities on both sides (Hibbert 249–50).

21. Abdul received the Eastern Star (Basu 130), the Hessian Order of 2nd Class from the Grand Duke of Hesse, the Star of India, the Order of the Red Eagle from the Kaiser (Basu 198), and the CIE Companion of the Order of the Indian Empire (Baird 449). In 1897 his request for KCIE Knight Commander of the Indian Empire, which would have given him the title "Sir," was denied (Basu 229–231). Victoria clashed with her ministers about giving him the Member of the Royal Victoria Order (MVO) and backed down only when Prime Minister Salisbury convinced her that this award could cause Hindu outrage (Basu 240). Ultimately, Victoria awarded Abdul the Commander of the Victoria Order (CVO) in 1899, a rank between member and knight. In 1905 George Prince of Wales visited Abdul in Agra and was surprised to see him wearing the CVO (Basu 290–91).

22. Reactions to *Victoria & Abdul* have been mixed. *The Times of India*, 29 January 2017, reported that the film production company encountered disruptions by a right-wing group during shooting in Agra where the company had set up a statue of Queen Victoria for the final scene where Abdul kisses the statue's feet. Film critics' reaction have noted *Victoria & Abdul*'s limitations. Andy Lea in the *Daily Express* for 17 September 2017 calls it a "knockabout farce," and the film shows "nothing about his politics, his motives or even his feelings" (Lea np). In *The Observer* for 22 September 2017, Rex Reed likes Dench's acting "Brittle but warm, stubborn but querulous, and

capable of both larky humor and touching vulnerability"(Reed). In *The Independent* for 16 September 2017, Amrou Al-Kadhi takes a highly negative political stance: "Period dramas such as this are dangerous. They are pitched as light entertainment: tonally soft with a peppering of low stakes conflict—but they are rooted in the merciless grip of British imperialism" (Al-Kadhi np).

23. The film is based on Theodore Bonnet's 1949 novel *The Mudlark* (Twentieth-Century Fox purchased the rights for $75,000), which in turn was loosely based on the historical character "the boy Jones," who broke into Buckingham Palace on multiple occasions between 1838 and 1841. The novel has more political context than the film; it shows Disraeli working on the purchase of the Suez Canal and luring the Queen back to public life with the title Empress of India, neither of which are mentioned in *The Mudlark*.

24. *The Mudlark* received an Academy Award nomination for Costume Design in a black and white film (Edward Stevenson, Margaret Furse). In contrast, its reception in UK was negative. "*The Mudlark* was chosen as the Royal Command Performance film, which enraged critics, viewers and actors. Clearly, British sensibilities were injured by the apparent annexation of their national history. *The Mudlark* could not fulfil any significant cultural function, however artistically competent it was" (Harper 180).

25. A few other films touch on the same theme of a child searching for Queen Victoria, where the emphasis is on the search itself and the Victoria character is shown as the object of a search, rather than a fully realized character. In *Stories from a Flying Trunk* (1979), the Hans Christian Andersen story "The Little Match Girl" is adapted to tell the tale of a little matchstick girl who wanders the streets of London searching for Queen Victoria and finds a living statue of the Queen (John Dalby). In *Marigold* (1938), a young girl runs away from home to appeal to Queen Victoria (Pamela Stanley). *Alice au pays des merveilles* (1949), directed by Dallas Bower, is a live action and stop-motion puppetry version of the Lewis Carroll 1865 novel *Alice in Wonderland*. The live action queen (Pamela Brown) is very haughty, with large nose and chin in air; she is also ignorant, needing coaching from Prince Albert about Christ Church college's collection of incunabula (she does not know the word means "old books"). The animated Queen of Hearts is ugly and irascible, with a grotesquely exaggerated nose (very Hanoverian) and is, of course, obsessed with chopping off heads. The film was kept out of Britain due to the perception that the Queen of Hearts was too close to Queen Victoria. It was not widely seen in the U.S. because of a legal dispute with Walt Disney Productions which released their animated *Alice in Wonderland* in 1951.

26. This plot twist in *From Hell* is complete fantasy. The film conveniently ignores the Royal Marriage Act of 1772 which required the heir to the throne to obtain the monarch's permission before marrying and forbade marriages with Catholics. Any marriage contracted without prior consent by the monarch was null and void, thus removing the film's key plot motivation for the royal family to cover up the Prince's marriage to Ann Crook. The rest of the film is highly fictionalized; there was no historical proof of Gull's complicity with the Ripper murders; he was elderly and frail at the time. Nor is there historical evidence for Prince Albert Victor's clandestine marriage or for Inspector Abberline's drug addiction.

27. Critical reception for *From Hell* is summed up by Roget Ebert as "a Guignol about a cross-section of a thoroughly rotten society, corrupted from the top down. The Ripper murders cut through layers of social class to insulate the sinners from the results of their sins" (Ebert np).

28. In the genre of horror films, the most limited portrayal of Queen Victoria is in the 1933 *Mystery of the Wax Museum*. Spunky girl reporter (Glenda Farrell in a precursor to her Torchy Blane film series) investigates suspicious disappearances that lead her to a wax museum, populated with historical figures created by the mad, obsessed owner. In several cases, including the scenes with Queen Victoria, the "wax" figures are actually live actors. In the scene where the Victoria figure is most clearly shown, it is possible to see the actress, Margaret Mann, blink once.

29. *The Pirates! Band of Misfits* is the USA title; the UK title is *The Pirates! In an Adventure with Scientists*. The concern for U.S. audiences was that the word "scientist" would hurt box office. In fact, *The Pirates* grossed worldwide over $123 million (against a production budget of $55 mil-

lion), making it the fourth highest grossing stop-animation film of all times. *The Pirates'* successful blend of CGI and stop-motion animation garnered an Academy Award nomination for Best Animated Feature. *Rotten Tomatoes* summed it up as "some of the smartest, most skillfully animated fare that modern cinema has to offer." (*Rotten Tomatoes* 2012 np).

30. Other films about adult obsessions include the Queen Victoria in small, almost cameo roles. *Pearls of the Crown* (1937), directed by Sacha Guitry, traces a fictional history of seven pearls from Henry VIII to 1937. Queen Victoria finds four of the pearls in a hidden casket, previously owned by Queen Elizabeth I (both queens played by Yvette Pienne). Victoria utters "we are amused" and has them set in her crown. In *The Wrong Box* (1966) the obsession is with money, specifically a tontine or survivors' annuity scheme, worth over a hundred thousand pounds. Queen Victoria (Avis Bunnage) appears in a brief "whoops" scene, where instead of knighting one of the tontine beneficiaries, she accidentally decapitates him ("We are frightfully sorry, Sir Robert"). Obsession with women's sexuality is the subject of *Hysteria* (2011), the story of Dr. Joseph Granville's invention of the vibrator (originally a machine sold to physicians) and its use on "hysterical" women to achieve relief, i.e., orgasm. During the end credits, widowed Queen Victoria (Sylvia Strange) is shown receiving a box containing the medical device "The Jolly Molly."

Chapter 4

1. There is no credible evidence that Queen Victoria actually said, "We are not amused," but like many an urban myth, this one persists. One source for this story was Caroline Holland's memoirs, which include, without supporting evidence, "a tale of the unfortunate equerry who ventured during dinner at Windsor to tell a story with a spice of scandal or impropriety in it. 'We are not amused,' said the Queen when he had finished." (Holland 269). In his book *Queen Victoria Was Amused*, Alan Hardy offers several sources and speculates, without evidence, that the most authoritative version is that Victoria uttered the phrase to Alick Yorke "who was sitting next to a German to whom he told a slightly risqué story. The German guffawed so loudly that the Queen asked Aleck to tell her what had caused such mirth. Alick thereupon repeated the story and received the classic snub" (Hardy 7). In a 1976 interview, Victoria's granddaughter Princess Alice, Countess of Athlone, maintained that the Queen denied ever using the phrase (BBC 1977). Regardless of historical precedence, the phrase has become firmly associated with the Queen.

2. As pointed out by James Downs, "In reality, protocol had prohibited Victoria and Albert from dancing the waltz together—their high status, combined with the physical intimacy of the dance, meant that this was considered improper" (Downs 94). In fact, Victoria's journal shows that they danced quadrilles together (Downs 104).

3. A variation on the dance motif shows up in a later scene in *Sixty Glorious Years* at the Balmoral Highland games presided over by the Queen and Prince Albert. Their son Bertie competes in a Highland dance contest, and Albert convinces Victoria to award second place to their son and first place to a local boy. Bertie's reaction is not shown, and the film avoids taking on the subject of tension between monarch and heir, thus keeping a tight focus on the Victoria-Albert relationship.

4. Contrary to *Victoria in Dover*'s introduction of "new" waltzes by Johann Strauss, Sr., the historical reality is that Strauss had written and performed his waltzes at a state ball held earlier, for the occasion of Victoria's accession in 1837 and at her coronation in 1838, though she wasn't able to dance them, due to royal protocol.

5. A couple of other films use the waltz motif, though with Queen Victoria as a secondary character. *Waltz War* aka *Walzerkrieg* (1933) features the competition between composers Johann Strauss, Sr., and Joseph Länner. In the German version of this film, Anton Walbrook appears as Johann Strauss. Also there is a French version of this same film *Court Waltzes (*aka *La guerre des valses)* in 1933. Queen Victoria's role is limited to inviting Strauss to play in England. In *Let's Make Up* (aka *Lilacs in the Spring,* 1954), Anna Neagle plays a WWII stage star who must choose between two suitors. After being injured during an air raid, she has several dreams, one of which puts her in the role of young Queen Victoria introducing

the waltz at Windsor Castle. This film was based on a stage musical *The Glorious Days*, which was a big hit for Neagle in 1953.

6. These operatic choices in *Young Victoria* are odd. Bellini's *I Puritani* premiered on 24 January 1835 and was a huge hit in its day. This opera's subject would seem suitable for a young princess; the libretto presents two lovers caught up in the conflicts between Oliver Cromwell's Roundheads and Royalists, with a happy ending where Cromwell's pardons all prisoners at the end. In contrast, Bellini's *Norma ou L'infanticide* is quite another story, and one wonders why a protective mother would allow her daughter to see it. Its lurid plot concerns a love affair between a Druid priestess and a Roman officer, two children in peril of being murdered by their mother, and tragic conclusion where Norma and her lover expire on a funeral pyre, sans children.

7. Albert's love of Schubert is rather advanced for 1836. The piece "Ständchen" is No. 4 of *Schwanensgesang* D957, published posthumously 1829. Schubert had a limited circle of Austrian admirers in his lifetime and only in the 1830s was beginning to gain recognition.

8. Victoria's highbrow entertainment is captured in another biopic *Melba* (1953). Queen Victoria (Sybil Thorndike) enjoys an operatic performance by Nellie Melba and meets Melba personally in another scene. *Melba* was operatic soprano Patrice Munsel's only feature film "that extensively showcases Munsel in roles that she and Melba shared" (Greten-Harrison np).

9. Biographer Alan Hardy records Victoria's fondness for *tableaux vivants* "Just as the young Vicky…had been Summer in *The Seasons*, so now the matronly Beatrice would appear as Queen Elizabeth, or as India in a tableau representing *Empire*. Victoria could not get enough of such spectacles" (Hardy 160). The Munshi appeared in multiple tableaux vivant such as *Empire* (Schoch 28) and *The Queen of Sheba* (Basu 83). He coordinated characters, costumes, and music for the *Oriental Bazaar* (Basu 127–28), directed *An Indian Bazaar* (Basu 155), and starred in *Rebecca* "his face capturing the expressions of the devoted servant Eleazar as he waited near the well for Rebecca to choose a bride for his master. Minnie Cochrane, playing the title role, would have been less enthusiastic starring opposite Karim" (Basu 104).

10. Biographer Hibbert makes the point that Victoria was much better read than she is given credit for. Her tastes included Cooper's *The Last of the Mohicans*, Irving's *The Conquest of Granada*, Dickens' *Oliver Twist*, Dumas' *The Three Musketeers*, Austin's *Northanger Abbey*, Eliot's *Adam Bede*, Trollop's *Barchester Towers*, Stowe's *Uncle Tom's Cabin*, and Brontë's *Jane Eyre*, among others (Hibbert, *Personal* 478). In May 1828, nine-year old Princess Victoria met Sir Walter Scott, who was struck by the strict isolation imposed on her by the Kensington System: "This little lady is educating with much care, and watched so closely that no busy maid has a moment to whisper 'You are heir to England'" (Gill 399 n63).

11. A 2010 exhibition featured a number of nude paintings collected by Victoria, including a replica of *Florinda* by German painter Franz Xavier Winterhalter. It depicts seminude female bathers, spied upon by the King of Spain. She hung a replica of this painting over the Victoria and Albert writing desks at Osborne House (Nikkah np). Whether this painting was distracting to the Prince is not known.

12. The historical record shows the Buffalo Bill's Wild West show performed for Queen Victoria as part of her Golden Jubilee celebration in 1887. The London opening drew a crowd of 28,000. The royal command performance was staged at the East Terrace at Windsor Castle before an entourage of 26 (Hibbert, *Personal History* 418). There are two versions of how the Queen reacted to the American flag: Cody maintained that she stood and bowed while it passed by; contemporary press reports have the queen nodding to a lowered American flag (King 1). In her journal, Victoria noted her pleasure: "An attack on a coach & on a ranch, with an immense deal of firing, was most exciting, so was the buffalo hunt & the bucking ponies" (Carlson 2).

13. Queen Victoria saw Tom Thumb three times in 1844 and was amused by the tiny General's merry performance and his defiance of stuffy royal protocol. The 1986 *Barnum* film shows the General speaking directly to the Queen to her amusement, but eliminates the funniest part of his first audience with Queen Victoria. In this biography, Barnum recalled the long walk backwards, "whenever the General found he was losing ground, he turned around and ran a

few steps;...running ... was an offense sufficiently heinous to excite the indignation of the Queen's favourite poodle dog, and he vented his displeasure by barking so sharply as to startle the General from his propriety. He, however, recovered immediately, and with his little cane commenced an attack on the poodle, and a funny fight ensued which renewed and increased the merriment of the royal party" (Barnum 94).

14. Throughout her life, Queen Victoria was fascinated by circus acts and menageries: "As a princess, Victoria and her mother, the Duchess of Kent, first visited Wombwell's menagerie on 3 May 1830." (Tait 55). Circus showman George Sanger (known as "Lord George") was another of her favorites. As a young queen, Victoria "was enthralled with the thrilling performances of Isaac Van Amburgh, "the American lion-tamer, at Drury Lane Theater...where ferocious lions, cheetahs, and leopards became as tame as kittens under the mesmerizing eye of Van Amburgh. After seven visits her fascination still burned bright, and she stayed after the performance ended to walk on stage and examine the huge beasts in in their cages" (Erickson 78).

15. The critical reception for *The Greatest Showman* was definitely mixed and at times turns the film's politically correct aspirations against it. Despite its strong box office performance, *Rotten Tomatoes* (2017) faults it for not showing "its complex subject's far more intriguing real-life story." In the *Huffington Post* (21 December 2017), critic Jackie Cooper liked the musical numbers, which are very contemporary in style (not at all reminiscent of any music that Victoria would have heard), and the "message that should resonate with today's world concerning acceptance and courage" (Cooper np). However, that very political correctness leaves the film open for attack. Jackie Mansky in *Smithsonian* (22 December 2017) downgrades the film for failing to deal with the larger context of Barnum's racism and crass exploitation of an African American— billed by Barnum as George Washington's former nurse– and "living curiosities"—so-called "freaks" like the Siamese twins (Mansky np).

16. This telephone demonstration scene in *The Story of Alexander Graham Bell* follows history, up to a point. Contemporary newspapers indicate that the 1878 demo resulted in installation first at Osborne House, and only later at Buckingham Palace (Erickson 221). Also, the film cuts off the demo, no doubt for reasons of narrative economy. Apparently, Victoria conversed with Sir Thomas and Lady Biddulph, who were at Osborne Cottage, and a Miss Kate Field sang several songs into the telephone. Letters between Bell and Biddulph indicate that the Queen decided "to purchase the 2 Instruments which are still here [Osborne House] with the wires attached. I think I understood the price would be about £25 each" (*Queen Victoria's Scrapbook* np).

17. Victoria's patronage of the Great Exhibition is briefly shown in *Steamboy* (2004).The inventions used by Victoria featured cutting-edge communication technology. She exchanged the first official transatlantic telegram (98-words) with President James Buchanan on 16 August 1858 (*Report of the Joint Committee* 232). Victoria also commissioned Guglielmo Marconi to install a wireless in Osborne House in 1898 and the royal yacht. When Bertie hurt his knee while onboard, she bombarded him with "150 bulletins" (Bathgate 12). There is some evidence that Queen Victoria recorded a few words in 1888 during a demonstration by Sydney Morse of the British Graphophone Company. This recording on a Graphophone cardboard cylinder is located in London's Science Museum by Paul Tritton and was transcribed via modern equipment in 1991. (Dash np).

Chapter 5

1. Laurence Houseman's 1934 play *Victoria Regina* has been adapted for radio and television multiple times. Helen Hayes recorded at 30-minute radio version of *Victoria Regina* for the Electric Radio Theater in 1948. Television adaptations include: 1947 with Sheila Beckett; 1951 (Episode 2.10 of *Robert Montgomery Presents* series) with Helen Hayes recreating her Broadway role; 1957 (for ITV Play of the Week) with Dorothy Tutin; 1957 (Episode 8.31 of the *Robert Montgomery Presents* series) with Claire Bloom; 1961 (Episode 11.2 of *Hallmark Hall of Fame* series) with Julie Harris; 1963 with Lola Brooks in an Australian television 60-minute version titled *The Young Victoria*; and 1964 for Granada Television

with Patricia Routledge. Prunella Scales toured in a one-woman stage show titled "An Evening with Queen Victoria," and her research for this stage role was the subject of a 2003 television documentary *Looking for Victoria*. A curiosity piece is a television recording of a 1976 stage version of Ellen Wood's 1861 novel *East Lynne* by the City Variety Theatre in Leeds. The play is framed by an audience dressed in Victorian costume with Queen Victoria in the Royal Box, thus lending royal prestige to this lurid tale of female infidelity, illegitimacy, and life-long repentance.

2. The "Responsible Government" episode of the Canadian television *Heritage Minutes* series actually conflates events between 1837 and 1849. In 1837–38, the Canadian Rebellions were fueled by local discontent with corruption in the colonial governments of Upper and Lower Canada. A recommendation to unify both Upper and Lower Canada into one province was implemented in 1840, and "responsible government" was granted in 1849, making the governor general a figurehead and giving power to the Canadian legislative assembly elected by the people.

3. The real Station Jim was a canine collector at the Slough railway station from 1894 to 1896. After his death he was stuffed and put on display at Slough Railway Station.

4. Shaka Zulu's opening episode "Epilogue" stacks the deck somewhat against Victoria. As historian Christopher Hibbert notes "It pained her, though, to have to approve of her soldiers fighting against such brave, black-skinned warriors as the Zulu King Cetshwayo who should be treated well, as she told the Government when the war was over" (Hibbert, *Personal* 365).

5. The Ian McShane *Disraeli* series is representative of several television treatments of Disraeli with Queen Victoria as a secondary character. For example, the biopic "The Invincible Mr. Disraeli" (*Hallmark Hall of Fame*, 4 April 1963, Episode 12.4) uses a series of vignettes to cover a 30-year span of Disraeli's life. Trevor Howard, with prominent forehead curl, plays Disraeli, and Kate Reid appears as Queen Victoria. The "Dizzy" episode of *Number 10* (20 March 1983, Episode 1.6) focuses on the private life of Disraeli, starring Richard Pasco as Disraeli and Zena Walker as Queen Victoria, who appears in a very limited amount of screen time.

6. In his review of the DVD release of *Disraeli: Portrait of a Romantic*, Paul Mavis noted the confusing presentation of historical events: "I know I was frequently stopping the film, and Googling certain names and terms that, while familiar to me, needed further explanation to get the context of what the filmmakers were trying to say." He characterized the series as "resolutely mid-seventies English TV…with the overwhelming emphasis on 'talking heads' drama…That being said, *Disraeli* is marvelous—in you're in the mood for a lot of talk, but talk delicately nuanced by terrific performances and a willingness to be thorough and deliberate in character development" (Mavis, *Disraeli* np).

7. *Edward the Seventh* was the original title from 1975. It was released in the U.S. as *Edward the King* in 1979. Annette Crosbie won the 1976 BAFTA award for Best Actress for her role as Queen Victoria. Critical reception was mixed. Blog reviewer "Woostersauce 2014" noted "the majority of the action takes place inside a studio set with painted scenes providing the backdrop," but that characterization is the strong point of this series: "The characters in *Edward the Seventh* are more credible as personalities of that era than those in *Downton Abbey* given their attitudes reflect more the twenty first century than the early twentieth…while later costume dramas may be more sophisticated in terms of locations and technical wizardry, *Edward the Seventh* remains noteworthy for …its respect for the values and behavior of an era very different from our own" (Woostersauce2014, np).

8. A parody of the *Edward the Seventh* series appeared in an episode of *The Phantom Raspberry Blower of Old London Town*, later adapted for the 1976 season of comedy sketch show *The Two Ronnies*. It features Ronnie Barker as browbeaten Bertie and Ronnie Corbet as domineering Queen Victoria ("God Bless Her"), who refuses to let Bertie out of the palace. The Queen's confrontation with Bertie, when she believes he is the Phantom Raspberry Blower, is staged much like the parallel scene in *Edward the Seventh*. Another skit for *Phantom Raspberry Blower* has the two Ronnies dressing up an entire squad of policemen as Queen Victoria, in

an attempt to capture the Phantom Raspberry Blower.

9. John Sinnott has similar reservations about the *Fall of Eagles* series. "The main point of contention that I have with the series is that some of the episodes don't really have anything to do with the main thrust of the program, tracing the fall of three empires. The second episode about Queen Victoria's' oldest daughter in Germany was a very good installment, but was basically padding... The last episode just mentions in passing the killing of Tsar Nicholas and his family" (Sinnott np).

10. Another Queen Victoria television biopic mentioned in television histories is the series *Happy and Glorious*, which aired in six episodes from September to October 1952. Recordings of these episodes were not made.

11. In general, critics were highly entertained by the 1978 *Lillie* series. Charlene Gianetti praises it as "a feast for the eyes with the costumes and scenery worthy of a Merchant and Ivory production... faithful to the period... The performances by Annis and the rest of the cast as Oscar worthy" (Gianetti np). Laurence Marcus states "the production was hailed as a great success due in no small part to the performance of Francesca Annis who portrayed Lillie from a young girl to an elderly woman of 76 years" (Marcus np).

12. "Daisy" was reviewed harshly by Paul Mavis "easily the worse episode of *The Edwardians* series. Frequently designed to look like a stage musical (complete with stylized sets and performers jumping around and throwing their hands in the air), Daisy utterly fails to engage the viewer in the 'plight' of its lead, with a thoroughly irritating performance by Virginia McKenna... by the time the Greek chorus of Cockney chimney sweeps (right out of Mary Poppins) started singling little asides to the main action, I dug my heels in" (Mavis, *Edwardians* np).

13. Rebecca Thomas' interview with *Victoria & Albert* producer David Cunliffe, "Victoria finds her passion" quotes the producer's view that Victoria and Albert were "a lusty couple" and that his decision to show them in bed on their wedding night raised some eyebrows (Thomas np).

14. Several other television series about the Victoria and Albert love story are not readily available for viewing today: "The Consort" Episode 2.19 of *Telephone Time*, aired 27 January 1957, as well as televised play by Farrukh Dhondy about Victoria and the Munshi "The Empress and the Munshi" (1984) and a television short "In Court with Queen Victoria" aired 18 February 2012, arguably precursors that sparked interest leading up to the 2017 film *Victoria & Abdul*. Another examination of the love/power dynamic between Victoria and Albert is explored in the recent docu-drama *Albert: The Power Behind the Throne* (29 September 2018). This production uses a scripted documentary-drama style and draws heavily from letters and historical accounts, with experts explaining and commenting on the story of Prince Albert's rise from poverty to power.

15. The Privy Council scene in *Victoria & Albert* has Victoria in a white dress, which is not historically correct; as noted for *The Young Victoria*, Emily Blunt wears the correct black dress to that meeting. However, the white dress does make a better visual contrast between the young Queen and all the old men surrounding her.

16. Critical reception for the *Victoria* miniseries noticed both the parallels to *Downton Abbey* and historical inaccuracies. Tim Goodman notes: "If PBS and Masterpiece were looking for that elusive post-*Downton Abbey* hit... they might have found it with the thoroughly enjoyable and addictive *Victoria* [which] delivers precisely two of the most essential elements of making historical fiction work: Is the cast—and particularly the lead—a group you want to spend hours with, and does the plot move at a brisk, entertaining clip?" (Goodman np). James Delingpole condemns the historical inaccuracies calling the series "silly, facile and irresponsible... fluffy escapism... Taking the odd liberty is one thing but doing so with such brazen shamelessness feels to me like one giant upraised middle finger to all of us—we're a minority but we do exist—who value history and who want to be informed as least as much as we want to be entertained" (Delingpole np).

17. Victoria and Albert were both convinced that Edward Oxford intentionally shot at them, that "he was not mad... [instead he was] a villain who deserved punishment" (Murphy 66). The Home Secretary and Victoria herself were "annoyed"

by the insanity verdict (Hibbert, *Personal* 422). Another point, not picked up by films or television series, is that one of Oxford's motives was that "he did not think a great country like England should be ruled by a woman" (Baird 155).

18. Taking her first railway ride on 13 June 1842 Queen Victoria really did love the experience, though not necessarily while pregnant and standing up in an open carriage, as *Victoria* Episode 1.7 portrays. "When the couple traveled on a train for the first time, a short trip from Slough to London ... Albert suffered motion sickness and was unsettled by the speed of forty-four miles per hour. Victoria loved it; 'I find the motion so very easy, far more so than a carriage and cannot understand how anyone can suffer from it'" (Baird 209, Hibbert, *Personal* 170).

19. The *Victoria* series takes broad license with the historical record to the point of total fiction in many key events unfortunately presented as factual to a television audience not familiar with the details of the Victorian reign. The conflict with Uncle Cumberland/ King of Hanover is completely made up; he was not in England repeatedly as the series shows (only one visit in 1843). There is no evidence of a conspiracy between Cumberland, Conroy, and the Duchess of Kent to have Victoria declared insane (Flantzer np). Melbourne was 40 years older than Victoria, and she viewed him as a father figure, not a potential husband. Historical events are conflated by moving later or earlier in time. For example, Episode 2.3 set in 1842 ends with two deaths: Lord Melbourne, who actually died in 1848, and Dash the spaniel, who died in 1840. Episode 2.8 conflates into a few months the ouster of Lehzen (actually 1841), the death of Drummond (actually 1843), and the repeal of the Corn Laws (actually 1846). While these date conflations can be justified as strategies to keep the narrative moving, the downstairs soap opera is entirely fictional. The romance of cook Francatelli and dresser Skerrett is simply made up. Francatelli's departure from royal service was in fact the result of a violent quarrel with another servant (Saunders np). The Nancy Skerrett character is so loosely based on the actual Marianne Skerrett as to be a total fabrication; Marianne was in her mid-40s during the period of this series and served as dresser from 1837 to 1863 (Erickson 65). On the other hand, the series is quite accurate in its comic presentation of the culinary disasters created by the interim chef (while Francatelli is gone), notably the vile cock-a-leekie soup, a real recipe including whole chicken, head and all, seasoned with prunes.

20. The *Victoria* series correctly points out that the Queen's courage in responding to the eight assassination attempts became a way to strengthen the monarchy. "Victoria, with unerring instinct and sheer gutsiness, converted each episode of near-tragedy into one of triumphant renewal for her monarchy, each time managing to strengthen the bond between herself and her subjects... Victoria, it becomes clear, was a canny politician who inherited a tainted monarchy and made it her life's work to create anew the stable, modern monarchy that endures to this day" (Murphy xi).

21. See William Constable's 5 March 1842 daguerreotype of Prince Albert. While badly faded, it shows a receding hairline (and a comb-over) surprising for man in his early twenties. It is considered the first surviving photograph of a member of the British Royal family. www.royalcollection.org.uk/collection/2932488/prince-albert-1819-1861. Accessed 13 September 2018.

22. Contrary to Episode 3.3 of the *Victoria* series, Queen Victoria was incensed by Palmerston's plan to host Hungarian anti-monarchist Lajos Kossuth. She deliberately overstepped the bounds of constitutional monarchy and wrote to Prime Minister Russell protesting "the official conduct of her Secretary of State since the arrival of M. Kossuth in this country" (20 November 1851), and again the next day "The Queen cannot suppose that Lord John considers the official reception by the Secretary of State for Foreign Affairs of addresses, in which allied Sovereigns are called Despots and Assassins, as within the 'latitude' which he claims for every Minister" (Hibbert, *QV Letters and Journals* 86). Palmerston's reception for Kossuth never happened as staged in the Victoria episode. The Prime Minister's cabinet voted against such a meeting. In defiance, Palmerston hosted a delegation of trade unionists who praised Kossuth and called the emperors of Austria and Russia "despots."

23. Another reference to Queen Victoria appears in *Blackadder* Episode 4.5 (1989) "General Hospital." Blackadder is com-

missioned to find the German spy in the hospital. Ignoring the patient with a thick German accent who is suspiciously asking military questions, Blackadder accuses Captain Darling of being the spy. Darling protests that he is "as British as Queen Victoria." Blackadder's reply is hilarious: "So your father's German, you're half German, and you married a German."

24. Another example of verbal farce appears in the "Under the Linden Tree with Queen Victoria" sketch in Episode 3.1 (2009) of *That Mitchell and Webb Look*, a series inspired by the duo's earlier radio show. An ambassador from the Confederacy (presumably, due to the Southern accent) presents 10,000 linden trees to Queen Victoria (Robert Webb), who takes her Prime Minister (David Mitchell) aside and objects to the bad smell: "Can you smell cum... Incredibly strong." They keep the verbal joke going for several minutes, with the Prime Minister going on a rant about Victorian values, the heat of Victorian clothing, and the Queen's obligation to accept the gift.

25. Queen Victoria also shows up in one farce produced in the United States. An unaired Episode 1.6 "Pigeon English" of the 1998 farce comedy series *The Secret Diary of Desmond Pfeiffer* (the "P" isn't silent) includes a passing reference to Queen Victoria (Irvin np). When Lincoln falls ill before a meeting with Queen Victoria (Wendy Worthington), Mary Todd Lincoln (Christine Estabrook) decides to hire a body double to impersonate the president. Little does the body double know that she also wants him to impersonate the president in the bedroom. Considered one of the worst television series of all times, this episode is not readily available for viewing.

26. A few other television shows consign the Queen Victoria to the background. *My Father Knew Lloyd George* (1965) is a satire where a young aristocrat (John Fortune) tries to distance his grandfather from a scandal involving the Prime Minister's wife, and Queen Victoria (John Bird) has a small role. Episode 1.2 (1969) of *The Flaxton Boys* has the 1854 generation of the Flaxton Hall boys meet Martin, the deserter, who effects a rescue in sight of Queen Victoria (Christine Ozanne). *The Young Visitors*, aired in 1965, is based on a 1918 novel by a 9-year-old girl Daisy Ashford and tells the story of a middle-aged man who tries to impress a social climbing woman by improving his manners at a gentleman's training school and is invited to a reception hosted by the Prince of Wales, where Queen Victoria (Janine Duvitski) is a background figure. The "Christmas with Morecambe & Wise" comedy skit show includes Glenda Jackson playing Queen Victoria in Ernie Wise's short play "Victoria and Albert." Pamela Kosh has a small role as Queen Victoria in "Baby Blues" (3 January 1994), Episode 5.11 of *Northern Exposure* about women who are about to become mothers. In "Annie Oakley" 24 December 1985), Episode 1.9 of *Tall Tales & Legends*, Lu Leonard appears briefly as Queen Victoria.

27. The historical record indicates that Queen Victoria found comfort in Tennyson's "In Memoriam A.H.H." after Prince Albert's death, in particular the lines: " 'Tis better to have loved and lost / Than never to have loved at all." The "Tooth and Claw" episode's script does not delve into Tennyson's more profound discussion of the conflict between faith in God versus a cruel Nature (relentless, impersonal, no life after death): "Are God and Nature then at strife / That Nature lends such evil dreams? "Man... Who trusted God was love indeed / And love Creation's final law / Tho' Nature, red in tooth and claw / With ravine, shriek'd against his creed."

28. This image in the *Doctor Who* "Tooth and Claw" Episode 2.2 foreshadows the image later in the same season, in the "Doomsday" Episode 2.13 where the Doctor and Rose, separated in parallel universes, press their ears to a dividing wall vainly listening for each other.

29. Three other time travel shows, not readily available for viewing, include the Queen Victoria character. In "Queen Victoria," Episode 1.30 (1995) of *A.J.'s Time Travelers*, Malloy, a teen-age time traveler, meets with Queen Victoria in one of his adventures in the time travelling ship Kryos. In *Timekeepers of the Millennium* (1999), two muppet-like workers must travel back in time to retrieve key parts of the Great Clock (scattered through different parts of history, including Queen Victoria's era) before the end of 1999 or there will be no millennium. In the 2004 series *Shadow Play*, a young boy's family takes refuge in an abandoned manor house where he starts filming the house and uncovers a mystery. His camcorder allows him to see the Victorian world; the Queen

Victoria character appears in four of the *Shadow Play* episodes.

Chapter 6

1. Queen Victoria has limited screen time in other *Black Butler* series. Based on the fourth *Kuroshitsuji* manga, the story arc in *Black Butler: Book of Circus* (2014) includes an interpolation coming after first season, 1.15 Episode of Queen Victoria and the curry contest. Ciel receives orders from the Queen via a letter, voice-over and image of the old, smiling Victoria on her throne. In her only appearance in *Circus*, she orders Ciel to investigate the travelling Noah's Arc Circus and its suspected role in the abduction of children. In the OVA two-episode *Black Butler: Book of Murder* (2014), the Queen Victoria character is an off-screen presence who delivers orders to Ciel via her two butlers, and is behind a plot to frame Ciel for a murder, as punishment for his disobedience at the end of *Book of Circus*. The Queen has a small on-screen appearance in *Black Butler: Book of the Atlantic* (2017, theatrical release). During the many battles against zombies running amok on a Titanic-like ocean liner, a flashback shows Queen Victoria in a ceremony where she invests Ciel as Earl Phantomhive.

2. Queen Victoria lends only the name of her era to two Empire building games: *Victoria: An Empire Under the Sun* (2003) and *Victoria II* (2010) by Paradox Entertainment. Classified as grand strategy games, both are set in 1837–1901 with an extension pack to 1936. These games allow the player to develop the economic system, by controlling resources, engaging in bilateral diplomacy, or engaging in limited warfare. The Queen Victoria character is not featured in the game and appears only on the cover of the media box in the Diamond Jubilee image.

3. Queen Victoria has a small role in *The Great Turnabout Trial: The Adventures of Ryūnosuke Naruhodō* aka *Dai Gyakuten Saiban: Naruhodō Ryūnosuke no Bōken* (2015). In this courtroom style game, the game is divided between investigation and courtroom. This game is set in the Meiji Period (in Britain the Victorian era). Ryūnosuke Naruhodō and his assistant Susato Mikotoba, travel to England to further their legal studies. They work beside Sherlock Holmes and his assistant Iris Watson, daughter of Dr. John Watson (deceased). Queen Victoria watches the climactic trial and strips the main villain of his position as chief justice. The Queen does not appear in court; instead, another character reads her decree to the court.

Works Cited

Afternoon Tea in the Gardens of Clarence House (1897). British Mutoscope and Biograph Co. (UK). 8 m. BFI Cat. 62658. www.imdb.com/title/tt2308461/?ref_=fn_al_tt_1. Accessed 28 February 2018.

Al-Kadhi, Amrou. "*Victoria and Abdul* Is Another Dangerous Example of British Filmmakers Whitewashing Colonialism." *The Independent*, 16 September 2017. www.independent.co.uk/voices/victoria-and-abdul-white-wash-british-empire-colonialism-poverty-slavery-a7950541.html. Accessed 19 June 2018.

"Alexander Graham Bell Demonstrates the Telephone to Queen Victoria." *Staffordshire Sentinel*, 17 January 1878. blog.britishnewspaperarchive.co.uk/2013/03/03/alexander-graham-bell/. Accessed 25 July 2018.

"Alhambra Theatre." en.wikipedia.org/wiki/Alhambra_Theatre. Accessed 28 December 2017.

Allan, Bruce. "Coronation at Denham." *Motion Picture Herald*, 22 May 1937. archive.org/details/motionpictureher127unse/page/n423. Accessed 6 January 2019.

American Film Institute Catalog of Feature Films: The First 100 Years 1893–1993. catalog.afi.com/Catalog/Showcase. Accessed 6 December 2018.

American Mutoscope & Biograph Picture Catalogue. American Mutoscope and Biograph Company, 1902. rucore.libraries.rutgers.edu/rutgers-lib/24582/PDF/1/play/. Accessed 6 December 2018.

"An American Queen: Extra Chins Help Irene Dunne Portray Victoria," *Life Magazine* 11 September 1950, p. 81. books.google.com/books?id=9U0EAAAAMBAJ&q=mudlark#v=snippet&q=mudlark&f=false. Accessed 7 January 2019.

Annie Oakley (1894). Thomas Edison Company (USA). archive.org/details/AnnieOakley. Accessed 27 July 2018.

"Auguste and Louis Lumiere." en.wikipedia.org/wiki/Auguste_and_Louis_Lumi%C3%A8re. Accessed 28 December 2017.

Baird, Julia. *Victoria the Queen: An Intimate Biography of the Woman Who Ruled an Empire*. Random House, 2016.

Baird, Julia. "Victoria's Secrets: What the Royal Archives Didn't Want You to Know About England's Queen." *New York Times*, 19 November 2016. www.nytimes.com/2016/11/20/opinion/sunday/victorias-secrets-what-the-royal-archives-didnt-want-you-to-know-about-englands-queen.html. Accessed 19 June 2018.

Barnes, John. *The Beginnings of Cinema in England*. Davie and Charles, 1976.

Barnes, John. *The Rise of the Cinema in Great Britain*. Bishopsgate Press, 1983.

Barnum, P.T. *The Life of P.T. Barnum*. New York: Redfield, 1855. archive.org/details/lifeofptbarnum5815barn/page/n7. Accessed 14 December 2018.

Barrett, Jerry. "Queen Victoria's First Visit to Her Wounded Soldiers." Oil painting, 1856. www.npg.org.uk/collections/search/portraitExtended/mw08509/Queen-Victorias-First-Visit-to-her-Wounded-Soldiers. Accessed 9 January 2018.

Barry, Matt. "Alfred Clark: Narrative and Special Effects Pioneer." artandcultureofmovies.blogspot.com/2010/03/-alfred-clark-narrative-and-special.html. Accessed 23 December 2017.

Basu, Shrabani. *Victoria & Abdul: The Extraordinary True Story of the Queen's Closest Confidant*. 2011. The History Press, 2017.

Bathgate, Gordon. *Voices from the Ether: The History of Radio.* Girdleness Publishing 2012.

Bayly, Paul. *David Livingstone: Africa's Greatest Explorer.* Font Hill Media, 2013.

Bombardment of Colenso by 4.7 Guns of HMS "Terrible" / Battle of Colensco (Boer War, 13–15 December 1899). British Mutoscope & Biograph Co. (UK). www.imdb.com/title/tt0344949/?ref_=fn_al_tt_1. Accessed 6 March 2018.

Bourke, Joanna. "History on Film: Queen Victoria's Funeral." *History Extra,* March 2013. www.historyextra.com/article/premium/queen-victoria-funeral-death-history-film. Accessed 7 December 2017.

Bradshaw, Peter. "The Young Victoria." *The Guardian,* 5 March 2009. www.theguardian.com/film/2009/mar/06/the-young-victoria-film-review. Accessed 7 January 2019.

British Film Institute: Collections Search. collections-search.bfi.org.uk/web. Accessed 15 January 2018.

British Pathé Catalog. www.britishpathe.com/. Accessed 15 January 2018.

"British Royal Train." *Wikipedia.* en.wikipedia.org/wiki/British_Royal_Train. Accessed 9 January 2017.

Brown, Geoff. "Balaclava (1928)." Film notes for a showing at the *19th British Silent Film Festival,* 15 September 2017. britishsilentfilmfestival.files.wordpress.com/2015/09/balaclava.pdf. Accessed 15 April 2018.

Brown, Richard, and Barry Anthony. *The Kinetoscope: A British History.* John Libbey Publishing, 2017.

Brown, Richard and Barry Anthony. *A Victorian Film Enterprise: The History of the British Mutoscope and Biograph Company, 1897–1915.* Flicks Books, 1999.

Carlson, Peter. "Encounter: Buffalo Bill at Queen Victoria's Command." Originally published in *American History Magazine,* www.historynet.com/encounter-buffalo-bill-at-queen-victorias-command.htm. Accessed 18 July 2018.

Chapman, James. *Past and Present: National Identity and the British Historical Film.* I.B. Tauris, 2005.

Children of the Royal Family Playing Soldiers I (1900). British Mutoscope & Biograph Co. Kinora reel 244. www.imdb.com/title/tt0299662/?ref_=fn_al_tt_1. Accessed 28 February 2018.

Children of the Royal Family Playing Soldiers II (1900). British Mutoscope & Biograph Co. www.imdb.com/title/tt0299663/?ref_=fn_al_tt_2. Accessed 28 February 2018.

Christie, Ian. *The Last Machine: Early Cinema and the Birth of the Modern World.* BBC Education, 1995.

Christie, Ian. "'A Very Wonderful Process': Queen Victoria, Photography and Film at the Fin De Siècle." *The British Monarchy on Screen,* edited by Mandy Merck. Manchester University Press, 2016, pp. 23–46.

Cinematek—Cinémathèque Royale De Belgique (CRB). www.filmarchives-online.eu/contact/cinematheque-royale-de-belgique. Accessed 6 December 2018.

Clayton, Zoe. "Stereographs." *Victoria and Albert Museum.* Blog published 29 January 2013. www.vam.ac.uk/blog/-factory-presents/stereographs. Accessed 9 January 2018.

Constable, William. "Prince Albert (1819–1861), Daguerreotype, 5 March 1842. www.royalcollection.org.uk/collection/2932488/prince-albert-1819-1861. Accessed 13 September 2018.

Cooper, Jackie K. "'The Greatest Showman' Is Movie Magic." *Huffington Post,* 21 December 2017. www.huffingtonpost.com/entry/the-greatest-showman-is-movie-magic_us_5a3c6921e4b06cd2bd03d98a. Accessed 23 July 2018.

Dargis, Manohla. "Poor Little Royal Girl: A Melancholy Monarch." *New York Times,* 17 December 2009. www.nytimes.com/2009/12/18/movies/18young.html. Accessed 7 January 2019.

Dash, Mike. "In Search of Queen Victoria's Voice." *Smithsonian.com,* 6 October 2011. www.smithsonianmag.com/history/in-search-of-queen-victorias-voice-98809025/. Accessed 25 July 2018.

David, Saul. "Victoria the Warrior Queen." *BBC History Magazine,* 4 May 2006. www.historyextra.com/period/victorian/-victoria-the-warrior-queen/. Accessed 12 April 2018.

"David Livingstone." *Westminster Abbey.* www.westminster-abbey.org/our-history/people/david-livingstone. Accessed 3 May 2018.

De Bary, Wm Theodore, and Richard Lufrano. *Sources of Chinese Tradition: From 1600 Through the Twentieth Century.* Columbia University Press, 2000.

Works Cited

Delingpole, James. "ITV's Victoria Is Silly, Facile and Irresponsible—I Blame the Feminization of Culture." *The Spectator*, 17 September 2016. www.spectator.co.uk/2016/09/itvs-victoria-is-silly-facile-and-irresponsible-i-blame-the-feminisation-of-culture/. Accessed 24 November 2018.

"Disraeli," *Variety*, 9 October 1929. archive.org/details/variety96-1929-10/page/n141. Accessed 27 April 2018.

Downs, James. "Walbrook's Royal Waltzes." *The British Monarchy on Screen*, edited by Mandy Merck. Manchester University Press, 2016.

Dubbelboes, Marieke. "Fifty Shades of Queen Victoria: The Year 1900 in La Caricature" *Poisonous Pens: Époque Media Culture*, 8 December 2014. poisonouspens.wordpress.com/2014/12/08/fifty-shades-of-queen-victoria-the-year-1900-in-la-caricature/. Accessed 4 May 2018.

Ebert, Roger. "From Hell." 19 October 2001. www.rogerebert.com/reviews/from-hell-2001. Accessed 7 January 2019.

Ebert, Roger. "The Young Victoria." 16 December 2009. www.rogerebert.com/reviews/the-young-victoria-2009. Accessed 7 January 2019.

"Empire, Leicester Square." en.wikipedia.org/wiki/Empire,_Leicester_Square. Accessed 7 December 2017.

Enoch, Nick. "Amazing Footage from 1897 Shows Queen's Great-great-grandmother Victoria During Her Diamond Jubilee Carriage Procession." *Daily Mail*, 6 June 2012. www.dailymail.co.uk/news/article-2155328/Diamond-Jubilee-Footage-1897-Queens-great-great-grandmother-Victoria-Diamond-Jubilee-carriage-procession.html. Accessed 10 January 2017.

Erickson, Carolly. *Her Little Majesty: The Life of Queen Victoria*. Simon & Schuster, 1997.

Evening Star (Washington, D.C.), 25 November. 1928. Image and caption "The Immortal Charge of the Light Brigade." chroniclingamerica.loc.gov/lccn/sn83045462/1928-11-25/ed-1/seq-108/. Accessed 17 April 2018.

The Execution of Mary, Queen of Scots (1895). Edison Manufacturing Company (USA). www.imdb.com/title/tt0132134/. Accessed 29 December 2017.

Ezra, Elizabeth. *Georges Méliès: The Birth of the Auteur*. Manchester University Press, 2000.

Farwell, Byron. *Queen Victoria's Little Wars*. Harper & Row, 1972.

Fells, Robert M. *The 1921 "Lost" DISRAELI: A Photo Reconstruction of the George Arliss Silent Film (The Arliss Archives Book 4)*. Arliss Publishing House, 2013.

Ferguson, Niall. *Empire: The Rise and Demise of the British World Order and the Lessons for Global Power*. Basic Books, 2004.

Ferris, Norman B. *The Trent Affair: A Diplomatic Crisis*. University of Tennessee Press, 1977.

Fielding, Stephen. "The Heart of a Heartless Political World: Screening Victoria." *The British Monarchy on Screen*, edited by Mandy Merck. Manchester University Press, 2016, pp. 64–85.

Flantzer, Susan. "What's Wrong with 'Victoria' Season 1?" *Unofficial Royalty*, 9 February 2017. www.unofficialroyalty.com/whats-wrong-with-victoria-why-the-alternative-facts/. Accessed 13 September 2018.

Fletcher, Tony. "The London County Council and the Cinematograph, 1896–1900." *Living Pictures: The Journal of the Popular and Projected Image Before 1914*. Flick Books, 1:2 (2001), 69–83.

Forster, E.M. *Aspects of the Novel*. Penguin, 1970.

"The Funeral of the Queen." *The Railway News*. 9 February 1901, pp. 203–204. books.google.com/books?id=_xo1AQAAIAAJ&pg=PA825&lpg=PA825&dq=railway+news+1901+vol+75&source=bl&ots=i4ovOPapSB&sig=jdz9Iv62sfjrhlrpd0i2dJTZ1T4&hl=en&sa=X&ved=0ahUKEwiJt-nL9-HYAhUPXK0KHRWHB10Q6AEILDAB#v=onepage&q&f=false. Accessed 18 January 2017.

Gallagher, Tag. "Brother Feeney—Francis Ford." sensesofcinema.com/2009/feature-articles/brother-feeney-francis-ford/. Accessed 30 March 2018.

George Méliès. en.wikipedia.org/wiki/Georges_Méliès. Accessed 7 December 2017.

Gernsheim, Alison. "The Rise and Fall of the Crinoline." *Victorian & Edwardian Fashion: A Photographic Survey*. Dover Publications, 1981.

Gianetti, Charlene. "Lillie." www.womanaroundtown.com/sections/playing-around/beauty-francesca-annis-as-beauty-lillie-langtry/. Accessed 16 August 2018.

Gibson, Charles Robert. *Wireless Telegraphy and Telephony Without Wires*. Philadelphia: Lippincott Co. 1914.

Gifford, Denis. *The British Film Catalogue: Fiction Film, 1895–1994*. 1999. Routledge, 2001.

Gill, Gillian. *We Two Victoria and Albert: Rulers, Partners, Rivals*. Random House, 2009.

Goodman, Tim. "'Victoria': TV Review." *The Hollywood Reporter*, 13 January 2017. www.hollywoodreporter.com/review/-victoria-review-964051. Accessed 20 January 2019.

Graves, Charles Larcom. *Mr. Punch's History of Modern England Vol. II—1857–1874*. Cassell and Company, 1921.

"Great North of Scotland Railway." en.wikipedia.org/wiki/Great_North_of_Scotland_Railway. Accessed 9 January 2018.

"The Greatest Showman." *Rotten Tomatoes*. www.rottentomatoes.com/m/the_greatest_showman_2017. Accessed 23 July 2018.

Green, Dominic. "This Oscar-Nominated Biopic Is an Act of Anachronistic Class Warfare." *The New Republic*, 17 February 2015. newrepublic.com/article/121078/-mike-leighs-mr-turner-distorts-artist-political-purposes. Accessed 19 July 2018.

Greten-Harrison. "Melba." *Opera News*, June 2012. www.operanews.com/Opera_News_Magazine/2012/6/Recordings/Melba.html. Accessed 16 July 2018.

"Guglielmo Marconi." *History.com*. www.history.com/topics/inventions/guglielmo-marconi. Accessed 25 July 2018.

Hampton, Janie. "Queen Victoria's First Railway Journey." *The History Girls*, 27 June 2017. the-history-girls.blogspot.com/2017/06/queen-victorias-first-railway-journey.html. Accessed 22 December 2018.

Hardie, Frank. *The Political Influence of Queen Victoria, 1861–1901*. Frank Cass & Co. 1935.

Hardy, Alan. *Queen Victoria Was Amused*. Murray, 1976.

Harper, Sue. *Picturing the Past: The Rise and Fall of the British Costume Film*. British Film Institute, 1994.

Hawkins, Kathleen. "The Real Tom Thumb and the Birth of Celebrity." *BBC*, 25 November 2014. www.bbc.com/news/-blogs-ouch-30034409. Accessed 20 July 2018.

Healey, John. "Anna Back to Song and Dance." *The Mail* (Adelaide, SA), 5 January 1954. trove.nla.gov.au/newspaper/article/57956666. Accessed 17 July 2018.

Heath, Victoria. "Was Queen Victoria a Borderline Nymphomaniac?" *Plaid Zebra*, 25 May 2016. theplaidzebra.com/queen-victoria-borderline-nymphomaniac/. Accessed 19 July 2018.

Her Majesty's Glorious Jubilee 1897: The Record Number of a Record Reign. Proprietors of *The Illustrated London News*, 1897.

Herbert, Stephen, and Luke McKernan, editors. *Who's Who of Victorian Cinema: A Worldwide Survey*. London: BFI, 1996. www.victorian-cinema.net/. Accessed 7 November 2017.

Hibbert, Christopher. *Queen Victoria in Her Letters and Journals*. Viking: 1985.

Hibbert, Christopher. *Queen Victoria: A Personal History*. Da Capo Press, 2001.

Higgens, Andrew. "China's Epic Exorcism: Britain Is the Arch-Villain of a Film to Purge the Imperial Legacy." *The Guardian*, 12 June 1997. tsquare.tv/film/Guardian01.html. Accessed 12 February 2018.

Holland, Caroline. *Notebooks of a Spinster Lady*. Cassell, 1919.

Holland, Clive. "A Chat with Mr. John Le Couteur." *The Idler, an Illustrated Monthly Magazine*, vol 13, February-July 1898. London: J.M. Dent, 1898, pp. 93–103.

Honeycutt, Kirk. "Film Review: The Young Victoria." *The Hollywood Reporter*, 6 February 2009. www.hollywoodreporter.com/review/film-review-young-victoria-92847. Accessed 7 January 2019.

Housman, Laurence. *The Unexpected Years*. Cape, 1937.

Huntley Film Archives. www.huntleyarchives.com/index.asp. Accessed 18 January 2018.

Irvin, Richard. *Forgotten Laughs: An Episode Guide to 150 TV Sitcoms You Probably Never Saw*. BearManor Media, 2012.

Jay, Bill. "Queen Victoria's Second Passion: Royal Patronage of Photography in the 19th Century." 1988. www.billjayonphotography.com/QnVictoria2ndPassion.pdf. Accessed 20 February 2018.

Jewell, Richard B., with Vernon Harbin. *The RKO Story*. Arlington House, 1982.

Johnson, Samuel. *A Dictionary of the English*

Language: In Which the Words Are Deduced from Their Originals and Illustrated in Their Different Significations by Examples from the Best Writers. Stratham, 1775. archive.org/details/dictionaryofengl01johnuoft/page/n6. Accessed 26 May 2019.

Jones, Kaye. "Netley: Queen Victoria's Great Hospital." *History in an Hour.* www.historyinanhour.com/2011/05/03/netley-hospital/. Accessed 9 January 2018.

The Kinematograph Year Book Program Diary and Directory 1914. Kinematograph & Lantern Weekly, 1914. www.bfi.org.uk/sites/bfi.org.uk/files/downloads/kinematograph-year-book-programdiary-and-directory-1914-2014-09-18.pdf. Accessed 22 December 2018.

King, Steve. "Buffalo Bill Meets Queen Vic." *Barnes and Noble Review,* 9 May 2012. www.barnesandnoble.com/review/buffalo-bill-meets-queen-vic. Accessed 18 July 2018.

Kingston, Anne. "Deadly Victorian Fashions." *Maclean's,* 9 June 2014. www.macleans.ca/culture/arts/deadly-victorian-fashions/. Accessed 8 May 2018.

"The Lady with a Lamp." *TV Guide,* 1951. www.tvguide.com/movies/the-lady-with-a-lamp/review/103686/. Accessed 21 April 2018.

"The Lady with a Lamp." *Variety,* 31 December 1950. variety.com/1950/film/reviews/the-lady-with-the-lamp-1200416857/. Accessed 21 April 2018.

Lawrence, Michael. *Sabu.* British Film Institute, 2014.

Lea, Andy. "Victoria and Abdul Review: An Interesting True Story That Feels Like a Cop-out." *The Daily Express,* 17 September 2017. www.express.co.uk/entertainment/films/855144/victoria-and-abdul-review-judi-dench-ali-fazal. Accesses 19 June 2018.

"Letter from Florence Nightingale to Queen Victoria Expressing Her Gratitude for the Brooch the Queen Had Sent Her" dated 1 December 1855. *Royal Collection.* www.royalcollection.org.uk/sites/royalcollection.org.uk/files/ra_vic_main_f_4_15.pdf. Accessed 21 April 2018.

"The Little Princess." *Variety,* 31 December 1938. variety.com/1938/film/reviews/the-little-princess-1200411974/. Accessed 1 May 2018.

London and South Western Railway. *Time Table of the Train Conveying Her Majesty the Queen and Suit, from Windsor to Portsmouth Dockyard on Thursday, 10th MARCH, 1898.* 4.bp.blogspot.com/-MFMVTDjDoRI/TzoVAUYtp_I/AAAAAAAABEE/6hxL2HkRvNY/s1600/Untitled-Scanned-04.jpg. Accessed 17 January 2018.

The London Gazette. 19 May 1899. www.thegazette.co.uk/London/issue/27081/page/3186. Accessed 13 December 2018.

Longford, Elizabeth. *Queen Victoria.* The History Press, 1999.

Lowe, Rachael, et al. *The History of the British Film, 1918–1929.* Vol. 4. Bowker, 1971.

Lyden, Anne M. *A Royal Passion: Queen Victoria and Photography.* Getty Trust Publications, 2014.

Mallet, Marie. *Life with Queen Victoria: Marie Mallet's Letters from Court 1887–1901.* Edited by Victor Mallet. Houghton Mifflin, 1968.

Manksy, Jackie. "P.T. Barnum Isn't the Hero the 'Greatest Showman' Wants You to Think." *Smithsonian.com,* 22 December 2017. www.smithsonianmag.com/history/true-story-pt-barnum-greatest-humbug-them-all-180967634/. Accessed 27 July 2018.

Marcus, Laurence. "Lillie (1978)." *Television Heaven,* 4 June 2007. www.televisionheaven.co.uk/lillie.htm. Accessed 15 January 2019.

Martin, Theodore. *The Life of His Royal Highness: The Prince Consort.* London: Smith, Elder, 1876.

Mavis, Paul. "Disraeli 1978." *DVD Talk,* 15 April 2008. www.dvdtalk.com/reviews/32951/disraeli-1978/. Accessed 15 April 2018.

Mavis, Paul. "The Edwardians." *DVD Talk,* 14 October 2008. www.dvdtalk.com/reviews/35096/edwardians-the/. Accessed 16 October 2018.

McGonagall, William. *Brief Autobiography.* www.mcgonagall-online.org.uk/life/brief-autobiography. Accessed 20 July 2018.

McGonagall, William. *William McGonagall: Collected Poems.,* edited by Chris Hunt. Birlinn, 2006.

McKernan, Luke. "Queen Victoria's Diamond Jubilee," 2012. lukemckernan.com/wp-content/uploads/queen_victoria_diamond_jubilee.pdf. Accessed 7 December 2017.

Meintjes, Johannes. *President Paul Kruger: A Biography*. Cassell, 1974.

Merck, Mandy, editor. *The British Monarchy on Screen*. Manchester University Press, 2016.

Meyer, H. "En Chine, Le Gâteau Des Rois Et... Des Empereurs." *Supplément Illustré Du Petit Journal*, 16 January 1898. www.researchgate.net/figure/En-Chine-Legateau-des-Rois-et-des-Empereurs-by-H-Meyer-Le-Petit-Journal_fig27_320536775. Accessed 19 November 2018. digital.library.cornell.edu/catalog/ss:3293809. Accessed 7 May 2018.

Moffat, Jamie. "*The Story of Gilbert and Sullivan* (Technicolor Film, 1953)." 29 October 2001. gasdisc.oakapplepress.com/greatgns.htm. Accessed 16 July 2018.

Montague, Jude Cowan. "Sixty Years a Queen (1913): A Lost Epic of the Reign of Victoria." *The British Monarchy on Screen*, edited by Mandy Merck. Manchester University Press, 2016, pp. 47–63.

"Movie of the Week: *Victoria the Great*." *Life Magazine*, 4 October 1937, p. 55. books.google.com/books?id=wkQEAAAAMBAJ&printsec=frontcover&source=gbs_ge_summary_r&cad=0#v=onepage&q&f=false. Accessed 7 January 2019.

"The Mudlark." *Variety*, 31 December 1949. variety.com/1949/film/reviews/the-mudlark-1200416538/. Accessed 22 June 2018.

Murphy, Paul Thomas. *Shooting Victoria: Madness, Mayhem and the Modernisation of the British Monarchy*. Pegasus, 2011.

Musser, Charles Musser. *Edison Motion Pictures, 1890–1900: An Annotated Filmography*. Smithsonian Institution Press, 1997.

"Netley Hospital." en.wikipedia.org/wiki/Netley_Hospital. Accessed 9 January 2018.

Neufeld, Charles. *A Prisoner of the Khaleefa*. London: Chapman & Hall, 1899.

Niewyk, Donald L., and Francis R. Nicosia. *The Columbia Guide to the Holocaust*. Columbia University Press, 2000.

"Nightingale Brooch." collection.nam.ac.uk/detail.php?acc=1963-10-280-1. Accessed 23 April 2018.

Nikkhah, Roya. "Queen Victoria's Passion for Nudity Goes on Display in New Art Exhibition." *The Telegraph*, 13 February 2010. www.telegraph.co.uk/culture/art/art-news/7228202/Queen-Victorias-passion-for-nudity-goes-on-display-in-new-art-exhibition.html. Accessed 27 July 2018.

O'Rourke, Chris. "London's Silent Cinemas." www.londonssilentcinemas.com. Accessed 7 December 2017.

"Our Future King at Play." *Harmsworth Magazine*, October 1900, pp. 195–200.

Pakula, Hannah. *An Uncommon Woman: Empress Frederick, Daughter of Queen Victoria, Wife of the Crown Prince of Prussia*. Simon & Schuster, 1995.

"Palace Theatre." en.wikipedia.org/wiki/Palace_Theatre,_London. Accessed 7 December 2017.

Parker, Louis N. *Disraeli*. www.ibdb.com/broadway-production/disraeli-7345. Accessed 27 April 2018.

Parrill, Sue, and William B. Robison. *The Tudors on Film and Television*. McFarland, 2013.

Perry, James. *Arrogant Armies: Great Military Disasters and the Generals Behind Them*. Castle Books, 2005.

"The Pirates! Band of Misfits." *Box Office Mojo*. www.boxofficemojo.com/movies/?id=pirates12.htm. Accessed 7 January 2019.

"The Pirates! Band of Misfits." *Rotten Tomatoes* (2012). www.rottentomatoes.com/m/pirates_band_of_misfits/. Accessed 7 January 2019.

Plunkett, John. *Queen Victoria: First Media Monarch*. Oxford University Press, 2003.

Porter, Laraine. "The Talkies Come to Britain: British Silent Cinema and the Transition to Sound, 1928–30." *The Routledge Companion to British Cinema History*, edited by I.Q. Hunter, Loraine Porter, Justin Smith. Routledge, 2017, pp. 91–92.

"The Prime Minister." *Variety* 9 April 1941. archive.org/stream/variety142-1941-04#page/n65/mode/2up/search/the+prime+minister. Accessed 27 April 2018.

"The Procession in London. Scene at Victoria Station. The Funeral Train Arrives. The Royal Mourners. Kaiser Easily Recognized. at Paddington Station." *New York Times*, 3 February 1901. query.nytimes.com/gst/abstract.html?res=9402E0D8133EE333A-25750C0A9649C946097D6CF&legacy=true. Accessed 9 January 2018.

"Queen Recreated Historic Train Journey." *BBC News*, 13 June 2017. www.bbc.com/news/uk-england-london-40248716. Accessed 16 January 2018.

Queen Victoria. *Leaves from the Journal of*

Our Life in the Highlands: From 1848 to 1861, edited by Arthur Helps. The Folio Society, 1973.

"Queen Victoria Became Mrs Brown, Diaries Suggest." www.smh.com.au/world/queen-victoria-became-mrs-brown-diaries-suggest-20030505-gdgpl8.html. Accessed 11 December 2018.

"Queen Victoria Survives Assassination Attempt." *The Guardian*, 4 March 1882. www.theguardian.com/theguardian/2013/mar/04/queen-victoria-assassination-attempt-1882 Accessed 4 June 2019.

"Queen Victoria Tries the Telephone." *Queen Victoria's Scrapbook*. www.queenvictorias-scrapbook.org/contents/6-2.html. Accessed 25 July 2018.

Queen Victoria's Journals. www.proquest.com/products-services/queenvic.html. Accessed 14 December 2018.

"Queen Victoria's Privy Council Dress." thequeenvictoriafiles.wordpress.com/2017/05/12/queen-victorias-privy-council-dress/. Accessed 7 January 2019.

"The Queen's Visit to Netley." *The Indian Medical Gazette*. Vol 32, No 2, February 1899, p. 56. www.ncbi.nlm.nih.gov/pmc/articles/PMC5145350/?page=1. Accessed 11 December 2017.

Rapp, Dean, and Charles W. Weber. "British Film, Empire and Society in the Twenties: The 'Livingstone' Film, 1923–1925." *Historical Journal of Film, Radio and Television*, vol. 9, no. 1, 1989.

Rappaport, Helen. *Queen Victoria: A Biographical Companion*. 2001. Clio, 2003.

Redivivus, Brunel. "The Funeral of Queen Victoria." *The Railway Magazine*, vol. 8, 1901, pp. 260–64. books.google.com Accessed 18 January 2018.

Reed, Rex. "Judi Dench Gives a Touching, Majestic Performance in 'Victoria and Abdul.'" *The Observer*, 22 September 2017. Observer.com/2017/09/review-judi-dench-is-majestic-in-victoria-and-abdul/. Accessed 19 June 2018.

Reid, John Howard. *500 Famous Films*. Reid Books, 2015.

Reid, Michaela. *Ask Sir James: The Life of Sir James Reid, Personal Physician to Queen Victoria*. Eland, 1987.

Report of the Joint Committee Appointed by the Lords of the Committee of Privy Council for Trade and the Atlantic Telegraph Company to Inquire Into the Construction of Submarine Telegraph Cables. London: Eyre and Spottiswood, 1861. Books.google.com/books?id=76HmAAAAMAAJ&pg=PA232#v=onepage&q&f=false. Accessed 25 July 2018.

Rice, Tim. "Livingstone," *Colonial Film: Moving Images of the British Empire*. www.colonialfilm.org.uk/node/1844. Accessed 3 May 2018.

Richards, Jeffrey. *Films and British National Identity from Dickens to Dad's Army*. Manchester University Press, 1997.

"Right Wing Group Stalls Shoot of Ali Fazal's 'Victoria and Abdul' in Agra Over Queen Victoria's Statue." *Times of India*, 29 January 2017. timesofindia.indiatimes.com/entertainment/hindi/bollywood/news/Right-wing-group-stalls-shoot-of-Ali-Fazals-Victoria-and-Abdul-in-Agra-over-Queen-Victorias-statue/articleshow/55497083.cms. Accessed 19 June 2018.

Robertson, David. "Victoria and Abdul—Re-Writing History to Indoctrinate Today's Society." *The Wee Flea*, 26 September 2017. Theweeflea.com/2017/09/26/victoria-and-abdul-re-writing-history-to-indoctrinate-todays-society/. Accessed 21 June 2018.

Rosen, Bruce. "Victoria on the Rails." *Victorian History*, 24 September 2015. vichist.blogspot.com/2015/09/victoria-on-rails.html. Accessed 17 January 2018.

Rosen, Miriam. "Méliès, Georges." *World Film Directors: Volume I, 1890–1945*, edited by John Wakeman. H. W. Wilson Company, 1987, pp 751–54.

Royal Collection Trust. www.royalcollection.org.uk/collection. Accessed 15 January 2018.

Salazar, David. "Opera Meets Film: 'The Young Victoria' Reminds Us of the Famed Monarch's Passion for Bel Canto." operawire.com/opera-meets-film-the-young-victoria-reminds-us-of-the-famed-monarchs-passion-for-bel-canto/. Accessed 15 July 2018.

Saunders, Tristram Fane. "Victoria Fact Vs Fiction: The True History Behind Series 2." *The Telegraph*, 28 August 2017. www.telegraph.co.uk/tv/0/victoria-fact-vs-fiction-true-history-behind-show/. Accessed 13 September 2018.

Schoch, R. *Queen Victoria and the Theatre of Her Age*. Palgrave Macmillan, 2004.

"7 Memorable Moments in the History of Buckingham Palace," *Historyextra.com*,

2 March 2016. www.historyextra.com/period/20th-century/7-memorable-moments-in-the-history-of-buckingham-palace/. Accessed 27 July 2018.

Sinnott, John. "Fall of Eagles." *DVD Talk*, 27 May 2006. www.dvdtalk.com/reviews/21906/fall-of-eagles/. Accessed 16 August 2018.

Spehr, Paul. *The Man Who Made Movies: W.K.L. Dickson*. Indiana University Press, 2008.

Spencer, Jesse Ames. *History of the United States: From the Earliest Period to the Administration of President Johnson*. Vol 3. New York: Johnson, Fry and Co. 1866. books.google.com. Accessed 25 July 2018.

Stanborough, Mark. "The Victorian Age," 21 March 2019. networkonair.com/features/2019/03/21/the-victorian-age/. Accessed 9 May 2019.

"Stereoscope." en.wikipedia.org/wiki/Stereoscope. Accessed 9 January 2018.

Strand, Ginger. "Selling Sex in Honeymoon Heaven." *The Believer*, January 2008. believermag.com/product/the-believer-january-2008/. Accessed 4 June 2019.

Sully, Andy. "Queen Victoria and Britain's First Diamond Jubilee." *BBC News*, 22 May 2012. www.bbc.com/news/uk-17368499. Accessed 10 January 2018.

Sungenis, Pab. *The New Adventures of Queen Victoria*. www.gocomics.com/thenewadventuresofqueenvictoria. Accessed 19 November 2018.

Tait, Peta. *Fighting Nature: Travelling Menageries, Animal Acts and War Shows*. Sydney University Press, 2016.

Tennyson, Lord Alfred. "In Memoriam A.H.H." www.online-literature.com/tennyson/718/. Accessed 2 October 2018.

Theodore Huff Memorial Film Society. "Balaclava" Film Program, 24 January 1972. www.nyu.edu/projects/wke/notes/titles/balaclava.php. Accessed 16 April 2018.

Thomas, Rebecca. "Victoria Finds Her Passion." *BBC News*, 24 August 2001. news.bbc.co.uk/2/hi/entertainment/1504266.stm. Accessed 17 August 2018.

Thomson, David. "Almost Famous." *The Guardian*, 6 November 2003. www.theguardian.com/film/2003/nov/07/1. Accessed 8 May 2018.

Tom Merry, Lightning Cartoonist, Sketching Bismarck. 1895. www.bfi.org.uk/films-tv-people/4ce2b800c22d8. Accessed 28 December 2017.

Tom Merry, Lightning Cartoonist, Sketching Kaiser Wilhelm II. 1895. www.bfi.org.uk/films-tv-people/4ce2b6a34c6b1. Accessed 28 December 2017.

Tom Merry, Lightning Cartoonist, Sketching Lord Salisbury. 1896. www.bfi.org.uk/films-tv-people/4ce2b800c28ce. Accessed 28 December 2017.

Tom Merry, Lightning Cartoonist, Sketching William Gladstone. 1896. www.bfi.org.uk/films-tv-people/4ce2b800c28ce. Accessed 28 December 2017.

"Tom Thumb." *Victoria and Albert Museum*. www.vam.ac.uk/content/articles/t/tom-thumb/. Accessed 20 July 2018.

Twain, Mark. "Queen Victoria's Jubilee." *San Francisco Examiner*, 20 and 23 June 1897. Reprinted in *Mark Twain: A Tramp Abroad, Following the Equator, Other Travels*. Library of America, 2010, pp. 1042–1052.

"The 24th Academy Awards: 1952." www.oscars.org/oscars/ceremonies/1952. Accessed 7 January 2019.

Woostersauce2014. "TV Review: Edward the Seventh (ITV, 1975)." 18 February 2015. enoughofthistomfoolery.wordpress.com/2015/02/18/tv-review-edward-the-seventh-itv-1975/. Accessed 21 August 2018.

Urban, Mark. *Generals: Ten British Commanders Who Shaped the World*. Farber and Faber, 2005.

Vallone, Lynne. *Becoming Victoria*. Yale University Press, 2001.

Vermilye, Jerry, and Deborah Kerr. *The Great British Films*. Citadel Press, 1978.

"Victoria and Albert Museum." en.wikipedia.org/wiki/Victoria_and_Albert_Museum. Accessed 9 January 2018.

"Victoria the Great." *Motion Pictures Reviews*, December 1937. www.archive.org/stream/motionpicturerev00wome_6#page/8/mode/2up/search/Victoria+the+Great. Accessed 14 November 2017.

"Victorian Circus." *Victoria and Albert Museum*, www.vam.ac.uk/content/articles/v/victorian-circus/. Accessed 20 July 2018.

Weintraub, Stanley. *Disraeli: A Biography*. Truman Talley Books, 1993.

Welch, David. *Propaganda and the German Cinema, 1933–1945*. Tauris, 2001, revised edition.

Wilkie, Sir David. "Victoria's First Privy Council." www.royalcollection.org.uk/

collection/404710/the-first-council-of-queen-victoria. Accessed 17 August 2018.

"William Mecham." Aka Tom Merry. en.wikipedia.org/wiki/William_Mecham. Accessed 28 December 2017.

Wilson, A.N. *Rise and Fall of the House of Windsor.* Norton, 1993.

Wilson, A.N. *Victoria: A Life.* Penguin Press, 2014.

Wilson, Robert. *The Life and Times of Queen Victoria.* Cassell, 1891.

Worsley, Lucy. *Queen Victoria: Daughter, Wife, Mother, Widow.* Hodder & Stoughton, 2018.

Wynne, May. *The Life and Reign of Victoria the Good, Produced in Conjunction with the Cinematograph Film 'Sixty Years a Queen': Cinema Books No.2.* Stanley Paul & Co, 1913.

Zone, Ray. *Stereoscopic Cinema and the Origins of 3-D Film, 1838–1952.* University Press of Kentucky, 2007.

Index

Numbers in **_bold italics_** indicate pages with illustrations

A-Pictures 166, 176
A&E Television 190
Aardman Animations 171
Abberline, Inspector 84–85, 167
Abdication crisis of 1936 59, 60, 62, 66
Abdul see Karim, Abdul
Abercorn, Duke of 105
Aberdeen 22
Acres, Birt 11, 12
actualités (short documentary silents) 1, 6, 10, 12, 11–35, 149–62
The Adventure of Sherlock Holmes' Smarter Brother (1975) 165, 202*n*27
Afgacolor 70
Afghanistan 125
Afternoon Tea in the Gardens of Clarence House (1897) 16
Agra 80
Ahmed, Rafuiddin 80
A.J.'s Time Travelers television show (1995) 185, 213*n*29
Aked, Muriel 96, 167
Akhtar, Adeel 78
Albemarle, Lord 115
Albert, Prince Consort, Prince of Saxe-Coburg and Gotha: anti-slavery activities 121, 127; Christmas traditions introduced by 116, 124; conflict with Lehzen 73–74, 109, 116, 126; courtship of Victoria 64–65, 69, 116; daguerreotype of 212*n*21; death of 49, 62, 66–65, 110, 116, 118–19, 200*n*11; design of Nightingale brooch 44; foreign policy involvement 47, 49; Great Exhibition 102, 118; Houses of Parliament, designed by Prince Albert 107; letters of 47; love story 1, 7, 8, 62–75; memorial 133–34; music 8, 65–66, 203*n*6; photography 14, 65, 127; prudery of 121; relationship with son 109–10, 116; sanitation efforts 125, 189; tension in marriage 65–66, 70, 74, 109–10, 118, 126, 189, 203*n*6; tomb of 112; Trent Affair 48–49, 119, 199–200*n*10; wedding 92, 116–17, 119, **_120_**, 211*n*13
Albert: The Power Behind the Throne television

docu-drama (29 September 2018) 175, 211*n*14
Alberta Conveying the Royal Bier (1901) 159
Aldershot 42
Alexandra, Princess of Wales 1, 25, 109, 112
Alfred, Lord Tennyson 41, 44, 48, 97, 130–31, 135, 162, 213*n*27
Alfresco television series 129, 180
Alhambra Theatre of Varieties 12, 13
Alice in Wonderland aka *Alice au pays des merveilles* (1949) 165, 206*n*25
Ambassadors (1897) 27, 154
Ameche, Don 101, 172
American Mutoscope and Biograph 12, 32
Amusement Park Films 169
amusements enjoyed by Queen Victoria 8, 91–102
android versions of Queen Victoria 137–38
Anglo-Afghan War 125
Anglo-Sikh Wars, First and Second 38
animation 7, 9, 89, 134, 192, 207*n*29; computer-generated 86; hand-drawn 2D 86, 140; stop-motion 86, 140
Animatograph device 12
anime series *see The Black Butler*
Annie Get Your Gun (1950) **99**, 165
"Annie Oakley" (1985) episode of *Tall Tales & Legends* 175, 213*n*26
Annis, Francesca 114, 182, 211*n*11
Anson, George 44, 118
Anthony, Barry 11, 12, 15, 16, 19, 25, 29, 31
anti–Britain attitudes 54–55, 104–106
anti-monarchism 7, 48, 104, 133–34, 138, 140–41
anti-slavery *see* slavery
appeasement 45–46, 50–54
Appleton, R.J. 29, 152
Arcadia Films 167
Arliss, Florence 50, 163
Arliss, George 50–51, 163
Around the World in 80 Days (1956) 87, 165
Around the World in 80 Days (2004) 165–66
Around the World in 80 Days television series (1989) 8, **87**, 103, 175

225

Index

Arrival of the Queen and Bodyguard (1899) 21, 157
Arrival of the Queen and the Emperor and Empress of Russia at Mar Lodge (1896) 15, 150
Arrival of the Queen from Windsor (1897) 21, 151
art, Queen Victoria's taste in 98, 177
assassination attempts on Queen Victoria 1, 6, 74, 76–77, 116, 120–23, 131, 138–39, 171, 186, 188, 189, 204*n*14, 211*n*17, 212*n*20
Assassin's Creed: Syndicate (2015) 9, **142-43**, 192
Associated British Picture Corporation 169
Associated Television (ATV) 178
Atkinson, Rowan 129
"Aunt Clara's Victoria Victory" (1967) episode of *Bewitched* 9, 132, **133**, 175
Austen, Jane 144
Australian Broadcasting Company 191
Avala Film 175
Avengers: End Game (2019) 145; infinity gauntlet 145, **146**
Aylesford divorce case 110
Aylmer, Felix 44
Azmi, Shabana **39,** 166

"Baby Blues" (1994), episode of *Northern Exposure* 175, 213*n*26
Baird, Julia 31, 80–81, 97, 212*n*17
Balaclava (1928) 7, 42, **43**; 162, 199*n*4; critical reception of 199*n*5
Balaclava, battle of 40–43, 162, 199*n*3
Ballater 22, 196*n*13
Balmoral 11, 14, **15**, 22, 26, 44, 49, 66–68, 76, 139, 197*n*15, 207*n*3
Barker, Ronnie 210*n*8
Barker Motion Photography LTD 164
Barnum (1986) 8, 99–100, 166
Barnum, Phineas T. 99–101
Barrett, Jerry 21
Barrie, Chris 137
Barry, Matt 13
Bartlett, Sabrina 127
Basil of Baker Street 85, 168
Bates, Kathy 88, 166
BBC 173, 177–78, 180–84, 186–87, 190–92, 193
BBC Manchester 178
BBC Scotland 179
BBC Wales 180
Beaconsfield, Lord *see* Disraeli, Benjamin
Beatrice, Princess, *see* Princess Beatrice
Beaumont, Debra 38, 170
Beaumont, Gunner/Bombardier 131
Beckett, Sheila 190, 209*n*1
Beckford, C.J. 128
Bedchamber Crisis 72, 74, 95
Beethoven 144
Bell, Alexander Graham 8, 101–2, 143, 172
Bennett, Joan 50, 167
Beresford, Evelyn 98, **99**, 165, 166

Bertie *see* Edward VII, King
Bettany, Paul 71, 174
Bewitched television series *see* "Aunt Clara's Victoria Victory" (1967)
BFI (British Film Institute) 169, 197*n*20, 201*n*24
Biddulph, Sir Thomas 101
Big Ben clock 88, 202*n*27
Bill & Ted's Excellent Adventures television series (1990) 134–35, 184
Biograph projector 12; *see also* British Mutoscope & Biograph Company
Bipps (Dr. Reid's nickname for Queen Victoria) 34
Bird, John 183, 213*n*26
Birmingham 4, 72
Birnbaum / Barber Productions 171
Bismarck, Otto von 13, 51–52, 109
Black, Jack (rat catcher) **140**
Black Penny stamp 38
The Black Butler (2008–9) 9, 140–41, 176
Black Butler: Book of Circus (2014) 176, 214*n*1
Black Butler: Book of Murder (2014) 176–77, 214*n*1
Black Butler: Book of the Atlantic (2017) 166, 214*n*1
Black Elk 5
The Black Prince (2017) 38–40, 166
Blackadder "General Hospital" episode (26 October 1989) 177, 212*n*23
Blackadder's Christmas Carol television special (23 December 1988) 9, 129, 177
Blackpool 29
Bloom, Claire 191, 209*n*1
Blunt, Emily 71, **74**, 93, 118, 174, 204*n*15, 211*n*15
Boer War *see* Second Boer War
Bogg, Phineas 134, 177
Boleyn, Ann 144
Bollywood 130
"The Bomb" *see Orson & Olivia*
books, Queen Victoria's tastes in 8, 78, 97, 206*n*25, 208*n*10
Bourke, Joanna 31
Boxer Rebellion 202*n*1
The Boy Jones *see* Jones, the Boy
Bremmer, Eve 86
The Bride of Lammermoor (1819) 97
Briggs-Owen, Lucy 143, 193
Brillstein Entertainment Partners 166
British Acoustic sound process 42, 199*n*4
British Cinematograph Company 26–27, 152
British Mutoscope & Biograph Company 15, 19–20, 22, 24–25, 29, 31, 32–32, 149–51, 153–59
British Pathé Company 16, 19, 31, 3, 33, 149, 154, 157, 159–61
British South Africa Company 105, 185
Broadbent, Jim 71, **88**, 129, 166, 167, 174, 177, 191
"Brocket Hall" episode of *Victoria* television series (2016/2017) 187

Index

Brooks, Lola 191, 209*n*1
Brooks, Michaela 71
Brosnan, Pierce 103, 175
Brown, John 55, 68, **75**–78, 81–84, 89, 93, 97, 131, 133, 170, 172–73, 177, 179, 186, 191, 198*n*24, 201*n*22; arrogance of 77; drinking 77, 83–84; memorials to 76, 97; tense relationship with Prince of Wales 76
Brown, Pamela 165, 191, 206*n*25
Brown, Richard 11, 12, 15–16, 19, 25, 29, 32
Browning, Robert 67
Brydon, Dr. William 125
Buckingham Palace 22, 25, 26, 28, 39, 53, 60, 66, 85, 102, 119–20, 124–25, 128, 130, 143, 157, 182, 189, 195*n*6, 206*n*23, 209*n*16; water closet installation 125
Buckley, Jessie 167
Buffalo Bill (1944) 8, 98, 166
"Buffalo Bill and Annie Play the Palace" episode of *Voyagers!* (1983) 177
Buffalo Bill Cody 5, 98–99, 134, 166, 177
Burma 103
Burnett, Frances Hodgson 56
Butler, Frank 99, 165
Byron, poetry of 118

C. Goodwin Norton Company 154
Cairo 53
camera work **39**, **41**, 42, 47, 53, 57–58, 60, 76, 100, 106, 109, 110, 112, 116–17, 119–20
Campbell, Eddie 84, 167
The Campbells Are Coming (1915) 36, 163
Canadian Rebellion 72, 104, 121, 198*n*1, 210*n*2
Canton 37
Capcom (Japan) 192
Carlson, Peter 4, 5
Carroll, Lewis 131
Carson, Ellen 40–**41**
cartes-de-visite 14
cartoon strip featuring Queen Victoria *see* New Adventures of Queen Victoria
Cat 137, 182
CBS 166, 192
Century of Humiliation (China) 37
Cetshwayo, King 105, 186, 210
CGI (computer generated imagery) 9, 86, 119, 124, 207
Chamberlain, Colonial Secretary Joseph 54–55, 172
Chamberlain, Prime Minister Neville 46, 51–52, 54
Chan, Jackie 88, 166, 171, 202*n*27
Chancellor of the Exchequer 107
Chapman, Graham 130
Chapman, James 45–46, 59, 60, 64, 201*n*25
Chard's Vitagraph Company 21, 150
Charge of the Light Brigade 36, 40, **41**, 42, 44, 48, 129, 162, 164, 198–99
Charge of the Light Brigade film (1912) 40
Charge of the Light Brigade film (1936) 36, 48

Charge of the Light Brigade film (1968) 40
Charing Cross 25
Charles, Craig 137
Charles, Prince *see* Prince Charles
Chartist Movement 72, 119, 121, 127, 173, 187, 189
Chernin Entertainment
chess 73
Children of the Royal Family Playing Soldiers (1900) 16
China 4, **6**, 37–38, 125, 164, 170, 199
Chinawood *see* Hengdian World Studios
cholera epidemic 119, 128, 189
Cholmo[n]deley, Lt. 40–42, 164
Christie, Ian 11–12, 15, 20, 29
"Christmas with Morecambe & Wise" episode of *The Morecambe & Wise Show* (25 December 1972) 177, 213*n*26
Churchill, Lady Jane 79, **96**
Cinéas 170
Cinématographe device 12
circus, Queen Victoria's taste for 8, 99, 100, 209*n*14, 214*n*1
City of London 29
Civil War, American 7, 48–49
Civilization VI game (2016) 9, 143, 192; denunciation 144, **145**; lead for England **144**
Clans Receiving the Queen (1898) 15, 154
Clark, Alfred 12
classism in films using the Queen Victoria character 7, 78–79, 143
"The Clockwork Prince" episode of *Victoria* television series (2016/2017) 187–88
clones of Queen Victoria 9, 137–38
Coburg 68, 71–72, 91, 93, 113, 133
"A Coburg Quarest" episode of *Victoria* television series (2019) 190
cock-a-leekie soup 145, 212*n*19
Cody, William Frederick *see* Buffalo Bill
The Coldstream Guards aka *The Military Review at Aldershot* (1897) 19, 151
Coleman, Jenna 119–**120**, **122**, **124**, 127–**128**
Collins, Pauline 135, **136**
Colonial Premiers and Colonial Troopers (1897) 27, 154
Columbia Pictures 168
comedy using the Queen Victoria character 9, 69–70, 129–31
"Comfort and Joy" episode of *Victoria* television series (2017/2018) 189
Compton, Fay **51**, 132
Compus Productions 191
Conan Doyle, Sir Arthur 140, 143, 168, 171
concentration camps in South Africa 55
Congress of Berlin (1878) 52, 109
Connell, Jane 132, **133**
Connolly, Billy **75**, 77, 93, 170
Conrad, Robert 138, 192
Conroy, Sir John 68–69, 71–73, 116–18, 173, 174, 187, 190, 212*n*19

228　　　　　　　　　　　　　　　Index

"The Consort" episode of *Telephone Time* (27 January 1957) 177, 211*n*14
Constable, William 212*n*21
Constantinople 52
Coogan, Steve 88, 166
Cooper, Gary 172, 201*n*27
Cooke, Alistair 106
Corbet, Ronnie 184, 210*n*8
Corn Laws, repeal of (1840 to 1846) 66, 119, 125, 172–73, 212*n*19
coronation of Queen Victoria 62, 71, 74, 94, 119, 130, 182, 203*n*12, 207*n*4
The Cortege on Its Way from Osborne to Trinity Pier (1901) 159
costuming in films about Queen Victoria 9, *39*, 70, 77–78, 81–84, 87, 92, 96, 109, 118–19, 121, 125, 127, 188, 202*n*1, 203*n*10, 206*n*24, 210*n*1, 211*n*11
Court Circular 4, 91
court photographer *see* Knight, Charles
Court Waltzes aka *La guerre des vales* (1933) 166
Courtemanche, Michel 138
Crew, Sara 56–57, 169
Cribb television series 8, 113–14, 181
Crimean War 7, 20, 36, 40–47, *48*, 129, 163, 169, 172, 174, 199; conditions in 44, 48
crinoline 70, 203*n*10
Crook, Ann 84, 167
Crosbie, Annette 109, *111*, 127, 178, 210*n*7
crosscut 42, 47, 55, 57–58, 60
Crowd Following the Queen's Carriage (1897) 27, 153
"The Crown Jewels" *see Orson & Olivia*
Crutchley, Rosalie 113
Crystal Palace 118, *130*
Cuffay, William 128
Cunliff, David 115, 178, 180, 211*n*13
Currie, Finlay 81, 170
A Curse on the House of Windsor (26 April 1994) 9, 132–33, 177
Curtiz, Michael 40, 170
Cyprus 51, 52, 109
Czar Nicholas 11, 14, 113
Czar of Russia 43, 47, 195*n*5; *see also* Tsar
Czechoslovakia 46, 56

daguerreotype 4, 14, 65, 127, 212*n*21
"Daisy" episode of *The Edwardians* (2 January 1973) 8, 114–15, 178; critical reception of 211*n*12
dancing 8, 62–64, 70, 91–94, 120, 125, 207*n*2, 207*n*3, 207*n*4
Daoguang Emperor of China 37–38
Darby, Lord 107
Darlton Company 168
Darwin, Charles 86–87, 143, 171, 192
Dash (spaniel) 124, 212*n*19
David Livingstone (1936) 57, 167
Dawley, J. Searle 40

Deary, Terry 129, 181
De Bary, Wm Theodore 37
Dee, Francis 201*n*27
de Havilland, Olivia 40
De Mallett De Donas, Alice 138
Demenÿ camera 26, 197
Demetral, Chris 138
DeMille, Cecil B. 164, 199*n*9
Dench, Judi *75*, 77–78, *79*, 81, 93, 95–96, 115, 170, 173, 205*n*22
Denmark 110, 179
Denton 37, 170
Departure from Folkestone of the Queen (1899) 22, 156
Depp, Johnny 84, 167
desks of Victorian and Albert 66, 75, 118
Dexter, Mark 84, 167
DG penny 85
Diamond Jubilee of Queen Victoria, 4, 11, 13, 22, 24–27, *28*, 29, *30*–31, 45, 60, 66, 78–79, 85, 91, 113, 151–54, 197*n*17; Diamond Jubilee photograph *5*, *30*
Diamond Jubilee Procession Taken from Apsley House (1897) 26, 152
The Diamond Jubilee Review at Aldershot, showing H.R.H. the Princess of Wales Taking Snapshots 25, 153
Dickens, Charles 131, 143, 183, 192, 208*n*10
Dickinson, Thorold 51
Dickson, William K.L. 19, 151, 154, 195*n*1, 196*n*8
Diehl, Karl Ludwig 68
digital media 1, 2, 3, 14
diplomacy, Queen Victoria's interest in 8, 103, 143
Disraeli (1911 play) 50, 163
Disraeli (1916 film) 50, 163
Disraeli (1921 film) 50, 163
Disraeli (1929 film) 50, 167; critical reception of 200*n*12
Disraeli, Benjamin 1, 7, 8, 36, 49–53, 59, 68, 77, 81–84, 106–7, *108*–10, 131, 163–64, 167, 170–73, 178, 182, 190–91, 205*n*17; 205*n*18, 206*n*23, 210*n*5
Disraeli, Mary Anne, Viscountess Beaconsfield 50–53, 106–8, 182
Disraeli: Portrait of a Romantic (1978, 1980) 8, 106–9; 178; critical reception of 210*n*5
Distinctive Productions 163
distribution of films and media 6, 12–13,16, 29–30, *32*, *39*, 140, 162, 174, 195*n*3
"Dizzy" episode of *Number 10* (20 March 1983) 178, 210*n*5
DNA Productions 185
Dr. Jekyll/Mr. Hyde 89
Dr. Who *see* "Tooth and Claw"
Doctor Who see "Tooth and Claw"
dogs in films about Queen Victoria 14–*15*, 33, 35, 104, 112, 149, 157, 160–61, 176, 179, 186, 197*n*21, 209*n*13

Index 229

Dolittle (2020) 167
"Doll" episode of *Victoria* television series (2016 / 2017) 187
Donahue, Troy 101, 168
Donizetti, Gaetano 94
Dover 68–70, 92, 173; *see also Victoria in Dover*
Downey, W. & D. 4, 11, 14–15, 30, 149–50
Downs, James 46–47, 92
Downton Abbey television series 120–21, 210n7
The Drama House 177
Droid *see* android versions of Queen Victoria
Drummond, Edward 127, 187–89, 212n19
Dublin 19, 20, 154, 157–58, 197
Duchess of Kent 64, 68–69, 71, 116–18, 121, 173–74, 187, 190–91, 209n14, 212n19
Duke Michael of Russia 134
Duke of Cumberland / King of Hanover 25, 120, 123, 212n19
Dunne, Irene 81, *82–83*, 170
Durbar Room 78, *79*, 98
Duvitski, Janine 186, 191, 213n26

Eadie, Dennis 50, 163
Early Films, 1900's (1901) 161
East India Company 107
East Lynne televised play (21 December 1976) 178, 210n1
Edinburgh 29, 79, 102, 169
Edison, Thomas 12, 33, 162
Edison Studios 40
Education Act (1880) 83
Edward VII, King 32–33, 76, 79, 109–10, *111*, 112, 178–79, 200, 201n26, 205n19; actualités of 32–33, 156, 158–61; affairs with women 8, 110, 114–16, 178, 180; childhood of 100; Derby winning horse 12; dislike of Abdul Karim the Munshi 79–80, 95, 205n20; dislike of John Brown 76; divorce case scandals 110; education of 110, 118; gambling scandal 110, 115; home movies 112; Internet 144–45; involvement in foreign events 75, 108, 167, 200n15; as prince of Wales 12, 14, 25, 27, 29, 55, 75–76, 80, 95, 100, 110, 119, 184; smoking 118; tension with mother 110, 118
Edward the Seventh television series aka *Edward the King* (1975) 8, 109–12, 127; 178–79; critical reception of 210n7; parody of 210n8
The Edwardians television series (1973) 8, 114–15, 178
Edwards, Mavis 113, 180
Egyptian Hall 12
Eiffel Tower 141
"1854: The Dog" episode of *The Flaxton Boys* (28 September 1969), 179
Elephant House Studios
L'Elisir d'Amore (1832) 94
Elizabeth I, Queen 144, 270, 177, 207n30
Elizabeth II, Queen 6, 9, 133–34, 170

Elles, Mike 113, 180
Elliot, Charles 37, 170
Elvey, Maurice 42, 162
Emei Film Studio 170
Emile 140
emoji 144
empire, British 1, 4, 6–9, 21, 25–26, 29, 36–61, 80, 84–85, 96, 103–109, 125, 131, 135–36, 141–44
Empire Theatre 12
"The Empress and the Munshi" televised play (6 November 1984) 179–80, 211n14
Empress of India 130, *131*, 135, 164, 167, 182, 184, 193; *see also Horrible Histories* television series
"En Chine, le gâteau des Rois et … Des Empereurs" 4, *6*
"Enemy of the Bane, Part 1" episode of *The Sarah Jane Adventures* (1 December 2008) 180
"Engine of Change" episode of *Victoria* television series (2016/2017) 188
"The English Princess" *see The Fall of Eagles* television series
Entente Cordiale 139, 188, 200n15
Entente Cordiale (1939), 167
"Entente Cordiale" episode of *Victoria* television series (2017/2018) 188
"Episode 1.2" of *Alfresco* (8 May 1983) 180
Erickson, Carolly 126, 203n12, 209n14, 209n16, 212n18
Erma-Film 173
Estabrook, Christine 213n25
"Et in Arcadia" episode of *Victoria* television series (2019) 189
Evans, Maurice 96, 167
An Evening with Queen Victoria (2003) 192
Everett, Chad 132, 184
The Execution of Mary Stuart 13
"The Eye of the Peacock" episode of *Young Sherlock: The Mystery of the Manor House* (19 December 1982) 180
Eyre, Peter 85, 167

"Faith, Hope & Charity" episode of *Victoria* television series (2017/2018) 188–89
The Fall of Eagles television series (1974) 8, 112–13, 180; critical reception of 211n9
family history of Victoria and Albert 8, 103, 113, 136
fantasy 12, 57; using the Queen Victoria character 8, 68, 70, 74, 78, 80, 84, 122, 127–28, 132, 206n26
farce comedy using the Queen Victoria character 9, 129–31
Farwell, Byron 53
fax machine, royal patronage of 133
Faye, Julia 164, 199n9
Fazal, Ali 78, *79*
féeries films 12

230 Index

Feodora, Princess of Leininger 119, 127–*128*, 189–90
Ferrell, Will 139, 168
Ferris, Pam 139, 168
Fêtes du Jubilé de la reine d'Angleterre (1897) 153–54
Fidget *86*, 168
Fielding, Stephen 48
Fife, Duke of 105
filmography: actualités (short documentary silents) 149–62; alternative media and miscellaneous 192–94; silent narrative films 162–65; sound narrative films 165–74; television 175–92
Finnegan/Pinchuk Productions 175
Firaxis Games 192
First Opium War 37–38, 125, 170
Firth, Jonathan 116–*117*, 190
Firth, Peter 120, 187
FitzPatrick, James A. 57, 167
flashback 38, 54–55, 71, 76, 94, 99, 105–106, 114, 116, 214*n*1
flashforward 71, 76
The Flaxton Boys (1969) 179, 213*n*26
Fleetwood, Kate 127–*128*, 187
Fletcher, Tony 12
"A Flicker at the Fairground" episode of *Shadow Play* (15 March 2004) 186
Flynn, Errol 36, 40, 48
Fogg, Phileas 88, 103, 138–39, 185
Fogg, Rebecca 138–39, 185
Folkestone 22, 156
Ford, Francis 36, 163
"Foreign Bodies" episode of *Victoria* television series (2019) 189
Foreign Office 46
foreign policy, Victoria's and Albert's involvement in 47, 49, 104, 108, 125, 189; Victoria's lack of interest in 75–76
Foreign Princes (1897) 27, 153
Forster, E.M. 3
Foundation TV Productions 186
Fox, Laurence 128, 187
Francatelli, Charles 123, 187–89, 212*n*19
France 4, *6*, 26, 50, 52, 110
Francen, Victor 165, 200*n*15
Francis, Kay 44, 174
Fredericks, Scott 113, 181
Friend, Rupert 71, *74*, 93, 174, 204*n*15
From Hell (2001) 7, 84–85; 167; critical reception of 206*n*27, historical inaccuracies in 206*n*26
From the Earth to the Moon (1865 novel) 101
Frye, Jacob and Evie 143, 192
Fuerst Brothers Company 154
Funeral of Her Late Majesty Queen Victoria (1901) 162
funeral of Queen Victoria 4, 11, 13, 31–35, 112, 158–62, 197*n*14, 197*n*21, 198*n*22, 198*n*23
Funeral of Queen Victoria A (1901) 32–33, 159

Funeral of Queen Victoria B (1901) 32–33, 160
Funeral of Queen Victoria C, and D (1901) 32–33, 160
Funeral of Queen Victoria D (1901) 32–33, 161
"The Funeral of Queen Victoria" poem 198*n*22
Funeral of Queen Victoria—The Marble Arch (1901) 33, 161

Gainsborough Pictures 42, 162
Gambon, Michael 79, 96, 173
garden parties in films about Queen Victoria 16, 150, 154, 195*n*6
Gaumont Company 26, 27, 152, 201*n*25
Gaylord 101
George Albert Smith Films 151
Germany 4, *6*–7, 46, 52, 56, 68, 131, 166, 172–75, 179, 183, 202*n*14
ghost story using Queen Victoria 9, 132, 184
Gielgud, John 40, 51, 171, 179
Gilbert, W.S. 79, 96, 167
Gilbert and Sullivan aka *The Story of Gilbert and Sullivan* (1953) 167
Gill, Gillian 22, 126, 203*n*7, 204*n*13, 208*n*10
GK Films 174
Gladstone, William Ewart 1, 13, 37, 50, 53–54, 108, 112, 130, 132, 164, 169, 172, 178, 181, 183, 196*n*12, 197*n*15, 200*n*17, 205*n*17
Glasgow 72
"God Save the Queen" 57, 60
God Save the Queen (1899) 157
Golden Jubilee 89
The Golden Legend (1886) 95, 168
The Gondoliers (1889) 96
Goodwin, Daisy 8, 187–90
Gordon, Artemus 8
Gordon, General Charles 53, 172, 180, 200*n*17; death of 201*n*18; *General Gordon's Last Stand*, painting by George Joy 53
Gordon, Julia Swayne 40
Gordon Highlanders aka *The Military Review at Aldershot* (1897) 150
"Gordon of Khartoum" episode of *BBC Play of the Month* (18 January 1966), 180
Graham, Heather 85, 167
Granada Television 180–81, 191
grandchildren of Queen Victoria 25, 31, 33, 84, 105, 112–13, 134, 167, 177, 193, 198*n*24, 207*n*1
Graves, Peter (English actor) 44
The Great Exhibition of 1851 25, 102, 118, 129, *130*, 172, 190, 197*n*20
The Great McGonagall (1975) 97–*98*, 168
The Great Mouse Detective (1986) 7, 85–*86*, 168
Great North of Scotland Railway 22
Great Review by the Queen in Phoenix Park (1900) 20, 158
The Great Turnabout Trial game (2015) 192, 214*n*3
Great Western Railway 22, 33–*34*, 196*n*12, 197*n*14, 198*n*23

Index

The Greatest Showman (2017) 8, 100, 168
"The Green Eyed Monster" episode of *Victoria* television series (2017/2018) 188
Green Pond Productions 181
Gregory, Count 138, 39
Gregory Powder 114
Grenville, Daisy, Countess of Warwick 8, 110, 114–15, 178
Guangzhou 37
Guinness, Alex 81–83, 170
Gull, Sir William 84–85
Gunga Din (1939) 1
Guoan, Bao 37

Hadland, Sarah 130, **131**, 181
Haldane, Bert 202*n*1
Hallmark Hall of Fame Productions 191
Hallsham, Lord 85
Halmi, Robert 166
Hamilton, Victoria 116–**117**, 190
Hammer Films 184
"The Hand That Rocks the Cradle" episode of *Cribb* (12 April 1981) 113–14, 181
Handel, George Frideric 94
Hands of a Murderer (1990) 132, 181
Hanna-Barbera Productions 184
Hanover 14, 16, 22, 120, 123, 187, 206*n*25, 212*n*19
Happy and Glorious television series (1952) 181, 211*n*10
Hardie, Frank 53
Hardy, Alan 91, 208*n*9
Harmsworth Magazine 16
Harper, Sue 66
Harriet, Duchess of Sutherland 123, 127, 187
Harris, Julie 191, 209*n*1
Harrison and Company 162
Hastings, Lady Flora 72, 187
Haydon & Urry Company 20, 22, 152, 155, 158
Hayes, Helen 190, 209*n*1
Hayes, Melvyn 131
Heale, Margaret 104, 185
Heath, Ida 202*n*1
Hengdian World Studios 37
Henry, Guy 132
Hepworth, Cecil 33, 157, 161, 162
Her Late Majesty the Queen's Funeral (1901) 162
Her Majesty Leaving Spittal Barracks Amid Cheers (1899) 156
Her Majesty, Queen Victoria Part 1 (1899) 156
Her Majesty, Queen Victoria Part 2 (1899) 156
Her Majesty, Queen Victoria, Reviewing the Honorable Artillery (1899) 156
Her Majesty, Queen Victoria, Reviewing the Household Cavalry at Spital Barracks (1899) 156
Her Majesty, Queen Victoria, Reviewing the Household Cavalry at Spital Barracks No 2 (1899) 156

Her Majesty the Queen and Her Escort (1897) 27–**28**, 153
Her Majesty the Queen Arriving at South Kensington on the Occasion of the Laying of the Foundation Stone of the Victoria & Albert Museum (1899) 24, 155–56
Her Majesty the Queen in State Carriage (1898) 21, 154
Her Majesty the Queen Inspecting Life Guards (1899) 155
Her Majesty the Queen's Diamond Jubilee Festivities (1897) 29
Her Majesty's Carriage (1897) 153
Her Majesty's Glorious Jubilee 1897, the Record Number of a Record Reign **30**
Herbert, Lord Sidney 44
Herbert Wilcox Productions 62, 169, 171, 173
Hero Films 164
Heritage Minutes 103–4
Hexum, Jon-Erik 134
Hibbert, Christopher 11, 14, 20, 36, 40, 44, 54, 72, 80, 91, 210*n*4, 212*n*17
Higgens, Andrew 37
Higgins, Paul 79
Highland reel 93
Hill, Harry 104
Historica Canada 185
historical inaccuracies in films and television about Queen Victoria 37, 39, 40, 49, 55, 70–74, 76, 78, 80, 88, 91, 100, 104, 106, 121–23, 125, 127–28, 134–35, 137, 189, 198*n*3, 199*n*7, 200*n*11, 200*n*14, 201*n*18, 201*n*22, 201*n*23, 201*n*26, 203*n*12, 204*n*13, 204*n*14, 204*n*16, 204*n*17, 205*n*20, 206*n*23, 206*n*26, 207*n*1, 207*n*4, 211*n*15, 211*n*16, 212*n*19
Hitler, Adolf 46, 138, 182
Höbiger, Paul **93**
Hohenzollern dynasty 112–13, 180
Holden, Fay 44, 174
Holland, Clive 28, 207*n*1
Holm, Ian 84, 167
Holmes, Sherlock 85, 131–32, 165, 168, 171, 180–81, 183, 192, 202*n*27, 214*n*3
Holmes & Watson (2018) **139**, 168
Holy Grail 139
home movies of the royal family 13–**15**, 112, 149
honeymoon of Queen Victoria and Prince Albert 65, 202*n*5
Hong Kong 37, 125
"Honourable Artillery Company Review, Queen in Carriage" 12
Horizon Pictures 169
Horrible Histories television series (2009–2015) 129, **130**–**31**, 181–82
The Horse Guards (1897) 153
The Hound of the Baskervilles 140
Housman, Laurence 31, 181, 190–92, 209*n*1
Hoven, Adrian 68, **70**, 92–**93**, 173
Howard, Trevor 40, 182, 210*n*5

Howe-Douglas, Martha **130**, 182
Howick, Jim **130**, 181
hugging woman in Queen Victoria's funeral film 32, 160
Hughes, Tom **120**-21, **124**, 127, 187
Huisman, Michiel 97
Hume, Benita 42–**43**
Humphrey, Sam 100
Hunt, Francesca 138
Huntley Film Archives 33
Hutton, Betty **99**, 165
Hyde, Jacquelyn 138
Hyde Park 25–26, 76
Hysteria (2011) 168, 207*n*30

"I will be good" 71, 203*n*11
Idle, Eric 103, 183
The Idler, an Illustrated Monthly Magazine 28
Illustrated London Mouse 86
Illustrated London News 4, 13, **17**–**18**, 26, **30**-31
Illustrated Times 13
Imperator Films 171
imposters of Queen Victoria 86, 141
"In Court with Queen Victoria" (18 February 2012) 182, 211*n*14
"In Memoriam A.H.H" *see* Alfred, Lord Tennyson
"In the Beginning" episode of *The Secret Adventures of Jules Verne* (18 June 2000) 185
The Indian Medical Gazette 20
Indian Rebellion (1857–58) 107, 131
industrialization 6, 22–25, 36–37, 59–60, 65, 101, 131, 143, 175, 193, 196*n*12
Informant Media 168
Innes-Smith, James 38, 170
Innocent, Mrs. 113–14, 181
Internet, Queen Victoria's attitude toward *see* New Adventures of Queen Victoria
"The Invincible Mr. Disraeli" episode of *Hallmark Hall of Fame* (4 April 1963) 182, 210*n*5
Ireland 11, 20, 24, 128, 187, 189–90, 197*n*19; potato famine 119, 124–25
iron petticoat worn by Queen Victoria **87**
Isle of Wight 32–33, 160–61
It Ain't Half Hot Mum television series (1976) 131, 191
ITV Network 187
Ivanhoe 95
Izzard, Eddie 79, 95, 173

J. Nevil Maskelyne Company 152
Jack the Ripper 84–85, 89, 143, 167, 171, 184, 206*n*26, 206*n*27
Jackman, Hugh 89, 100, 168, 173
Jackson, Glenda 177, 213*n*26
Jackson, Gordon 44, 169
Jameson, Leander 54–55
Jameson Raid 54

Jannings, Emil 54, 172
Japan 4, **6**, 176, 192
Jennings, Mrs. 121
Jindan, Maharani **39**, 166
John Wrench & Son Company 152
John-Jules, Danny 137, 182
Joly, Henri 26, 197*n*18
Joly-Normandin camera 26–27
Jones, Gemma 112, 171, 202*n*27
Jones, Jeffrey 134
Jones, Terry 130
Jones, the Boy 116, 206*n*23
Jouer Films 165
journal and letters of Queen Victoria 11, 14, 36, 43, 67, 197*n*17, 204*n*16, 205*n*20, 212*n*22; edited by Princess Beatrice 76
Journey to the Unknown (1968) *see* "Poor Butterfly"
Jubliee Procession (1897) 152
Jules Verne Films Ltd. 168
Jules Verne's Rocket to the Moon aka *Those Fantastic Flying Fools* (1967) 8, 101, 168
J.W. Rowe's Pictorialgraph Company 152

Kabul 125
Kaiser Wilhelm 13, 31–33, 110, 158, 160–61, 205*n*21
Kalmus, Natalie 45
Karim, Abdul (the Munshi) 8, 78, **79**–81, 95–**96**, 173, 211*n*14; medals awarded to 205*n*21
Kastner, Ina 202*n*1
Kay, Charles 113
Keel, Howard 99,165
Kelly, Mary 85
Kelvin, Lord 88
Kennedy, John 42–**43**
Kensington 21, 24, 71–73, 94, 133, 154–55, 177
Kensington system 71, 73, 94, 208*n*10
Keppel, Alice 110, 115
Keyser, Agnes 110
Khartoum 53–54, 172, 180, 181, 198*n*2, 201*n*19
Khedive of Egypt 50, 53
Khyber Pass 125–26
Kilgarriff, Michael 133, 177
Kine Weekly Magazine 42, 199*n*4
kineopticon device 12
kinetoscope device 11
King Arthur or the British Worthy (1691) 94
King Edward VII *see* Edward VII
King George III 144
King of Hanover *see* Duke of Cambridge
King of Persia tableau 8, 78, **96**
"The King Over the Water" episode of *Victoria* television series (2–17/2018), 189
King William IV 71, 116–18
kinora device 16
Kitchener, Field Marshall Herbert 54–55; scorched earth policy of 200*n*20
Klagemann-Film GmbH 173
Knight, Charles 91, **92**, 193

Koh-i-Noor diamond 135, 187
Kosh, Pamela 175, 213*n*26
Kossuth, Lajos 128, 212*n*22
Kretschmann, Thomas 71, 174
Kruger, Paul 54–55, 201*n*22
Kryten 137, 182

"Ladies in Waiting" episode of *Victoria* television series (2016/2017) 187
Lady Emily 84
The Lady with a Lamp (1951) 7, 44, **45**, 169
Lancaster, Burt 99, 166
Landers, Ash 141, 176
Landmann, Professor **93**, 173
Langtry, Lillie 8, 110, 179, 182
"The Last Tsar" episode of *The Fall of Eagles* (12 April 1974) 113, 180
Leach, Rosemary 106, ***107–108***, 178
League of Darkness 138, 185–86
Le Couteur, John 26–28, 152
Lee, Christopher 186, 202*n*27
Leeds **17**, 18, 26, 178
Lehzen, Baroness Louise 64, 68–70, 72–74, **93**, 109, 116, 118, 121, 124–26, 173–75, 181, 187, 189, 190, 212*n*19
Leicester Square 12
Lenin 113, 180
Leonard, Lu 175, 213*n*26
Leopold I, King of the Belgians 70, 71, 73, 114, 117, 121, 125, 127, 173, 187–89, 196
Let's Make Up aka *Lilacs in the Spring* (1954) 169, 207*n*5
Lieutenant Charles 84
Life and Death of Queen Victoria (1901) 162
Life Guards and Dragoon's Band (1897) 27, 151, 154
Life Magazine 63, 81
"A Light at the Window" episode of *Shadow Play* (1 March 2004) 186
Lighting Cartoonist 13
lighting effects 71, 73, 76–77, 81, 83–84, 93, 112
Lill, Denis 112, 182
Lillie television series (1978) 8, 114, 182; critical reception of 211*n*11
Lin, Zexu 37–38, 170
Lincoln, Abraham 49, 185
Lincoln, Mary Todd 185, 213*n*25
Lion Television 181
Lister 137, 182
Lister, Dr. Joseph 199*n*7
literature, Victoria's taste in 8, 78, 97, 206*n*25, 208*n*10
The Little Princess (1939) **56**–57, 169
Liverpool **18**
Livingstone (1925) 57–**58,** 164; safari footage in 201*n*24
Livingstone, David 57–**58**, 164, 167
Llewellyn, Robert 137, 182
Lloyd's Weekly Newspaper 13

Lobengula, King of Matabeleland 54, 104
London 9, 11–12, 21–22, 25, 33, 89, 124, 128, 141–43, 189; Diamond Jubilee in 24–31; early cinema theaters in 12, 195*n*1; Soho 119
London and South Western Railway **23**, 33, 197*n*14
"London Bridge Is Falling Down" episode of *Victoria* television series (2019) 189
London Film Productions 167
London Gazette 24
London Stereoscope Company 150
London Weekend Television 182
long shot 14, **18**, 26, 33, 41, 53, 60, 76, 119, 124
Long Valley 42
Longford, Elizabeth 3, 133
Lord Roberts Unveils Statue of Queen Victoria (1899) 157
Lorne, Marion 132–**33**, 175
Louis Philippe, King of France 124, 127, 189
love story of Victoria and Albert: in films 1, 7–8, 62–75; in television 8, 115, 190, 211*n*14
Loveless, Dr. Miguelito, Jr. 138, 192
low angle shot 33
Lubin, Siemund 162
Lucknow, siege of 36, 163
Ludgate Circus 25, 28
Ludgate Kinematograph Company 152
Lufrano, Richard 37
Lumière, Auguste and Louis 11–12, 26–27, **28**–29, 153–54
"The Luxury of Conscience" episode of *Victoria* television series (2017/2018) 189
Lyden, Anne 4
Lytton, Mrs. Henry 50, 163, 164, 202*n*1

MacDonald, Jean 42–**43**, 199
Mädchenjahre einer Königin see *Victoria in Dover*
Mafeking, siege of 56
Maharani Jindan *see* Jindan, Maharani
The Mahdi, Muhammad Ahmad bin Abd Allah 53, 201*n*19
makeup for Irene Dunne 81, **83**, 170
male actors playing Queen Victoria: John Bird 183; John Dalby 172, 206*n*25; Melvyn Hayes 131, 191; Peter Sellers 97–**98**, 168; Robert Webb 187, 213*n*24; Ronnie Corbett 184; Terry Jones 130, 183
Mammoth Screen 187
Manchester 24–25, 157
Mann, Margaret 50, 167, 170, 206*n*28
Mantel, Bronwen 100, 104, 166, 185
Marble Arch 32–33
Mardayn, Cristl 68
Margolyes, Miriam 129, 132, 177
Marian, Ferdinand 54
Marigold (1938) 169, 206*n*25
Marmont, Percy 57, 167
martial arts 87–88, 135, 139
Martin, Ross 138, 192

234 Index

Marx, Karl 143
Mary, Queen of Scots 13, 144; see also *The Execution of Mary Stuart*
Mason, Brewster 109
Masse, Anna 103, 175
Masterpiece Theatre 106, 211n16
Matabeleland 104-5
Maureen, Mollie 115, 178, 202n27
Maximilian, Emperor 110
McConnell, Marina 132, 180
McCrea, Joel 98, 166
McDonalds 129, 145
McGonagall, William 97-98, 168
McKenna, Virginia 115, 178, 211n12
McKernan, Luke 26-28, 202n1
McLaglen, Cyril 42-**43**, 162
McLeod, Gordon 68, 172, 173
McShane, Ian 106, **108**, 178
Mecham, William 13
mechanical replicant of Queen Victoria 7, 85-**86**
media and the monarchy 1, 3-6, 13-14, 24, 65
medium shot 33, 41-42, 85, 99, 100-1, 106, 113, 117, 120
Meier, Sid 143
Melba (1953) 169, 208n8
Melbourne, Lord William Lamb 38, 62, **64**, 68-69, 72-73, 75, 104, 116, 124, 171, 173-75, 179, 185, 187-88, 190-91, 204n13; age of 212n19; Mrs. Melbourne insult 94
Melbourne-Cooper, Arthur 12
Méliès, Georges 12, 195n2
"Meltdown" episode of *Red Dwarf* (1991) 9, 137-38, 182
Mercer, Beryl **56**, 101, 169, 172
Merry, Tom 12
Mexico 110
MGM (Metro-Goldwin-Mayer) 165, 201n24
Michaelis, Sebastian 140, 166, 176-77
The Military Review at Aldershot (1897) 19, 150-51, 153
Miller, Steve 132, 184
Milligan, Spike 97-**98**, 168, 184
Milton, John 107
Mirisch Films 171
miscellaneous appearances of Queen Victoria 192-93
mistaken identity 69, 203n9
Mr. Turner (2014) 98, 169
Mitchell, David 187, 213n24
Mitchell & Kenyon Company 158
Modern Screen Magazine 82
Moffat, Jamie 96
Mohammed (Indian attendant) 78, 80, 173
montage 48, 55, 60, 88, 98, 100, 110, 123, 182
Montague, Jude Cowan 198n2, 202n1
Montgomery, Elizabeth 132, 175
Monty Python's Flying Circus 9, 130-31, 183
Moore, Alan 84, 167
Mordaunt divorce case 110

Moriarty, Professor 85, 132, 139, 165, 168, 181, 202n27
Morlay, Gaby 167, 200n15
Morley, Robert 96, 167
Morton, Andrew 133
Moscrop, Liz 84
Motion Picture Reviews 65
Moto-Supply Company 152
Mouse Queen 85-**86**, 168
Mrs. Brown (1997) 7, 8, **75**-78, 93, 97, 115, 170; historical inaccuracies in 204n16, 204n17; humor in 205n18; physical relationship of Victoria and John Brown 93, 205n19
The Mudlark (1950) 7, 81-84, 170; costumes 206n24; critical reception of 206n24; novel 206n23
Munich Agreement 46, 52, 54, 200n15
Munsel, Patrice 169, 208n8
The Munshi *see* Karim, Abdul
Murphy, Paul Thomas 6, 211n17, 212n20
Musgrove, Lady 114
music 8, 12, 35, 57, 65-66, 91-96, 115, 123, 132, 154, 174, 199n5, 203n6, 207n5, 208n9
musicals 99, 100, 165, 199n6, 202n27, 209n15, 211n11
My Father Knew Lloyd George (1965) 183, 213n26
Mystery of the Wax Museum (1933) 170, 206n28

narrative structure 12, 42, 71, 73, 87, 106, 122-25, 202n1, 202n2, 205n17, 209n16, 212n19; flashback 54, 71, 76, 116; flashforward 71, 76; multiple story lines 122-24; parallel scenes 67-68, 78
Nation, Carry 144
Naval Field Battery and Guns (1897) 27, 154
Nazi propaganda films 7, 54-55, 68, 172, 201n21, 203n8
NB Films 163
Neagle, Anna 7, 8, 44, **45**-**47**, 48, 59, 62, **63**-68, 71, 91-92, 106, 169, 171, 173, 202n4, 207n5
Neilson, Perlita 113, 180
Neptune Productions 191
Netley Hospital 20-21, 155, 158, 196n10, 196n11
New Adventures of Queen Victoria (2006-) 9-10, 144-45, **146**, 192-93, 195n2
New York Times 26, 204n15
Newport 72, 121
News of the World 13
newspapers 13, 25, 43, 47, 69, 72, 85-86, 88, 197n16
Nightingale, Florence 7, 40-44, 129, 143, 165, 169; insistence on sanitation 44, 169
Nightingale brooch 44, 48
Niven, David 88, 165
Norma opera 94, 208n6
Northern Photographic Works 20, 151, 158

Index 235

Oakes, David 121, 187
Oakley, Annie **99**, 134, 165, 175, 177, 213n26
obsessions with Queen Victoria 7, 81–89, 207n30
O'Casey, Ronan 83, 170
O'Connor, Arthur 76, 179
O'Connor, Sinead 94
opera, Queen Victoria's taste for 8, 91, 94–95, 208n6, 208n8
The Opium War aka *Yapian zhanzheng* (1997) 7, 37–38, 170
Order of Merit 44
Order of the Garter 53
"An Ordinary Woman" episode of *Victoria* television series (2016/2107) 188
O'Rourke, Chris 12, 195n1
Orson & Olivia television series (1992) 131, 183
Osborne House 31–32, 78–79, 98, 101, 128, 159, 192, 208n11, 209n16, 209n17
Our Friend the Atom (1957) see *Your Friend the Rat*
Oxford, Edward 116, 121–23, 174, 211n17
Ozanne, Christine 179, 213n25

Paddington 27, 33, 35, 123, 153, 162, 196n12, 198n23
Page, Joanna 84, 167
Paget, Lord Alfred 127, 187, 188, 189
paintings: collected by Victoria and Albert 208n11; dislike of Turner painting 98; Duchess and baby Victoria 204n14; Duleep Singh 39; General Gordon 53; hospital visit 21; Privy Council 204n14, 212n22
Pakula, Hannah 52, 97, 200n14
Palace Theatre of Varieties 12
Palmerston, Lord Henry John Temple 38, 43–44, 47, 49, 110, 119, 128, 162, 169–70, 172–73, 181, 187, 189–90, 212n22
Paradox Development Studio 193
parallel structure 43, 78, 122
Paramount Network Television 185
Paramount Pictures 172
Parker, Louis N. 50, 163, 167
Pasco, Richard 170, 178, 210n5
Passepartout 88, 138–39, 165, 175, 185
Paul, Robert 11–12, 20–21, 26–27, 157–58
Paul's Animatograph Works 21–22, 150–52, 154
"peace with honor" 46, 52
Peacock throne **79**; see also Durbar Room
Peach, Mary 106, 178
Pearls of the Crown (1937) 170, 207n30
Peck, Bob 37, 170
Peel, Prime Minister Robert 65–66, 71–72, 74, 107, 116, 122, 124–25, 172–73, 175, 178, 182, 187–89
Peluce, Meeno 134, 177
Penge 124–26, 128, 187
The Phantom Raspberry Blower of Old London Town (1971/1976) 184, 210n8

Phantomhive, Ciel 140–41, 166, 176–77, 214n1
"Phantoms and Photographs" episode of *Shadow Play* (22 March 2004) 186
Phipps, Miss 79, 95–**96**, 173
Phoenix Park 20, 157–58, 197n19
photography, royal patronage of 6, 14, 65
Piccadilly 12, 25
Pickard, Helena 44, 169
Pigott-Smith, Tim 79, 173
Piper, Billie 135, 187
Pirate Captain 86–**87**, 171
The Pirates! In an Adventure with Scientists! aka *The Pirates! Band of Misfits* (2012) 7, 86, 87–88, 171, 206n29
Plunkett, John 4, 13–14, 16, 18, 24, 31
"Pocket Watch Full of Miracles" episode of Bill & Ted's Excellent Adventures (10 November 1990) 184
"Poetry Reading" skit see *Monty Python's Flying Circus*
Poland 46, 56
politically correct attitudes 7, 78, 120–22, 124–25, 209n15
politics, Queen Victoria's interest in 8–9, 45, 104, 123; Bedchamber Crisis 72
Polly, pet bird 87, 171
"Pomp and Circumstance" (Elgar) 60, 201n26
Ponsonby, Sir Henry 79–80, 96, 170, 173, 204n17, 205n19, 205n20
"Poor Butterfly" episode of *Journey to the Unknown* (9 January 1968) 9, 132, 184
Postcard of Smiling Queen Victoria (1898) 193
Praed, Michael 138, 185
"Praise God from Whom All Blessings Flow" 60
Presentation of the New State Colours to the Scots Guards: Arrival of her Majesty the Queen (1899) 155
Presentation of the New State Colours to the Scots Guards: Review of the Scots Guards by Her Majesty the Queen (1899) 155
Presenting Bouquet to Queen in Phoenix Park (1900) 20, 158
Prestwich Manufacturing Company 21, 28, 152, 154
"The Price of My Blood" episode of *Rhodes* (6 October 1996) 185
The Prime Minister (1941) 7, 51–53, 170; critical reception of 200n16; historical inaccuracies in 200n14
Prince Albert Edward see Edward VII
Prince Albert of Saxe-Coburg and Gotha see Albert, Prince of Saxe-Coburg and Gotha
Prince Arthur, Duke of Connaught 19, 25, 151, 156, 159–61
Prince Charles 134, 144
Prince Edward Albert Victor 84–85, 167
Prince Ernest of Saxe-Coburg and Gotha 74, 91, 97, 121, 123, 126–27, 173, 187–89
Prince Frederick of Prussia 68, 112, 172, 180

Prince Henry of Battenberg 113
Prince Leopold 114–15, 204n17
Prince of Wales *see* Edward VII
Princess Alice, Countess of Athlone (granddaughter of Queen Victoria) 193, 207n1
Princess Alice, daughter of Queen Victoria 107–8, 118, 195, 208n9
Princess Beatrice 8, 15, 76, 113–14, 155, 178, 181, 208n9
Princess Christian of Schleswig-Holstein 25
Princess Diana 133
Princess Feodora of Leiningen *see* Feodora
Princess Helena 25
Princess of Wales *see* Alexandra, Princess of Wales
Princess Victoria, granddaughter of Queen Victoria 134, 177
Princess Victoria of Saxe-Coburg-Saalfeld *see* Duchess of Kent
Princess Victoria (Vickie, daughter of Queen Victoria) *see* Victoria, Princess of England and Empress of Germany
print images of Queen Victoria 5, 6, 13–14, 28, 30, 56, 59, 70, 82, 92, 122, **123**, 195n3
Printer's Register 16
The Private Life of Sherlock Holmes (1970) 171, 202n27
Privy Council meeting 118, 204n14, 211n15
Professor Ratigan 85–86, 168
Promio, Alexander 27, 153
propaganda films: China 7, 11, 19–20; France 200n15; Germany 7, 54–55, 68, 172, 201n21, 201n22, 203n8; Great Britain 11, 19, 20
Prussian-Danish War 110
public engagement films of Queen Victoria 4, 6, 11, 13, 16–24; Diamond Jubilee 24–31; funeral of Queen Victoria 31–35
"A Public Inconvenience" episode of *Victoria* television series (2019) 190
Punch Magazine 4, 203n10
Punjab 38–39, 166
Purcell, Henry 94
I Puritani (opera) 94, 208n6

Qing dynasty of China 37–38, 170
quadrille 91–92, 179, 207n2
quarrels between Victoria and Albert 65–66, 74, 126, 183, 203n6
Queen and Escort in Churchyard (1897) 21, 151
The Queen and Princess of Battenburg (1899) 15, 155
The Queen and Royal Family (1897) 15, 150
Queen and Royal Family Entering Their Carriages (1899) 22, 154
The Queen and Royal Household with Bodyguard (1899) 21, 154
The Queen and the Emperor and Empress of Russia at Balmoral (1896) **15**, 150
The Queen Arriving and Leaving the Lawn (1899) 21, 154

The Queen at Sheffield (1897) 21, 150
Queen at State Garden Party (1897) 150
The Queen at Temple Bar (1897) 21, 150
Queen Elizabeth *see* Elizabeth I, Queen
Queen Elizabeth *see* Elizabeth II, Queen
The Queen Entering Phoenix Park (1900) 20, 157
The Queen Entering the Borough (1897) 21, 150
The Queen in Her State Carriage (1901) 22, 158
The Queen Leaving Buckingham Palace (1900) 22, 157
The Queen Leaving Netley Hospital (1901) 20, 158
The Queen Leaving Windsor Castle (1900) 22, 157
Queen of Destiny see Sixty Glorious Years (1938)
The Queen, Princess and Escort (1897) 15, 21, 150
The Queen Reviewing the Guards (1900) 157
Queen Victoria (1942) 171; *see also Sixty Glorious Years; Victoria the Great*
"*Queen Victoria*" episode of *A.J.'s Time Travelers* (1995) 185
Queen Victoria and Royal Family at State Garden Party (1897) 150
"Queen Victoria and the Giant Mole" episode of *The Secret Adventures of Jules Verne* (25 June 2000) 185
Queen Victoria at Aldershot (1989) 154
Queen Victoria at Garden Party (1898) 16, 154
Queen Victoria Driving to Laffans Plain (1898) 154
Queen Victoria Funeral Procession (1901) 33, 161
"Queen Victoria Handicap" *see Monty Python's Flying Circus*
Queen Victoria in Dublin (1900) 157
Queen Victoria in Ireland (1900) 20, 158
Queen Victoria Laying Corner Stone aka *The Queen Arriving at South Kensington* (1899) 24, 155
Queen Victoria Presenting Colours to Gordon Highlanders (1898) 154
Queen Victoria Reviewing Household Cavalry (1899) 155
Queen Victoria Reviewing the Life Guards (1899) 155
Queen Victoria Reviewing Troops at Aldershot (1898) 154
Queen Victoria with Horse Guards (1899) 19, 155
Queen Victoria's Arrival at Ballater (1897) 22, 150
Queen Victoria's Carriage Passing Along the Thames Embankment (1900) 157
Queen Victoria's Departure from Ballater for Balmoral (1897) 22, 150
Queen Victoria's Diamond Jubilee (1897) **28**, 151

Queen Victoria's Diamond Jubilee from York Road (1897) 28–29, 151
Queen Victoria's Diamond Jubilee full version (1897) 151
Queen Victoria's Diamond Jubilee location unknown (1897) 29, 152
Queen Victoria's Diamond Jubilee—No Sound (1897) 152
Queen Victoria's Diamond Jubilee—Paul—St. Paul's South—Arrival of the Queen's Carriage (1897) 151
Queen Victoria's Diamond Jubilee Procession (1897) 26–27, 29, 152–53
Queen Victoria's Diamond Jubilee Procession: Queen in Carriage (1897) 152
Queen Victoria's Diamond Jubilee Procession: Queen's Carriage (1897) 151
Queen Victoria's Diamond Jubilee Procession: Colonials (1897) 151
Queen Victoria's Diamond Jubilee short version (1897) 151
Queen Victoria's Funeral (1901) 161
Queen Victoria's Funeral [Number 1] (1901) 158
Queen Victoria's Funeral [Number 2] (1901) 159
Queen Victoria's Funeral [Number 3] (1901) 159
Queen Victoria's Funeral: Ships Fire a Salute in the Solent (1901) 162
Queen Victoria's Jubilee Procession (1897) 151
Queen Victoria's Last Visit to Ireland (1900) 20, 158, 197n19
The Queen's Arrival at Netley (1899) 20, 155
Queen's Arrival from Windsor at Paddington (1897) 27, 153
The Queen's Carriage (1897) 150
The Queen's Carriage and Escort (1897) 21, 150
Queen's Carriage and Indian Escort Arriving at St. Paul's (1897) 21, 150
The Queen's Drive Through Windsor (1899) 22, 155
The Queen's Entry Into Dublin (1900) 20, 158
The Queen's Funeral (1901) 162
The Queen's Funeral Pageant Enters Hyde Park (1901) 162
Queen's Funeral Procession at Cowes (1901) 162
Queens's Jubilee (1897) 153
Queens's Jubilee No 2 (1897) 153
"The Queen's Husband" episode of *Victoria* television series (2016/2017) 188
The Queen's Visit to Dublin (1897) 19, 154
The Queen's Visit to Dublin (1900) 20, 157–58
The Queen's Visit to London (1900) 22, 157

racism 3, 7, 78–80, 100, 146, 209n15
Railway News 33
railways, royal patronage of 6, 22, **23**–24, 28, 33–35, 38, 59, 65, 104, **122**–**23**, 186, 188, 196n12, 197n14, 197n15, 198n23, 212n18
Rankin, Gayle 100, 168

Rapp, Dean 57
Rappaport, Helen 97
Rare Creature Dining Club 87
Ratatouille (2007) see *Your Friend the Rat*
Ratigan, Professor 85–86, 168
Ray, Andrew 81, 170
reading, Queen Victoria's taste for 8, 78, 91, 97, 206n25, 208n10
Red Dwarf see "Meltdown" episode of *Red Dwarf* (1991)
Redgrave, Corin 37, 170
Redman, Joyce 116, 190
Redmond, Siobhan 129, 180
Regent's Park 76
Reid, Hal 40, 164
Reid, Dr. James 31, 33–35, 79–80, 161, 173, 195n5, 196n9, 198n24, 201n23, 205n20
Reid, John Howard 172
Reid, Kate 182, 210n5
Reid, Michaela 31, 80, 198n23
Reid, Sheila 114, 182
Reid, Wallace 40, 164
Reilly, John C. **139**, 168
religious discrimination 78, 107
Remy 140, 193
"Responsible Government" episode of *Heritage Minutes* (31 March 1991) 103–4, 185, 210n2
Restoring the Queen Victoria Recording of 1888 (2017) 193
Returning from St. Paul's (1897) 150
Returning, Part Two (1897 150
reverse shot 18, 32, 160
reversed images 32
Review of Berkshire Volunteers by the Queen (1900) 158
Review of the Life Guards by the Queen (1899) 19, 155
reviewing the troops films 12, 18–19, 20, 25, 150–52, 154–58, 195n7
revolution in France (1848) 119, 127, 189
Rhodes, Cecil 54–55, 104–5, 172, 185
Rhodes television series (1996) 8, 104–5, 185
Rhodesia 104–5, 201n24
Richard, Irene 113, 181
Richardson, Miranda 71, 174, 204n14
Richardson, Tony 40
Rigg, Diana 118, 187
Riley Brothers Company 21, 150
Rimmer 137, 182
Ripper, Jack the see Jack the Ripper
Robertson, David 80
rocket to the moon 8, 101, 168
Romana Film 174
Romanov dynasty 112–13, 180
Romeo and Juliet 69
Root, Amanda 38–**39**, 166
Rosmer, Milton 42, 162
Routledge, Patricia 191, 210n1
Royal Carriages Arriving at St. Paul's (1897) 152

238　Index

Royal Carriages Passing Westminster (1897) 151
Royal Horse Artillery with Guns (1897) 27, 154
Royal Photographic Society 12, 14
Royal Proclamation of the Death of Queen Victoria, Blackburn (1901) 158
royal yacht Alberta 32, 160, 209n17
"Rule Brittania" 57
Russell, Lord John 47, 187, 212n22
Russia 4, **6**, 9, 14–15, 42, 47, 51, 52, 109, 113, 134, 150, 163, 164, 167, 177, 180, 192, 195n5, 200n14, 212n22
Russo-Turkish War 109
Ruud Concession 104–5

Safety Last (1923), homage to 171, 202n27
St. George's Chapel 32, 160, 161
St. George's Church 29
St. James's Street 27
St. Paul's Cathedral 21, 25–28, 60, 150–52
St. Thomas' Hospital 44
Salamander Film Productions 174
Salazar, David 94
Salisbury, Lord Robert 13, 79, 96, 105, 114, 173, 178, 205n21
Salisbury Plains 42
Samantha Stevens character in *Bewitched* television series 9, 132, 175
San Francisco Examiner 26
Sands Films 172
Sandwich, Lord 129
sanitation 51, 57, 197n16; Albert's efforts for 125, 189; Nightingale's insistence on 44, 169
Sarah (African princess) 127
Sartaaj, Satinder 38–**39**, 166
"Saving Mr. Lincoln" episode of *The Secret Diary of Desmond Pfeiffer* (19 October 1998) 185
Scales, Prunella 104, 186, 192, 210n1
Scenes at Balmoral (1896) 14, 149
Schleswig-Holstein 25, 110, 156
Schneider, Magda 68, 92–**93**, 173, **93**
Schneider, Romy 7–8, 68, **70–71**, 92–**93**, 173
Schubert, Franz 8, 94–95, 121, 208n7
science, Queen Victoria's interest in 8, 24, 166
scorched earth policy, British use of 54–55, 201n20
Scotland 11, **15**, 44, 124, 135, 189
Scotland Yard 141
Scott, Sir Walter 8, 95, 97, 208n10
Screen Gem 175
Scutari 44, 199n3
Sebastopol, siege of 40, 42, 47, 162, 198n2
Second Boer War 19–21, 54–56, 79, 110, 155, 169, 172, 179, 195n1, 196n8, 201n20, 205n20
The Secret Adventures of Jules Verne (2000) 9, 138–39, 185
"A Secret Comes to Live" episode of *Shadow Play* (29 March 2004) 186
The Secret Diary of Desmond Pfeiffer (1998) 185, 213n25

"Secret of the Realm" episode of *The Secret Adventures of Jules Verne* (7 April 2000) 186
self-reflexive 25
selfie stick **139**
Sellers, Peter 97–**98**, 168, 174
Seward, William, U.S. Secretary of State 48
sex, obsession with 3, 8–9, 121, 127, 183, 185, 204, 207
Shadow Play television show (2004) 186, 213n29
Shaka Zulu television series (1986) 8, 105–6, 186, 210n4
Shanghai Knights (2003) 171, 202n27
Shaw, Martin 104, 185
Shooting Victoria (history) 6
"A Show of Unity" episode of *Victoria* television series (2019) 189
Showtime 175
Sikh 38–39, 166
Silberer, Geza 68, 173
silent films 4, 6, 13; actualités 149–162; featuring Queen Victoria as a character 162–65
Singh, Duleep 38–40, 182
"The Sins of the Father" episode of *Victoria* television series (2017/2018) 188
Sir Wilfred Laurier and the New South Wales Lancers (1897) 153
Sixty Glorious Years aka *Queen of Destiny* (1938) 7, 8, 45, **46–47**, 48, 50, 53–54, 60, 62, 66–68, 92, 171–72, 199n7, 201n18, 202n2, 203n6, 207n3; critical reception of 199n8, 202n2; death of General Gordon 200n13; historical context of Victoria's conflict with Gladstone 200n17; technicolor 199n6
Sixty Years a Queen, lost silent film (1913) 164, 198n2, 202n1; critical reception of 199n8
Skerrett, Nancy 123–24, 127, 187–89; loosely based on Marianne Skerrett 212n19
Slattery (footman) 83, 170
slavery 57, 72, 127, 185, 188, 202n27; Albert's campaign against 121; Livingstone's attitude towards 57–58, 164
Small, Timothy 98, 170
smiling Queen 29, 39, 57, 77, 84–87, 91, 95, **92**, **98–99**, 100, 102, 105, 133, 158, 193, 197n19, 205n19, 214n1
Smith, Grace 71, 174
Smith, Dr. J.H. 26
social reform 51, 59, 83, 121
"A Soldier's Daughter" episode of *Victoria* television series (2017/2018) 188
Souls at Sea (1937) 172, 201n27
South Africa 8; 54–55, 105, 155–56, 172, 185, 186, 196n8; scorched earth in 55, 201n20
South African Broadcasting Company 186
South-Western Rail 33
Spencer, Jessica 113, 181
Spital barracks 155–56, 196
Spitalfields silk 125, 188
split image **89**

"Ständchen" see Schubert, Franz
Standish, Lady 116
Standish, Pamela 171, 172, 200n13
Station Jim (2001) 104, 186, 210n3
Staunton, Imelda 86, 171
steampunk genre 9, 138–39, 185
stereoscope 6, 150, 197n20
Sterndale-Bennett, Joan 101, 168
Stewart, Patrick 113, 180
Stockmar, Baron Christian Friedrich 71, 73, 94, 97, 110, 116–18, 175, 181
Storey, Edith 40–*41,* 164
Stories from a Flying Trunk (1979) 172, 206n25
The Story of Alexander Graham Bell (1939) 8, 101–2, 143, 172, 209n16
The Story of Gilbert and Sullivan (1953) 8, 95, 167
Strange, Sylvia 168, 207n30
Strauss, Johann 91, 93, 166, 174, 207n4, 207n5
Strong, Mark 71, 174
subjective experience 74
Sudan Campaign 45, 53–54, 62, 172, 198n2, 201n19
Suez Canal 7, 50–52, 66, 108, 163, 167, 171–72, 178, 182, 206n23
Sullivan, Arthur 79, 96
Sully, Andy 24–25
Sungenis, Pab 144, *146,* 192, 195n2
Supplément illustré du Petit Journal 4, *6*

tableaux vivants 8, 14, 78, 95–*97,* 208n9
Talisman Films 185
Talking Pictures 182
Technicolor 45–*46,* 48, *56*–57, 59, 199n6
technology, Queen Victoria's interest in 8, 24–25, 38, 65, 101, 133, 196n11; selfie 139
telecommuting 204n16
telegraph, royal patronage of 6, 25, 31, 53, 59, 204n16; Diamond Jubilee telegram 24–25; first official transatlantic telegram 101, 209n17; uncoded telegram to Gladstone 53
telephone, royal patronage of 6, 101–2, 134, 144, 172, 177, 209n16
telescope 135, 187
television programs and series about Queen Victoria 174–91
Templars 143–43
Temple, Henry John *see* Palmerston, Lord
Temple, Jane 114, 181
Temple, Miss 113–14, 181
Temple, Shirley *55*–57, 169
Tennant, David 135, 171
Tennyson, *see* Alfred, Lord Tennyson
Terry, Ellen 14
Tesla 144
Thames River 81, 87, 157, 170
Theatrograph device 12
Theodore Huff Memorial Film Society 43
Thompson, Emma 129, 167, 180
Thompson, Sir William 101

Thorndike, Sybil 169, 208n8
Thornton, Frank 113, 180
Those Fantastic Flying Fools (1967) see *Jules Verne's Rocket to the Moon*
threats to the monarchy 7, 85, 105, 139, 143; *see also* assassination attempts on Queen Victoria
Thumb, General Tom 99–100, 166, 168, 208n13
ticket sales for silent films about Queen Victoria 29, 32
Time Table of the Train Conveying Her Majesty the Queen and Suite, from Windsor to Portsmouth Dockyard **23**, 24
time travel films and television 8, 9, 103, 128, 132–36, 175, 177, 184–85, 187, 213n29
Timekeepers of the Millennium television show (1999) 186–87, 213n29
title cards 41–42, 47, 49, 51, 53, 57–60, 66–68, 71, 75–76, 78, 91, 106, 109, 118, 124–25, 198n1, 204n14
Tobis Filmkunst 172
Toboso, Yana 140, 166, 176–77
"Tooth and Claw" episode of *Doctor Who* (6 October 2006) 9, 135–36, 180, 187, 213n27; visual parallel to "Doomsday" episode 213n28
Torchwood 9, 135–36, 187
Trader Horn (1931) 58, 164, 201n24
Trafalgar speech by Queen Victoria 126
Trafalgar Square 60
Trail, Dr. 125
Tranby Croft gambling scandal 110, 115
Transvaal 54–55, 172, 195n1, 198n1; *see also* South Africa
Treaty of Nanking (1842) 37, 125, 170
Trent Affair 48–49, 62, 66, 119, 173, 199–200n10
"Tricky Queen Vicky" 130, *131,* 182; *see also Horrible Histories* television series
Tsar 43, 113, 162, 180, 211n9; *see also* Czar
Tsarevich Nicholas *see* Czar Nicholas
Turkey 52
Turner, Abigail 127, 187
Turner, J.M.W. 98, 170
Tutin, Dorothy 191, 209n1
Tuttle, Lurene 134, 177
TV Guide Magazine 44
Twain, Mark 25–27, 60, 197n16
Twentieth Century-Fox 81, 165–70, 72, 206n23
twentieth-century perspectives 3, 7, 103–4, 128, 133, 136–37, 141, 146, 210n7
twenty-first century perspectives 2–3, 6, 9–10, 73–74, 78, 100, 104, 120–22, 125–28, 135–*136,* 137–47
typhoid fever 76, 179, 200n11

Ubisoft Quebec 192
Uncle Kruger aka *Ohm Kruger* (1941) 7, 54–57,

172; historical inaccuracies of 201n22, 201n23
Uncle Leopold *see* Leopold I, King of the Belgians
"Under the Linden Tree with Queen Victoria" sketch in episode of *That Mitchell and Webb Look* (11 June 2009) 187, 213n24
"Uneasy Lies the Head Tha cxsaqzsxt Wears the Crown" episode of *Victoria* television series (2019) 189
United States 7, 27, 98, 110, 119, 165, 199n9, 199–200n10, 201n24, 213n25
Universal Cartoon Studios 172
Universal Pictures 163, 172
Universal Television 175
Universum Film (UFA) 167, 174
Upstairs Downstairs television series 37, 122

Van Helsing: The London Assignment (2004) 7, **89**, 172
Vanity Fair Magazine 79
Vansittart, Sir Robert 46
Variety Magazine 44, 57, 199n5, 200n12, 200n16
Velograph Syndicate 150, 152, 195n6
Verne, Jules 8–9, 101, 138–39, 165–66, 168–69, 175, 185
Victoria: An Empire Under the Sun game (2003) 193, 214n2
Victoria & Abdul 7, 8, 78–81, 95–**96**, 173, 190, 211n14; critical reception of 205n22; historical inaccuracies in 205n20; medals award to Abdul 205n21
Victoria and Albert Museum 24
Victoria & Albert television series (26 August 2001) 8, 115–16, **117**, 118–19, 211n13; historical inaccuracies in 211n15
The Victoria Cross (1912) 7, 40–42, 164
Victoria Cross medal 40, 48, 164
Victoria Falls 57
Victoria in Dover aka *Mädchenjahre einer Königen* (1936) 68, 173
Victoria in Dover aka *Mädchenjahre einer Königen* (1954) 7–8, 68–70, 91–**92**, 173, 203n9; historical inaccuracies in 207n4
Victoria, Princess of England and Empress of Germany (Vicky, daughter of Queen Victoria) 52, 68, 75, 97, 110, 112–13, 116, 126, 178–80, 188, 200n13, 200n14, 203n10, 208n9
Victoria, Queen and Empress—The Princess Alice Interview (1977) 193
Victoria Regina (1964) 191
"Victoria Regina" episode of *Hallmark Hall of Fame* (30 November 1961) 191
"Victoria Regina" episode of *ITV Play of the Week* (26 June 1957) 190
"Victoria Regina" episode of *Robert Montgomery Presents* (15 January 1951) 190
"Victoria Regina" episode of *Robert Montgomery Presents* (8 April 1957) 191

Victoria Regina play (1934) 31, 190–91, 209n1
Victoria Regina radio play (1948) 190
Victoria Regina television play (20 November 1947) 190
Victoria television series (2016–19) 8, 115, 119, **120**–21, **122**–23, **124**, 125–27, **128**, 187–90; critical reception of 211n16; historical inaccuracies in 211n16, 212n17, 212n18, 212n19, 212n22
Victoria the Great (1937) 7–8, 48, **59**–60, 62–**67**, 91–92, 173–74, 198n1; combined with *Sixty Glorious Years* 172, 202n2; critical reception of 202n2; dialect coach for Anton Walbrook 202n4; historical inaccuracies in 200n11, 201n26; similarities to Gaumont-British newsreel 201n25; Trent Affair, 199–200n10
Victoria II game (2010) 193, 214n2
"The Victorian Candidate" episode of *The Secret Adventures of Jules Verne* (9 December 2000) 186
Victoria's Funeral, 1900's (1901) 161
Visit of the Queen to South Kensington (1899) 21, 154
visual space, use of 72–73
Vitagraph Company 21, 40, 150, 164
Vogel, Rudolf 69, 173
voice-over 71, 73, 77, 95, 112, 123, 130, 133–34, 214n1
voice recording by Queen Victoria 193, 209n17
Von Bulow, Professor 101
Voyagers! television series 9, 134, 177

"Wacky Queen Skit" *see* Monty Python's Flying Circus
Walbrook, Anton 7–8, 45, **46–47**, 48, **59**, 62–68, 91–92, 172–74, 202n4, 203n8, 207n5
Walden Media 166
Walker, Zena 178, 210n5
Walker Company 150, 154
Walt Disney Pictures 168, 193
Walt Disney Productions 165, 206n25
Walturdaw Company 162
waltz 74, 91, 94; inappropriate for royalty 92–**93**; on roller stakes 97–**98**
Waltz War aka *Walzerkrieg* (1933) 167, 174, 207n5; *see also* Court Waltzes
Wangel, Hedwig 54, 172
war films without a Queen Victoria character 198n1
War Office 45
War Propaganda Bureau 20
Warner Brothers 40, 167, 170–71, 174, 200n12
"Warp and Weft" episode of *Victoria* television series (2017/2018) 188
Warwick Trading Company 15, 19–22, 32, 150–51, 154–58, 162, 195–196n7
Watson, Dr. **139**, 168, 171, 181, 192, 214n3
Watson & Sons Motorgraph 15, 21, 150, 152, 195n6

Index 241

Wax Droid Theme Park 137
wax museum 170, 206*n*28
"we are not amused" 8, 49, 89, 91, 100, 130, 132, 135, 137, 144, 146, 183, 193
"We Are Not Amused" episode of *It Ain't Half Hot Mum* (1976) 131, 191
Webb, Robert 187, 213*n*24
Weber, Charles W. 57
Weekly Times 13
Wellington, Duke of 71–73, 100, 126, 129, **130**, 164, 172–74, 180–81
werewolf 9, 135, 187
West, Jim 138
West, Timothy ***111***, 178, 184, 186, 192
Westminster Abbey 58, 119, 151
Westminster Bridge 28
Wetherell, M.A. 57, **58**, 164, 201*n*24
WGBH 170, 185
Wheeler the mudlark 81–84, 170
whiskey 54, 83
The White Angel (1936) 44, 174
"The White Elephant" episode of *Victoria* television series (2019) 190
Whitechapel 84
Whitrow, Benjamin 38, 170
Wilcox, Herbert 45–46, 59–60, 62, 66, 68, 169, 171, 173, 202*n*2
wild west shows, Queen Victoria's love of 8, 98–**99**, 134, 177, 208*n*12
The Wild Wild West Revisited (1979) 9, 138, 192
Wilde, Oscar 144
Wilder, Gene 165, 202*n*27
Wilding, Michael 44, 169
Williams, Olivia 79, **96**, 173
Williams, Simon 37, 170
Williamson Kinematograph Company 20, 158
Wilson, A.N. 133, 205*n*19
Wilson, Owen 171, 202*n*27
Wilson, Robert 126
Windsor 11, 14, 21–**23**, 24, 27, 32–33, **34**, 38, 49, 54, 65, 81, 83, 88, 91, 95, 105, 107, 116, 118, 132–34, 151, 153, 155–57, 160–61, 165, 169–70, 177, 180, 198*n*21, 198*n*23, 204*n*16, 207*n*1, 208*n*5, 208*n*12; Blue Room 116; fire 134
Winter Gardens Theatre 29

wireless, royal patronage of 209*n*17
women doctors, Queen Victoria's opinion of 114
women's suffrage, Queen Victoria's opinion of 114
"Work Out with Queen Victoria" *see Horrible Histories* television series
Woolgar, Fenella 79, 95, **96**, 173
World War I 7, 20, 40, 43, 53, 171, 202*n*27
World War II 7, 46, 48, 51, 52, 57, 131
Worthington, Wendy 185, 213*n*25
The Wrong Box (1966) 174, 207*n*30
Wynyard, Diana 51, 171

Xie, Jin 37, 170

Yankee Clipper (1927) 164, 199*n*9
Yeomen Warders (Beefeaters) 32, 160
York Road 28, 151
Yorkshire 21, 119
Yorkshire Television (YTV) 178–79
Young, Freddie 45, 60
Young, Loretta 101, 172
"Young England" episode of *Victoria* television series (2016/2017) 188
Young Sherlock: The Mystery of the Manor House television series (1982) 131–32, 180
The Young Victoria (2009) 7–8, 71–75, 93–94, 118, 174; critical reception of 204*n*15; historical inaccuracies in 203*n*12, 204*n*13, 204*n*15, 211*n*15
The Young Victoria television play (1963) 191
The Young Visitors (26 December 1965) 191, 213*n*26
Your Friend the Rat (2007) **140**, 193

"Zadok the Priest" *see* coronation of Queen Victoria
Zexu Lin *see* Lin, Zexu
Zorro in the Court of England (1969) 174, 202*n*27
Zulu (1964) 36
Zulu Dawn (1979) 36
Zulu, Shaka *see Shaka Zulu* (1986)

www.ingramcontent.com/pod-product-compliance
Lightning Source LLC
Chambersburg PA
CBHW032038300426
44117CB00009B/1102